English Pageantry
An Historical Outline

The Guildhall, London, E. C.

English Pageantry
An Historical Outline

BY

Robert Withington

VOLUME I

BENJAMIN BLOM, INC.

NEW YORK

First published 1918, Harvard University Press.
Reprinted 1963, by arrangement with the Harvard University Press.
Published by Benjamin Blom, Inc., New York 52.
L. C. Catalog Card No.: 63-23193

Printed in U.S.A. by
NOBLE OFFSET PRINTERS, INC.
NEW YORK 3, N. Y.

PATRI · MATRIQVE
PARENTIBVS · AMATIS
HOC · OPVS · FILIVS
DEDICAT
A · D
MDCCCCXIV

PREFACE

IT were, perhaps, too much to ask of any human work that it be without short-comings, and I take full responsibility for such sins — both of commission and of omission — as may be found herein. That the number of such is not much greater than it is, is due to the kind help of many friends, which I gladly acknowledge. My debt to Professor George P. Baker, under whose guidance I began my researches at Harvard, and to Professor George L. Kittredge, with whose help I carried them on during Mr. Baker's absence from Cambridge, can never be repaid. Only men who have worked with them can realize how grateful I am for their encouragement and criticism.

To the members of the Harvard Library staff — especially to the late Mr. Thomas J. Kiernan, and to Mr. T. Franklin Currier — I owe much. My obligation is all the greater because my demands on their courtesy came at a time of turmoil and confusion. The moving of so great a library with so little inconvenience to those who were constantly using it, was a marvel to all of us.

To my friend Louis N. Parker, Esq., I feel deeply grateful for much valuable information, and many suggestions. To the kindness of J. Dixon Taylor, Esq., of the Guildhall, London, I owe the programs of nineteenth century Lord Mayor's Shows, now in the Harvard Library, and the opportunity of seeing the rehearsal of the 1913 Show. I am indebted to Dr. F. W. C. Lieder of Harvard for the collection of Hudson-Fulton Pageant postcards now in the Treasure Room of the Harvard Library. President William Allan Neilson has given me many fruitful hints, and Mr. Frederic Schenck, Dr. Howard R. Patch, and Dr. Archer Taylor have brought material to my notice which otherwise might have escaped me.

My researches in England have been aided by many library and town officials. Bernard Kettle, Esq., and D. J. Hile, Esq., of the Guildhall Library; Dr. Reginald R. Sharpe, late Records Clerk in the office of the Town Clerk of the City of London, and the officials of the British Museum Reading, Manuscript, and Newspaper rooms; the Librarians of the Society of Antiquaries, and of Corpus Christi College, Cambridge, have been very kind; the Town Clerks of Norwich, York, and Chester have given me ready access to their records. I heartily appreciate the helpfulness of many others, whom I do not mention by name; I have indicated, at particular points in the text, those to whom I am indebted for specific services.

My colleague, Professor Paul R. Lieder of Smith College, has helped me greatly in reading proof; and I am also indebted to Mr. C. C. Lane of the Harvard University Press for much friendly aid.

I have, at various places, suggested opportunities for further research along lines which it has been impossible for me here to take up. If any one is moved to follow me in exploring this absorbing field, I hope he may find my work of service. The subject is interesting because it is close to the people. One root is in folk custom; and from the beginning, the populace has claimed pageantry for itself. As a form of artistic expression it is not, perhaps, so high as the masque; but of late years, from the soil cultivated by pageantry for centuries, a new form has arisen, calling itself by the same name. And this bids fair to play a considerable part in the community life of our country, as well as of England, for some time to come.

R. W.

CONTENTS

CHAPTER II

REMARKS ON THE TOURNAMENT AND EARLY MASQUE: TOGETHER WITH A
DISCUSSION OF THE INFLUENCE OF THE MORALITY, AND OTHER MATTERS   85

CHAPTER III

CHAPTER IV

CHAPTER V

ILLUSTRATIONS

INTRODUCTION

AN historical outline of English pageantry must, of necessity, suggest many questions which cannot there be carefully considered. The field to be covered is so wide, that I can merely touch on some matters which, in themselves, would make good subjects for an entire work.

In the following pages I shall, with the exception of a chapter on pageantry in the United States, limit myself to England. There are, however, certain continental influences which cannot be ignored; these I have, so far as possible, dismissed to the footnotes. We are here more concerned with the development of pageantry in England than with international influences, which must be considered elsewhere.

The " æsthetic pageant " of earlier days still exists; as such may be considered the carnivals with floats, the " antiques and horribles," the modern Lord Mayor's Shows of London, and such parades as those at Boston on Columbus Day. Beside this " æsthetic " pageantry, however, there has arisen the " educational pageant " which we all know — in which many of us have taken part. I do not mean, in making the distinction, to imply that the " æsthetic " pageant fails to teach, or that the " educational " pageant makes no appeal to our sense of beauty. Quite the contrary; but the emphasis of the older pageantry is on the aim to entertain by means of lavish display, while the purpose of the modern is to instruct by means of entertainment.

I may here remark that, in view of the two pronunciations of the word current today, the *New English Dictionary* seems to prefer the vowel (*a* as in *man*) to the diphthong (*ai* as in *rain*). The old spellings of the word show that both pronunciations have long existed side by side. Such forms[1] as *padzhand, padgion*, are far from ambiguous, but the majority of the forms given in the *New English Dictionary* might be pronounced either way. *Pageon, pageunt*, etc., prove nothing, though the *e* which follows the *g* is probably not meant to modify the vowel, making it like that in *page*, but rather to indicate that the *g* has the value of *j*. The *i* in such a form as *paiaunt* does not indicate the *ai* of *rain*; it is merely *y* or *j*. Occasionally we find such a form as *paygente*,[2] which allows but one pronunciation — that said to have been insisted on by Tennyson; but of the forms where the spelling allows only one pronunciation, i. e., with a *d* or a modified vowel clearly indicated, there are in the *New English Dictionary* eight showing the vowel of *pad* to two showing the pronunciation *pay*.

---

[1] See L. T. Smith, *York Plays*, p. xxxv.

[2] Of 1587. See *The Presentation in the Temple*, p. 26; cf. *paidgion* (L. T. Smith).

The word *pageant* has been so loosely used of late years, that it is well to have clearly in mind just what we mean when we use it in its strict sense. I have not planned a history of " gorgeous processions " — which is one of the acquired senses of the word. It is not worth while to consider the various etymologies which have been suggested for *pageant*;[1] as Sharp points out, " in the first instance [it] was certainly applied to the vehicle of exposition,[2] and afterwards to the exhibition itself." The development is a natural one. " Those scaffoldings [on which miracle plays in England were performed] were usually called *pageants;* a loose term, applied also to the wooden stage, the text of the drama, and the *ensemble* of the *fête* or theatrical display."[3] In Tennyson's " Lead out the pageant" (at the beginning of the *Ode on the Death of the Duke of Wellington*), the word refers to the gun carriage on which the Duke's coffin rested. The connection shows that it could not refer to the procession of soldiers — the " spectacle " — as we might expect.

Connected with *pango*, and our *pact*, a pageant was, in its primary sense, something " compacted together." We shall consider processions which were accompanied by something of that sort. The giants, animals, and folk mumming, which date from very early times, lead us to discuss the folk-element in pageantry. The saints' images show an early Church influence; and as time went on and the shows became less primitive, angels, Biblical characters, and not infrequently (in the provinces) the pageant-cars of the miracle plays[4] made their appearance: on them stood historical, allegorical, or Biblical figures. Sometimes the actual stage or moving wagon drops away, leaving the pageantic figures without the pageant. Such processions, with the allegory or symbolism expressed by riders or marchers, are really pageants. The " angels," or even the undisguised minstrels,

---

[1] Any one interested is referred to the collection published by Sharp, p. 2. The gem of this collection is undoubtedly Dr. Johnson's suggestion that the word comes from *payen geant*, (*a pagan giant*) which was, as we shall see, a common feature of these shows. Cf. also on this matter, Collier's *Annals of the Stage*, ii, p. 151, and Hazlitt's edition of the *Dramatic Works* of John Webster, iii, p. 227. Also, of course, *New English Dictionary, s. v. pageant*. The word does not, apparently, antedate the fourteenth century.

[2] Cf. Dekker, 2 *Honest Whore*, iv, iii, 178: " Let me not be carried through the streets like a pageant."

[3] Jusserand in the *Furnivall Miscellany*, p. 183. He describes the kinds of pageants used in the miracle plays — both stationary and movable — and reproduces two pictures by Jean de Grise, made before 1344, from MS. Bodl. 264, fols. 54 b and 76. The wheels — if there were any — and " lower room " are hidden by flowing drapery as " in our own age, those modern ' pageants ' used in cavalcades or *vachalcades*, figuring at need Olympus or Montmartre, are hung with draperies concealing their lower part and their wheels." (*Ibid.*, p. 192.)

[4] These miracle plays would be pageants themselves, were they not something more. The " pageant-cars " of the miracle plays were merely stages on which the Biblical characters played their parts; the " pageants " of the royal-entry were little more than stages, though at times a certain amount of symbolism was expressed in the decorations, or explained by means of " scriptures " fastened on the platforms.

furnished the " raw material " for allegory, which, after 1432, became an integral part of pageantry.

What may be called the *body* of pageantry is the cars — but a procession of cars is only a corpse. The allegory or symbolism or history which the living characters bring, may be called the *soul* of pageantry — and is much the more important part. The real pageant has both body and soul; and though sometimes the latter is expressed by inanimate figures or even by painted pictures, it is still important as showing the element which appeals to the intellect of the spectator.

The *technique* of this form of artistic expression is the procession. In our own day, the technique has changed, so far as the Parkerian pageant is concerned, becoming more that of the theatre; but the pageantic soul remains, in the history that lives and the cities which speak.

Both the early and more modern forms have a " popular " quality which may be called the *spirit* of pageantry. This distinguishes the earlier " pageant " from the " masque," as today the " pageant " may be distinguished from the show given by and for a limited group in the community. All have some elements in common — the differences are in spirit and in technique.

Beside the folk-elements, which lie at the foundation of pageantry, we find contributions from other sources. The castles built on conduits, from 1377 on, open the field of chivalry and tournament, and occasionally characters appear in pageantry from the metrical romances. The influence of the Church made itself felt; and not only court " disguisings," but the mummers' play of the commons, are suggested by the " dressing-up " of the characters in the pageant. Some of the " folk-elements " — the St. George figure, for instance — which are treated in the first chapter, need a separate investigation.

There is nothing in the word *pageantry* which should limit it to the trade-guilds or to the Church; but as a matter of fact it is practically confined to these two bodies,[1] which were the two institutions in the community around which processions centered, and which have left records telling of their activities in this direction. In fact, the pageantry of the Church, save in the earliest times, is almost negligible, so completely did the guilds[2] take charge of those processions which indicated the joy of a community on a holiday occasion. The clergy often combined with the guilds, it is true; but the pageants were provided by the latter.

---

[1] Even in folk celebrations like the " Midsummer Show " the guilds appear to have furnished the pageants. I am, of course, referring to the earlier pageantry. That newer " folk play " or " historical pageant " which, under Mr. Parker's direction, came into existence at Sherborne in 1905, is not limited to any class; indeed, Mr. Parker holds — as we shall see — that a pageant must, of necessity, be a community affair, given of the town, by the town, for the town, and only incidentally for the strangers that are within the gates.

[2] Some of them " sacred " rather than " commercial," organized for the purpose of honoring some saint.

I have already referred to the spirit of " popularity " which is common to the pageantry of the past and that of today. A pageant is essentially of the people. Whether the stages moved with the procession, or the procession passed before one platform after another, the " show " took place outdoors; spectators thronged the streets, and there was none of the seclusion which characterizes the masque. Not until the present century does pageantry become rooted to one spot: but even now it has not lost its " popular " characteristic. Indeed, it has gained a deeper popularity. For in the old days the community took a free interest in the " finished product " of the guilds' labors; now, the pageant is at its best when produced, not by one group or set in a community, but by all; not by paid performers but by the townspeople in voluntary coöperation.

The main root of pageantry is in folk custom; but we find this form of expression developed by Church and guild. No section of a community where class lines are sharply drawn as they are in England, was so well fitted to carry on and develop this form as the merchant class. When the Church gave up miracle plays, the guilds took them over for commercial reasons; when the municipal governments fell into the hands of the merchants, they were the natural hosts of visiting sovereigns. No other class was so near all classes of the people: kings and nobles held membership in one of the Livery Companies an honor; and the apprentices could look forward to becoming influential merchants, aldermen, mayors, and even knights.

It is hard to determine just what the relation between the morality play and the pageant may be. I shall touch upon this subject in a later chapter. Allegory appears definitely in the pageant of 1432, and it looks as if this were the great contribution of Lydgate to this form of art. Did he apply literary conventions to the pageant, making the abstract qualities, already personified in literature, real flesh and blood ? Did the morality play draw its living abstractions from the pageant ? Or did the pageant draw, perhaps indirectly, from the morality play ? Or are both independent developments of the same tendency ? These are troublesome questions.

Another important matter is the relation of the pageant-car to scenery, already elaborate in the Elizabethan and Jacobean masques. As early as 1494 a contrivance much like a pageant-car was wheeled into the hall at a court " disguising," and the dancers stepped forth and danced. M. Reyher has dealt with the question in much more detail than I can here; he makes it plain that this gift of pageant to embryonic masque was the beginning of scenery which in our theatres is so elaborate.

Having traced the rise of pageantry to Elizabethan days, and given the history of the London Lord Mayor's Show, which attained its most glorious period in the seventeenth century, I shall devote a chapter to modern survivals of the older pageantry. Some of these survivals have been influenced, or kept alive, by the interest in mediævalism characteristic of the last part of the nineteenth century;

perhaps, also, by the Parkerian work itself. I shall then consider the modern "community drama," which came to life at Sherborne (Dorsetshire), in 1905, fathered by Mr. Louis N. Parker. These "pageants" of Mr. Parker and others have no real right to the name, though I believe there is a connection between them and the earlier form of pageantry. That the two are quite different in technique, we must admit; and it is to be regretted that an already overworked word is forced to stagger under a new load. But Mr. Parker's original suggestion of "folk play" failed to arouse an interest which was immediately stimulated by the substitution of a word which every one knew; though what it meant was delightfully vague. Because this new use of the word *pageant* has apparently come to stay, we must make the best of it.

As with *romance* and some other words denoting forms of literary expression, we have in *pageant* a term which is extremely elastic. Since it has not, for a long time, been used exactly, it cannot be exactly defined. We shall see what some of the elements of this form are: we shall start our investigations, not with sacred processions (with or without images) nor with mere processions of joyful reception, but with folk processions which include giants, animals, and a certain amount of "dressing-up"; with processions into which came monologues; which absorbed the movable wagon from the miracle plays, and put a romantic castle from the tournament on a conduit.

The old name for these processions was *riding*; when pageantic features came to be added, *triumph* or *show* took its place. For a long time the word *pageant* was applied only to the car or platform; later it was transferred to the whole parade. The modern, careless use of the word to denote any gay or splendid procession, is a further generalization, the reason for which is obvious, and the result of which is confusing. Our confusion is increased, as has been said, by a modern specialization of the word to "historical folk play."

Circumstances have made it advisable to print this survey of the subject in two parts; the present volume deals with the elements of pageantry; the pageantic features of tournament and early masque; the development of the "royal-entry" from 1300; and the growth of Elizabethan pageants. Later chapters will trace the history of the civic procession known as the "Lord Mayor's Show" and the growth of the pageant of the present day. Since 1432 the royal-entry has included not only Biblical, but historical and allegorical characters, which, with a later mythological element, are the chief ingredients of the Lord Mayor's Show. This civic "triumph" emerged from folk custom in the middle of the sixteenth century, and reached its height a hundred years later; speech left these shows with that planned by Settle in 1702 — after which they did not cease to be pageants, but obviously became a lower form of art. *Tableaux* or *tableaux vivants* remained on the cars; then, in the eighteenth century, they were borrowed from the pageants and transported into halls, where scenes from the past, with an allegorical flavoring, were shown by means of "living pictures." When these representations were of historical subjects, they were still felt to be pageantic, and the name sometimes clung to them.

These scenes, or historical episodes, shown by means of "living pictures" mark an intermediate stage between the earlier and the later pageantry. Originating in the German *Festspiel*, this latter is really a "folk play" or, more exactly, a "community drama." It was begun by Mr. Parker at Sherborne; and it may be found, together with survivals of the earlier processional type, and the *tableaux vivants*, in America.

The pageant is the lowest form of dramatic expression;[1] but it is a form deeply rooted in the heart of the people. It appeals strongly to a characteristic we all share — the love of display — and it is only recently that a serious effort has been made to harness this instinct to higher aims.

Since the above was written, the Great War has broken out, and the course of pageantry has been interrupted. That it will be changed is possible, but unlikely; for England has seen many wars without losing her love of splendor; and her pride in her history will not diminish in the decades to follow the noble chapter she is writing now. In the United States five thousand people took part in a spectacle, produced in the Harvard Stadium for the benefit of the Red Cross, three months after we had joined the belligerents. Useful as it may be in times of stress to raise money for national needs, pageantry must return to an uncommercial basis if it is to keep its spontaneity; and there is little reason to doubt that it will do so. *Caliban* lost money, instead of making it; and hard feelings were aroused. Pageantry is not a good source of revenue; but the fact that a big spectacle was produced in war-time is significant.

"LAND'S END,"
LITTLE COMPTON, RHODE ISLAND,
August, 1917.

[1] This is more true of the earlier, than of the Parkerian, type. We shall see that this latter is not very far removed from the theatre, especially when it is historical, rather than symbolic. Strictly speaking, the symbolic pageantry, which is characteristic of America, cannot be called "Parkerian." Cf. chapter viii, infra.

ENGLISH PAGEANTRY

CHAPTER I

ELEMENTS OF THE PAGEANT

PROFESSOR Sir Adolphus Ward, in his *History of English Dramatic Literature*,[1] defines pageants as " moving shows devoid of either action or dialogue, or at least only employing their aid by way of supplementing and explaining the living picture." This definition is, in the main, satisfactory;[2] it is with these " moving shows " that a large part of this work has to deal. A pageant is primarily something " compacted together "; but, as I noted in the Introduction, the characters which give a symbolical or historical significance to the float or wagon are more important than the wagon or stage which bears them; and symbolism and history may be expressed by the image of a giant or of some animal.

Later chapters will trace the development of the pageant from the thirteenth century down to our own times; it is the task of this to treat some of the elements that have been drawn from folk-custom, modified by the Church, or borrowed from the metrical romance. The root of a " moving show " is obviously the procession — but we are not concerned with processions pure and simple. Giants, animals, figures of saints, and wagons bearing characters dressed up to represent something they are not in real life, give these processions a pageantic aspect.

I shall disregard chronology, partly because one must, in dealing with folklore material, and partly because chronology is here not a thing of great importance. The unfortunate result, however, is that the chapter may seem chaotic; this is also partly due to the fact that the elements of pageantry are not homogeneous.

---

[1] (1875) i, p. 79; (1899) i, pp. 145 f. "These exhibitions," he continues, "formed an important part of the public life of the later Middle Ages, and . . . were to a large extent allegorical in character. . . . In England, and more especially in London, this pageantry obtained an extraordinary hold over the popular taste. . . . The refining fancies of chivalry introduced in the Norman period gave variety to these exhibitions, but their fuller development was owing to our commercial relation with Flanders which began and rose to its height in the Plantagenet reigns." It is worthy of note that the French language has no word to translate *pageant*. Says Magnin, *Hist. Marionnettes en Europe*: " . . . une action muette, expliquée par une exposition verbale ou une cantilène narrative, ce que les Anglais appellent une *pageant*." The word does not appear in Littré; but *cortège historique* furnishes an equivalent.

[2] We shall see, however, that usually in the pageantic " royal-entry " and sometimes in the Lord Mayor's Show, the platforms were stationary, and the movement obtained by the progress of the city's royal guest from one stage to the next.

3

§ 1 FOLK MUMMING

The element of " disguising " in pageantry leads us first to folk mumming —
the " Plough Monday " and Christmas mummers' plays. It is supposed that
the sword dance which lies behind them goes back to a contest typifying the
fight between winter and summer. This is a common feature of the folk custom
of many countries, and connects itself with various festivals. We shall consider
the processions of Plough Monday later; here we will limit ourselves to remarks
on the earliest kind of " folk play."

Says Olaus Magnus,[1] " The southern Swedes and Goths . . . have another
custome, that on the first day of May, when the sun is in Taurus, there should be
two horse troops appointed of young and lusty men; as if they were to fight some
hard conflict. The one of these is led on by the captain who is chosen by lot,
who hath the name and habit of Winter, and is clothed with divers skins, and
armed with fire forks, casting about snowballs and pieces of ice, that he may pro-
long the cold; and thus he rides up and down in triumph, and he shews and
makes himself the harder. . . . On the other side the captain of the other troop
is for Summer, and is called Captain Florio, and is clothed with green boughs
and leaves . . . and summer garments that are not very strong; and both these
ride forth of the field into the city . . . and with their fire spears they fight, and
make a publike shew, that Summer hath conquered Winter."

And again,[2] " Moreover the northern Goths and Swedes have another sport to
exercise youth withal. . . . And this play is shew'd especially about Shrovetide,
called in Italian, *Maschararum*. For before Carnivals all the youth dance for 8
dayes together, holding their swords up: but within the scabbards for 3 times
turning about, and then they do it with their naked swords lifted up: after this
turning more moderately . . . they change ranks and place themselves in an
hexagonal figure; and this they call *Rosam:* and presently they dissolve it, by
drawing back their swords and lifting them up, that upon every one's head there
may be made a square *Rosa*, and then by a most nimble whisking their swords
about collaterally, they quickly leap back and end the sport; which they guide
with pipes or songs, or both together, first by a more heavy, then by a more
vehement, and lastly by a most vehement dancing. But this speculation is
scarce to be understood but by those that look on, how comely and decent it
is . . ."

Sometimes what may be called " pageants " appeared in these dances. The
same Bishop of Upsala records,[3] " There is also another kind of dance or play,
where, upon a woodden Engine men are carried in the ayr by the motion of
wheels: or else they sport otherwise, being very nimble of body: as with spears,
about which they will turn themselves. . . ."

---

[1] *Hist. Goth.*, Bk. xv, ch. ii.   [2] *Ibid.*, ch. vi.   [3] *Ibid.*, ch. vii.

These Scandinavian folk dances show what may be a development of military exercises; we shall see, later,[1] that the tournament of mediæval times became softened to a " silken war," in much the same way. H. H. Child[2] notes that " disguise has its origin in the clothing of leaves and flowers or of the skin and head of the sacrificial animal[3] with which the worshipper made himself a ' garment of the god,' thus bringing himself into the closest possible contact with the spirit of fertilization . . ." The sword dance " seems to have had its ritual origin in the primitive expulsion of Death or Winter, the death and resurrection of Summer. . . . It was, moreover, a natural mode of play for warlike peoples. Like all dancing it became mimetic in character. Its chief personages are the fool, who wears the skin of a fox or some other animal, and the ' Bessy,' a man dressed in woman's clothes — figures in which folklore finds the survival of the ritual of agricultural worship . . ."[4]

The garments of leaves and flowers may have been influenced by Bacchic rites. " And when the feast of Bacchus was kept, the Jews were compelled to go in procession to Bacchus, carrying ivy."[5] It is not impossible to imagine in the disguise of the Scandinavian dance an influence from Greece or Rome, though both may be independent developments of the same nature worship. The root of the northern custom is generally considered to be in pre-Christian religion. Says Ditchfield, " In connection with Pace-egging, there is the Pace-egg or Easter play, which resembles in its main features the Christmas mumming play. In this piece of ancient drama folklorists see a relic of old Norse mythology — the contest of Thor[6] and Balder, of spring with winter. Beau Slasher is the champion of winter, and his iron head, steel body, and hands and feet made of knuckle bones, are descriptive of the frost-bound earth. These interpretations seem somewhat fanciful."[7]

In the north and northwestern parts of England, the sword dance used to be a part of the Plough Monday observance.[8] The fight which lies behind some of these dances has been, by certain folklorists, carried back to the days of the human sacrifice. " The attack or killing — or merely the symbolical surrounding or approach — goes back to the sacrifice: and this became the principal point of action in the St. George plays which developed from the sword dance. The invariable incident of the death and restoration of one of the characters is the point upon which has been based the descent of this play from pagan festivals celebrating the death and resurrection of the year." The fixing of Christian eccle-

---

[1] Cf. below, pp. 95 and 100.

[2] In *Camb. Hist. Eng. Lit.*, v, p. 33.

[3] We shall return to this point soon.

[4] *Ibid.*, pp. 34 f. Cf. Chambers, ch. ix.

[5] 2 *Maccabees*, vi, 7.

[6] Does he mean Loki ?

[7] *Old Eng. Customs*, p. 81.

[8] See Drake, *Shakspere and his Times*, i, p. 137. It may not be out of place to refer to the Gothic Christmas play which combined dancing, singing, and fighting. This is discussed by Carl Kraus (*Das Gothische Weinachtsspiel*) in Paul-Braune's *Beiträge zur Geschichte der Deutschen Sprache und Literatur* (Halle, 1895), xx, pp. 224 f.

siastical feasts has shifted the seasons of the festivals, which accounts for the performance of these plays at Christmas.[1] They seem to have been widespread, falling at different seasons at different places.[2]

The ground work of the sword dance is conjectured to be an actual sacrifice. Though some authorities do not hold this view, those who do suppose that when the sacrifice was done away with, it was replaced by a symbolic dumb show. Even in these dumb shows the symbolism is slight, for it is subordinated to the evolutions of the dance.[3]

---

[1] H. H. Child in *Camb. Hist. Eng. Lit.*, v, p. 35. Further (*ibid.*, p. 33), "Writers on folk-lore point out that such games as football and hockey descend from the struggles for the possession of the head of the sacrificial victim."

[2] On the custom in Bavaria and elsewhere, see Beatty, *The St. George, or Mummer's Plays* in *Trans. Wis. Acad.*, xv, pt. 2 (October, 1906), p. 290, etc.; Frazer, *The Dying God*, p. 254 f. He says that the contest between representatives of Summer and Winter degenerated into a mere dramatic performance with the Esquimaux (p. 259); that it may also be found among the Canadian Indians (p. 260), and that at Zürich an image of winter " is still burned." (pp. 260 f.) Trevelyan, *Folk-Lore and Folk Stories of Wales*, pp. 25 f., notes: " In Wales, as in England, the May Day festivities were not complete without the customary fight between Summer and Winter " — which is described. Cf. also *ibid.*, p. 24: " It was said that Gwythyr, the son of Greidawl, fought with Gwyn ab Nudd for the fair Cordelia, daughter of Lear, every first of May, and they were to continue doing so until the day of doom. . . . May Day contests were probably held in this belief." (Miss Trevelyan refers to the *Mabinogion*, pp. 251, 263.) After a procession, there was a mock fight between the two parties, the captains of each of which were dressed to symbolize winter and summer. Summer always won the fight, his weapons being birch branches, willow wands, and young ferns. After the victory, Summer selected a May King, the people a May Queen, and the rest of the day was given up to feasting, dancing, and games. (Trevelyan, pp. 25 and 26.) Cf. *The Dying God*, p. 211, where Frazer notes that the leaf-clad mummers represent the spirit of vegetation, and are in the same class with the King of the May. H. H. Child (*op. cit.*) says " The Maypole . . . stands for the sacred tree, and the dance around it for the ritual dance of the pagan worshipper." Cf. also Schelling, *Eliz. Drama*, i, pp. 48–49.

[3] Chambers, *Med. Stage*, i, p. 206 f. His chapter x, *The Mummers' Play*, and Appendix J (ii, p. 270) treat the subject in more detail than I can here. Cf. also Beatty, *The St. George, or Mummers' Plays*. Ordish, in *Folk-Lore*, iv, p. 164, holds that the groundwork of the Easter, or Pace-egg play, the Plough Monday play, and the Christmas Mumming play, was the sword dance; he points out (*ibid.*, p. 161) that the sword dance originated in the sacrifice and says that in Gothland a sacrificial play is still performed, acted by young fellows in disguise. Cf. Hazlitt's Brand (1870), i, pp. 281 f., for *Fool, Plough and Sword Dance*; Kelly, *Notices of Leicester*, pp. 51 f. On p. 53 he gives the text of the play performed in the neighborhood of Lutterworth at Christmas, 1863: cf. Chambers, ii, p. 276 (Appendix K); Ditchfield, pp. 310 f. — who prints some Berkshire and Oxfordshire mumming plays; Leather, *The Folk-Lore of Herefordshire*, pp. 141 f., for the Herefordshire play; Manly, *Spec. pre-Shaks. Drama*, i, pp. 296 f., for the Revesby Sword play, and *ibid.*, i, pp. 289 f., for another version of the Lutterworth play. On Christmas mummers in Dorsetshire see Udal in *Folk-Lore Record*, iii, i, pp. 87 f.; on the mumming play in Wales, see Trevélyan, pp. 30 f. On Christmas mumming plays in general see Ditchfield, chapter i (pp. 8–15). Cf. R. Chambers, *Book of Days*, ii, pp. 739 f. (under 24 December) for a description of mummers together with an illustration

Whatever is the origin of these folk mummings, which later developed into " folk plays," [1] they may be said to combine the spirit of pageantry with the technique of the masque, being a dance with a great popular appeal, in much the same way that the modern " festival " combines the spirit of the masque with the technique of the modern pageant. The element of " dressing-up " is common to both mumming and pageant; and among the characters shared by both, St. George stands out prominently.

The May games are supposed to have originated in the Floralia of pagan Rome, though there may be a trace of the Druidical worship of Bel therein.[2] Mr. H. H. Child says that the May game developed into the Robin Hood play; the names Robin and Marian — type names of the shepherd lover and his lass — may have been brought over from France and become confused with Robin Hood, or à Wood, of *Piers Plowman* and the ballads. Mr. Child suggests that the origin of this figure is purely fictitious, or that he may be a personification of Woden.[3]

---

of a group, showing various masks, and one character with the dragon's head. The Scotch *guisers* are referred to in the same work (ii, p. 789 — under 31 December); masked, and each attended by a man in woman's clothing, (the " Bessy,") they go from house to house on Hogmanay night, and sing or perform a play not unlike that of the English mummers.

A text of a mummers' play is printed in the *Book of Days*, ii, pp. 740 f. Three players, can, by changing their make-up, play all the parts. St. George fights the Turkish Knight who is twice revived by the doctor. The exposition is of the simplest kind.

[1] The " Plowboys' or Morris dancers' " performance at Revesby, in Lincolnshire, shows a transition between the sword dance and the play. The mummers' play shows another advance. The central incident is still the killing, and restoring to life, of one of the characters, and there is still enough dancing to show a descent from the sword dance. The presence of " St. George " (" prince " and " king " are Hanoverian " improvements ") implies the influence of literature. His advent is a matter of some obscurity. Mr. Child suggests that he comes from the George " ridings " — which we shall consider anon — and the miracle plays on the subject; or " the name of St. George may have come into them [these plays] by way of Richard Johnson's *History of the Seven Champions* (published in 1596–97)." H. H. Child, *op. cit.*, p. 37. (This last statement is hard to accept.)

In the Robin Hood plays, fighting seems to furnish the chief interest. (For these plays, see Manly, Part III.) The St. George plays of Oxfordshire and Lutterworth, and the Revesby sword play, combine dancing and fighting, with less emphasis on the latter. The Christmas mumming plays included a mixed cast — Old Father Christmas, St. (or Prince) George, Old King Cole, the Giant Blunderbore, Little Jack, a doctor, the Old Dragon, the Merry Andrew or the Clown, Morrismen, Beëlzebub, a Turkish Champion or Knight, Captain Slasher, etc. King Alfred was sometimes King of England, or King William — sometimes both appeared. In these plays are fighting, dancing, and singing: the dialogue is of small value, and the fun is farcical.

The Revesby play includes the Dragon and a Hobby Horse; the Fool is the chief character, and his five sons mingle dancing with their insipid dialogue; there is a little mock fighting. The chief emphasis of this play is on the dancing; it is built up around the sword dance, and must be given by skilled performers. There is plenty of singing, as well.

[2] Kelly, *Notices*, p. 58.

[3] H. H. Child, *op. cit.* Cf. Chambers, i, pp. 175 and 176. For remarks on, and quotations

On New Year's Eve " it was customary . . . for the young men and women to exchange their clothes, which was termed *Mumming* or *Disguising;* and when thus dressed in each others' garments, they would go from one neighbour's cottage to another, singing, dancing, and partaking of their good cheer. . . ." [1]

As an instance of mumming to which political significance was given, a passing reference may be made to the so-called " Gladman's Insurrection," which took place at Norwich early in 1443.[2] On this occasion it was alleged that John Gladman, a merchant of Norwich, " rode on Horseback as a King, with a Paper Crown on, and a Scepter and Sword carried before him by three Persons unknown," and twenty-seven riders preceded him, " with Coronets on their Arms, and Bows and Arrows in their Hands, like Valets of the Crown to our Sovereign Lord the King, and 100 others unknown, on Horseback and Foot with Bows and Arrows, then and there following the said John Gladman, and calling the Citizens to Arms in a riotous Manner." [3] As to the insurrection, the city pretended that Gladman, " who was ever and at thys our is, a Man of sad Disposition, & trewe & feythfull to God and to the Kyng, of Disporte as hath been accustomed in ony Cite or Burgh thorowe alle this reame, on Tuesday in the last ende of Cristemesse viz. Fastyngonge Tuesday, made a Disporte with hys Neyghbours, havyng his Hors trappyd with tynn foyle, & other nyse disgisy things, coronned as Kyng of Crestemesse, in tokyn that seson should end with the twelve Monethes of the yere, aforn hym (went) yche moneth dysguysed after the Seson requiryd, and Lenton [4] clad in whyte & red Heryngs skinns, and his Hors trapped with Oystyr-shells after him, in token that sadnesse shuld folowe, and an holy Tyme, and so rode in diverse Stretes of the Cite, with other People, with hym disguysed makyng Myrth, disportes and plays." [5]

DECAY OF FOLK CUSTOMS

Of late years many of these English folk customs have unfortunately passed out of existence. This is due to many causes, perhaps the chief of which is the

referring to, May Day customs, morris dancers, the Robin Hood play, etc., see Drake, *Shakspere and his Times,* i, pp. 152–174.

Brewer, *Dict. Phrase and Fable,* p. 542, *s. v. Maid Marian,* derives the words from *Mad Morion* — a boy in the morris dance who wore a " morion." He says that it is a corruption first of the words, and then of the sex of the character.

[1] Drake, *Shakspere and his Times,* i, p. 124.

[2] For full details see Hudson, *Records of Norwich,* i, pp. 343 f.; Blomefield, *Hist. Norf.* (1745), ii, pp. 107 f.; Herrig's *Archiv,* cxxvi, p. 185; MS. 9 c. in Muniment Room printed in full by Goddard Johnson, in *Norf. Arch.,* i, p. 294 (cited by Hudson). Cf. also Hudson, i, pp. lxxxviii f.; Blomefield (1805–10), iii, pp. 149 and 155; and Sir George Croke, *Reports* (1657), p. 183, who refers to this case.

Hudson, i, p. xc, discusses the perplexing mention of Shrove Tuesday, as the riot surely took place on 24 or 25 January.

[3] Blomefield (1745), ii, p. 108.

[4] " A man representing Lent," notes Blomefield.   [5] Blomefield, *op. cit.,* p. 111.

movement of the rural population to the cities. Then, with the increased facility of travel, people do not stay at home so much, and are not so dependent on home pleasures; villages are no longer detached from the outside world. Itinerant cinematographs come to the country centers at fair-time, and the people, relying less on themselves, find their entertainment already provided. In places where the old customs still remain, crowds of staring tourists are brought by the ubiquitous motor-car, and the country folk who dislike to be gazed at keep away from the old celebrations; while those who remain grow self-conscious, and lose their spontaneity. Professional morris dancers take the place of the spontaneous folk dancing in many places; and there has come, in the attitude of the present day, a change which makes what were undoubtedly excesses, though, softened by distance, they are covered with the glamour of poetry, distasteful to many.

In some places, the reason for the local festivals has been removed by Parliamentary legislation, and the celebrations have lapsed. Many went out of existence in 1835 when the Municipal Corporations Act was passed. At Lichfield the " Greenhill Bower " has persisted, long after the need for the " Court of Array " had been done away with — but this is an exception to the rule.[1]

Survivals and Revivals

There are, to be sure, some survivals of old customs in England. The " Plough Monday " play — the chief interest of which lies in the fact that men dress as women [2] — is still a popular pastime in parts of England. It is a proof of its early origin that the police do not interfere with a flagrant breach of the law in this case. The ceremonies in connection with the Dunmow Flitch of Bacon, have been revived.[3]

Such ceremonies as that on ships which carry passengers and sailors over the equator for the first time, seem to be survivals, or revivals, of folk plays; but they have a certain pageantic element in such a figure as Neptune. They show

---

[1] For further consideration of this ceremony, see chapter vii.

[2] On men in women's clothing see Frazer, *Adonis, Attis, Osiris*, pp. 428 f. (Appendix IV); Trevelyan, p. 250; Cf. also mention of this custom, above p. 5.

[3] On this, see William Andrews, *History of the Dunmow Flitch of Bacon Custom*, London, 1877; Strutt, *Manners and Customs*, iii, pp. 155 f.; the London *Mirror* for Saturday 11 November 1837 (no. 861), and *ibid.*, vol. v., p. 213; Ditchfield, p. 175, who refers to Harrison Ainsworth's novel, *The Flitch of Bacon*, and his reviving a lapsing custom in 1855. " The annual court which awards the Dunmow flitch of bacon " is referred to by G. B. Shaw, in his *Preface for Politicians* prefixed to *John Bull's Other Island* (New York, 1907, p. liii); cf. also *Our Mutual Friend*, Book ii, ch. xvi, for another reference to it. In the *Illus. Lond. News* for 10 Aug. 1912, p. 209, are pictures of the ceremonies which " took a new lease of life on August Bank Holiday. There was a wordless Pageant of Dunmow, morris dancing, and, of course, a trial. . . . Both couples were successful in winning a flitch — sign of a strifeless wedded life." The two pictures show the ceremony as it was in 1751 and 1912. The earlier occasion was reproduced by modern actors.

the rough fun — intensified because the victim of it is not " behind the scenes," so to speak — characteristic of the folk play; and the element of disguising makes them worth noting.

In recent years folk dancing has been revived in England, and the interest in this revival has spread to the United States.[1] But the conscious revivals of folk dancing, seem to have left the folk untouched. Children trained in Maypole dancing, and other kinds, gave in 1914 an exhibition at the " Royal May Day Festival " of Knutsford, after the morning procession; a troop of professional morris dancers accompanied the procession and danced in the streets; boy morris dancers appeared in the 1914 Greenhill Bower procession at Lichfield.[2] But when the townspeople danced on the green in both places, they danced the ordinary dances of the present day.

GUY FAWKES

One other folk-custom, now moribund, deserves mention. The festivities of Guy Fawkes' Day are linked to pageantry through the image which was some- times carried in procession.[3] This anniversary used to be elaborately observed at Hampstead; on one occasion a car, representing the British Isles and the Colonies, was provided.[4] This links pageantry closely to folk festivals. Effigies are burned at Rye; Folkestone has decorated carts with *tableaux vivants*, ancient Britons, etc. Political " guys " are sometimes shown, and occasionally a huge fancy-dress procession combines the spirit of carnival with " groups allegorical of local tradition." [5]

---

[1] In January, 1914, the Revesby sword play " from a MS. of 1779 " was performed at the Agassiz House Theatre at Cambridge, Massachusetts, by a group of students. A note on the program calls it " the only extant sword play known. Its centre is the nonsense of Pickle Herring about the nut or glass made by the sword dancers. In the play, however, country men, as a means of exhibiting their skill in sword, folk, and morris dancing, have brought to- gether survivals or reminiscences of (1) the Christmas Play — in the opening by the Fool and his sons; (2) the Robin Hood play — in the Knight of Lee and his relations to Church and peasant; and (3) a jig such as the Elizabethan theatre used between acts — in the rivalry for the hand of Cicely."

[2] The Knutsford and Lichfield processions will be considered in chapter vii.

[3] In connection with Guy Fawkes, cf. the Pope-Burnings mentioned in chapter vii. Cf. also Ditchfield, chapter ix (pp. 160 f.), for much material on Guy Fawkes' Day celebrations. The images carried in procession are treated in the following section of this chapter.

[4] Ditchfield, p. 163.

[5] Ditchfield, p. 164. "Building the Guy" is pictured in the *Illus. Lond. News*, 5 Nov. 1853; an article entitled "Recollections of the Fifth of November" accompanies it. "Burning Guy Fawkes " is pictured, *ibid.*, 8 Nov. 1851, p. 573. I append the first and last paragraphs of an article from the London *Standard*, 5 Nov. 1913, on "The Passing of the Old-Time Celebra- tions ": " Noisy street urchins busily soliciting coppers for ' our guy ' served to remind Londoners last night that today is Guy Fawkes' Day. The passing of the Children's Act, with the restrictions which it contains, has materially decreased their receipts, but many children

§ 2. PROCESSIONS

The discussion of Guy Fawkes leads us naturally to consider folk processions, in which the main root of pageantic technique may be found. These processions are common to all lands, and date from very early times. No rural merrymaking was complete without them.[1] In Germanic countries they were often accompanied by the image of some god or goddess;[2] " a doll is set on the garland, or some popular ' giant ' or other image is carried round."[3] This " doll " or image of a deity, which Chambers says is " a common, though not an invariable element in the lustration," is by some folklorists conjectured to be an " anthropomorphic representation of the fertilization spirit."

PLOUGHS AND SHIPS

Chambers points out that " at the early spring festival which survives in Plough Monday, the plough itself, the central instrument of the opening labour, figures. A variant of this custom may be traced in certain maritime districts where the functions of the agricultural deities have been extended to include the oversight of seafaring. Here it is not a plough but a boat or ship that makes its rounds when the fishing season is about to begin."[4]

---

last night managed to make themselves the richer by two shillings or more after ' rendering ' a few songs, commencing with ' Guy, Guy, Guy! ' . . .

" The parading of effigies is nowadays almost as obsolete as the lighting of bonfires. A hundred years ago, however, bands of youths would parade the streets bearing their ' creation ' in triumph. When two bands met often a royal fight ensued, which ended in one party obtaining possession of the other's effigy. These old-world celebrations have fallen into decay, and now fireworks almost alone are used to celebrate the anniversary of the discovery of the great plot. The diminution of religious intolerance probably has had much to do with the decreased popularity of the Guy Fawkes celebration, and the liberal provision of varied forms of public amusement may also have assisted. People no longer are driven to find amusement for themselves in the perpetuation of an obsolete observance." It may be added that Ditchfield, (p. 1 f.) gives an adequate summing up of the reasons for the decline of folk customs.

Cf. Leather, *Folk-Lore of Herefordshire*, p. 146, for accounts of mummers' faces blackened; on p. 130, the author notes blackened faces, with white patches, at a Christmas dance of 1909. The mummers in Yorkshire were disguised, wore masks, and carried an image of a white horse. Cf. Chambers, i. pp. 89 f. (Book ii, *Folk-Drama*) for the subject of folk drama and folk custom in general. In many places in the United States the Hallowe'en disguisings of the children preserve these folk customs far from the land of their origin.

See below, chapter vii, for further notes on pageantic " Survivals and Revivals."

[1] Cf. Chambers i, pp. 118 f., 120.

[2] *Ibid.*, p. 118. Cf. Hazlitt's Brand, (1870 ed., i, p. 111) on the Ascension Day perambulation.

[3] Chambers, i, p. 120. See below, § 5 — the discussion of giants — for further development of this point.

[4] *Ibid.*, i, p. 121. " Ship processions are to be found in various parts of Germany " (see Chambers' authorities, i, p. 121, n. 1); " at Minehead, Plymouth and Devonport in the west

" In the northern and northwestern parts of England, the entire day [Plough Monday] was usually consumed in parading the streets, and the night was devoted to festivity. The ploughmen . . . went about collecting what they called ' *plough-money* for drink.' They were accompanied by a plough, which they dragged along, and by music, and not unfrequently two of the party were dressed to personate an *old woman*, whom they called *Bessy*, and a *Fool*, the latter of these characters being covered with skins, with a hairy cap on his head and the tail of some animal pendent from his back. On one of these antics was devolved the office of collecting money from the spectators . . ." [1] We see here characters from the sword dance taking part in the procession, and collecting money while other marchers danced.

" A rude custom," says Ditchfield, " prevails at Minehead on May Day. The men fashion a cardboard ship, about ten feet long, with sails trimmed with flags and ribbons. This is carried on a man's shoulders, his head coming through a hole in the deck of the ship. . . . The origin of this custom is said to date from the beginning of the eighteenth century, when a ship was sunk off Dunster, and all hands lost." [2]

Mr. Worth describes the Millbrook May Day ship: in Devonport, the " ship-garland " was brought from Millbrook. " The ship, as I recollect it first, was a large and handsome model of a man-of-war, fullrigged, and perhaps five to six feet long, resting on a perfect sea of flowers, and carried shoulder high by four men. . . . It is interesting to note that there are lines of evidence that would make the festival [in] its present form a survival of very early days indeed. The carrying of a ship through the streets was one of the chief features of the celebration of the feast of Corpus Christi in old Plymouth. The Reformation put an end to the Corpus Christi festival, but it was not a very great change to transfer the pageant to May Day. . . . I have no doubt, therefore, that the Millbrook ship is the lineal descendant of the ship at Corpus Christi, the chief feature in the chief pageant of mediæval Plymouth; and as little that the latter was itself the survival of the ship-carrying of the elder Teutonic races. . . . The early Christian Church, if it could not abolish pagan rites and festivals, adapted them to its own purposes. . . ." [3]

---

of England, and probably also at Hull in the north." The ship of the Fishmongers in 1313, which has an obvious trade symbolism, may be a development of some such early custom. (See chapter iii.)

[1] Drake, *Shakspere and his Times* i, p. 137.

[2] *Old Eng. Customs*, p. 103, cited by Chambers, i, p. 121. The latter also cites R. N. Worth, in *Trans. Dev.'Assoc.* xv, p. 104, from whom I quote the following paragraph.

[3] Mr. Worth suggests that the "silver boat of the crescent moon became the ship of Corpus Christi." I prefer the more obvious connection with the trade of fisherfolk, which amply accounts for the rise of this folk custom.

Quenson (p. 10, n. 3) notes at Malines, on 15 August, 1838, among other things in the " grande procession de *Notre Dame d'Answick*," " un navire, symbole du bien-être de la patrie."

RELIGIOUS RIDINGS

Many folk customs were absorbed into the Church processions;[1] the older images of deities became images of Saints; the Christmas festivals were grafted on to the Roman Saturnalia,[2] and Easter was fastened to the Aryan spring festival — the immortality of the soul being substituted for the regeneration of Nature, celebrated before the Christian Era.[3]

Brand says:[4] "It was a general custom formerly, and is still observed in some country parishes, to go around the bounds and limits of the parish, on one

See also Madame Clément, *Histoire des Fêtes Civiles et Religieuses de la Belgique méridionale, et d'un grand nombre de Villes de France* (Avesnes, 1846), p. 249. The writer describes the "marche triomphale, et réjouissance publique pour honorer le martyre de Saint Rumold, apôtre et patron de la ville de Malines," on 28 June, 5 and 12 July, 1825 (pp. 225 f.). On the three-masted vessel, *La Prosperité du Pays*, were St. Catherine, the captain, and an angel, an American and two Chinamen — a real pageantic *mélange*. Mme. Clément, citing M. Quenson, notes the appearance of the ship in 1838 (p. 251).

Burckhardt, ii, p. 146, mentions the naval car (*carrus navalis*) which had been inherited from pagan times — strictly, the ship of Isis, which entered the water on the fifth of March, as a symbol that navigation was reopened. (For Germanic analogies, he refers to Jakob Grimm, *Deutsche Mythologie*.) This ship, has, he says, permanently left its name on one festival — the carnival. I may note that the *N. E. D.*, *s. v. carnival*, gives the apparent origin of the word as the Latin *carnem levare*, or an Italian descendant of this phrase. It does not mention *carrus navalis* as a possibility.

Burckhart continues: "Ein solches Schiff konnte freilich als heiter ausgestattes Prachtstück die Beschauer vergnügen, ohne dass man sich irgend noch der frühern Bedeutung bewusst war, und als z. B. Isabella von England mit ihrem Bräutigam Kaiser Friedrich II. in Köln zusammenkam, fuhren ihr eine ganze Anzahl von Schiffwagen mit musicirenden Geistlichen, von verdeckten Pferden gezogen, entgegen."

[1] Cf. Ward, *Hist. Eng. Dram. Lit.* (1899) i, p. 145. For an example outside England, see Étienne de Bourbon, p. 168: "Accidit in dyocesi Elnensi [Elne in Roussillon] quod, cum quidam predicator in terra illa predicasset et vigiliis sanctorum cum in quadam parrochia quidam juvenes consuevissent venire et super equum ligneum ascendere, et larvati et parati choreas ducere in vigilia festivitatis illius ecclesie, in ecclesia et per cimiterium, cum propter verba illius predicatoris et inhibicionem sui sacerdotis dimissis choreis, vigilarent homines in ecclesia in oracione, venit quidam juvenis ad socium suum, invitans eum ad solitum ludum." The editor notes, (p. 168, n. 4) "Les danses devant les églises, et même dans leur enceinte ou dans celle des cimitières qui les entouraient, étaient encore très repandues au XIIIᵉ siècle. . . . Mais cette coutume de célébrer la fête patronale par des déguisements et des danses équestres" [cf. the hobby-horse of the Plough Monday play] "sur des montures en bois semble particulière au Roussillon — il serait curieux d'en retrouver la trace chez les montagnards de ce pays." Cf. also, *ibid.*, p. 162, note and references. Chambers, i, p. 327, in summing up the characteristics of the Feast of Fools, notes processions or cavalcades through the streets of Laon, Châlons-sur-Marne, etc.

[2] As Davidson points out, p. 42.

[3] See Ordish in *Folk-Lore* iv, no. 2, p. 156. On the connection of the ecclesiastical New Year's revels with the pagan Kalends, see Chambers, i, pp. 330 f.

[4] *Observations on Popular Antiquities* (1777) ch. xxvi, p. 263. Cf. Hazlitt's Brand (1905) ii, p. 476, *s. v. Parochial Perambulations*.

of the three days before Holy Thursday, or the Feast of our Lord's Ascension; when the minister accompany'd with his churchwardens and parishioners, were (*sic*) wont to deprecate the vengeance of God, beg a blessing on the fruits of the earth, and preserve the rights and properties of their parish.

" The original of this custom is dated from the times of the heathen. For from the days of Numa Pompilius, they worshipped the god Terminus, whom they looked upon to be the guardian of fields and landmarks and the keeper-up of friendship and peace among men; upon this account the feast called *Terminalia* was dedicated to him; instead of which it is a very ancient custom to surround the bounds of parishes every year: and instead of heathenish rites and sacrifices to an imaginary god, to offer praises and prayer to the true God, the God of the whole earth. The custom was, the people accompanied the bishop, or some of the clergy into the fields, where litanies were made, and the mercy of God implor'd, that he would avert the evils of plague and pestilence, that he would send them good and seasonable weather, and give them the fruits of the earth in due season.

" The litanies or rogations, which were then made use of, and gave name to the time of Rogation-week, were first observed by Mamertus, Bishop of Vienna, in the year 550 . . ." [1]

---

[1] On early Italian religious processions, with masks, and the encroachment of the secular elements, see Burckhardt, *Die Kultur der Renaissance in Italien* (5th ed., 1896), ii, pp. 145 f.: " Ohne Zweifel gewährten die kirchlichen Processionen seitdem Mittelalter einen Anlass zur Maskirung, mochten nun Engelkinder das Sacrament, die herumgetragenen heiligen Bilder und Reliquien begleiten, oder Personen der Passion im Zuge mitgehen, etwa Christus mit dem Kreuz, die Schächer und Kriegsknechte, die heiligen Frauen. Allein mit grossen Kirchenfesten verbindet sich schon frühe die Idee eines städtischen Aufzuges, der nach der naiven Art des Mittelalters eine Menge profaner Bestandtheile verträgt."

Middlemore, ii, pp. 196 f. (Burckhardt, ii, pp. 146 f.): " But the religious processions were not only mingled with secular accessories of all kinds, but were often replaced by processions of clerical masks. Their origin is perhaps to be found in the parties of actors who wound their way through the streets of the city to the place where they were about to act the mystery; but it is possible that at an early period the clerical procession may have constituted itself as a distinct species. . . . The secular ' trionfi ' were far more frequent than the religious. They were modelled on the procession of the Roman Imperator. . . . All the festive processions, whether they celebrated any special event or were mainly held for their own sakes, assumed more or less the character and nearly always the name of a ' trionfo ' . . .

" At the Venetian festivals the processions, not on land but on water, were marvelous in their fantastic splendour . . . Genii with attributes symbolising the various gods, floated on machines hung in the air [in 1491]; below stood others grouped as tritons and nymphs . . . the Bucentaur was followed by such a crowd of boats of every sort that for a mile all round the water could not be seen . . ." The Carnival in Rome — where its character was most varied in the fifteenth century — is described by Burckhardt, ii, p. 153 (Middlemore, ii, p. 205). At Florence, allegorical figures were not uncommon; they went on floats or horseback through the crowd (Burckhardt, ii, p. 154; Middlemore, ii, p. 207). Not only allegory, but mythology, appeared; but these are perhaps rather masquerades with a pageantic element, than

FEAST OF THE ASS

In the twelfth and thirteenth centuries, the Feast of the Ass was used to stimulate the devotion of the people.[1] "On Palm Sunday . . . a wooden ass with an image on it, being placed on a platform, with wheels, and drest up, was drawn by the people bearing boughs and branches of palm to the church door. . . . The ass with the figure being moved along, the people cast branches upon both, and it was drawn into the church in procession, the priests going before; the people followed, struggling for the holy boughs over which the pageant had passed."[2] The celebration of Palm Sunday in Wales is described by Miss Trevelyan.[3] In South Wales an image of a donkey was made of wood; a stuffed effigy was placed on it,

---

real pageants. This description might be applied to the numerous carnival processions of today.

"The Procession, in the broad, level and well-paved streets of the Italian cities, was soon developed into the 'Trionfo,' or train of masked figures on foot and in chariots, the ecclesiastical character of which gradually gave way to the secular. The processions at the Carnival and at the feast of Corpus Christi" (which, says a note, was not established at Venice until 1407) "were alike in the pomp and brilliancy with which they were conducted, and set the pattern afterwards followed by the royal or princely progresses. Other nations were willing to spend vast sums of money on these shows, but in Italy alone do we find an artistic method of treatment which arranged the procession as a harmonious and significative whole . . ." Burckhardt, ii, p. 133; Middlemore, ii, pp. 177 f.

"Die rein oder überwiegend Aufführungen waren besonders an den grösseren Fürstenhöfen ganz wesentlich auf die geschmackvolle Pracht des Anblicks berechnet, dessen einzelne Elemente in einem mythologischen und allegorischen Zusammenhang standen, soweit ein solcher sich gerne und angenehm erraten liess. Das Barocke fehlte nicht; riesige Thierfiguren, aus welchen plötzlich Schaaren von Masken herauskamen, wie z. B. bei einem fürstlichen Empfang [1465] zu Siena, aus einer goldenen Wölfin ein ganzes Ballet von zwölf Personen hervorstieg . . ." Burckhardt, ii, pp 142 f; Middlemore, ii, pp. 190 f.

[1] Cf. Chambers's remarks on the Boy Bishop, (Med. Stage, chapter xv), the customs of which revel were in the main parallel to the Feast of Fools. A processional character was common at the celebration.

Cf. also Hone, Anc. Mys., chapter vii (Origin of Mysteries — Feast of Fools — Feast of the Ass, etc.), pp. 148 f., and chapter viii (The Boy Bishop — English Mysteries), pp. 193 f. Cf. Davidson, Eng. Mystery Plays, p. 43; Kelly, Notices, p. 27. Both Hone and Kelly refer to Barnaby Googe's translation of The Popish Kingdome, and Brand's Popular Antiquities. Hazlitt, Dict. Faiths and Folk-Lore, i, p. 20, gives vulgar superstitions regarding the ass.

On Palm Sunday observances in general, see Brand (ed. Hazlitt, 1870), i, pp. 71 f. "Upon Palme Sondaye they play the foles sadely, drawynge after them an Asse in a rope, when they be not moche distante from the Woden Asse that they drawe" is quoted from the Pylgremage of Pure Devotyon newly translatyd into Englishe (1551); cf. also Fulke (quoted, i, p. 76): "Thus you turn the holy mystery of Christ's riding to Jerusalem to a May-game and pagent-play." See Leather, p. 141, for notice of a laborer going through Hereford in Passion Week, 1706, clothed in a long coat and periwig, and seated on a donkey, shocking people by his travesty on the Entry into Jerusalem.

[2] Hone, Anc. Mys., p. 162, n. a.

[3] Trevelyan, pp. 245 f.

and these were glued to a wheeled platform. Both effigy and donkey were decorated with flowers and bunches of evergreens; they were brought to the church
door by the people in procession carrying evergreens or seasonable flowers. After
the clergyman's blessing, the people kept the sprigs as a charm against evil
spirits.

"On Easter Monday at Ashton-under-Lyne there is the custom of ' Riding
the Black Lad '; in which case the effigy of a black boy, after being carried round
the town and shot at, is finally burned." [1] Ditchfield also notes that " the curious
custom of flogging Judas Iscariot, though not an English practice, may be witnessed in any of our ports, if any Portuguese or South American vessels are in the
harbour. An effigy is made of the Betrayer, which is ducked in the dock, and
then kicked and lashed with knotted ropes, amid the shouts and the singing of a
weird, rude chant by the spectators." [2]

In these examples we see the Church sharing in a popular custom, and the old
folk habit of marching with images of men or models of animals connected with
Biblical material. We shall return to this old folk custom later in discussing
giants. Effigies given a political, rather than a religious, significance were — as we
shall see — burned at London in the seventeenth, and at Boston in the eighteenth,
century.[3]

A description of the solemn Whitmonday procession from the Church of St.
Mary within the Castle to St. Margaret's without the walls of Leicester is given
by Kelly.[4] "The image of the Virgin Mary . . . was, on these occasions,
carried through the streets under a canopy, borne by four persons and preceded by
ministrels . . . . Then followed twelve persons representing the twelve apostles,
each of whom had the name of the apostle whom he personated written on parch-
ment,[5] and fixed on his bonnet." [6]

Davidson says that the Church had processions from the first century; [7] that
the royal ridings and these processions simulated each other, and were sometimes
combined (especially in England, in the procession of St. George). Many processions after the thirteenth century contained one or more pageants carried on
moving wagons; and sometimes, in place of these, groups afoot personated
characters.[8] The Whitmonday procession at Leicester, to which we have just

---

[1] Ditchfield, p. 87.
[2] Ibid., p. 76.
[3] See below, chapter vii.
[4] Notices of Leicester, p. 7.
[5] Cf. the " scriptures " of the royal entries, below, chapter iii.
[6] This seems to have been going on in 1490; the earlier parochial records are lost. See
Kelly, pp. 7 and 9. The St. Giles procession at Edinburgh (see Extracts from the Records of the
Burgh of Edinburgh, ii, p. 220, for that of 6 September, 1555) was probably a church procession
with a saint's image. As Chambers points out (i, p. 119) the Church found room for the
summer lustrations in its scheme, and often the statue of some local saint was carried round.
[7] Davidson, pp. 90 f.
[8] See Magnin, Hist. marionnettes en Europe (1862 ed., pp. 51 f.), book ii, chapter i, for a
consideration of the adoption by the Church of popular and pagan marionettes.

referred, shows a larger religious element than does the mumming in Wales at Christmas, where the Holy Family appeared with a throng of motley dancers. Mummers, dressed up in all kinds of costumes, made up the " Mari Llwyd " or Holy Mary. Boys dressed as bears, foxes, squirrels, and rabbits, swelled the throng: in some places a woman impersonated the Virgin, while Joseph and the child Jesus were prominent. Later these were omitted, and a kind of Punch and Judy substituted.[1]

The Beverley guild of St. Mary was founded in 1355 and that of St. Elene in 1378.[2] " Every year on the Feast of the Purification of the blessed Mary, all the bretheren and sisteren shall meet together in a fit and appointed place away from the Church; and there one of the gild shall be clad in comely fashion as a queen, like to the glorious Virgin Mary, having what may seem a son in her arms; and two others shall be clad like to Joseph and Simeon; and two shall go as angels.... With much music and gladness the pageant Virgin with her son and Joseph and Simeon shall go in procession to the Church . . . and when they have got there, the pageant Virgin shall offer her son to Simeon at the high altar . . ." [3] The Beverley guild of St. Elene chose " a fair youth " to be clad as a queen like to St. Elene; and he was preceded by two old men carrying cross and shovel. There were " sisters " in this guild also — as in many others of like sort.[4] The guild of St. William at Norwich paraded a " knave-child " between two men holding candles in honor of the youthful martyr.[5]

These early Church processions with pageantic features are not unlike — as Sir George Forrest has pointed out to me — the Mussulman " mourning festival " of the *Muharram*. The *taziya* is, strictly speaking, a pageant — as, indeed, is the Ark of the Covenant, carried around in religious procession.[6]

---

[1] Trevelyan, pp. 31 f. When the procession started out, all doors were locked; then a house was chosen, and the procession exchanged banter, sarcasm, and wit with those inside the house: if the *Mari Llwyd* party defeated the householder by superior wit, the conquerors were admitted and entertained.

The skeleton head and shoulders of a horse, carried in this procession, have been variously explained (p. 32).

[2] Smith, *English Gilds*, pp. 148, 149. [3] Quoted in Smith, p. 149. [4] See Smith, p. 148.

[5] Smith, p. 30, and Chambers, ii, p. 164.

" At York, the proclaiming of Yule by ' Yule ' and ' Yule's wife ' on St. Thomas's day was once a notable pageant." Chambers, i, p. 261.

[6] For descriptions of the *Muharram* see Fanny Parkes, *Wanderings of a Pilgrim in Search of the Picturesque* (2 vols., London, 1850); one on 19 May, 1834 is described, i, pp. 295 f.; another on 29 April, 1835, ii, pp. 17 f.

Connected with this kind of religious pageantry may be mentioned — as an example of many others — " the great funeral machine builded within the Cathedral of St. Peter in Rome," for the obsequies of His Holiness Pope Alexander VII. There were many inscriptions and elegies on this structure, with pictures of the late Pope, and other magnates of the Church, together with " four great silver'd Statues representing the foure Vertues, *Prudence, Justice, Fortitude,* and *Temperance.*" For a full description of this, see a pamphlet entitled: *A Short*

Corpus Christi

Sometimes the Church pageantry was very elaborate — particularly in the ridings of the guilds of St. George and at Corpus Christi.[1]

Account of the Life and Death of Pope Alexander VII, with a Description of his Funeral Machin, and Elegies erected in St. Peter's Church in Rome. . . . Translated out of the Italian Copies printed at Rome, by P. A., Gent., London, 1667. (This is in the Fairholt collection at the London Society of Antiquaries.)

Engravings of a car, containing allegorical figures, which appeared in the funeral procession of Charles V, may be seen in the Musée Plantin at Antwerp.

Cars, or pageants, appeared in Roman triumphs. We cannot, of course, do more than touch upon these here: Menestrier, *Traité des Tournois*, etc. (Lyons, 1669) pp. 25 f., describes a "pomp" of Ptolemy Philadelphus at Alexandria — "Cent quatre-vingt hommes tiroient vn grand Char à quatre roües, sur lequel estoit placée l'Image de Bacchus . . . . Soixante hommes tiroient vn autre char, sur lequel estoit l'Image de Nyse . . . . Ce char estoit suivi d'vn autre chargé de raisins que soixante Satyres fouloient chantant les chansons qu'on avoit pour lors coûtume de chanter, quand on pressoit la vendange. Ils alloient sous la conduite d'vn Silene, & le moust qu'ils exprimoient des raisins couloit par toutes les rües. Six cens hommes tiroient encore vn autre char d'une grandeur extraordinaire, sur lequel estoit porté vn Outre, de prés (*sic*) de deux cens muits de vin, faite de plusieurs peaux de Pantheres cousües ensemble, dont il couloit du vin par divers tuyaux. Six vingt Satyres . . . accompagnoient ce char . . ."

At the same triumph, " Sur vn Char de quatre roües on voyoit la representation de Bacchus, qui pour se mettre à couvert des poursuites de Iunon, cherchoit vn azile près de l'Autel de Rhea. Les Images d'Alexandre Ptolomée, estoient en ce mesme Corps avec des Couronnes d'or à fueilles (*sic*) de lierre, & l'image de la Vertu representée en pied devant Ptolomée avoit vne couronne d'or, à feuilles d'olive. La Ville de Corynthe sous l'Image d'vne Nymphe estoit à son costé. . . . Sur le mesme Char estoient les Images de toutes les Villes d' Ionie, & de toutes les autres où l'on parle la langue Grecque . . . chacune avec . . . vne Inscription, qui la faissoit connoitre . . ."

This shows several parallels to English pageantry in its developed form. The flowing wine, the mythology and allegory — personified by images or living people — the personification of cities, the historical element, and the explanatory "scriptures," will all be treated in due course.

[1] Mr. Smith, in *English Gilds* is corrected by his daughter (*York Plays*, p. xxx, n. 2). She points out that the York processions had nothing to do with the Corpus Christi plays, and says: " My father made a natural error, (in which Drake preceded him, followed by Skaife and Klein,) in confusing the procession of the gild and the Corpus Christi pageants together, and supposing them both to have been brought out by the gild." On these plays — which are outside our field — see, beside Miss Toulmin Smith's authoritative book, the dramatic histories of Collier, Ward, and Schelling.

At Leicester, in 1477 and earlier, a " passion play " was given on pageants by the crafts. (Bateson, *Records of the Borough of Leicester* (1899–1901), ii, p. 297). A petition of the Norwich Guild of St. Luke for the aid of the Guilds in the pageantic procession of Pentecost week, may be found in *Norf. Arch.* iii, pp. 6 f. The aid was granted. (The date of the petition was the Feast of St. Matthew the Apostle, 19 Henry VIII.)

The Corpus Christi plays were given by the crafts, and were not a growth from the guild processions.

The Feast of Corpus Christi was instituted by Pope Urban IV in 1264;[1] from the first, the leading feature of the celebration was the procession of priests and laymen, in which all civic bodies took part, with tapers, banners, shields of the guilds, and later with pageant *tableaux*. Individuals personated characters, at first Biblical, then legendary. The Guilds of Corpus Christi arose — as did the Guilds of St. George later — to take the procession under their care; they did not foster plays, " and were, indeed, sometimes necessary to preserve the splendor of the processions after the popular interest had turned to the plays." [2] The same writer continues: " How early pageant *tableaux* were introduced, it is impossible . . . to state, but it must have been at an early date, and in close connection with the royal entry,[3] The body of Christ received in a sense royal honors, and it may be that at first stationary pageants, a marked tribute to royalty,[4] were sometimes used. It seems evident that moveable pageants were carried by the gild in connection with the gild banner, and usually bore the insignia or arms of the gild; also that at first they presented a connected Bible story,[5] but afterwards passed through nearly the same developmental stages as did the pageants of the royal entry. These changes, like those of the royal entry, were in the main the same throughout western Europe, although the intrusion of the civic element doubtless contributed to local variations." [6]

Shortly after the confirmation of the Feast in 1318,[7] pageants of the Bible story were introduced [8] in conjunction with the banners of the craft. " These at

---

[1] Cf. Schelling, *Eliz. Drama* (1908), i, p. 14. It "is supposed" that "the performance of plays or pageants during the festival of *Corpus Christi* " was introduced into England in 1268, says Collier (*Hist. Eng. Drama Poetry* (1879), i, p. 18).

[2] Davidson, p. 92.

[3] It will be shown in the third chapter that the earliest reliable account of a pageantic " royal-entry " is that planned by the Fishmongers in 1298; and in this, the " animals " (really fishes) which had a trade significance, were combined with the figure of St. Magnus. The Corpus Christi procession was presumably existing in 1264 or shortly after.

[4] The reason for this statement is not clear; although they are more common in the " royal-entry " than in the Lord Mayor's Shows, I cannot see that stationary pageants are " a marked tribute to royalty." There were stationary pageants in sixteenth-century Lord Mayor's shows.

[5] But cf. below, p. 21 — the craft-guild plays rivalled the " riding." I do not see sufficient cause for the statement that these religious guilds presented " a connected Bible story." Often there were few Biblical characters included; and while it might, perhaps, be allowed that the celebration of the Purification of the Virgin at Beverley combines narrative and procession, I think this is rather the exception than the rule.

[6] Davidson, p. 92. We shall see that in the London " royal-entry," the civic element was the most important.

[7] In 1313 Philip the Fair gave a splendid show at Paris, which Edward II and Isabella saw. (*Histoire de la Ville de Paris*, ii, p. 523, cited by Davies, *Extracts from the Municipal Records of the City of York* (1843) p. 229.)

[8] No Corpus Christi Guild was founded as early as this. — That at York was founded in 1408; in 1368–69 the Leicester Guild paid rent for a room; in 1425 the Bristol Guild

first were mute mysteries, expressed by action. In a short time, however, spoken drama necessitated frequent halts by the procession, as it was impossible to act satisfactorily in motion. Indeed, connected pantomimic action would seem impossible in a moving procession; therefore this custom [1] may be older than the spoken drama. These halts prolonged the procession beyond reasonable limit, and were avoided by transferring the pageants to the rear of the procession. A division of the procession immediately arose through the slower movement of the pageants, but the plays, though much belated, followed the traditional course of the procession through the city." [2]

These craft-guild plays — taken from the churches and put on pageants [3] — must not be confused with the religious-guild processions. As has been pointed out

was old. For the "constitucion for Corpus Christi Procession and for the Maundy," see the citation (1325) from *Liber Quartus* of the Great Domesday Book of Ispwich, in Gross, *Gild Merchant*, ii, pp. 125 f.

Henry Harrod, in *Norf. Arch.* iii, p. 11, describes the Corpus Christi plays at Norwich from documents in the Record Room of the Corporation. See p. 12 for mention of the York play corresponding to the Norwich "paradise." He says they "seem to have been in dumb show, and several sets of actors required to set forth one incident." The "tree" of the Grocers' Play later became secularized. The exhibition of Whitsun pageants at Norwich was suspended in the last year of the reign of Henry VIII (Hudson, *Records, Norwich*, ii, p. 171.) They were revived in 1565 (ii, p. 135. Cf. also ii, p. lv). The *Mayoralty Court Book* (1540–49), p. 216 (4 June, 32 Henry VIII), is cited by Hudson; the *Folio Assembly Book* (1491–1553), fol. 206 b, records the minutes of an assembly held on the Friday after Ascension Day, 1 Edw. VI (11 May, 1548): "And as touching any elecion of Wardens of misteryes & the wateryng or for the Master of Beggers or for settyng forth of pageants this yeere ben differryd upon divers consideracions." The *Folio Assembly Book* for 1553–83, fol. 112 b, contains this entry (13 April, 7 Eliz. [1565]): "Allso it is agreyd that souche Pageauntes that wer wont to go in this cittie, in the tyme of Whitson holy dayes shalbe sett furth by occupacions as in tymes past haue been usyed." Cf. Hudson, ii, p. 230, for the order of the 1449 Corpus Christi procession at Norwich.

[1] Of stopping? Davidson does not seem to take into account the need of getting to larger audiences than one place could accommodate. As the drama was spoken in the churches before the craft guilds undertook to present the plays, I do not see any necessity for assuming pantomime. The difficulty of hearing does not enter into the question: otherwise, the movement would have been toward pantomime, rather than away from it.

[2] Davidson, pp. 93 f. Cf. also Chambers, ii, p. 161: "In some places the play was suppressed, and reduced to a dumb-show."

[3] Cf. "Here Erode ragis in the pagond and in the strete also," the oft-quoted stage direction in the *Pageant of the Shearmen and Taylors* printed in Manly, i, p. 147. The word then spread to the show given on each car; cf. "Pagina Quinta de Mose," of the Chester Whitsun plays (Manly, i, p. 66) and "explicit pagina pastorum" (p. 119). A discussion of the miracle plays is, as I have remarked, outside our field; I shall merely cite a passage from Davidson (p. 76) who notes that on the continent the plays were given on a stationary platform. "To this, the English cycles presented a marked contrast. The guild plays of England changed the station of the Continental stage into a movable pageant, or platform, and instead of calling the population of a city to the stage, rolled the platform through the streets in orderly succession from audience to audience."

these were quite distinct.[1] " Up till 1426 the procession of Corpus Christi and the plays had [at York] both been taken on the same day, but in that year (it is entered on the records) one William Melton . . . induced the people to have the play on one day and the procession on the second . . ."[2] The York Corpus Christi guild was founded in 1408, " in order to do honour to the feast of that name by a procession, which rapidly became rich and popular; it has nothing to do with the plays performed on Corpus Christi Day, which . . . were produced by the crafts . . . ; but in 1446 William Revetor, a chantry priest . . . bequeathed to the gild a play called *The Creed Play* . . . to be performed through York every tenth year. . . . The gild was abolished in 1547, but . . . the city council tried in 1568 to have it [the play] performed again " against which Dean Hutton protested.[3]

As early as 1368–69 the Leicester Corpus Christi guild paid a shilling rent for a room over the East Gate.[4] In the early part of the sixteenth century the guild was very prosperous;[5] and in March, 1540, the guilds of Corpus Christi and St. Margaret received a grant of £10 each.[6] In *Hall Papers*, i, no. 146[7] (temp. Elizabeth), is a reference to the cottages and parcels of land "sometyme belonging to the late dissolved Guylde of Corpus Cristi," and a charter of Queen Elizabeth, dated 17 February, 1589, gives the property of the guilds of Corpus Christi and St. Margaret to the town.[8]

In 1425 the celebration of this feast was an ancient custom at Bristol,[9] but there seems to have been no religious guild; the craft guilds apparently carried on

---

Lydgate's *Processioune of Corpus Cristi*, printed by Halliwell-Phillipps (*Minor Poems of Lydgate*, p. 95), from Harl. MS. 2251, fol. 250 *et seq.*, is a description of the miracle-plays given on that feast. It is not a pageant in any sense of the word, though it is the kind of explanation that might be repeated by an " expositor " or " doctor."   [1] See above, p. 18, note 1.

[2] L. T. Smith, pp. xxxiv f., citing the York Records, Book A, fol. 269; Davies, p. 243; F. Drake, *Eboracum*, appendix, pp. xxix f. Drake notes that the play was to be performed on the vigil of the feast. (Cf. p. 223.)

[3] L. T. Smith, p. xxx. Such entries as that in the York *House Book*, i, fol. 59 b (22 Oct., 17 Edw. IV), dealing with a fine, "an halfe [to go] to the vse of the Coialtie of this Citie and the other halfe to the vphaldynge of the pageante of the said Dyers," refers to the craft-guild plays. Miss Smith (p. xxxi) gives a mention of the Bakers' fines of 1378 and shows (p. xxxii) that the plays had then been in use for many years.

[4] *Mayor's Account*, Box 5, no. 124, in Bateson, ii, p. 143.   [5] Bateson, iii, pp. 11, 35, etc.

[6] *Book of Acts*, p. 1, printed in Bateson, iii, p. 45.   [7] Bateson, iii, p. 235.

[8] Bateson, iii, p. 251. Davidson, p. 92, notes that the guild of Corpus Christi at Leicester " contributed to the most splendid procession in the city except that of St. George."

[9] Mr. Frederick Schenck has called my attention to the ordinances regarding the feast of Corpus Christi in *The Little Red Book of Bristol* (ed. Bickley). Cf. this work, ii, p. 145 (a new ordinance for the Cordwainers, 26 June, 1425): As masters and servants of this craft "ount auncienment vses devoir lour lumier en le fest de Corpus Christi ardant, en la procession generalle en lonour de sacrement et auxi daler deuaunt leȝ Mair et Viscont en les veilles del natiuitee de Seint John Baptiste et des Appostles Petre et Paule en lonour de mesmes les seints . . . leȝ quelle lumier et autres affair as ditȝ temps ne purront estre sustenuȝ sauns

the celebration. The craft guilds of Dublin gave Corpus Christi plays,[1] and did not confine themselves to religious subjects. The regulations [2] were " made by an old law, and confermed by a semble [3] in 1498." Beside Biblical subjects, the " courteours " [4] showed King Arthur and his knights; the butchers showed " tormentours, [5] with their garmentis well and clenly peynted." The " Mayor of the Bull Ring " and bachelors of the same showed " the Nine Worthies ridyng worshupfully with ther followers accordyng." The " Hagardmen and the husbandmen to berr the dragoun and to repaire the dragoun a [*i. e.* on] Seint Georges day and Corpus Christi day." [6]

In Coventry, " the procession upon Corpus Christi Day (which preceded, and must be carefully distinguished from the exhibition of Pageants) was conducted with no small degree of splendour, and called for express Acts of Leet." [7] The first entry is dated 1444: " Pur le Ridyng on Corpus xp̄i day and for Watche on midsomer even." [8] In 1446: " Et quod le Ruydyng in festo Corporis Christi fiat prout ex antiquo tempore conserverint." [9]

---

graundes costages et ces en commune par toute la mestier a lour commune assemble; et sont diuers persons de dite mestier queux ne voullent venir as tels assembles pur lexploit des busoignes auauntditʒ, Que plese . . ." to grant that anyone who shall absent himself shall pay 12*d.* fine. Cf. also ii, pp. 148, 149, 151, etc., for further rules regarding this feast. By the early years of the fifteenth century, interest in the Corpus Christi procession at Bristol was apparently waning.

[1] J. C. Walker, *An Historical Essay on the Irish Stage*, in *Trans. Royal Irish Acad.* (Antiquities), 1787, vol. ii, pp. 82 f.; Sir John T. Gilbert, *Calendar of Ancient Records of Dublin*, preface, p. x, and i, pp. 239 f., where the *Chain-Book* account is reprinted.

[2] Printed from the *Chain-Book* in Gilbert, i, pp. 239 f.   [3] Assembly.

[4] Ed. notes " MS. indistinct." Qy: *couturiers ?* The *cowtyoures* could apparently choose between Arthur and the worthies. (Cf. i, p. 241.)   [5] Ed. notes "executioners."

[6] Sir Richard Torkington describes the Corpus Christi feast at Venice in 1517. (Addl. MS. 28,561, fol. 20 b (p. 38), *et seq.* [His *Diary* has been edited by W. J. Loftie. For this extract see that edition, p. 14.]): " Ther went Pagents of the old law and the new law Joynyng to gedyr. . . . And betwyne every of the Pagents went littyll childern of both kynds, gloriusly and rechely Dressed beryng in ther handys ryche Cuppes or other vessales of gold and silver Rychely inamelyd and gylt ffull of plesaunt fflowers and well Smellying which chyldern kest the flowers vpon the lords and pylgrymes. They war Dressed as Aungellis with clothe of gold and crymsyn velvet. . . . The forme and manner thereof excedyd all other that ever I saw, so much that I canne nott wryte it."

[7] Sharp, *Diss. on Pag. at Coventry* (1825), pp. 159 f. He quotes, p. 170, from Barnaby Googe's translation of Naogeorgus' *Popish Kingdom*, the account of Corpus Christi ceremonies. Torches were provided in the parade of the companies; and the cresset-bearers of the Dyers' Company wore surplices and straw hats. (Sharp, p. 165: this costume suggests the Commencement season at at least one New England University. Cf. the straw hats at London in 1540 and 1542 (see p. 38, n. 5).

[8] Cf. also Harris, *Coventry Leet Book*, i, p. 220 [*sub anno* 1445].

[9] Sharp, p. 160. (Harris, i, p. 231, *sub anno* 1447, reads *consueuit.*) Sharp gives Trinity Guild accounts for 1459, 1468, 1518; Corpus Christi and St. Nicholas Guild inventories for 1493, 1502; and notes various expenses, 1448–1554. (See pp. 161 f.)

The Corpus Christi procession took place in the morning: the order of the companies was from the youngest to the oldest. The members of each rode, and their journeymen walked. The members were preceded by their torchbearers; the religious bodies followed the laity; the Trinity Guild bore the Host, which was attended by priests, and the fraternity of the Corpus Christi Guild did special honor to the solemnity.

The Mayor and the Aldermen with their attendants, and the civil and religious fraternities, and all the ecclesiastics of the city would join in the procession.[1] Sometimes Herod, and perhaps the chief persons in the other craft plays, rode in it.[2]

There seem to have been pageants in the Corpus Christi processions at Bungay and Bury St. Edmunds, but " the notices are too fragmentary to permit of more than a conjecture as to whether they were accompanied by plays. The *tableaux* shown at Dublin, Hereford, and London were of a continuous and cyclical character, although at Hereford, St. Katharine, and at Dublin, King Arthur, the Nine Worthies and St. George's dragon were tacked on at the tail of the procession." [3] In the " Decree Arbitral " (19 May, 1531) between the Edinburgh " Wobstaris," the " Walkaris and Scheraris," and the " Bonetmakaris," arrangements were made about settling disputes, " and in speciall anent the ordering of thame to pas in the processioun on Corpus Christi Day and the octauis tharof, and all vthir generall processionis. . . ." [4]

Before we pass to a consideration of the civic processions that are survivals of the craft plays at Corpus Christi, as well as of the habit of " perambulating boundaries," let us consider the other chief procession of the religious guilds [5] — that of St. George.

St. George

We have already seen that one of the important characters in folk mumming is St. George. It is possible that his name was attached to a figure in the sword

---

[1] For items concerning the craft plays at Coventry, see Harris, *Leet Book*, ii, pp. 555, 556, 558, 564, 565; iii, 625, 708, etc.

[2] We shall see that it was not uncommon to find characters from the craft plays in provincial " royal-entries." Chambers, ii, p. 163, notes that the Coventry procession outlived the Corpus Christi feast.

[3] Chambers, ii, p. 162. He quotes Sharp, p. 172; the latter, citing a contemporary writer, shows that the Dublin procession, like those of Coventry and Shrewsbury, lasted to a recent date. " The Fringes was a procession of the trades and corporations, performed in Ireland on Corpus Christi day, even within the author's recollection. King Solomon, the Queen of Sheba, with Vulcan, Venus, and Cupid were leading persons on this occasion."

[4] *Extracts from the Records of the Burgh of Edinburgh*, ii, p. 49.

[5] Cf. Brentano's introduction to Toulmin Smith's *English Gilds*, pp. lxv f.; C. Gross, *The Gild Merchant*, i, appendix A, and Sullivan's introduction to O'Curry, *Manners and Customs of the Ancient Irish* (1873), i, pp. ccvi f., for a discussion of the origin of guilds, and the different kinds — religious, mercantile, etc.

dance because of a fancied resemblance between the struggle of the Fool with the "Wild Worm," and St. George's battle with the Dragon. While this is conjectural, we may, I think safely, assume that it was from the folk custom that St. George appeared in pageantry.[1] The natural current is from folk-custom to pageantry, rather than in the other direction. It is probable that the name was fastened on the folk figure by the religious "riding," which may have given its St. George to the pageant directly.

Not only in England, but on the Continent as well, did St. George often figure in mediæval pageants.[2] In England the St. George "riding" was very common.

---

[1] He may, of course, have come into pageantry through the Church, *via* the religious "riding"; or there may be here an influence from chivalry. The ultimate source seems to have been a folk figure on whom the name was fastened. The whole subject needs a separate treatment; I add a few references.

Fairholt, *L. M. Pag.*, pt. i, pp. xxxviii f., gives an account of St. George and the Dragon at Mons, as well as other French dragons, referring to a list of similar processions given in *Recherches Historiques sur Gilles, Seigneur de Chin, et le Dragon* (Mons, 1825); he notes (p. xl, note) that "the author of this pamphlet is inclined to consider these legends of saints overcoming dragons as nothing more than a symbol of the reclaiming of marsh lands left to the Church." This suggestion may be of interest to the future investigator of St. George; it suggests Müllenhof's exploded theories concerning *Beowulf*.

On the legend of St. George, see J. E. Matzke, in *Publ. Mod. Lang. Assoc.*, xvii, pp. 464 f. and xviii, pp. 99 f. Cf. also Beatty, p. 279: "The life of the saint must have been very well-known in England. He appears in the old English Martyrology after the ninth century . . . and he displaced St. Edward as the patron saint of England in 1349." On St. George, see also Frazer, *The Magic Art*, ii, chapter xix, pp. 324 f. He was the patron of wolves and cattle.

The pageant of St. George in the fourteenth and fifteenth centuries had its place among the miracle plays. Ordish, in *Folk-Lore*, iv, 2, p. 152, says, "The representations invariably took place by a well or water conduit." (This may be due to the fact that the conduit, running wine, could be made to suggest dragon's blood, and so add verisimilitude to the killing; or because the best pageants were built on the most prominent sites.) The slaying of the dragon in Bavaria ("descended from a magical rite designed to fertilize the fields") is described by Frazer, *The Magic Art*, ii, pp. 163 f. In view of the fact that St. George's Day falls on 23 April, it is, perhaps, worth noting that (as Frazer points out), May Day and Whitsuntide are closely associated with ceremonies for the revival of plant life in spring (*ibid.*, ii, 103). In some instances, says Kelly (*Notices*, p. 63) St. George and the dragon became confused with the May games; and the names "king play" and "king game" were also applied "to the pageant of the 'Three Kings of Cologne' — and the sport or pageant of the 'Lord of Misrule' . . . also partook very much of the same character."

[2] Cf. Fairholt's translation (pt. i, pp. x f.) of Albrecht Dürer's account of Antwerp's "Groote Ommeganck." In 1520 Dürer saw a great dragon led by St. Margaret and her maidens. These, as well as St. George, says Fairholt, seem to have disappeared later.

Kelly, *Notices*, pp. 43 and 44, records that St. George was exhibited in Russia and Portugal. In the latter country a colossal figure is carried around Lisbon on the festival of Corpo de Dios "even to the present day" (*Notes and Queries*, 2d Series, vol. viii, p. 214). This shows the confusion between St. George and Corpus Christi celebrations.

Stevens, *The Giant and Hob Nob and their Story*, in the Salisbury *Festival Book* (1914), records three items relating to the dragon from the Churchwardens' Accounts in the parish of St. Mar-

Says Chambers: " These performances generally took the form of a ' riding ' or procession on St. George's day, April 23. Such ridings may, of course, have originally, like the Godiva processions or the midsummer shows, have preserved the memory of the pre-Christian perambulations of the fields in spring,[1] but during the period for which records are available, they were rather municipal celebrations of a semi-ecclesiastical type. St. George was the patron saint of England, and his day was honored as one of the greater feasts, notably at court, where the chivalric order of the Garter was under his protection." [2]

" The conduct of these ridings," continues the same writer, " was generally, from the end of the fourteenth century onwards, in the hands of a guild, founded not as a trade guild but as a half-social, half-religious fraternity, for the worship of the saint, and the mutual aid and good-fellowship of its members." [3] These guilds sprang up during the fourteenth century, so that the development of the " religious riding " — if we may call it that — was nearly parallel to the elabora-

---

garet, Westminster, under dates of 1491 and 1502. He considers that the dragon and the hobby horse are both survivals of Scandinavian sacrifices.

[1] We shall see, later, that the present Godiva procession in Coventry, does not go back so far.

[2] Chambers, i, pp. 221 f.

[3] *Loc. cit.* In 1385 the Guild or Company of St. George was founded at Norwich; it received a charter from Henry V in 1418 (Smith, *Eng. Gilds*, p. 443; cf. Chambers, i, p. 222 n. 2, and Davidson, p. 85). The aldermen and masters were to meet before the day of St. George and choose a George and a man to bear his sword and " be his Keruere to fore him " (Smith, p. 446).

I may add that the dates of the foundation of the Norwich Guild of St. George are not agreed upon. It will be enough, here, to point out that Kelly, *Notices*, p. 48, says it was founded in 1324 and received a royal charter in 1416. He must be wrong on both dates; Blomefield, *Hist. Norf.* (1805–07), ii, pp. 734 f. — cited by Fairholt, *Civic Garland*, p. xxii — Chambers, and Smith agree on 1385 as the date of foundation. Smith says the charter was granted in 1418 — the MS. he prints is dated 5 Henry V (which Blomefield dates 1416): Hudson, i, p. lxxvi (referring to Smith, p. 17) says, " According to its own return in 1389 it had been founded in 1385, with perhaps something of a military character. . . . In 1417, the year when King Henry V gave his charter to the municipality, he conferred a charter on this gild, licensing it to hold property to the extent of £10."

The original charter of foundation, the Town Archivist of Norwich tells me, is no longer in existence. The guild accounts begin in 1421, and there are no other records of the guild until 1505.

The St. George's Company, from Mackerell's MS. *History of Norwich*, is described in *Norf. Arch.* iii, p. 315 f. Here it is noted that the fraternity was begun in 1324 (p. 316); Mackerell cites the charter from a MS. book belonging to the company, and says it was given them in the reign of Henry V (1417 — *op. cit.*, p. 327).

On " the Corporation and St. George's Guild," see Hudson, i, pp. xcix f. The guild lasted until 1732.

In Chester, at an assembly on 17 April, 1612, the " sports and recreations " of St. George's Day were put under the sole direction of the mayor. (Chester, *Assembly Book*, 1539–1624, fol. 318.)

tion of the " royal-entry " which, as we shall see, began to be pageantic at the end of the thirteenth century, and by 1377 was a clearly defined pageant.

The St. George riding at Norwich was one of the most famous. The guild was founded at the end of the fourteenth century,[1] and lasted until 1732,[2] while the procession continued after the guild had been dissolved.[3] This procession was a survival of folk custom fostered and developed by a religious guild. When it ceased to exist in 1835, killed by the Municipal Corporations Act, it was a civic pageant.

There are no assembly books of St. George's Guild before 1505, and there are no city assembly books between 1386 and 1413, nor any guild accounts before 1421 now in the Norwich archives. In 1460 the image of St. George was carried around Norwich on St. George's Day, accompanied with torches, candles, a standard, etc.[4] As early as 1534–35, the " Lady " — sometimes called " the Maid " or " the Margaret " — appeared. In that year, " payd for vj payer shoes for the ladye iiij henchemen and the standard berer, iijs. iiijd." [5]

---

[1] See preceding note.

[2] On 24 February, 1731–32, the Guild of St. George gave up all its property to the Corporation, " which being done, the Corporation signed a deed to pay all debts due from them as a Company." Mackerell, cited in *Norf. Arch.* iii, p. 374. Cf. also Blomefield (1806) iv [ii of *Norwich*] p. 351.

[3] Blomefield, ii, p. 737 notes that the effects of the guild " were put under the care of the city committee . . . which committee were impower'd to order the procession on the day of swearing the mayor . . ." R. Chambers, *Book of Days*, i, p. 541 (under 23 April), says: "In the ancient processions [of the Church, on the festival of the Rogations] there was always carried the image of a dragon, the emblem of the infernal spirit, whose overthrow was solicited from heaven, and whose final defeat was attributed to the saint more particularly revered by the people of the diocese or parish. On the third day of the processions, the dragon was stoned, kicked, buffeted and treated in a very ignominious, if not indecent, manner. . . . The processional dragon has descended down even to our own day. Previous to the Municipal Corporations Act of 1835, Snap, the famous Norwich dragon, annually went in procession with the mayor and corporation on the Tuesday preceding the eve of St. John the Baptist. Snap was a magnificent reptile, all glittering in green and gold. He was witty, too, bandying jokes on men and things in general, with his admiring friends in the crowd. Guarded by four *whifflers*, armed with drawn swords, Snap seemed to be quite at home among the bands and banners of the procession. . . . But the act previously referred to has ruthlessly swept away Snap, with all the grand corporate doings and feastings for which the East Anglian city was once so famous . . . ." Cf. Fairholt, *Civic Garland*, pp. xxv f. On *whiffler*, see § 7 below.

[4] See the St. George *Guild Accounts*, for the years 1460–61, in the *Surveyors' Account Rolls*, 1421–1592 (not in unbroken sequence), now in Norwich Castle. From the *Account Rolls* of the Norwich Guild of St. George for 1532–33 I take these items: " Payed . . . to the berers [4d written over this word] of the iiij torches to the berers [4d written over this word] of the crosse candelstyks & haly water stop, to the berers of too Judas [again 4d over *berers*] the branche [2d over this word] canopie [4d over this word] iij angells beryng the helmet cote armor and target " [6d over *angells*] — total, two shillings.

This shows the guild marching with the guild priest and the George. Here, apparently, the Judases were images.

[5] MS. *Surveyors' Account Rolls* (1534–35), sheet 5. Other expenses this year were: for

It is sometimes hard to tell whether the George and the Margaret were images or living people. The same difficulty applies to the Judases,[1] which made their appearance in these processions.[2] Angels also were provided.[3] Long before this date, as we shall see, the angels had given way to allegorical figures in the London " royal-entries."

It is hard to keep the " ridings " of this guild apart from the Norwich Whitsun plays; the interruption of the pageants noted by Hudson refers to these latter,[4] though it is quite possible that the George ridings were also interrupted during the reigns of Henry VIII and Edward VI. Hudson says they started again after Mary came to the throne, but " it seems that shortly after the accession of Elizabeth the Edwardian rule was restored, and St. George's pageant was then abolished with the exception of the dragon." [5] It is possible that Edward and Elizabeth felt that the celebration contained too large an element of Romanism.[6]

In the *Guild Book* for 1645, we read — under date of 14 June — " It is ordered and thought fit that the Gunnes and the Trumpeters be forborne and the Snappe Dragon and the foole and that ther shalbe noe hanginge of the Streetes for this yeare and that the standard of the George shalbe likewise forborne." [7] Bills of the

---

gloves for the George and his company, 18*d*; paid to Adrian for his horse for the George for two days, 12*d*; to the footmen of the lady, 8*d*; " payed for the makyng of the dragon to Roose Steyner, v*s*, and payed for canvas for his nekke & for a new staffe, viij*d*." [In the MS. 6*d* is written over *canvas* and 2*d* over *staffe*.]

Other items from this account roll are: " Payed to John Mannys servaunt for his horse and his labor ryding for to borowe for the Mary, xij*d* " and " Payed for rebonds for the Marget and for the Georges horse and the dragon, x*d*."

[1] Cf. the effigy of the Betrayer, flogged at seaports by foreign sailors (above p. 16).

[2] The MS. *Account Rolls* for 1535–36, sheet 6, record four Judases who received a penny each. Another item reads " Judas & ij processionalls, xiiij*d*." Needless to say, if the Judases were images, it was the bearers who were paid.

[3] " Payd to ffen for the angells, xij*d* " (Accounts for 1535–56, sheet 6); the accounts for 1537–38 (sheet 7) show that Robert Fenn received 12*d*. for " setting forth " three angels. This same year, a lamb was provided, as well as a dragon.

[4] Hudson, ii, pp. lv and 171.   [5] Hudson, ii, p. cxliii.

[6] Cf. Ewing, *Notices and Illustrations of the Costumes, Processions, Pageantry, etc., formerly displayed by the Corporation of Norwich.* (Illus.) Norwich, 1850. This work is usually cited under the name of the publisher, Charles Muskett. A MS.-note in the Norwich Museum copy shows it was prepared by W. C. Ewing, a well-known antiquarian of that city. On page 15 he gives an inventory and appraisement of the Norwich Guild of St. George, which includes two coats of Bruges satin, and two worsted coats of St. Thomas's, for the henchmen; also two " horse's harness " for the George and one " for the Lady."

In 1553, " it was fully consented to and agreed, that on the Feast day next to be holden for the Company and Fellowship of St. George (for divers good causes weighed and considered) there shall be neither George nor Margaret; but for pastime, the Dragon to come and shew himself as in other years." Ewing, p. 16. (I have not seen the originals of these entries; they are not in Norwich Castle, where the accounts of the Company show an interruption from 1547 to 1581.)

[7] *St. George's Guild Book*, fol. 104 b, cited by Ewing, p. 18.

Company of St. George, including some expenses of the guild-day, dated 17 June, 1698, note that the City Waits received £2, 10s " for their service as usuall "; the four whifflers received, " as usual," £2; the " Clubb-bearer & his Man," 10s., and the " Dragon-bearer and his Man," 7s. 6d.[1] In the seventeenth century, apparently, the religious element had died away, leaving the original folk element; and the guild was growing into closer relationship with the civic authorities, as is shown by an item of the 18 December, 1702, when the Company decided to get a new scabbard for the mourning sword and a new blade for the mayor's sword of state.[2]

The last of these accounts is dated 1729,[3] and in 1732 the Company ceased to exist. The town authorities received its property, which included " a new dragon, commonly called the *Snap-dragon*," valued at £3, 3s.[4] Among other items in the list given is " two habits, one for the club bearer, another for his man, who are now called *fools*, 10s. 6d." When the old corporation was legislatively abolished in 1835, these " properties " went out of active service.

" The manner of the Procession on the Guild Day " may be found in Ewing's volume.[5] " The last Dragon was made but a few years ago, and was so contrived as to spread and clap his wings, distend or contract its head . . . ." This — or its successor, built on the same model — is now in the Castle Museum at Norwich, together with whifflers' and standard-bearers' costumes — the last relics of the old pageantry.[6]

---

[1] *St. George's Guild Book*, pp. 502, 503. Cited by Ewing, pp. 18 f: he misdates the entry 21 June.   [2] *Guild Book*, p. 557. Cf. Ewing, p. 19.

[3] See the same MS. *Guild Book* under 16 June, 1729 (the pages are not numbered at the end). Bells were rung and guns fired; five whifflers received £2, 10s; two Dick-Fools, 10s; the dragon bearer and his man, 15s. I may add here that the " Dick-Fool " is the descendant of the " Wild Man " whom we shall discuss in a later section of this chapter.

For further references to the usual payments of the Guild, see the same *Guild Book*, pp. 509 (1699); 597 (1708); 707 (1722); and 764 (1727). It is possible that the date of the procession was shifted from April to June when the figures of St. George and St. Margaret disappeared. The records are too fragmentary to allow a definite statement on this matter.

[4] Blomefield iv (ii of *Norwich* [1806]), p. 351; Fairholt, *Civic Garland*, p. xxv, citing Blomefield. Snap is illustrated in Ewing's volume.

[5] Printed from Mackerell's MS. *History* [which (Mr. Ewing notes in his preface) was written in 1737] by Ewing, pp. 20 f.

[6] Besides Snap, the following are in the Castle Museum: mayor's Robe of Justice, mauve silk, 1817; sheriff's cloak, black velvet lined with red, 1817; also black cocked hat and scarlet gaiters worn with the above; standard-bearer's blue costume with fringed trimmings and gilt buttons, the mitre-shaped hat bearing the city arms; standard-bearer's costume (red), with mitre-shaped hat bearing figure of Justice; standards of red and blue silk, with the city arms and figure of Justice. Also whiffler's costume of red trousers and white jacket trimmed with red braid; gilt buttons with city arms. Ditto with blue trousers and white jacket, without trimming. Whifflers' hats of red silk, brims caught up at the side with a cockade of feathers and ribbons; whifflers' swords decorated with tassels.

For accounts of the procession under the civic authorities see the MS. *Chamberlains' Accounts* at Norwich. In the volume from Michaelmas, 1759, to Michaelmas, 1760, p. 23, we

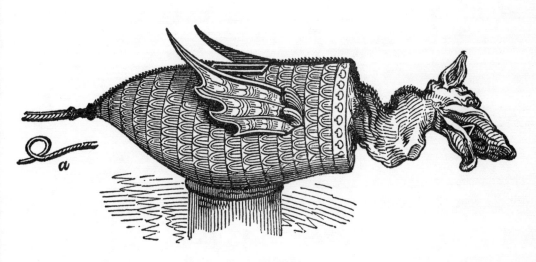

Snap Dragon

A writer in the Edinburgh *Review* [1] laments the passing of Snap. " The civic life of England, as such, is extinct. Municipal institutions remain, but the pomp, pride and circumstance that surrounded them are gone. What is more, the spirit that inspired them is extinct. . . . In London, indeed, the Lord Mayor's Show is kept up — as a show; but in other corporate towns the antique and traditional pageants, and the peculiar customs, have been abolished.

" Who that has seen a Norwich guild twenty years ago, does not remember *Snap Snap*, as necessary to the Mayor as his gold chain ? — the delight and terror of children, the true representative of the dragon slain by St. George, patron of the city, who used to be borne, like a barbarian monarch in a Roman triumph, at the heels of the civil power, opening his wide and menacing jaws with no more felonious intent than the reception of the half-pence which it was the touchstone of courage to put into that blood-red and fearful gulf. These were the perquisites of the inner man, the *spiritus rector* who walked under the scaly hide, flourished the long forked tail, and pulled the string which moved the dreadful head and jaws. The religious significance of *Snap* had been lost for ages. The Protestant and prosaic people saw in him nothing but a child's toy; the enlightened thought such toys absurd and disgusting — and he is no more. With him are gone the whifflers, the last depositaries of an art so long forgotten beyond the walls of the venerable city, that the commentators on Shakespeare were at a loss for the meaning of the word . . ." [2]

That St. George was a familiar figure in the seventeenth century, is shown by the following passage in the Duke of Newcastle's *The Country Captain:* [3] " . . . all thy tennants shall at their owne charge make them selfes fine & march, like Cavaliers with tyltinge feathers gaudy as *Agamemnons* in the playe after whom thou like a *St. George* on horseback, or the high Sheriffe, shallt make the Country people fall downe in Adoration of thy crupper & silver sturrup . . ."

Norwich was not the only town that had ridings of the George. Details of the Leicester George may be found in Miss Bateson's volumes. Under date of 21

---

read " Paid Michael Hutchinson for mending the snap-dragon, 5s. 9d." In 1791 the expenses were £12, 6s., for the procession (vol. 1790–91, p. 24), — in 1800, £13, 11s. (vol. 1790–1800, p. 23); in 1833, the expenses of the guild procession and ringers at St. Peter's Mancroft, St. Andrew's, and St. George Tombland, totalled £23, 8s. 8d., (vol. from April, 1833–April, 1834, p. 25.)

[1] February, 1843 (vol. 77) p. 143 f.

[2] Cf. Chambers's lament for Snap (above, p. 26, n. 3). Like Snap, Hob-nob, the Salisbury Hobby-Horse, is preserved in the local museum. With him is the local giant; the last public appearance of both was made in 1911, on the occasion of King George's coronation. Mr. Stevens (*The Giant and Hob Nob and their Story*) records the existence of " three of these strange monsters " at Norwich; beside that in the Castle Museum is one " in the ' Strangers' Hall,' while the third is in the hands of Colonel Back at the ' Hall of John Curat.' "

[3] *The Covntry Captaine, a Comoedye Lately Presented By his Majesties Servants at the Blackfryers.* (The Hague, 1649). Act ii, sec. 1 (p. 22).

September, 1523, we read: [1] "*Nota Bene. Nota for the Rydyng of the George.* Allso it is enactyd at the same comon hall be the seyd meyre & his brether the XXIIII^ti and the XLVIII^ti electyd of the commyns that this acte foloyng to be of effect and euer more to theym that shall cum hereafter, to be ferme and stable, that whoso-ever be the maister off Seynt Georgis Gylde shall cavse the George to be rydyn accordyng to the olde auncient costome, yat ys to sey betewyx Sent Georgys day and Wytsondey, except a caussse reassonnable; and he or they that make deffaute in rydyng of the seyd George of ye seid maister or maisters to forfet frome the day of this acte forthward v *li* and that to be levied of ye seid maister or maisters to ye behewe & wse of the seyd gyld by the meire for the tyme beyng and the chambur-leyns, and yf ye seyd meyre & chamberleyns be necligent a lachius [2] in levyeng of ye seid forfet, that then the meire to forfet xxvi*s*. viii*d*. and eyther chamburleyn to forfet vi*s*. viii*d*. and to be peyd to the profet of the same gyld.

" Moreover it is agreyd at the same acte that all forfettes mayd by the masters that haue bene seyth the laste tyme that the George was ryden shall be browght in and payd to the behowe and profet of the same gyld of euery maister beyng behynd xxvi*s*. viii*d*."

This seems to imply that in 1523 the riding of the George was revived, after having been allowed to lapse for a while. In 1543, on 5 October, the master of St. George's guild " paid to Hew Barlo & Will Alsope becawse the George was nat rydyn xl*s*." [3]

That the riding of the George was established at Leicester later than 1467 is suggested by the Borough Ordinances of 22 October, 1467, [4] where it is provided that all men of the town summoned to "attend uppon the Maire to ryde ayenest the Kyng or for [riding of the George or] eny other thing that shalbe to the plesure of the Maire and worshyppe for the town " shall obey or be fined. The editor notes that the words in brackets were " added later." On 29 September (1499) it was recorded [5] " yat it was condecended, agreed & stablyshed at a comen hall holden xxi day of Septembre a. r. r. H. septimi quartodecimo that euery of xlviii yat hathe ben chamberleyns shall pay to the up holdyng of Saynt Georgys gild by yere vi*d*. & the[y] yat hathe not bene chamberleyns shall pay at the leyst iiii*d*. or more if the[y] pleasse." On 5 April, 1533, [6] " yt is agred be the wole assentt off ye XXIIII^ti the v daye off Apryll in ye reene of Kyng Henry ye viiith ye xxiii thatt master Chrystofer Clughtt schud nott ryde ye George, nott y^ys yere, for dyueres considdaerasuns, so yat ye holde hacted schall stand in ful strenghtt as he hasse done aforetyme." The Chamberlains' accounts of 1537-38 record that four shillings were " paid for dryssyng of the dragon." [7]

---

[1] *Hall Book*, i, p. 160, printed in Bateson, iii, p. 24.   [2] *Ed's. note*: or neglectful.

[3] *Hall Book*, i, p. 400, in Bateson, iii, p. 50.

[4] Printed from p. 236 of the *Hall Book* by Bateson, ii, p. 293.

[5] *Hall Book*, p. 65, printed by Bateson, ii, p. 355.

[6] *Hall Book*, i, p. 290 in Bateson, iii, p. 33.

[7] Bateson, iii, p. 42. Cf. Kelly, *Ancient Records of Leicester* (read before the Literary and

St. Margaret's guild, at Leicester, seems to have been founded by the reign of Richard II, if not earlier; the name of the guild appears in a rental of Lord de Grey.[1] It was dissolved in the reign of Elizabeth, at the same time as the Leicester guild of Corpus Christi.[2] Kelly notes that the guild of the George at Leicester continued to the end of the reign of Henry VIII; was temporarily revived during Mary's reign, and finally abolished at Elizabeth's accession.[3]

Many other towns had their St. George ridings, but it will be enough for us here to consider but one more — that at Dublin.[4] Here, " it was ordered, in maintenance of the Pageant of St. George, that the Mayor of the foregoing year should find the Emperor and Empress with their train and followers, well apparelled and accoutered; that is to say, the Emperor attended with two doctors, and the Empress with two knights and two maidens richly apparelled to bear up the train of her gown.

" Item, 2dly. The mayor for the time being was to find St. George a horse, and the wardens to pay 3s. 4d. for his wages that day: The bailiffs for the time being were to find four horses, with men mounted on them, well apparelled, to beare the pole-axe, the standard, and the Emperor and St. George's sword.

" Item, 3dly. The elder master of the Guild was to find a maiden well attired to lead the dragon and the clerk of the market was to find a good [5] line for the dragon.

" Item, 4thly. The elder warden was to find for St. George four trumpets; but St. George himself was to pay their wages.

" Item, 5thly. The younger warden was obliged to find the King of Dele and the Queen of Dele, and two maidens to bear the train of her gown, all being

---

Philosophical Society of Leicester on 24 February, 1851, and printed in a selection of papers included in the report of the Council of the Society, presented to the annual general meeting in June, 1855) pp. 31–103. On p. 41 of this article we find a description of the ridings: " On these occasions the figure of the Saint, armed in complete steel and mounted on horseback, which at other times occupied a prominent position in St. George's chapel at the west end of St. Martin's Church, was drawn through the town, in the presence of the Master and brethren of the Guild, the Mayor and Corporation, and many of the nobility and gentry of the county. The peculiar ceremonies in use on the occasion are not recorded, although many entries connected with ' the riding of the George ' occur in the accounts, and in one instance a payment was made for providing a dragon for the pageant." Cf. Kelly, *Notices*, pp. 37 f.

[1] Printed in Bateson, ii, p. 202.   [2] See above, p. 21.   [3] *Notices*, pp. 50, 51.

[4] From a seventeenth century transcript of the *Chain Book* [which " is believed to have acquired its name from having been chained in the Dublin Guildhall for reference by the citizens." (Gilbert, preface, p. x.) Several parts "are faded, obliterated and stained. Many of its leaves have long been missing. The contents of [a] portion of one of the absent leaves have been preserved in a transcript of the seventeenth century . . ." (*ibid.*, p. xi)] in the B.M. (Addl. MS. 4791, fol. 149 [new numbering]) reprinted by Gilbert, i, p. 242, and by Walker, *Trans. Royal Irish Acad.* (1788) ii, pp. 80 f.   Cf. also E. K. Chambers, i, p. 224 and Davidson, pp. 90 f.

[5] Walker reads *golden*.

entirely clad in black apparel. Moreover, he was to cause St. George's chapel to be well hung in black, and completely apparelled to every purpose, and was to provide it with cushions, rushes, and other necessaries for the festivity of that day."

In these St. George ridings, the influence of the Church is clearly seen; and the fact that often the figure of St. George is an effigy, seems to show its origin in a saint's image, transferred from an ecclesiastical procession to a folk festival. That sometimes the George was a living man — as at Dublin and Chester — suggests an influence from the St. George play [1] which may have grown out of the riding, or have come direct from folk mumming.[2] Another element in the origin of this riding may be the military training common in English towns — the most important development of which was the Midsummer Watch.[3] This may account for the fact that a military saint was attached to this celebration; or the saint may have come to the procession as a result of the military nature of the exercises. Perhaps the riding developed differently in different places. Once in, it is not hard to understand how other knights — perhaps from the romances of the time — were absorbed; it is hard to tell where the Dublin Emperor and Empress came from, they being unnamed. We have seen King Arthur and the Nine Worthies in Corpus Christi plays at Dublin; and no doubt the people there were as ready to draw from chivalric as from legendary sources.

St. George appeared at Chester in an elaborate welcome to Prince Henry on 23 April, 1610,[4] and probably the date had a good deal to do with his presence.

Secular Developments

We have seen how, in England, the religious ridings which survived the Reformation grew nearer and nearer the civic processions, finally — as at Norwich — becoming merged with them. The " Shrewsbury Show " [5] says Chambers,

---

[1] This is outside our field. I may refer to L. T. Smith, pp. xxxi and xxxv; Davies, p. 263; Kelly, *Notices*, pp. 41 f.; Beatty, pp. 321 f.; Chambers, i, p. 225. Ten Brink, *Gesch. Engl. Lit.* ii, p. 293 — cited by Beatty — says: " The play of St. George was widely spread in England, and was usually performed on St. John's Day, when a solemn procession was formed. In many places, the drama may have absorbed the remains of native traditions of a very early date." The play was not confined to England, though sometimes on the Continent, the name of St. Clement, or another saintly dragon killer, was substituted for St. George.

[2] Beatty shows that the village mumming is widespread, and is based on the attempts of man to force the powers of nature to his will, to produce abundant harvests. The magic idea passed out of Europe, but the play was kept up, a traditional custom. To it came Christian influence; and the mock struggle attached St. George to itself. But the name may have come through the religious riding.

[3] E. K. Chambers, i, p. 223, n. 4, mentions the formation of the guild at Coventry by journeymen; and (i, p. 224, n. 2) that the Fraternity of St. George at Chester was founded for the encouragement of shooting, in 1537.

[4] See Chapter v where Amory's show is described in detail.

[5] See Sharp, p. 171; Chambers, ii, p. 163 and Fairholt, *Civic Garland*, pp. xix f.

" continued the tradition of an older Corpus Christi procession " until a recent date; and at it Saints Crispin and Crispinian rode for the shoemakers. Sharp dates its origin *circa* 1450, and describes how each guild moved in procession down the principal street of the town to a field called Kingsland, preceded by a man on horseback " dressed after a manner intended to be emblematical of some circumstance referring to the trade of the company which follows him." At Kingsland were small enclosures or arbors, appropriated to the several trades. An hour after the arrival of this procession, the Mayor and Corporation rode to Kingsland, and took a glass of wine and some refreshment at each of the arbors. " Lately," says Sharp, writing in 1825, " few companies observe the custom, and those who do attend are the apprentices." The by-laws of all the trade guilds contained, in the middle of the fifteenth century, regulations for this procession.[1]

Aberdeen had two great processions, which were maintained by the guilds.[2] The " Haliblude " play, " which existed in 1440 and 1479 " had apparently given way by 1531 to a procession in which pageants of the Crucifixion, Resurrection, the Coronation of the Virgin were eked out by others of Saints Sebastian, Laurence, Stephen, Martin, Nicholas, John, and George. The other procession, says Chambers,[3] seems to have originated as an episode in a play of the *Presentation in the Temple* on Candlemas Day. " Its ' personnes ' or ' pageants ' are such as might furnish out the action of a short Nativity cycle, together with ' honest squiares ' from each craft, ' wodmen,' and minstrels." He says that the play seems to have vanished, in this case also, early in the sixteenth century, while the procession certainly endured until a much later date.

The Worcester Guilds ruled on 14 September, 1467 " that v pagentes amonge the craftes to be holden yerly, shuld not be to seche when the[y] shuld go to do worshippe to god and to the citie, and to [be] better and more certainly kept than they haue be bifore this tyme, vppon peyn of euery crafte founde in defaute of xls." [4] " Also that yerly, at the lawday holdyn at hokday that the grete enquest shalle provide and ordeyn wheþer the pageant shuld go that yere or no." [5]

---

[1] Drawings of the trades' arbors in Kingsland, Shrewsbury (including the Butchers' arbor, and the Tailors', and Shoemakers' arbors), may be found in Mr. Fairholt's scrapbook iv in the Society of Antiquaries (opposite p. xxii of the text). Fairholt, *Civic Garland*, p. xxi, mentions this show (in 1845) in the present tense, and notes that the procession includes " St. Crispin in the dress of a cavalier of Charles I, and Crispinian in the costume of George II, both on horseback."

[2] Chambers, ii, p. 163.

[3] *Loc. cit.* He notes that there was no other English religious dumb show outside the Corpus Christi processions so elaborate as the Candlemas procession of Aberdeen.

[4] Smith, *Eng. Gilds*, pp. 376 f, gives the *Ordinances of Worcester*. For these quotations, see p. 385.

[5] Cf., p. 407, where it is ordered that the crafts which have pageants, lights, etc., shall maintain them. This probably refers to Corpus Christi.

Chambers notes that the pageant of St. Thomas the Martyr was shown at Canterbury on 29 December.[1] Knights, played by children, and the saint on a cart, and an altar, and a device of an angel, and a " leder bag for the blode " are mentioned.

St. John the Baptist was patron of the Preston *guilda mercatoria*,[2] which began in the reign of Henry II. At the end of the seventeenth century (c. 1685) the Smiths, Saddlers, and Cutlers produced " a man on horse-back armed Cap-a-pe, brandishing a naked sword." [3] An illustration in *The History of Preston* [4] shows the Wool-Combers' company, with a mounted figure who may represent Bishop Blaise. He has a mitre, a perruque of the time of Charles II, and holds a comb for wool stiffly in his right hand. At the guild of 30 August, 1802,[5] the marshal was armed cap-a-pie; he was followed by twenty-four mill girls whose dress consisted entirely of the manufacture of the town. Gentry and manufacturers followed in the procession; the mayor and corporation were there in their robes; the companies marched with bands and flags: "the tailors' company was attended by a man and woman decorated with fig-leaves, an emblem of the very high antiquity of their business." [6] The Farriers' company was led by a fully armed knight mounted on a stately horse. " This personage represented Vulcan; he was followed by eight boys, with their hair powdered, without coats and waistcoats . . . they carried white staves." Most of the companies, on this occasion, wore a uniform costume; the ladies' procession came the next day.

The arrangements for the Guild of 2 September, 1822 are given in *The History of Preston*.[7]

We see how secular elements crept into the guild " ridings " as time went on. Godiva appeared in the Coventry procession in the seventeenth century,[8] and by

---

[1] Chambers, ii, p. 164. (His authority is *Representations, s. v. Canterbury*.) He mentions other pageants, and adds, " Probably this list could be largely increased, were it worth while."

[2] See *The History of Preston* (1882); John Taylor, *Description of Preston* (1818); Fairholt, *Civic Garland*, pp. xvii f. (citing the *History*).

[3] John Taylor, p. 60. The " Guild Merchant " is described, pp. 47 f.

[4] Plate 7. This may be placed c. 1762; it is not dated, but several others in the collection are. [5] *Hist. Preston*, pp. 110 f. [6] P. 113.

[7] P. 119 f. Both the Mayor's and Mayoress's processions are arranged for.

Fairholt, *Civic Garland*, pp. xvii f. notes among the characters of the Guild Merchant, " two nondescript figures, partially armed, with hats and feathers and long mantles, probably meant for Crispin and Crispianus. The weavers carried aloft a small loom, with a boy at work; the wool-combers exhibited their patron saint, Bishop Blaise. . . . The celebration of this Guild lasted about fourteen days.

" In 1802, the tailors' company was attended by a man and woman decorated with fig-leaves to personate Adam and Eve. . . . A spinning jenny, with a boy at work, and a loom at which was a girl at work with bobbins, were each drawn on sledges . . . in the procession, as well as a miniature steam-engine . . ."

[8] See below, chapter vii.

the nineteenth century the Preston Wool-Combers had a shepherd and shepherdess, their patron Bishop Blaise, and Jason with the Golden Fleece. At Norwich the grocers had a " tree, which may have been the tree of knowledge from
their Whitsun play of Paradise, but which was converted by festoons of fruit
and spicery into an emblem of their trade." [1] The pageant was used on various
secular occasions. [2]

CIVIC PERAMBULATIONS

There were other processions, even when the religious " riding " was at its
height; and these civic perambulations undoubtedly helped to secularize the
latter. In 1457 at the Norwich Mayor's Riding, " the Perambulation was left off
(which of old times they used) during five years." [3] The magistrates of Edinburgh perambulated the marches of the city in the sixteenth century, [4] and in
1773 the Mayor and Guilds of Dublin marched around the Liberties of the city. [5]

---

[1] Chambers, ii, p. 163. On this tree, see R. Fitch in *Norf. Arch.* v, pp. 11 f. — and *The
Grocers' Play of Norwich* (1856) pp. 4 f. The Norwich Grocers' records have all been lost —
there only remain trade by-laws of 1698 which are in the archives at Norwich Castle. A
MS. of the Grocers' play (of Adam and Eve) is in the Castle: it was made by John Kirkpatrick, an antiquary of Norwich, early in the eighteenth century. Fitch reprinted this MS.,
(in *Norf Arch.*, v, p. 31, and in *The Grocers' Play*, p. 24); he owned it, and on his death it
came into the archives of the city. We may note that even when the tree represented Paradise,
it had a trade significance.

[2] See *The Grocers' Play*, p. 18. " Item, thys yere ye pageant went not at Wytsontyde,
howbeyt ther went oute in costs in makyng thereof redy & also yt went that yere in Octobyr in
ye Procession for ye Byrthe of Prynce Edward. So yt ye charges both tymes dyd amownte to
14s. 4d." (From the Grocers' records of 1537, copied by Kirkpatrick). Cf., p. 22 — records
of 13 May, 1563, also copied by Kirkpatrick — " It was enquyryd by Mr. Aldriche for yee
Provysyon of ye Pageant to be preparyd ageynst ye daye of Mr. Davy his takyng of his
charge of ye Mayralltye . . ."

In 1557, the Guild paid 10d. " for oranges, figs, almonds, dates, raisins, prunes, and apples
to garnish the tree with," and 2d. " for collerd thryd to bynd ye flowers" (Fitch, *Grocers' Play*,
p. 22). The same kind of items appear in 1558; see p. 23, for a description of the pageant in
1565: " a Howse of Waynskott paynted & buylded on a Carte wt foure whelys."

On the last page of Kirkpatrick's MS., we read: " Item yt is to be noted, that for asmuch
as for ye space of 8 yeris, ther was neyther Semblye nor metyng in ye meane season ye Pageant
remaynynge 6 yeris in ye gate house of Mr. John Sotherton of London, vntyll ye ferme came
to 20s. and bycaus ye surveiors in Mr. Sothertons tyme wold not dysburs ani moni therefor ye
Pageante was sett out in ye strete," where it remained until it rotted, and no one would buy it.
This was in 1570, John Aldrich being mayor.

In connection with the " tree " of the Norwich Grocers, see the " royal-entries " of 1392,
1432 and the Lord Mayor's Shows of 1616 and 1659 (chapters iii and vi, below).

[3] Goddard Johnson in *Norf. Arch.*, i, p. 142, citing from the City Archives of Norwich.

[4] *Extracts from the Records of the Burgh of Edinburgh*, ii, p. 254; iv, pp. 124, 310, 341.

[5] " The Whole Order and Procession of the twenty-five Corporations of Dublin, with a
survey of it's (*sic*) Liberties and Franchises, as they are to be ridden and perambulated on
Tuesday the 10th of August, 1773, by the Right Hon. *Richard French*, Lord Mayor, *James
Sheil* and *James Jones*, Esqrs., Sheriffs, with the names of the Masters and Wardens of said

A " Poem on the twenty-five corporations, etc., who are to perambulate the said Liberties and Franchises " is also published in the British Museum broadside;[1] it calls the procession "a glorious Cavalcade," and notes

> The City Prætor, mounted on a Steed
> With Ribbands drest, leads on the Cavalcade,
> Before his Lordship with a solemn Grace,
> Are borne the Sword of Justice and the Mace. . . .
> In awful Pomp and State on either Side
> The City Sheriffs in like Triumph ride
> Attended by a Band . . .

after which each marching company is named and characterized.

Molloy[2] records—without mentioning his authorities—that "the procession of the Trades was a spectacle . . . witnessed once every three years, when people not only from the provinces but from England and France assembled to enjoy the sight. According to the terms of their charter, the Corporation were bound to perambulate the limits of the Lord Mayor's jurisdiction, to make stands at various points, and to skirt the Liberties of the Earl of Meath. . . . These processions, which were held on the first day of August, were not only composed of the Lord Mayor and Corporation, but of the various trade-guilds . . . all of them having immense platforms with high canopies, gilded . . . and drawn by six richly bedecked horses. These platforms were fitted as workshops whereon the respective trades were exhibited. . . . Behind these cars came the masters on splendid horses . . . followed by the journeymen on foot, they in turn succeeded by the apprentices . . . ."

MIDSUMMER WATCH

The chief of these civic processions — and one that is particularly important for us in that it drew much from folk custom — is the " Midsummer Watch." We have seen it mentioned in the Coventry records, as early as 1444;[3] its origin, according to Stow,[4] dates from 1253 when " Henrie the third commanded Watches in Cities, and Borough Townes to be kept, for the better observing of peace and quietnesse amongst his people." [5] Midsummer had long been an important festival. The ceremonies of setting the watch not only preserved many

---

Corporations, and the various colours in each worn cockade," is the title of a broadside preserved in the British Museum (press-mark, 1890. e. 5. no. 108). The route of the procession is given, but there is no sign of pageantry.

[1] See preceding note.   [2] *Romance of the Irish Stage*, (1897) i, p. 55.

[3] In connection with the Corpus Christi procession. See above, p. 22.

[4] *Survey* (1618), p. 158.

[5] For folk-customs on this evening see Brand (ed. Hazlitt, 1905), ii, pp. 346 and 410 f., s.v. *St. John's Vigil* and *Midsummer Day*; Brand (1777), p. 279 (cited by Major Rooke in *Archæologia*, viii, pp. 215 f., who misprints p. 297) gives the origin of the fires of St. John as a " *feu de joie* kindled the very moment the year began; for the first of all years, and the most antient

folk-customs, but were instrumental in causing them to be adopted by the municipal authorities as regular features of civic pageantry. We shall see [1] that the Lord Mayor's show sprang from the Midsummer Show about the middle of the sixteenth century: and were this festival of no other interest to us, it would be important as a contributor to one pageantic entertainment which still flourishes.

AT LONDON

Stow [2] describes the bonfires in the streets after sunset, the feasting, and continues: " On the Vigill of Saint Iohn Baptist, and on Saint Peter and Paul the Apostles, every mans dore beeing shadowed with greene Birch, long Fennell, Saint Iohn's wort, Orpin, white Lilies, and such like . . . had also Lamps of glasse, with Oyle burning in them all the night, some hung out branches of yron curiously wrought, containing hundreds of Lamps lighted at once, which made a goodly shew, namely in new Fish-street, Thames-street, &c. Then had yee besides the standing watches, all in bright harnesse, in every Ward and street of this Citie and Suburbs, a marching watch, that passed through the principal streets thereof, to wit from the little Conduit by Paules gate,[3] through West Cheape, by the Stocks, through Cornehill, by Leaden hall to Aldgate, then backe downe Fenchurch streete, by Grasse-church street into Cornehill, and through it into West Cheape againe, and so broke up. The whole way ordered for this marching watch extended to 3200 Taylors yards of assize, for the furniture whereof with lights, there were appointed 700 Cressets, 500 of them being found by the Companies, the other 200 by the Chamber of London. . . .

" There were also diuers Pageants, Morris dancers, Constables . . . the Waytes of the City. . . . The Sheriffes watches came one after the other in like order, but not so large in number as the Maiors: for where the Maior had besides his Giant three Pageants, each of the Sheriffes had besides their Giants but two Pageants, each their Morris Dance and one Hench-man . . ." [4]

---

that we know of, began at the month of June; thence the very name of this month, *Junior*, the *youngest, which is renewed;* while that of the preceding one is *Mag, major*, the *antient* . . ."

Toland, *Works* (1747), i, p. 73 (*History of the Druids*) is also cited by Major Rooke (*Archæologia*, viii, p. 216). He maintains that the fires are Druidical. " These Midsummer fires and sacrifices were to obtain a blessing on the fruits of the earth, now becoming ready for gathering; as those of the first of May, that they might prosperously grow: and those of the last of October, were a thanksgiving for finishing their Harvest."

Cf. also Strutt, *Sports*, p. 278, note k. Trevelyan mentions the bonfire in Wales. On Midsummer Day in general, see Brand (ed. Hazlitt, 1870), i, pp. 169 f. This feast was a counterpart of those of the winter solstice and Yule; and the pagan rites of this festival gave rise to most of the folk-custom surrounding this day.

[1] In chapter vi, below.   [2] *Survey* (1618) pp. 160 f.

[3] Built in 1442 (Stow, *Survey*, p. 19); the great conduit in West Cheap was " begun to be builded " in 1285 (*ibid.*).

[4] On *henchman*, see Dean Milles's citation of the Wardrobe Account for 1483 in *Archæologia*, i, p. 369 and note k. " To seven of oure sayde Souverain Lorde the Kyng's Hengemen

In 1377 was made a " precept for a proper watch and ward to be kept on the eves of the nativity of St. John Bapt [24 June] and the Feast of SS. Peter and Paul [29 June] and for precautions to be taken against fire." [1] In 1474 " was a grete watche upon Seint Petres nyght, the kyng beyng in the Chepe; and ther fill affrey bitwixt men of his household and the constablis, wherefore the kyng was gretely displeasid with the cunstablis." [2]

The Grocers' Wardens' Accounts for 1386 contain the following item: "paie al chaundeler pur torches le velle de Seint Johan Baptist, iij *li*." [3] The MS. Churchwardens' accounts of St. Andrew Hubbard (in the Guildhall Library) show, in the first half of the sixteenth century, many items for "byrch" on Midsummer Eve. [4] The chief burden of these celebrations was, however, borne by the guilds. [5]

. . . for theire apparail ayenst the day of the grete solemnitee " [Richard III's coronation]: the note explains *henchman* as " an old English name for a Page, or rather an Equerry, derived from the Saxon word *henʒest*, which signifies a horse." Cf. *N.E.D. s.v. henchman*: it is not clear how or whence the compound made its appearance in the fourteenth century. *Henchman* means a squire, page or attendant to a great man, who walked or rode beside him in processions or marches.

[1] R. R. Sharpe, *Letter-Book H*, p. 308.

[2] A contemporary MS. cited by Tyrrell, *Chron. Lond.* (1827), p. 145.

[3] Kingdon, *Facsimile MS. Archives of Grocers* (1886), i, p. 67.

[4] Cf. other churchwardens' accounts — those edited by Littlehales and Overall, for example — for similar items.

[5] See Jupp, *History of the Carpenters' Company* (1887), pp. 40 f., for an account of the participation of that company in the Midsummer Watch. Various extracts from sixteenth-century records are reprinted, full entries being given for the revival in 1548 (2 Edw. VI). Firth, *Hist. Coopers' Company* (1848), pp. 96 f., gives items from the Coopers' accounts illustrating the expenditures of that company for the Midsummer Watch in the sixteenth century. The items include cressets, and cresset-staves, scouring of the harness by the armorer, etc. W. M. Williams (*Annals of the Founders* (1867), p. 212) notes from the city records that in 1 Richard III (1483) various companies should watch from eight in the evening to six in the morning, "and mete in the Chepe." None of the Twelve Companies were included in this order.

Nicholl, *Some Account of the Ironmongers* (1866), p. 95, gives some of the Ironmongers' midsummer expenses for 1567. Cressets, birch, and men in harness are mentioned, but no pageants. Cf. p. 63, for the expenses of this company in 1540; among the items is " ffor j. doss. strawe hattys, xd." Subsequent midsummer night expenses may be found, *ibid.*, pp. 64 f. In 1542: " Payd to x. crosset berers and iij baggs for both nyghts, xiijs. Payd for xij strawe hatts for them, xijd." In 1531 the Ironmongers " payd to iiij men for goyng in harness in the mayres watche upon Saynt John and Saynt Petrs nyght, iis. viiid." (Appendix, p. xii.)

Cf. C. Welch, *Hist. Pewterers*, i, pp. 49, 153, 268 for accounts of the Pewterers' company in regard to the Midsummer Watch of 1477, 1547, and 1571. There is no mention of pageants.

C. M. Clode, *Hist. Merch. Taylors* (1888) ii, p. 114, notes from the Merchant-Tailors' records that in Sir Thomas White's mayoralty the company paid " to the Lord Mayor in support of his charges, and for discharging this house of all charges concerning the having of a watch at midsummer, if any such to be, 40l."

In 1535–36, the Skinners ordered two new pageants — King Solomon and St. John the Evangelist — and had two others new trimmed, at a total cost of £12, 10s. (see the Renter Wardens' accounts, printed by J. F. Wadmore, *Account of the Skinners Company* (1902) p. 77.)

Beginning in folk-custom, with an element of the civic muster added, perhaps in the thirteenth century (certainly by 1377), these civic shows reached their height early in the sixteenth century.[1] On 10 May, 1502 [Shaa, mayor], it was appointed " that the comyners which have the oversight of movyng of the pageants be warned to bee at this courte a thyrsday next comyng every of theym seuerally to be charged wt the sellyng of the stuff of the pageants that they have rule of." [2]

The books of the Drapers' Company show that in 1516 the sum of £13, 4s. 7d. was paid towards " Sir Lawrence Aylmer's pageant." [3] " There does not, however, follow any account of what it consisted," says Herbert. Fairholt[4] calls this, one of the earliest notices of a pageant exhibited on Lord Mayor's day; Herbert does not give the exact date of the entry, which may refer to a midsummer pageant — by this time a recognized feature of the setting of the City Watch.

In 1522 the London Drapers resolved that they would have " ' no Mydsom^r pageant becaus there was so many pageants redy standyng for the emperors [Charles V] coming into London; ' and afterwards ' that for divers considerations,' they will ' surcease the said pageants, and find xxx men in harness instead.' They, however, previously to the day of the spectacle, abandon both resolutions, an entry of subsequent date informing us that the court and bachelors had agreed —

These seem to be midsummer pageants rather than for Corpus Christi. The company also paid " for the refresshynge of the gyant & his mamettes. And for the refresshynge of the same pageantes after Midsomer. And for vij men for waytinge on the seyd pagentes, whereof vj were workemen, for bothe the nyghtes . . ."

Welch, i, p. 153 mentions cressets and cresset bearers from the Pewterers' accounts of 1546–47; and a " precept " from the mayor for six cressets, their bearers, and " two discrete persones to attende vppon the saide Cressett-bearers, called wyfflers," in 1570–71 (i, p. 268).

[1] J. G. Nichols, pp. 6 f., refers to Stow who recounts how in 1510 Henry VIII watched the procession in disguise, and liked it so much that on St. Peter's Eve he came again with the queen, royally riding with the nobles, saw the watch of the city, and returned to the palace in the morning. See Stow, *Annals*, p. 488, cited also by Strutt, *Sports*, pp. 267–269. Cf. Chambers, ii, pp. 165 and 382–383 for further remarks on the Midsummer Show.

[2] *Repertory* i, fol. 100. (The *Repertories* are the MS. records of the court of Aldermen of the corporation of London; they are kept in the Guildhall Archives.)

Unless the pageants of Katherine's entry in November, 1501, were not dismantled until May, 1502 — which is, of course, possible — this entry must refer to the pageants of the Midsummer Show. (It probably does not apply to the wedding of Margaret and James IV of Scotland in January, 1502–03.) It is not impossible that the men who had the oversight of the pageants were " charged with selling of the stuff " of them a month or six weeks before the show took place.

[3] W. Herbert, *Hist. Livery Cos.* (1834–36), i, p. 457.

[4] Fairholt, *L. M. Pag.*, pt. i, p. 14. He refers to Herbert's cautious utterance (*loc. cit.*); says the latter: " *Lord Mayor's Show* is not mentioned by name, but besides the procession there was very early a scenic spectacle, as we learn from an entry in 1516," etc. Fairholt misprints this date 1510.

" To ' renew all the old pageants for the house; including our newe pageant of the *Goldyn Flees* [1] for the may^r against midsom^r; also the *gyant*, Lord *Moryspyks*, and a morys daunce as was used last year.'

" From a long bill of expenses which follows, it appears that this Lord Moryspyks, or ' Marlingspikes,' as he is afterwards called, was an allegorical personage . . . as was also ' the King of the Moors,' and other characters whose dresses are charged for." [2]

The Golden Fleece has an obvious trade connection with the Drapers; it had had a significance of another kind when used, in this same year, to greet Charles V, on 6 June. The King of Denmark attended this Midsummer Show, and the pageants of the Assumption and St. Ursula were shown.[3] Here Biblical and legendary material are added, and folk custom is represented by the giant.[4]

" The King of the Moors " appeared in this show; his pavilion was borne over his head, a child with harness attending; "payment of 5s. to John Wakelyn for playing the King of the Moors (the company finding him his apparell, his stage and his wyld fire)" is noted.[5]

Puttenham uses the Midsummer Show to point a lesson. He says: " But generally the high stile is disgraced and made foolish and ridiculous by all wordes affected, counterfait and puffed up, as it were a windball carrying more countenance than matter, and cannot be better resembled then (*sic*) to these midsommer pageants in London, where to make the people wonder are set forth great and vglie Gyants marching as if they were aliue, and armed at all points, but within they are stuffed full of browne paper and tow, which the shrewd boyes vnderpeering, do guilefully discouer and turne to a great derision." [6]

---

[1] Provided for the emperor's reception.

[2] Herbert, i, p. 455, making extracts from the records of the Drapers' Company. Cf. Davidson, p. 88.

[3] Herbert, i, p. 457; Chambers, ii, p. 165. Herbert records that " the King of Denmark being here," it was agreed that Mr. Rudstone the Sheriff should have two pageants at midsummer — one of the Assumption and one of St. Ursula — " but to be no precedent hereafter." Andrew Wright received 22s. 8d. for repairing the Assumption, and for a new pageant of St. Ursula. " These sums speak little for the renewal of this show, which must have been miserably poor. . . . But these mummeries were evidently fast getting out of fashion. Most of the charges indicate, by their smallness, the deteriorated quality of the spectacle." Herbert, i, pp. 455, 456.   [4] On the giant, see below, pp. 50 f.

[5] The " wild fire " seems to connect the " King of the Moors " with the *wild-* or *green-man*, on whom, see below, pp. 72 f. See *The Dying God*, p. 208, for a Moorish King in Bavarian Whitsuntide processions; cf. the Moor in Peele's 1585 pageant (chapter vi, below) where he is given a trade significance.

In 1523–24 there is another long list of expenses in the Drapers' records for the Midsummer Watch; but here " the pageantry is made subservient to the more solid entertainment of feasting. . . . ' The hire of the gyant of Barking, for both the nights,' forms an item of the spectacle." Herbert, i, p. 457.

[6] George Puttenham, *The Arte of English Poesie* (1589), p. 128; cited by Hazlitt's Brand (1905), ii, p. 411, and by Sharp, p. 203.

It will be noted that the giants referred to are " armed at all points," which shows the folk element adapted to the muster. We shall return to this matter in discussing the armed-men; here it is enough to call attention to the fact.

In 1534 the Ironmongers had an elaborate Midsummer Show.[1] There were a castle,[2] a pageant of William the Conqueror, and another of Our Lady and Saint Elizabeth. A giant and a puppet appeared;[3] mummers bore torches before the Saint's pageant, and there were men in harness — including the Conqueror and the " French king." The former may have been chosen because the sheriff's first name was William.

This Midsummer Show is important, because it shows a blend of legendary material — perhaps from the miracle play — with history and romance. This latter — represented by the castle — appears in the " royal-entry " as early as 1377.

On 22 June, 1539, John Husee wrote to Lord Lisle that " no solemn watch will be held in the city this year on Midsummer night, at which some of the citizens of London are not a little dissatisfied." [4] Wriothesley records: "Allso this yere

---

[1] See the items extracted from " the accompte of Thomas Lewyn & Richard Hall, wardens of the craf of Iremongers of the cetye of London," 9 July, 1534, printed in Nicholl, appendix x (p. xv f.). The charges " thet was payd at midsom^r when Mr. Willm Denham alderman was sheryff of London," include the following:

" Item, payd to Seger for a complett harnes & for his chylde that stode in the castell of Denhm at the dowre both ye nyghts, ii*s*. Item, payd to Wellow for the harnes that King Willm had on both nyghts, ii*s*. Item, payd for the harnes that the man had on that played the frenche kyng both the nyghts, vii*j*d. . . . Item payd for Rocketts & Reds to shott a bowte the castell, iii*s*. Item payd to iiij chylderyn In the Castell for ther labore for boyth nyghts, ii*s*. vii*j*d. Itm. payd to Thomas brownschanke for syñg (*sic*) of the propertes for the Castell boyth nyghts, ii*s*. . . Item payd to Cater & hys chyldre for playing & syngyng in the pagent of oure lady & seynt Elyzabeth boyth nyghts, xiiij*s*. Itm. payd to Rychard Alen for playing w^h the fflagge boyth nyghts, v*s*. Item payd to the berrers of the geant & the popett berers, x*s*. Itm. payd for the mendyng of the gyant & geants, ii*s*. Item payd to xxiiii porters for the beryng of the ii pageants at xi [Nicholl asks, 10½ *d*. ?] a pece of them a nyght, s'ma xlii*s*.

" Itm payd bakhowse for makyng of the ii pagents on of Wyll'm Congquerer & another of Seynt Elyzabeth, vj*li*. xiij*s*. iiij*d*.

" Itm. payd to iiij momars (mummers) to bere the torches boyth nyghts abowt Seynt elyzabeth, iiii*s*. viii*d*.

" Itm payd for the hyre of the garments for the iiii momars boyth nyghts, ii*s*." (Appendix, p. xvii.)

Horses, minstrels, cressets, etc., were also part of the show.

[2] The " castell of Denhm " refers to the sheriff. Nicholl (p. xv, note) suggests that " this pageant had evidently some allusion to the family history of Mr. Sheriff Denham." It may, of course, only have been named out of compliment to him; I doubt if any family history were given.

[3] Why a distinction should be made between the " gyant " and the " geants," is not clear. The *puppet* may be a smaller giant — the forerunner of Corineus. Cf. the " gyant and his mamettes " of the Skinners (above p. 38, n. 5 — on p. 39).

[4] Brewer and Gairdner, *Letters and Papers of Henry VIII*, xiv, pt. i, p. 515 (entry 1144), cited by Kingsford in his edition of Stow's *Survey*, ii, p. 284.

[1539] the watche kept in London at Midsommer was put downe by the kinges commaundement because the citizens had bene at great charge in their muster; howebeyt the mayor and sheriffes had prepared divers pageantes with lightes and other thinges for to have had the said watche, and had no knowledge till two dayes afore Midsommer that it should not be kept, which was a great losse to poore men."[1] In 1542 (34 Henry VIII) the London Court of Aldermen ruled that the sheriffs were to have pageants not exceeding three in number " upon the nights of St. John and St. Peter next coming." [2] That this revival did not last long is shown by the fact that in 1548, the Mayor, Sir John Gresham, revived the show again.[3]

" In 1567 the merchant-tailors' books state that company to have provided ' at the muster and show on Midsummer Eve, 12 persons with comely cressets . . . with straw hats upon their heads,'" etc.[4] No pageants seem to have been provided. In 1569 the citizens tried to have the custom abolished, but the Queen wished it kept up.[5] A precept for " mydsomer showes " (inter alia) was issued " by the Queen " on 18 March, 1584 (27 Eliz.).[6] The Show continued, on a more economical plan, as the " standing watch," till the force was finally superseded by the City Trained Bands, now the Artillery Company.[7] The pageants, as we shall see,[8] seem to have been taken from the Midsummer Show about the middle of the sixteenth century, by the Lord Mayor's Show.

---

[1] *Chronicle* (ed. Hamilton, 1875–77), i, p. 100; referred to in Kingsford's Stow, ii, p. 284.

[2] *Repertory* x, fol. 259. In 1545 " there was no watch kept at Midsommer in London, but with constables in theyr wardes " because the king had three great armies away from home. (Wriothesley, i, p. 156.) In 1546 " the watch was laid downe by a court of aldermen for eaver, but my lord major rode on Midsommer Even and Sainct Peeters . . . the tow sherives and their officers followinge my lord major and after them fortie constables more with their cressitt lightes which was a proper sight " (i, p. 166). In 1550 " was noe watch kept at Midsommer nor St. Peters tyde " (ii, p. 41).

[3] Kingsford's Stow, i, p. 103; the 1618 ed. of the *Survey*, p. 161, and Strype's Stow, Book i, p. 256; Wriothesley, ii, p. 3. The Midsummer Show should not be confused with the musters of citizens which were not pageantic, and which continued when the other was interrupted. Kingsford, in his notes to Stow's *Survey* (ii, p. 284) cites from Harl. MS. 530, fol. 119, a contemporary account of the muster on 8 May, 1539; he also refers to Wriothesley's *Chronicle*, i, pp. 95 f., and *Letters and Papers*, xiv, pt. i, pp. 438 f. (entry 940). Cf. also p. 440 (entry 941) where John Husee recounts to Lord Lisle a muster of from twenty to twenty-five thousand men reviewed by the king. These are, evidently, not midsummer shows. With the transfer of the pageants to the Lord Mayor's day, the midsummer show became little more than a muster.

[4] Herbert, i, pp. 196 f.

[5] Strype's Stow, book i, p. 257.

[6] *Journal* xxi, fol. 421 b, *et seq.* The MS. bears a marginal date, 18–3–(?5) 1584. (The *Journals* are MS. minutes of the Court of Common Council of the Corporation of London, in the Guildhall Archives.)

[7] Herbert, i, p. 197.

[8] Below, chapter vi.

Provincial Midsummer Shows

London was not the only English city to have a Midsummer Show. At Chester the city paid for the pageants, and it may have done so at Coventry, too; though in 1542 the Drapers paid for a pageant [1] — perhaps in addition to the regular ones, as the master of the company was then mayor. The yearly Christmas watches at Chester had no pageantic accompaniment; [2] but the midsummer show there included several pageants. [3] It began at the end of the fifteenth century; in 1497 " the wach on Midsummer Eve was first sett outt and begonne." [4] By 1566 the Midsummer Show, already pageantic, [5] had begun to borrow features from the Whitsuntide plays. In that year the Smiths paid " for gloues for the docters & litle god on midsomer euen, vjd. gilding Gods face xijd. other ordnary expences for midsomer euen as before." [6] This marks a new departure. In 1568

---

[1] Sharp, p. 200, note h. Chambers, ii, p. 165, assembles much information concerning the part played by the crafts in the midsummer shows at various places.

[2] Ormerod, *Hist. Chester* [ed. Helsby (1882)], i, pp. 382 f.

[3] Strutt, *Sports*, p. xxviii; Sharp, p. 200 (quoted by Axon, *Chester Gleanings* (1884) p. 175): on the Midsummer Show see also Ormerod, i, pp. 380 f.; Lysons, *Chester* (1810) pp. 583, 584, and notes; Strutt, *Sports*, p. xxv; R. H. Morris, *Chester in Plantagenet and Tudor Reigns* (1894), pp. 323 f. The latter, pp. 326 f., reprints many extracts from Mr. Holme's accounts, Harl. MS. 2150, fol. 373, *et seq.* (pencilled numbering, 202), "The Auntient forme & payments of midsomer wach or show."

[4] Randle Holme's *Chronology of Chester*, Harl. MS. 2125, fol. 206 (pencilled number, 32), cited by R. H. Morris — who misprints fol. 203 — on p. 323. The exact year is more a matter of interest than importance to us: I may point out that it is variously set at 1497, 1498, and 1499 by Ormerod, Lysons, and Webb, in King's *Vale Royal*.
The Whitsun plays were first given in 1339; they were played by the guilds, and dealt with Biblical material. (See Ormerod, i, pp. 384 f.). They were licensed by the Pope between 1342 and 1352 (iii, p. 651, n.). The Smiths' accounts for 1554 (in Harl. MS. 2054, fol. 14 b, *et seq*, some items from which are printed by Morris, p. 323, n. 3), include many items concerning the Whitsun plays, but they are not then connected with midsummer. The items in the records which deal with the expenses at midsummer do not imply pageantry. In 1565, the Smiths paid " for guildinge of litle gods face xijd. for 3 payre of gloues & horses for the docters & litle God xvjd. more to the Doctors & litle God for theyr paynes xijd. more when we went about the towne to the prisoners at Castle, 4d."
Archdeacon Rogers (Harl. MS. 1948, fol. 62 b; printed by Ormerod, i, pp. 380 f.) is wrong in supposing that the Midsummer Watch antedates the Whitsun plays.

[5] The treasurer's accounts printed in Morris, p. 325, n. 2, show various items in connection with the Midsummer Show. For instance, in 1555: " For mydsommer wache for the caredge of the pagions and paynters xxviijs. vjd." We do not know what these pageants were; of course they may have been from the craft plays. In 1564 " Houghe Gillome for dansing at Midsomer by Mr. Mayors appointment," received 6s. 8d. and " Thomas Yeaton for goune powder at the triumthe by Maister Mayres appoyntment," was given fourteen shillings. " Paid Mr. Mayre at Midsomer for the triumthe, xxvjs. viijd." Other items for various years to 1593 are cited, *ibid.*

[6] Harl. MS. 2054, fol. 18.

the same accounts include an item " for gylding Gods face on midsomer euen xij*d*."; [1] and in 1569 " for hernesse to the horses at midsomer iij*s*. to the docters and some of the company iiij*d*. minstrells ii*s*." [2]

In 1572 the Smiths gave sixpence for the " gere for the child that ridd on midsomer euen "; [3] in 1574 the apparell " for him that ridd " cost eightpence. In 1575 or '76 [4] the " first banner they had at Midsomer " was displayed; [5] this year " for dressinge the child " they paid thirteen pence; " for hose & shewes for chyld xiiij*d*." [6]

By 1589 civic pageantry had appeared at Chester. In the *Treasurer's Rolls* for 1589–90 we find the following item: " Payd to Tho Poole paynter for dressing Mr. Maiores mount and the geyantes and beastes at Midsomer xliij*s*. iiij*d*." It is, of course, possible that the " pagions " of 1555 [7] were civic; the word might apply to giants or beasts. [8]

With occasional interruptions the Midsummer Show continued well into the seventeenth century, in the first half of which it was at its best. [9] In 1599 the mayor, Henry Hardware, " . . . a goodly and zealous man . . . caused the Gyauntes in the mydsomer show to be put downe & broken and not to goe. The devill in his fethers he put away . . ." substituting a man in armor. [10] The

---

[1] Fol. 19.

[2] *Loc. cit.* Other expenses at midsummer in 1569 may be found on fol. 19 b; they include " things that went to dresse our child vij*d*." Perhaps the " 2 dougters & litle god " mentioned on fol. 19, appeared on this occasion. The " litle god " was usually not far away from the " docters "; he may be the " Cupitt " of 1657, and the " naked boy " of 1633 — or a youthful Christ with the Doctors' at the Temple, from a craft-guild play.

[3] Fol. 20.   [4] Fol. 21, " no yere sett."

[5] Cf. fol. 19 b: in 1569 was paid " for our syne xvj*d*; " in 1572 " for our signe ij*s*. 4*d*." (fol. 20); in 1574, " dressinge of our signe vj*d*." (fol. 20); the " sign " may have been a forerunner of the banner.

[6] See Morris, pp. 323 and 324 for extracts from other guild records showing other characters from the Whitsun plays marching on Midsummer Eve. The Barbers and Barber-Surgeons, for instance, furnished Abraham and Isaac; the Bricklayers contributed Balaam and his ass in 1602.   [7] See above, p. 43, n. 5.

[8] See Morris, p. 325, (citing the *Treasurer's Accounts*, for various years from 1555 to 1593), for items concerning giants. Strutt, *Sports*, p. xxviii, Sharp, p. 204, note o, and Morris, p. 325, refer to an ordinance of 1564 which includes four giants, a unicorn, a dromedary, a luce (perhaps a *luzern*, like that which appeared in Peele's London pageant in 1585; but cf. the " flower de luce " of the seventeenth century show [Harl. MS. 2150, fol. 203; Morris, p. 329]) a camel, an ass, a dragon and sixteen naked boys.

[9] Sharp, p. 204, records the 1599 cessation, and says the show was revived in 1601. After a suspension during the Puritan *régime* it was revived again in 1661 and in 1670 was moved to Whit-Tuesday. In 1678 it was abolished. Cf. also Ormerod, i, pp. 380 f. The last accounts in Harl. MS. 2150 are those of 1661 (fol. 216, printed in Morris, p. 328). Cf. also Strutt, *Sports*, p. xxviii.

[10] Harl. MS. 2125 fol. 45 b. Cf. *ibid.*, fol. 123; Morris, pp. 318 f.; Ormerod. i, p. 380; Fairholt, *Gog and Magog*, pp. 53 f.; Sharp, p. 204, etc.

pageants were restored by the next mayor; [1] " this midsomer showe had diuers things in it which weare ofenciue in anchant times (as Christe in stringes) men in womens apparell with diuells attendinge them called cuppes & cannes with a diuell in his shape ridinge there with preachers of God's worde and worthye diuines there spake against as unlawfull and not meete with diuers other thinges which are now reformed " [2] . . . we read in Archdeacon Rogers's manuscript.

In 1610, " for paynting of the beastes . . . at midsomer, xliijs. iiijd." [3] were paid; " harness men," who evidently carried halberts, appear in these accounts, and serve to perpetuate the memory of the marching watch. In 1628 were paid these items: " to 4 men that carried the 2 beastes 4s. vjd. to the 5 men that held the boys that ridd ijs. vjd. to the 2 boys that danced the hobby horses [4] . . . for payntinge the beastes at midsomer . . . ." [5] In the 1632 account are recorded " giants and other payntinge at midsommer show, xliijs. iiijd. Payd for fitting of the maiors mount xxvjs. viijd." The show for 1633 was very elaborate; [5]

---

[1] Harl. MS. 2125, fol. 45 b.

[2] Harl. MS. 1948, fol. 62 b (pencilled numbering); cited by Ormerod. There were devils in the mid-sixteenth century Mayors' shows at London (see below, chapter vi).

[3] Harl. MS. 2150, fol. 202.   [4] A blot has obliterated the sums paid.

[5] MS. *cit.* fol. 202 *et seq.* For carriage of the mayor's mount, 2s. 6d. was paid; and on the sheriff's bill appear the following:

" payd 2 porters to Carry Elophant my p[ar]t Mr byrd pa[i]d as much xijd.

" to the boy that ridd out my pt vjd.

" payd R. Thornley for my pt paynting the Elophant vs. Mr. byrd payd as much.

" vpon conference with Jo Wright about makinge the 4 Giants & other things for midsom^r . . . we compute great hoopes dale bords Couper worke nayles . . . xxli for one Giant wth an other to be wth workmanshipp the least to be vli a peece. all beinge new to be made & the stronger & firmer will be better for the future to saue the Citty charge.

" for the Elophant wth the Castell for hoopes cloth cullers & makinge Tinfole for Castell.

" 10s. for Arrows & skyns for the naked boy & workmanshipp all new wrought.

" the beaste wth workmanship will be 1s.

" vli the 4 beastes for the leauelookers the Antilope flower de luce vnicorne & camell all matterialls this yeare to be new will be about 36s. a peece.

" the maiors mount new made this yeare wth all matterialls will be at least 1s. beside bays to be hired & a man to carry it.

" 50s. for the Marchant mount all to be new made wth maior men etc & the shipp 50s. beside cloth to be hired & men to carry it.

" 2li for the 4 hobby horses for the leauelokers xiijs. 4d. peece . . .

" jli 1s. for garlands for Mr. Maior 6 harnesse men as vsuall hath byn xviijd. a peece & sheriffs 4 a peece.

" The Maior Sheriffs Threasurers & leauelokers pay yearly among them 7. 10. 8d. to the paynters the rest on the paynters charges.

" this to be this yeare to goe on the generall charge because of new makinge and an order for future the thinges made to be payd according to ould custome.

" or if this to be contynued by them as Auntiently then the same is to be deducted out of the generall charge of agreement.

" payd yearly to the paynters for new triminge of the Marchants mount by the company of marchants, xxxiijs. 4d."

many of the things were new; there was an elephant and castle, all tin-foil; the usual animals of the leavelookers [1] were new made, and the giants, also new, were not to cost less than five pounds apiece.[2] In 1657 a new outfit was again required;[3] there was a mayor's mount, a merchants' mount (which had a ship that turned round as it was carried) [4] there were also four giants; an elephant with a castle on his back, and Cupid looking out of it; the usual four beasts — unicorn, antelope, "flower de luce" and camel; a dragon baited by six naked boys; and morris dancers completed the show.[5]

Sharp gives much information about the Midsummer Shows at Coventry.[6] The marching watch was chiefly composed of men in light armor, attended by children bearing spears. Minstrels, waits, and "every species of musical accompaniments" attended the show. There were also giants; these, like the giants at Chester, seem to have been of both sexes.[7] Bonfires, torch-parades, garlands of flowers worn on the head, were features of the Coventry midsummer celebration, both before the show was established, and after it was given up.[8] It was well established by 1421; we may note that at Coventry the mayor watched on Midsummer night, and the sheriffs on St. Peter's.[9]

---

[1] *Leavelooker*, "a municipal officer in several boroughs of Lancashire, Cheshire and North Wales having certain duties of inspection." The word comes from *leave*, sb. (? in the sense of *license*) and *looker*. See the *N.E.D.*

[2] It is not clear whether the "naked boys" who appear from time to time in these accounts are images or alive. The 1633 entry is ambiguous — the "workmanship" might apply to the skins and arrows; the passage cited by Lysons, *Mag. Brit.* (1810) p. 583, n. 2, suggests images. In 1657 (Harl. MS. 2150, fol. 203 — see R. H. Morris, p. 329) "for makinge anew the Elaphant & Castell & Cupitt . . ." is recorded; here again we have an image, apparently. But "for the makinge new the dragon . . . & for the 6 naked boys to beat at it," suggests living figures (*MS. et fol. cit.*) and so does the entry (MS. *cit.* fol. 200 b) "for the carriage & payinge 6 naked boys at the sheriffs & leaulokers charge." One does not pay images; but the money may have gone to the porters.

[3] See Harl. MS. 2150, fol. 203 (which is undated). "A compute of the charges about midsomer show all thinges to be made new by reason the ould modells were all broken which was Mr. Holmes & Jo Wryghts goods & yearly repayred heretofore by the Citty Threasurer one part and the maior sheriffs & leauelokers the rest."

[4] "for makinge anew the marchant mount as auntiently it was with a shipp to turne hyringe of bays & 5 to carry it iiij *li*." (*MS. et fol. cit.*) Cf. fol. 213: "for an Iron handle & spindle to turne the ship, 1*s*. 6*d*."

[5] See Harl. MS. 2150, fol. 203, for detailed accounts; one item reads "Mrs Maiores berage" or "bereage." Perhaps it refers to those who carried the lady's sedan-chair. Morris, p. 329, prints it "barage," which he explains as "drink-money."

Other accounts (some undated) may be found in the same MS., fols. 204–216. The average yearly charge for the Midsummer Show seems to have been about £45.

[6] Sharp, pp. 174 f.

[7] Sharp, pp. 201 f., gives items concerning the giants from the Cappers' and Drapers' accounts. He is cited by Fairholt, *Gog and Magog*, pp. 59 f.

[8] Sharp, pp. 175 and 180. For the watch in 1555, see *Coventry Leet Book*, iii, p. 813.

[9] Sharp, pp. 180 f., 184.

Smith gives some ordinances of Worcester providing for this anniversary.[1] " . . . Every crafte havyng the name of pageant, shullen fynde oon cresset yerly brennynge, to be born biforne the Baillies of the seid cite in the Vigille of the natiuite of Seynt John Baptiste, at the comyn Wacche of the seid cite . . . ."

Deering is quoted by Hazlitt[2] on the Midsummer Show in Nottingham; marching and garlanded watchmen were apparently unaccompanied by pageants. " This custom is now quite left off. It used to be kept in this town even so lately as the reign of King Charles I."

Many other places had their Midsummer Shows,[3] but this is evidence enough to indicate its character. It links civic authorities with folk-custom; it drew from the miracle play and kept alive folk-giants and animals. It is one of the immediate ancestors of the London Lord Mayor's Show, which developed from it about the middle of the sixteenth century; so that, while the custom is dead, it has left results still felt today.

§ 3. MEN IN ARMOR

The marching watch, made up of such a muster as that which lies behind the Lichfield " Greenhill Bower," or the " Midsummer Show " we have just been considering, is the obvious starting point for a consideration of the " men in armor " which appear often in the earlier pageants, and which were the chief element in the Lord Mayor's show of the first two-thirds of the nineteenth century. On the 17 September, 1469, there was a " muster of the crafts showed in London," and the numbers of each company are recorded by Williams.[4] In a time when there was no police, these musters of armed men must have been frequent, even if the king were not preparing to wage war; and as soon as they became pageantic, the name of some famous warrior must have been attached to the chief figures in such a procession. Probably the influence of the Church is seen in the adoption of St. George, who is — after all — nothing but an armed knight. We have seen that in 1599 a man in armor replaced the Midsummer pageants at Chester; there were armed men in the Lord Mayor's Show very early — but these were probably no more than the militia. The " knight " of later times is presumably a descendant of the St. George figure.

The anonymous author of *The Gigantick History*[5] suggests a connection

---

[1] *English Gilds*, pp. 407 f. Cf. p. 27, where it is recorded that the Norwich Barbers shall provide candles and torches for midsummer.

[2] Brand (ed. Hazlitt, 1870) i, pp. 183 f. " ' In Nottingham,' says Deering, upon some authority which he does not specify, ' by an antient custom, they keep yearly a general watch every Midsummer Eve at night.' "

[3] It is possible that the pageants at Norwich in 1540, 1545, and 1546 (recorded below, chapter vi) had been used at Midsummer Shows in that city.

[4] W. M. Williams, *Annals of the Founders*, p. 211.

[5] *The Gigantick History of the two famous Giants and other curiosities in Guildhall, London* (2 vols.; [vol. i (third edition " corrected "), London, 1741; vol. ii (second edition), London,

between the " men in armor " and St. George. I quote the seventh chapter of his second volume:

" Chap. vii. *Of the Man in Armour.*

This champion bold in bright aray
Looks like St. George who did the dragon slay.

He is clothed with armour of polished steel, which covers his whole body, legs, arms, fingers and toes, made with such partitions, so as to bend any part of his body, excepting his feet; which, for want of proper joints, if by any accident he should be unhorsed, he would be unable to remount himself: and upon his head he wears a strong helmet.

" This armour he has from the Tower: it weighs about a hundred and a half; which the horse he rides on chiefly sustains.

" This heavy armour was made use of by valiant knights in former times, who voluntarily offered to vindicate in single combat their country's honour.

" About twelve a clock this mighty champion,[1] mounted on his horse, with a great drawn sword in his hand, advances at the head of the worshipful company of armourers who set out from their hall in Coleman-street, and proceed to a large house near Trig stairs, belonging to that company; where having regaled themselves, they set out again; going through St. Paul's church-yard, Ludgate, and so on to Salisbury court in Fleet-street; where, having just show'd themselves, they return back, and march before my Lord's company through the city to King-street, and then to their own hall in Coleman-street: and after this bold champion hath seen the worshipful company safe hous'd, he dismounts his prancer; and so concludes the ceremony."

It is possible that St. George — originally a saint's image — was attached to a figure in a pageantic armed-watch by the Church. I doubt if there is any influence from chivalry other than that played by real knights in organizing bands of retainers. We shall see that in the early fifteenth-century royal-entries, the giants sometimes appear armed, as " champions "; and Puttenham's description of the giants " marching as if they were alive, and armed at all points " may show a development of the " giant-champion," with a possible influence of the armed-watch. The trade significance given these figures by attaching them to the armorers, is an obvious development.[2]

1741]) is kept in the safe of the Guildhall Library. The volumes measure one and a half inches by two and a half; they are very rare, if not unique.

The book was evidently written for children, and is slightly satirical. (It is referred to by J. E. Price, *Desc. Acct. of Guildhall* (1886), pp. 91 f.; by Fairholt, *Gog and Magog*, p. 16, and by Hone, *Anc. Mys.*, p. 265, etc.). While the volumes are not, of course, "scholarly," their account of a contemporary Lord Mayor's Show is probably trustworthy.

[1] This paragraph seems to suggest first a chivalric, and then a trade origin for this figure, which had become an important feature of the Lord Mayor's Show by 1740. Perhaps there is an element of both chivalry and trade here; and there may be a hint of the St. George as well. In pageantry, all things are possible.

[2] Such figures as the Dublin " Emperor " and " Empress " — the latter attended by two

§ 4. MINSTRELS

Before passing to a consideration of the giant, let us briefly mention the minstrels, who played a part in these shows. Sharp tells us that minstrels and waits were essential to the processions, pageants, and entertainments of our ancestors; and we shall see, in later chapters, how large a share musicians — both singers and players — took in royal-entry and Lord Mayor's Show.[1] The city minstrels of Coventry were appointed first in 1423,[2] and continued until 1780. Music is a natural accompaniment of the procession; and as minstrels often helped in the performance of miracle plays,[3] they might easily have come into pageantry with the characters and cars of the religious drama.

Before the fifteenth century minstrels appeared in London ridings,[4] and they

---

knights — may show an influence from the chivalric romance, similar to that exerted by the Church, which resulted in the St. George figure.

" A few years ago St. George had his votaries — so had St. Patrick, St. Andrew and St. David; and provincial towns on the days assigned to these worthies used to ring with merriment. In fact, they presented all the appearance of a tournament, even to the knights in brass and the shield and lance borne by the faithful squire." *Weekly Times*, 13 November, 1853.

The " armed men " of the present day Greenhill Bower, at Lichfield, are survivals of the older muster, and serve to keep alive the memory of the way the present festival originated. In May, 1559 (1 Eliz.), " the Ironmongers sent forty-two men in armour to the May-game that went before the Queen's Majesty to Greenwich " (Nicholl, p. 75 — presumably from the Ironmongers' records).

[1] See Arundell, *Hist. Rem. Lond. and Liv. Companies* (1869), chapter xix (pp. 210 f.) for remarks on minstrels in connection with guild feasts; Ewing, p. 4, note, mentions the waits at Norwich, giving extracts from the chamberlain's books. On the duties of minstrels and waits in general, see Kelly, *Notices*, pp. 125 f.

The Historie of Promos and Cassandra (1578) by George Whetstone is quoted by Strutt, *Sports*, p. xxv: a carpenter, employed in preparing the pageants for a royal procession, is commanded to " errect a stage, that the wayghtes in sight may stand." One of the city gates was to be occupied by the four Virtues, together with " a consort of music."

[2] Sharp, pp. 207 f., gives a description of their clothing, information as to their remuneration, hours of performance, etc. A *minstrel* was a player of instrumental music; there were other charges for singers. Among the instruments played were the trumpet, harp, lute, drum and flute — and a " wysseler " is mentioned by Sharp, on p. 215. (The last is not to be confused with the " wyffler " or " whiffler.")

[3] Kelly, *Notices*, p. 41: " A mynstrel and three waits of Cambridge assisted at the play of ' The Holy Martyr of St. George ' at Basingborne in 1511." See *The Grocers' Play of Norwich* for various entries from the Grocers' accounts regarding payment to waits and minstrels; " in the MS. series of pageants at Chester and Coventry, ' ministrels ' are not unfrequently spoken of," says Collier (i, p. 21); but he finds no evidence to prove that minstrels ever acted in such representations. As these plays were given by the guilds, it is not likely that the minstrels would be called on to furnish additional actors.

[4] Kingdon, *Facsmile*, i, p. 83 — the Wardens' accounts of the Grocers' company — under 1399: " Paye pur vij menstrell quant nostre Seignour le Roy Fuist coroune, xlviijs. iiijd." " Paye a lez menstralls quant nous cheuachams oue le maire, xlvjs. viijd." In 1386, " Item

were common in the provinces.[1] We need not linger over them; we need only
point out that they formed an important part of these shows.[2]

§ 5. GIANTS

The chief folk-figure in pageantry is the giant; we have seen him in the Coventry, London and Chester Midsummer Shows; have noted that he was perhaps
influenced by the " armed-watch," and shall see him again in the " royal-entry "
and the Lord Mayor's Show. He is not especially an English figure; indeed,
Fairholt traces " all these English giants to the much older guild observances of
the continental cities." [3] While it is, perhaps, outside the field of this work to try
to establish the origins of these folk-elements — indeed, the only thing we can be
sure of is the fact of their existence — I cannot let this statement of Fairholt's
pass without a remark.

Human sacrifices were at one time common in all lands.[4] Later, as times grew
more civilized, images of men were burned, instead of the men themselves;

---

paie alle menstrals et por lours chaperouns et pur lour costes all cheuache dell Viscounts,
xxvij*s.* iij*d*," and in 21 Richard II, "Item paie pur vj mynstralles pur le cheuache de le maire
Richard Wedynton, summa xliij*s.* iiij*d*." (pp. 67 and 78. Cf. for similar items, pp. 81, 96,
137, etc.)

[1] On the town waits of Leicester, see Kelly, *Notices*, pp. 131 f.

[2] Ned Ward's *London Spy* (4th ed. 1709), pp. 35 f., contains a humorous picture of the City
Waits (c. 1700). " We heard a Noise so dreadful and surprizing, that we thought the Devil was
Riding on Hunting through the City. . . . At last bolted out from the Corner of a Street, with
an *Ignis Fatus* Dancing before them, a parcel of strange *Hobgoblins* cover'd with long Frize
Rugs and Blankets, hoop'd round with Leather Girdles . . . and their Noddles button'd up
into Caps of Martial Figure, like a *Knight Errant* at Tilt and Turnament, with his Wooden-
Head lock'd in an Iron Helmet; one Arm'd, as I thought, with a lusty Faggot-Bat, and the
rest with strange Wooden Weapons in their hands in the shape of *Clyster-Pipes*, but as long,
almost as *Speaking-Trumpets*. Of a sudden they clap'd them to their Mouths, and made such
a frightful Yelling, that I thought the World had been Dissolving, and the Terrible Sound of
the last Trumpet to be within an Inch of my Ears.

" Under these amazing apprehensions, I ask'd my Friend what was the meaning of this
Infernal outcry ? Prithee, says he, what's the matter with thee ? Thou look'st as if thou wert
Gally'd; why these are the *City Waites* . . . the Topping Tooters of the Town; and [they]
have *Gowns, Silver-Chains*, and *Sallaries*, for playing *Lilla Bolaro* to my *Lord Mayors Horse*
thro' the City."

[3] *Gog and Magog*, p. 64.

[4] See *The Golden Bough*, especially — for Roman sacrifices — *The Dying God*, pp. 143 f.
Slaves, captives, or needy freemen who volunteered themselves, were slain at tombs; slaves,
hostages, and animals were burned at the funerals of dead Irish warriors, to keep them company (see Sullivan in O'Curry, i, pp. cccxx f.). Tacitus tells of the drowning of slaves at the end
of the progresses of the goddess Nerthus in Germany (cited by Chambers, i, p. 118). The
burning of giants in French festival fires are survivals of the Druidical habit of burning
human victims in colossal images of hollow wickerwork (Chambers, i, p. 139 and note 2);
I may call attention in passing to the puppet attendants for the dead in China (a custom pic-

finally, the figures received the name of the divinity in whose honor the feast was held; and these, in time, became saints' images. Other figures, unnamed, became folk-giants. The contest between winter and summer [1] may owe something to the human sacrifice.[2]

The " Early Inhabitant "

Every people regarded the " early inhabitant " of its territory as gigantic,[3] and the memory of these early races was preserved in legendary history and romances.

---

tured in the *Illus. Lond. News* for 3 August, 1912, p. 177, and in *l'Illustration* (Paris) for 23 July, 1912, p. 33). In the funeral procession of the Princess Tsin " were the ' servants ' shown in the photograph; large dolls of paper and bamboo, holding the teabowl, teapot and pipe of their mistress. These were burnt at the cemetery during the final ceremony." Cf. J. J. M. de Groot, *Religion of the Chinese* (1910), p. 71: " Slaves and servants, wives and concubines are also burned, i. e., in paper imitations. They point back to the time when actual human sacrifices were the custom." Professor Barrett Wendell tells me that there are two " giants " at Shanghai, which accompany funeral processions; they are not, however, destroyed, but are used over and over again. Perhaps the royal funeral effigies, preserved in Westminster Abbey, have a folk origin. [1] See above, pp. 4 f. and 6, n. 2.

[2] On the " mock sacrifices " see *The Dying God*, p. 214, etc. Cf. the " King " beheaded on Whitmonday in Pilsen (p. 210); the burying or drowning of the Carnival, as practiced in many European countries (pp. 220 f.); the mock execution of the tree spirit, personified in the leaf-and flower-dressed boy in Bavaria (p. 207) which is seen also in the English " sword-dance "; and the mock death and resuscitation of the " wild-man " in Saxony and Bohemia (p. 208). Hone, *Anc. Mys.*, p. 264, mentions the two giants of Guildhall, in Lowman's narrative of the fireworks in honor of James II on 24 April, 1685, when likenesses of them were burnt; a political significance was given to the burning of images in London in the seventeenth century, and in Boston in the eighteenth; indeed, the practice still continues — the American current press records the burning of more than one senator in effigy in 1917. The Judas-burning of foreign sailors in English ports (cf. above, p. 16) shows a religious significance in this kind of thing.

[3] " Chez tous les peuples, on le sait, et sous toutes les religions, on a créé des géants chaque fois que les arts, la poésie ont eu besoin de reproduire au-devant des masses un grand effet de crainte ou d'admiration. Les hommes du passé, d'ailleurs, n'apparaissent aux vivants que, comme l'ombre d'un corps, presque toujours plus grands que l'original; et l'imagination des peuples en avait dû, rehausser encore la stature. De là ces géants de la fable, de l'écriture sainte, ces géants de la Gaule, ceux du moyen-âge surtout, si fameux dans nos romans de chevalerie, si souvent mis en scène dans nos tournois du 15⁰ siècle." Quenson, *Le Géant de Douai* (1839), pp. 9 f.

Cf. *Genesis*, vi, 4, and the Titans and Giants, offspring of Ouranos; giants were the enemies of the Scandinavian gods. In the *Chanson de Roland* (Clédat's edition, line 3518) we read, " Turs et Enfrons Arabiz et Jaianz."

" The gods and kings of early Egypt were giants among men. . . . The national heroes of Greece and Rome were endowed with gigantic frames. . . . The heroes of knight errantry were similarly vast." Fairholt, *Gog and Magog*, pp. 1, 2.

Cf. C. M. Jopling in *Archæologia*, xxxi, p. 452: " The two small barrows on Heathwaite (Lancashire) are close to two small stone circles, called ' Giants' Graves,' which on being excavated . . . were found to contain the bones of men, covered by a flat stone. . . . There is

There were three types of " romantic giants " [1] — the gigantic men, men with traces of the giant, and real " jaiants." [2] The pagan giants are not ugly or deformed; they seem to be merely giant men. The influence of Celtic material seems to be strong in bringing giants into French romance; there was also a Germanic element; but little straight French (thinks Wohlgemuth) as the French epics were based on history, and therefore giants were not a natural growth, save where national heroes became gigantic. This development is, I may add, akin to the " early inhabitant " type of giant; for if the gigantic " early inhabitant " were routed by a national hero, it might easily — though not necessarily — follow that the hero himself became a giant in the popular mind. It must also not be forgotten that the hero was often, without doubt, a large and powerful man; and his physical strength was exaggerated as his deeds passed into saga.

---

a tradition amongst the old inhabitants that giants formerly lived at the place, and were buried there. The last of the race is said to have been shot with an arrow upon the adjacent hill of Blawithknott." Says Francis Grose (in *Archæologia*, v, p. 237) ". . . a bold head-land or cliff, called Hengist-bury head, *i. e.*, Hengist's, or the Stone Horse Hill; whether from some now forgotten story of the Saxon leader of that name, or from some fancied resemblance to a horse; a conceit not uncommon in the neighboring counties, of which the Giant in Dorsetshire, and the White Horse in Wiltshire, are well-known instances." Governor Pownall, in *Archæologia*, vii, p. 271, note c, records that " the humour of converting heroes into Giants is natural to the half-civilized ideas of antient nations: nor is it totally undescriptive of the persons."

Thomas Wright, *On the Legend of Weland the Smith*, in *Archæologia*, xxxii, pp. 315 f., says: " Our forefathers . . . looked with . . . reverence on cromlechs, and barrows . . . because their own superstitions had taught them to attribute such structures to the primeval giants of their mythology, who were objects of dread even to the gods themselves. . . . The mythic legends were still current as romances, and continued to exist under altered forms as romances of chivalry, and under various subsequent degradations, until they were at last hawked about the streets in the still humbler form of penny chap-books and nursery tales. It was in this manner, and by such gradations, that the mighty deeds of the god Thor against the giants of Jotenheim became transformed into the exploits of *Jack the Giant-Killer* . . ."

Wright cites Leland who mentions " a place caullid Colecester, wher hath beene a forteres or castelle. The peple there say that ther dwellid yn it one *Yoton*, whom they fable to have beene a gygant." In the first chapter of his fifth book, Olaus Magnus deals with the gigantic " early inhabitant," and tells of the descent of " champions " from giants.

Six gigantic figures stood over the gate of the castle to welcome Queen Elizabeth to Kenilworth, in 1575 (see chapter iv). They carried trumpets — and real trumpeters were stationed behind them to sound as the Queen approached. " This pageant was childish enough," says Nichols (*Prog. Q. Eliz.*) in his note, " but not more so than the reason for its being placed there. ' By this dumb show,' says my author (Laneham), ' it was meant that in the daies of King Arthur, men were of that stature; so that the castle of Kenelworth should seem still to be kept by King Arthur's heirs and their servants.' Laneham says these figures were eight feet high."

[1] F. Wohlgemuth, *Riesen und Zwerge in der altfr. Erzählenden Dichtung* (1906) makes this classification.

[2] The tall man " muss daher immer genau nach grösse u.s.w. beschrieben werden, während bei dem eigentlichen *jaiant*, wie bei unserem *riesen* der blosse name genügt um dem leser bezw. hörer sofort ein bild zu geben."

Professor Harris H. Wilder, of Smith College, tells me that he has found, among the uneducated who have watched him unearth the bones of Indians, a belief that these early New Englanders were of uncommon stature. His explanation of this fact is simple: the thigh-bone is easily recognized, and when a man places it against his groin, he finds that it projects several inches beyond his knee, and he assumes that the Indian to whom it belonged must have been of more than average size. Were he to place the thigh-bone against his hip, where it belongs, he would find that it is no longer than his own. The Englishman of the dim past, finding bones under a cromlech or barrow, may possibly have concluded, by a similar process of reasoning, they belonged to a giant.

The giant-hero is common;[1] men with traces of the giant are found in such figures as the " giant herdsmen " of *Ywain* and *Aucassin and Nicolette*.[2] The giant Langbane, who was killed by Vidrick Verlandson,[3] seems to be either a giant-man, or a man with traces of the giant. Cain is connected with the giants, often being considered the father of the race.[4] The real *giants* in romances are

---

[1] I may refer to a few examples: Judas Maccabeus " gat his people great honor, and put on a breast-plate as a giant." (1 *Maccab*. iii, 3.) Says Havelock, " I am now no groom, I am well waxen and well may eat More than ever Grim may get, I eat more by God alive, Than Grim and his children five." Cf. also *Havelock*, l. 986: " Havelock stood over them als a mast. Als he was high, al he was long." Sir Valentine, in Thomas Chester's *Launfal*, " was wonther strong, Fyftene feet he was long." Beowulf, Horn, Thomas Hickathrift, and many others might be cited, but it is needless to multiply these random references. Almost every hero was endowed with gigantic strength.

[2] These figures suggest the " wild-man " which we shall touch upon (see below, § 8). On these stock incidents of the " other-world journey " from the Celtic, see A. C. L. Brown, *Iwain*, in the Harvard *Studies and Notes in Philology and Literature*.

[3] Prior's *Ancient Danish Ballads*, vii, (i, pp. 69 f.). Langbane (Etgeir) raises with ease a stone to show Vidrick (Widja) a treasure cave, in a vain effort to purchase his life.

[4] See O. F. Emerson, *Legends of Cain*, in *Publ. Mod. Lang. Assoc.*, xxi, pp. 831 f.; esp. pp. 878 f., *Cain's Descendants*. Professor Emerson points out that in *Beowulf* (ll. 111 f.) giants are numbered among Cain's offspring; he refers to *Genesis* vi; the Cædmonian *Genesis*, lines 1245–1284; and the Old Saxon *Genesis*, in all of which Cain is connected with the giants. He also notes, "a very clear reference to the giant descendants of Cain" in Wyntown's *Original Chronicle* of Scotland. (Scot. Text Soc. ed., Bk. i, ll. 297 f.):

> " Intill þis tyme þat I of tell
> Wer gyandis wakkand ferss and fell,
> That like till men war in figure,
> Bot þai were fere maire in stature. . . .
> . . . Sethis sonis, as þai say,
> Luffit Canys douchteris stout and gay
> And gat upon þaim bodely
> Thir gyantis þat were sa forsy."

Mr. Emerson gives (pp. 888 f.) many references, from mediæval literature, to Cain's "giant brood " — a common mediæval tradition. The gods of the heathen were, in the middle ages, considered to be giants; and were connected with the descendants of Cain (pp. 926 f.).

big, strong, ugly, and they carry heavy weapons.[1] A few are handsome; many are black,[2] some have a big head or a little head — at all events, out of proportion — or big ears; animals' heads are sometimes found — or horns. Most have red eyes; some, one red and one black; some have much room between the eyes; most have big mouths and big white teeth. In short, almost all differ, in some respect other than size, from the normal man; all tend to approach the monstrous.

Monsters are related to giants, though not of them.[3] I may note here that the pageant giants have no trace of the supernatural about them; they seem to belong to the " early inhabitant " type, deriving their names from historical — or pseudo-historical — characters, like Gogmagog; from Biblical history, like Samson; or from classical mythology, like Hercules. Giants with several heads are found in Germanic myths, and English tales,[4] but not in pageants. Romances have metallic giants — automata — which stand beside a gate or bridge to attack those who approach.[5] All pageant giants are, of course, artificial; but there seems to be no connection between these two sets of automata. Whatever the source of these giants in literature,[6] the pageantic giant originated in folk-custom.[7]

CONTINENTAL AND ENGLISH GIANTS

The custom of carrying effigies at various festivals was, as has been pointed out,[8] widespread, not only in England, but on the Continent. The rise of the

---

[1] Wohlgemuth illustrates each characteristic from French romances.

[2] Cf. Lebeaus Disconus, who " rod toward the fyer And whan he nyghede ner Two geauntes he saw ther That one was red and lothlych And that other swart as pych Grysly bothe of chere." The knight rescues a maid from them; they had stolen her from a castle. It looks as if this might be a development of the " early inhabitant " type.

[3] Cf. the *genius* of the *Arabian Nights*. Grendel, of the race of Cain, shows, perhaps, the " early inhabitant " type mingled with the magic element. He is called " giant " more than once — " *eoten wæs ûtweard.*"

"One of them [*i. e.*, Grendel and his mother] was like unto a woman; the other miscreated being, in the image of a man wandered in exile (save that he was larger than any man) whom in the olden time the people called Grendel."

Wohlgemuth says that man-eating giants are rare in Germanic *sagen*, but that the invulnerability of giants is due to Germanic influence.

[4] Cf. *Jack the Giant-Killer*.   [5] Sometimes this figures is a giantess.

[6] Some authorities consider that they have a mythical origin in nature personifications.

[7] I do not wish to assume responsibility for the usual explanation of these giants as relics of past " fertilization spirits " or survivals of the human sacrifice. I accept the researches of folk-lorists, who seem to agree that such are the origins of this folk-figure. For our purposes, it is enough that we find the giants in folk-custom; how they got there is outside the present field. There may have been two sets of giants — or else the " fertilization spirit " developed from the figure which took the place of the human sacrifice.

I disagree with Mr. Frank Stevens, who in his paper, *The Giant and Hob Nob and their Story*, finds that the Continental giants " would seem for the most part to have derived their origin from one or other of the old thirteenth-century ' *chansons de gestes* . . .' " That they derived their names, and in that way their individuality, from these sources is, however, quite likely.   [8] See above, § 2.

merchant in the Low Countries, " resulted," Fairholt [1] says, " in the overthrow of the feudal system, the establishment of commerce on a firm basis, and the rise and prosperity of great cities with a free trade. . . . Their prosperous traders rivalled the glories of the old nobility in the palaces they constructed for their Guildhalls; and having no pride of ancestry, they chose the legends of their old cities for display on public occasions. Hence they typified the legendary history of Antwerp in the giant Antigonus; that of Lyderic the Forester of Flanders; of the gigantic horse Bayard, upon which ride the four sons of Aymon; of Goliath, the giant of Ath. . . . On solemn occasions of great popular observance . . . there is a reunion of giants. They are lent by the corporations of each town to swell the public shows. The only giant who has not visited his friends is he of Antwerp: the reason being that there is no gate in the city large enough for him to go through." [2]

The Continental giants drew their individuality from romance or history; and it is possible that this influenced the " personality " — if I may so express it — of the English giants. I see no reason, however, for assuming that the figure itself was imported from Europe: the folk-custom in which it has its origin, was as

---

[1] *Gog and Magog*, p. 64.

[2] Ward, *Hist. Eng. Dram. Lit.* (1875), i, p. 79, says that pageantry " seems to have been introduced [into England] from Flanders . . . and in particular from Antwerp, where a procession of the trades (*die groote Ommeganck*) was customary from an early date." Quenson notes several towns in Flanders and Belgium which have their civic giants; Malines showed her giants, and the " grand-père des géants " on 15 August, 1838 (p. 10, n. 3, referring to the *Journal des Débats*, 12 August, 1838). He explains (pp. 20 f.) the origin of the Douai giant, which commemorates " un seigneur du voisinage " who lost his life in the siege of the town by the Normans in 881. " C'est ce seigneur, tué sous les murs de Bavai . . . dont les Douaisiens reconnaissants ont conservé la mémoire et l'image, sous la forme d'un guerrier et la stature d'un géant." This giant probably dated from the fifteenth or sixteenth century (p. 35); but there is no documentary evidence of his existence before the seventeenth century (p. 36); when he apparently replaces the *mannequins* of former times. I may note that in the extract " du compte de la ville de Douay, de l'an 1577 à l'an 1578," (printed by Quenson, p. 86), Louis Sampson and others received 24 *sols* " pour avoir porté les torses de la ville a icelle procession." This seems to refer to giants.

My friend Professor Hazard, of the University of Lyons, has told me that almost every city of northern France has its giant, which, until the war broke out, were carried round at local *fêtes*. Among the most famous may be noted, beside that of Douai, those of Lille and Valenciennes, which have names.

In *Gog and Magog* are pictured Antigonus of Antwerp; Gayant and his family, of Douai; the giants of Brussels, Goliath and his wife of Ath; Lyderic, the giant of Lille, and St. Christopher, of Aix.

Mr. Frank Stevens, in *The Giant and Hob-Nob and their Story*, records that " the Processional Giant is to be found freely distributed over western Europe, in Flanders, Belgium, Westphalia, France, and Spain; and effigies similar to that in the Salisbury Museum may be seen in the Kermesse Processions at Brussels, T'serclaes, Mons, Hasselt (Limburg) and Termonde, as well as in some parts of Spain." How many will be in existence after the war, it is impossible to say.

English as it was Continental. It is unnecessary to assume a European origin for the English giant; and it seems impossible to prove one.

It is, however, quite possible that the idea of connecting the civic giant with civic history is an importation from abroad.[1] Pageants absorbed material readily from all quarters, and were sensitive to all influences. The giant of folk-custom made an admirable champion; and it is natural to develop a champion into a local hero. But when the London giants were first named — in 1522 — they were appropriately called Hercules and Samson;[2] had the influence of Europe on the English figures been very marked, we might expect a sign of it before this year. It was a common belief that the early inhabitants were gigantic; and the tendency to name the local giant, after it had been used enough to gain an individuality, was natural,[3] and may well have sprung up independently in England.

---

[1] We shall, in a later chapter, see that giants appeared in the London royal-entries early in the fifteenth century as half-giant, half-champion. But they did not receive names until a hundred years later, and were not connected with the accepted history of London until the time of Queen Mary.   [2] See below, ch. 3.

[3] The midsummer giant of the London Drapers was distinguished by a name — Lord Moryspyks. Trevelyan, p. 25, notes that in Wales effigies were carried around the villages on May Day. " These would be named after any man or woman who had made himself or herself notorious, ridiculous or scandalous. The effigy with laughter and shouts of derision was pelted with various missiles. This was done as late as the sixties." At Llantwit, 3 May was celebrated (Llantwit's Anwyl, Pet or Darling, Day) in memory of the capture of the Irish pirate, O'Neil. This celebration lasted until about 1850–1855, and was observed by the Odd Fellows — with a church parade and dinner — until 1907. An effigy of the pirate was burned annually in Colhugh meadows; and a king and queen were chosen. (See Trevelyan, p. 26.) The Tailors' giant at Salisbury (illustrated in the frontispiece of *Gog and Magog*) was called St. Christopher; Fairholt (*op. cit.*, pp. 62 f.) says this was " the last of the old perambulating English giants." His popular name was " the giant " — naturally enough, if there were only one. Sharp, p. 202, notes that he saw St. Christopher exhibited in 1814; a man danced inside and two attendants danced around, with his sword and club, watching carefully to check any deviation from the perpendicular position (note m). Cf. Stevens: *The Giant and Hob Nob and their Story* [in the *Salisbury Festival Book* (1914) pp. 62–64]. St. Christopher is illustrated, opp. p. 59, with Hob-Nob; and is shown " in procession " (1911), opp. p. 64.

The Salisbury giant — named St. Christopher, on account of an heroic size figure of the saint which existed in the chapel of St. John the Baptist, the patron of the Merchant Tailors' Guild — is still preserved in the Museum there. Under date of 28 October, 1914, Mr. Stevens writes me: ". . . From 1496–1760 it may safely be assumed that the giant came out every year, on the eve of St. John in Harvest. About 1760, the Tailors' guild began to get into low water. The trade of the town was going north. . . . The records from 1760 onwards mark *national* events — previous to that, the giant was a purely guild figure.

" I sincerely hope the giant may never again appear in public; he gets a rough time, and the men who carry him usually become very unsteady towards the end of the procession. . . . If the giant does not go out again, it is my intention to redress him in more congruous costume. At present, he sports a Georgian Hat, Stuart Ruffle and Baldrick, and a dress of no period, all of which is an abomination to me, who am supposed to have some knowledge of historical costume . . ." St. Christopher's last public appearance was in 1911, on the occasion of the coronation of George V.

Perhaps the Aberdeen Bruce of 1511 [1] combined the giant-champion of London with the Continental practice of naming giants after local or national heroes; I do not feel any necessity, however, for assuming such an influence, and only suggest it as a possibility.[2]

The saints' names, sometimes attached to giants, show the influence of the Church exercised through the guilds. It would be natural for the guilds to give their giant the name of their patron saint, and the figure of St. Magnus — if he be not a living person — who marched with the London Fishmongers in 1298, may show some such development. As in the case of St. George, it is not always easy to tell whether a character mentioned is a living person, or an effigy.[3] Mr. Frank Stevens has explained the origin of the name of Salisbury's St. Christopher, who was the patron of the Merchant-Tailors' Guild.

---

[1] See below, p. 170.

[2] It must be admitted that many English giants remained unnamed. Even where there were four, as in the Chester Midsummer Show, no distinction was apparently made; and though the names Gogmagog and Corineus were attached to the London giants in 1554, there were two giants, apparently unnamed, in 1606 — when King Christian IV came to London. In the Lord Mayor's Show of 1656 the walking giant is unnamed, nor does Jordan give any name to the two giants who appeared in the 1672 show. Nameless giants greeted Queen Elizabeth Woodville at Norwich in 1469, and in 1661 (from Harl. MS. 2150, fol. 216 — John Wright's charges for the Chester giants) we find expenses concerning the still unnamed Chester midsummer giants: " for a payre of old sheetes to cover the father and mother gyantes Armes & shoulders and repayre the heades, 4s. for two sheetes more to cover the 4 gyantes boddies, 3s." (On the expenses of the Chester midsummer giants in detail, see R. H. Morris pp. 325 f.) The London giants mentioned by Puttenham are unnamed.

In the *Churchwardens' Account* of St. Andrew Hubbard (Guildhall MS. 1279/2), occur these two entries (cited by Price, p. 92): " Receyved for the Jeyantt, xixd " and " Receyved for the Jeyantt ij viijd." Both are on the same folio — the first one of the accounts which run from the " natyvyte of our lord god xv c xxxiij vnto the fest off ower lord god xv c and xxxv," John Chylderly and Thomas Surbutt being churchwardens. It is not clear to what " giant " refers — perhaps to a saint's image. Various mentions of images — not called " giants " — occur in the records of St. Mary at Hill [ed. by H. Littlehales for EETS. (1905)]. Cf. especially p. 271: " Ress' (received) of Sir Thomas of Gravisend and of harry herd for the olde Rode (rood) and Mary and John þat stode in the chirch, xxs." (This was in 1509–10). Over-all's edition of the *Accounts of the Churchwardens of the parish of St. Michael, Cornhill*, mentions images frequently; but they are not called " giants."

It is possible that the Saints Crispin and Crispinian who " rode " in the Shrewsbury Show were images (or " giants ") carried by riders.

[3] Cf. Magnin (1862), pp. 216 f. " Dans les Mystères et les *Miracle-plays* joués à Chester, à Coventry, . . . etc., la statuaire mobile avait particulièrement pour emploi de rendre possible l'introduction de quelques personnages gigantesques de l'Écriture et des légendes, Samson, Goliath, saint Christophe, ou celle de quelques animaux monstrueux, tels que la baleine de Jonas, le dragon de saint Georges, etc., colosses que l'on représentait à l'aide de mannequins d'osier, qu' un homme placé dans l'intérieur faisait mouvoir avec adresse et à propos.

" D'autres grandes machines avaient aussi et ont conservé longtemps un rôle considérable dans les *pageants* municipaux ou populaires, tels que la procession annulle pour l'élection du Lord-maire et les *May-games*. Dans la première des ces solennités, on voyait défiler, entre

CORINEUS AND GOGMAGOG

In 1554 the names Gogmagog and Corineus were attached to the London giants for the first time.[1] This shows the appearance of an historical element; whether it is authentic history or not, does not concern us here.[2] Brutus, the great-grandson of Æneas, fled from Troy and after various adventures arrived in

---

autres divertissantes mascarades, quelques figures de géants fabuleux armés de pied en cap. A Londres, c' était Gogmagog et Corinœus, aujourd'hui immobiles sur leur piliers de Guildhall. . . ."

[1] See below, chapter iii. Lydgate gave, as we shall see, allegorical names to the *paginæ persones* of 1432; Biblical characters had appeared in the miracle plays; the romance had contributed King Arthur. We should be surprised, not that the giants received names, but that they did not receive them sooner. There were, to be sure, Hercules and Samson in 1522; that these names did not remain those of the London giants may be due either to the fact that these particular giants passed out of existence, or to the custom of naming the giants for local historical celebrities, which caused a substitution of names. The male and female giants of 1415 (see below, chapter iii) seem to have given way to the giant champion of 1432; some accounts of the 1415 reception of Henry V do not, it is true, mention the giantess — but both male and female giants were common; and no one mentions a female giant in 1432.

[2] Geoffrey of Monmouth, *Hist. Reg. Brit.*, lib. i, cap. xvi, tells the story of Gogmagog; Mathew Paris, *Chron. Majora*, i, p. 21, 22, repeats it; as does Robert Manning of Brunne in his *Chronicle*, i, pp. 62 f. (ll. 1737–1944), " de ludo inter Coryneum & Gogmagogum," ll. 1803 f. Cf. also the *Chronicle* of Robert of Gloucester, i, p. 36 f. (ll. 480–539). The *Gigantick History*, to which I have referred before, tells the story; (Hone, *Anc. Mys.*; Price; Fairholt, *Gog and Magog*, allude to this version). Hone, *op. cit.*, p. 272, retells the story. Fairholt, p. 13, refers to " the old tragedy of *Locrine* " where " the same story is detailed."

Cf. *Chronica* Thomæ Sprotti (ed. Hearn, Oxford, 1719), p. 84: Albyna, daughter of a certain Greek King Cicropes, being come to England — " Quod Dæmones incubi perpendentes oppresserunt eas [Albyna and her companions] & sic quælibet concepit de Dæmone suo & partum peperit gigantinum, & cum gigantes adolescerent, matres de filiis, sorores de fratribus genuerunt. Et erat generacio monstruosa & magnitudinis excessivæ. Et duraverunt gigantes in ista terra ii c. lx. annis. Quorum ultimo Brutus fugiens excidium belli Trojani cum ii c. xx. navibus Angliam peciit, quæ tunc Albyon vocabatur à prædicta Albyna, plena gigantibus, quos Brutus & Coroneus frater ejus occiderunt vel in cavernas moncium fugaverunt." The name *Gogmagog* does not occur in Sprott — who derives (p. 85) Albania (" Scocia ") from the name of Brute's son Albanactus — but the tradition of early gigantic inhabitants is there continued. Brute and Gogmagog are mentioned in Tyrrell, *Chron. Lond.* (1827), p. 184, and often elsewhere. Heywood refers to this mythical history in the preface to *Londini Speculum*, his Lord Mayor's Show for 1637 (see the 1874 ed. of his *Works*, iv, p. 305) saying that London derives her antiquity from " *Brute*, lineally descended from *Æneas*, the sonne of *Anchises* and *Venus*, and by him erected about the yeare of the world two thousand eight hundred and fifty-five: before the nativity of our blessed Saviour one thousand one hundred and eight: first called *Trinovantum*, or *Troy-Novant*, New Troy, to continue the remembrancer of the old, and after, in the processe of time *Caier Lud*, that is, *Luds Towne*, of King Lud . . . and so from *Luds Towne*, by contraction of the word and *dialect* used in those times, it came since to be called *London*." Munday, in the 1605 Show, calls James a second Brute, and " Britannia " retells some of this history. *Troia Nova* is used in but one title of the Lord Mayor's Shows — that by Dekker in 1612. (See below, chapter vi.)

England, to which he gave his name — Britain. One of his band was Corineus, an able warrior; he received Cornwall [1] and here fought the last of the " giant brood " who inhabited the land. Gogmagog, Corineus slew in single combat, throwing him headlong from a high rock into the sea; and the rock " has been ever since called Langoëmagog, that is, the giant's leap." [2] Brutus afterwards built Troia Nova, which changed in time to Trinovantum, and is now called London.[3]

The author of *The Gigantick History* supposes that as " Corinæus and Gogmagog were two brave giants, who richly valued their honour, and exerted their whole strength and force in defence of their liberty and country; so the city of London, by placing these their representatives in their Guildhall, emblematically declare, that they will, like mighty giants, defend the honour of their country, and liberties of this their city; which excels all others, as much as those huge giants exceed in stature the common bulk of mankind." [4]

GOG AND MAGOG

It is possible that the Biblical or romantic Gog and Magog may have influenced the modern names of these giants; [5] originally, however, they were clearly historical characters. Once given a name, they achieved an individuality which helped to endear them to the people.

---

[1] Cf. Monmouth, lib. i, cap. xvi: " At Corineus portionem regni quæ sorti suæ cesserat, ab appellatione sui nominis Corineiam vocat, populumque Corineiensem, exemplum ducis insecutus: qui cum præ omnibus qui advenerant electionem provinciarum posset habere, maluit regionem illam quæ nunc vel a cornu Britanniæ, vel per corruptionem prædicti nominis Cornubia appellatur."

[2] *The Gigantic History*, i, p. 50 (cited by Hone). Cf. Monmouth, lib. i, cap. xvi: " Locus autem ille a præcipitatione gigantis nomen adeptus Lamgoëmagot, id est saltus Goëmagot, usque in præsentem diem vocatur." Professor E. D. Snyder has called my attention to Dissertation I, prefacing Hazlitt's edition of Warton, *Hist. Eng. Poetry* (London, 1871), i, pp. 102 f. Here Monmouth is cited.

[3] Cf. Sprott's *Chronica*, p. 85; Monmouth, lib. i, cap. xvii; and the extract from Heywood, cited above, p. 58, n. 2.

[4] *The Gigantick History*, i, pp. 53 f., quoted by Hone, *Anc. Mys.*, p. 275; the latter adds, " Each of these giants, as they now stand, measures upwards of fourteen feet in height: the young one is believed to be Corineus, and the old one Gogmagog."

[5] For an example of these names in a romance, see Ulrich von Eschenbach, *Alexander* (ed. Wendelin Toischer, Tübingen, 1888) lines 20903–4:

> " under in ein künic der hiez Gog
> was, der ander hiez Magog."

I am indebted to Dr. R. W. Pettengill for further references to Gog and Magog in Heinrich von Neustadt's *Apollonius* (ed. S. Singer, Berlin, 1906), line 2939 f.:

> " Ain volck Gock und Magock
> Ist gehaissen ungestalt,
> Das fewlet veld und wald
> Und ödet im das gut land."

In 1605 Munday alludes to the giants, who appeared in the procession on Lord Mayor's Day,[1] as Corinæus and Gogmagog; there was a giant in 1656 which is mentioned in Bulteel's pamphlet;[2] " a Gyant being twelve foot in height going before the [first] Pageant for the delight of the people "; but this giant is, it will be remarked, not named.   There seems to be no other mention of giants in the descriptive pamphlets of the Lord Mayor's Show, until 1672, when Jordan refers to them as " two exceeding rarities." [3]

Cf. l. 10953, and the references in the *Index of Names* (pp. 470, 474) to lines 3175, 3341, 3347, 3366, 3446, 3516, 3646, 3990, 4000; and in *Gottes Zukunft*, to lines 5550, 5808, and 5858. The names are used not only of kings, but also of the folk.

It may be remarked that Mr. Price is also not satisfied with the suggestion that the London figures of Gog and Magog have a Continental origin.   He cites the Biblical Gog and Magog, and notes that the mountains in the district between Caucasus and Mesopotamia bear the names Ghogh and Moghef to the present day; he draws attention to the bow borne by Gog's effigy — the national weapon of the Biblical people; but if there is any connection between this and *Ezekiel*, xxxix (showing that the loss of this weapon was one of the judgments foretold as coming on Gog and his kingdom), it may not antedate 1708.   These giants were undoubtedly connected with English history through Geoffrey of Monmouth; the later division of Gogmagog's name into two parts, may be due to Biblical influence, people having forgotten that the giant — so often unnamed — was Cornish.

[1] See below, chapter vi.

[2] This pamphlet, describing the Lord Mayor's Show of 1656, is in the British Museum [C. 33. e. 10].   I shall refer to it in more detail later — see chapter vi, below.

[3] Cf. the pamphlet of the 1672 show, by Jordan (p. 12): " I must not omit to tell you, that marching in the van of these five pageants, are two exceeding rarities to be taken notice of: that is, there are two extreme great giants, each of them at least fifteen foot high, that do sit and are drawn by horses in two several chariots, moving, talking, and taking tobacco as they ride along, to the great admiration and delight of all the spectators: at the conclusion of the show, they are to be set up in Guildhall, where they may be daily seen all the year, and I hope never to be demolished by such dismal violence as happened to their predecessors; which are raised at the peculiar and proper cost of the city."   Cited by Fairholt, *L. M. Pag.*, pt. i, p. 76; *Gog and Magog*, p. 30.   Cf. *Repertory* lxxvii, fol. 266 b (cited by Price, p. 93); on 15 October, 1672, " upon the request of the right honorable the Lord Maior Elect, This Courte doth thinke fitt & order That the two Gyants now preparing to be sett upp in the Guildhall shall be vsed upon the next Lord Maiors Day for such purpose as his Lopp shall thinke fitting, His Lopp now ingageing to restore them againe in as good plight and condicōn as they shall bee in when hee shall receive them."

For a brief history of the London giants after 1554, see *Gog and Magog*, pp. 28 f.   Hone, Fairholt, and Sharp quote Marston's *Dutch Courtezan*: " Yet all will scarce make me so high as one of the Gyant's stilts that stalks before my Lord Maior's pageants."   For various references to the giants in literature see *Gog and Magog* and Hazlitt's Brand (1905), i, p. 279, art. *Gog and Magog*. Cf. also *L. M. Pag.*, pt. i, p. 76, n.: " Bishop Corbet, who died 1635, in his 'Iter Boreale' written about the middle of James the First's reign, alludes to them [the giants] when speaking of those at Holmby, the seat of Sir Christopher Hatton, the ' dancing chancellor ' of Queen Elizabeth.

' Oh, you that do Guildhall and Holmby keep
Soe carefully, when both their founders sleepe
You are good giants.' "

By the end of the seventeenth century the two giants had been given their present names; but Hone shows an amusing *naïveté* when he deduces that the oath of the cabman of 1700 shows that " the city giants were far more popular than now." [1]

Edward Ward, writing about 1700, describes the City Giants ironically. " . . . we Jostled thro' a parcel of Busie Citizens, who blunder'd along with as much speed towards the *Change*, as Lawyers in Term time towards *Westminster-Hall*, till we turn'd down *King-Street*, and came to the place intended; which I enter'd with as great Astonishment, to see the Giants, as the *Morocco* Ambassador did *London*, when he saw the Snow fall: I ask'd my Friend the meaning and design of setting up those two Lubberly Preposterous Figures; for I suppose they had some peculiar End in't: Truly, says my Friend, I am wholly Ignorant of what they intended by 'em, unless they were set up to show the City what huge Loobies their Fore-fathers were, or else to fright Stubborn Apprentices into Obedience; for the dread of appearing before two such Monstrous Logger-heads, will sooner Reform their Manners, or mould 'em into a Compliance with their Masters Will, than carrying 'em before my Lord-Mayor, or the Chamberlain of *London*; for some of them are as much frighted at the names of *Gog* and *Magog* as little Children are at the terrible Sound of *Raw-Head* and *Bloody-Bones*." [2]

In 1708 the present giants were carved to take the place of those mentioned by Ward and in Jordan's 1672 pamphlet, which apparently had succumbed to time, and a number of city rats and mice.[3] These are the giants described in *The Gigantick History* (about 1740) where the names Gog and Magog are used.[4]

[Cf. *Gog and Magog*, p. 36.] Fairholt also refers to George Wither, who " in his ' Joco Serio; strange news of a Discourse between two dead Giants ' (1661) alludes to them as —

    ' Big-bon'd Colbrant and great Brandamore
    The giants in Guildhall . . .
    Where they have had a place to them assign'd
    At publick meetings, now time out of mind.' "

[1] Hone, *Anc. Mys.*, p. 264, citing Edward Ward's *London Spy* — a satire on the London life of the times — also quoted in *Gog and Magog*, p. 41. The fourth edition of this work appeared in 1709: from it I quote the oath referred to: The coachman, afraid of getting " bilked " of his fare, cries, " Pay me my Fare, or by *Gog* and *Magog* you shall feel the smart of my whipcord before you go a Step further " (p. 174.) *Gog* is evidently a harmless corruption of *God*: *Magog* is added for emphasis, or to make the oath even more innocuous. The same oath appears in the *Lamentation* of " Dybdynne " in 1830. " By Gog, no more will I." It can hardly be proved that this shows the giants to be still popular (seven years after Hone's book appeared!) for the verses are written in a colloquial and ironic style, and the author may have supposed he was inventing the oath.

[2] *The London Spy*, p. 93; see Price, p. 93; Magnin (1862), p. 216, n. 2, citing Hone's *Anc. Mys.*; the latter refers to *The London Spy*.

[3] Fairholt, *L.M.Pag.*, pt. i, p. 76, n. Cf. *Gog and Magog*, p. 28 f; Hone, *Anc.Mys.*, pp. 262 f; Bieling, *Zu den Sagen von Gog und Magog* (1882), pp. 15 f., and Price, p. 94.

[4] The first book of this work deals with the giants. The third chapter deals with " the two ancient giants that were in Guildhall," which were made " only of wickerwork and paste-

A Frenchman travelling in England in 1765,[1] writes: "Le goût anglois, goût universel, mais indécis, pour tous les objets des arts, n'exclut pas même aujourd'hui le gothique; il règne encore, non-seulement dans des ornemens de fantaisie, mais dans des bâtimens très-modernes qu'il a entièrement dirigés. La maison de ville de Londres doit à ce goût la conservation des deux géants que porte un baldaquin qui couronne le perron par lequel on passe de la grand' salle, dans la chambre d'audience. Ces géants, en comparaison desquels le Jacquemard de S. Paul de Paris est un bijou, ne semblent placés là que pour faire peur aux enfans: pour qu' ils remplissent mieux cette destination, on a soin de renouveller souvent l'enduit dont leur visage & leurs armes sont grossièrement enluminés. On auroit quelque raison de les conserver, s'ils étoient d'une haute antiquité, ou si, de même que la pierre qui servoit de premier trône aux rois d'Ecosse & que l'on conserve précieusement à Westminster, le peuple les regardoit comme le *palladium* de la nation; mais ils n'ont en leur faveur que l'étonnement qu' inspire leur première vue aux étrangers, à qui elles (*sic*) semblent prèsenter la barbarie danoise en alliance avec la barbarie saxonne." [2]

---

board." " Those two terrible original giants had the honour yearly to grace my Lord Mayor's shew, being carried in great triumph in the time of the pageants; and when that eminent annual service was over, remounted in their old stations in Guildhall, which their successors the present giants possess, till by reason of their very great age, old time, with the help of a number of City rats and mice, had eaten up all their entrails; so that being no longer able to support themselves, they gave up the ghost and died." The fourth chapter tells " of the present giants, their birth, parentage, and advancement in the world." They were made by Captain Richard Saunders (an eminent King Street carver) in 1708; and in the next chapter we read that since they were erected in Guildhall, they never quit their stations. The seventh chapter — " why the Giants are by some people called *Gog* and *Magog* and by others *Jupiter* and *Mars* " — says that the mythological names were given them " because the spiked ball at the end of the staff which the former holds in his hand [some people] say, is a thunderbolt; and that the habiliments of war which the latter has about him, are the ensigns of Mars." The eighth chapter tells us that others call the old giant, Brutus — and gives, briefly, the Brutus story: in the ninth chapter we find the author's theory that the older giant represents Gogmagog and the younger Corineus; and the book closes with a chapter describing " the mighty giant Og, King of Bashan."

Among the numerous places where illustrations of Gog and Magog may be found, are Fairholt's *Gog and Magog*, Hone, *Anc. Mys.* (facing p. 262) and Price, p. 90. For remarks on the Guildhall giants by J. T. Smith and F. Douce (in a review of Mr. Smith's *Ancient Topography of London*) see the *Gentleman's Magazine*, lxxxvi, pt. ii, pp. 41 f. (July, 1816). See also Bieling, *Zu den Sagen von Gog and Magog*, to which I have already referred.

Apparently the giants had no official names in the seventeenth and eighteenth centuries, and were called whatever the people chose to call them.

[1] See Pierre Jean Grosley, *Londres*, published at Lausanne in 1770; translated by Thomas Nugent under the title, *A Tour to London, or New Observations on England and its Inhabitants*, in 1772. The above date of the visit is that given by Dr. Nugent, p. 1, preface.

[2] Grosley, iii, pp. 57 f.; cf. Nugent's translation, ii, p. 88—cited by Price, pp. 94 f. (Did M. Grosley forget the giants of northern France and Flanders ?)

A satire — faintly Swiftian — which appeared in 1823, describes the departure for Africa

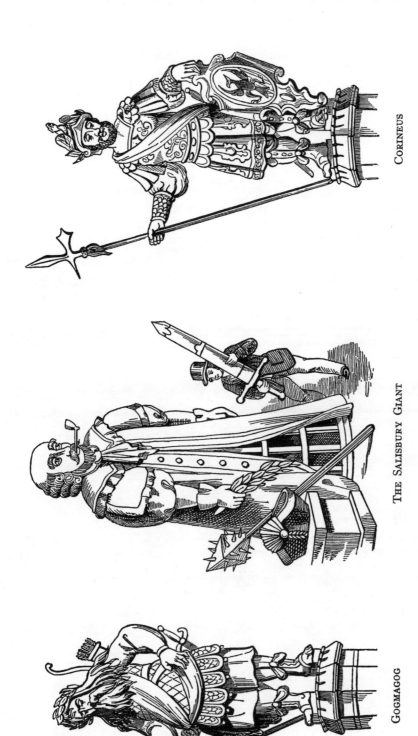

CORINEUS

THE SALISBURY GIANT

GOGMAGOG

In 1827 giants again appeared in the Lord Mayor's Show: "each walked by the aid of a man within them (*sic*) and they from time to time turned their faces to the spectators who lined the streets. It was the final exhibition of the olden glories of that day." [1] The *Times* for 10 November, 1827, remarks "some deviations . . . from the usual order, which deserve mention." The Mayor, being the Alderman of the Tower ward, embarked from the Tower stairs, instead of from Blackfriars bridge, as usual; "the second, and far more attractive novelty of the day, was the exhibition of two colossal figures representing the well-known statues Gog and Magog (as they are called) of Guildhall. They were extremely well contrived, and appeared to call forth more admiration and applause than fell to the share of any of the other personages who formed part of the procession." [2]

The popularity of the giant as a figure in the Lord Mayor's Show was demonstrated again in that of 1913. Many of the large crowd which lined the streets of London in November of that year to see the annual procession, supposed that he represented Magog, to whom he bore a surprising resemblance; but he was intended to symbolize the "River God" which Hugh Middleton had chained three hundred years before. Led captive by a miniature St. George, the gigantic

---

of Baron Münchausen, accompanied by a Sphinx from the Tower, Gog, Magog, and a large train of attendants. In chapter ix of *A Sequel to the Travels and Adventures of Baron Munchausen* (London, 1823 — printed as volume ii of *The Surprising Travels and Adventures of Baron Munchausen. . . . A new and complete edition. . . . London, 1823*) we hear how "The Baron's Retinue is opposed in a heroic style by Don Quixote, who in his turn is attacked by Gog and Magog. — Lord Whittington with the Lord Mayor's Show" [which consists of "armour antique of chivalry, and helmets old, and troops, all streamers, flags and banners glittering gay, red, gold and purple . . ."] — apparently a description of an early nineteenth century show] "comes to the assistance of Don Quixote. — Gog and Magog assail his Lordship. — Lord Whittington makes a speech and deludes Gog and Magog to his party. — A general scene of uproar and battle among the company follows; until the Baron, with great presence of mind, appeases the tumult" (pp. 35 f). Reminiscent of Swift is the Baron's journey to the Moon and the Dog Star, his arrival at an Island of Cheese, surrounded by a Sea of Milk, etc. (in part i). The work has little to do with our subject, but is, perhaps, interesting as showing Gog and Magog still connected with the Lord Mayor's Show in a nineteenth century satire.

[1] Fairholt, *Gog and Magog*, p. 50, and *Lord Mayor's Pageants*, pt. i, p. 138, misprints 1837. There were no giants when Queen Victoria attended the Lord Mayor's banquet in the first year of her reign.

In the second volume of Faitholt's scrapbooks (preserved in the Society of Antiquaries) is a woodcut representing the 1827 procession. Underneath it is this MS. note: "This woodcut representing the procession of 1837 (*sic*) passing through Cornhill, was drawn for the Penny Magazine, but so wretchedly engraved that the cut was cancelled, and the above proof impression the only one ever taken from it."

[2] J. G. Nichols, *London Pageants*, p. 121, records in addition that the giants "were constructed of wickerwork; each walked along by means of a man withinside (*sic*) who ever and anon turned the faces; and as the figures were fourteen feet high, their features were on a level with the first floor windows."

figure stalked through the London streets; he was nine feet tall, and hollow — the man who carried him walked inside, looking out through a lace covered shirt-front. Although there seems to be no historical basis for such a figure,[1] the popular approval he evoked was ample excuse for his existence; and it is possible that a gigantic figure will be a part of more than one Lord Mayor's Show yet to come.[2]

§ 6. ANIMALS IN PAGEANT AND ROMANCE

Whether or not the giants are survivals of human sacrificial customs, or of pagan images, of both or of neither, certain it is that they appear in folk-celebrations at an early date. Just when they were attached to the Midsummer Show, we do not know; it was, however, not later than the early part of the sixteenth century, and probably was much earlier; for they were in the royal-entry by 1415. From the Midsummer Show they were taken over by the Lord Mayor's Show when that arose in the mid-sixteenth century.

Closely connected with giants are the animals which have played a symbolic part in pageantry since the end of the thirteenth century. The welcome of Edward I by the Fishmongers in 1298 included animals whose trade symbolism is obvious.[3] Folk-custom in every country had its animals,[4] and the Church included animals in its processions — adapting them to the Biblical or legendary material used — as in the Feast of the Ass. Perhaps the folk animals suggested the Biblical stories or Saint's legends to be used; given a " wild worm " is it natural that the figures of St. George should be adapted to it. The reader will recall the various unicorns, dromedaries, camels, luces, dragons, asses, and hobbyhorses of the Midsummer Shows at Chester, London and elsewhere. These are the "raw material" from which a fabric of trade-symbolism was woven in later

---

[1] The 1913 show was announced as a " reproduction " of that of 1613: we shall return to this later — see chapter vi, below.

[2] An illustration of the 1913 giant may be found in the *Illus. Lond. News*, 15 November, 1913, p. 783.

[3] See my paper on *The Early " Royal-Entry,"* in *Publ. Mod. Lang. Assoc.* for December, 1917. Animals have been explained as a survival, in folk celebrations, of sacrificial beasts, the artificial being substituted for the real, as in the case of giants. Cf. Chambers, i, p. 139, n. 2. C. J. Billson, writing in *Folk-Lore* for December, 1892, " has shown a connection between the Christian festival of Easter and the worship or sacrifice of hares. . . ." He " brings forward much evidence to prove that ' the hare was originally a totem, or divine animal . . . and that the customs at Leicester and Hallaton are relics of the religious procession and annual sacrifice of the god.' " Ditchfield, *Old Eng. Customs* (1896), pp. 86 and 87.

[4] On " grandes marionnettes demi-religieuses et demi-populaires " see Magnin, book ii, ch. i, § 4 (1862 ed., pp. 60 f.). He deals with the dragons, giants and monsters of Continental processions. On animals in Italian mediæval processions see Burckhardt, ii, pp. 142 f. Sharp, p. 202 (quoting the *Life of Friar Gerund*, i, 111), mentions " the figures of gigantic men and a large serpent " which " are carried about . . . by way of shewing the conquest of Christ over the powers of earth and hell." Cf. the description of the *groote Ommeganck* of Antwerp in *Gog and Magog*, pp. 67 f. and in *Lord Mayor's Pageants*, pp. ix f.

Lord Mayor's Shows; the weaving had begun in the welcome to Edward I by the Fishmongers of 1298.

In such folk festivals as May Day, it is very probable that the animals determined the characters assumed by the mummers — at least to some extent.[1]

Mr. Frank Stevens, in his paper on *The Giant and Hob-Nob and their Story*,[2] says: " The Hob-Nob, Hobby Horse, ' Hooden ' or ' Old Snap ' as he is variously called, deserves something more than passing notice since his origin is even more remote than that of the Giant. He was always regarded as essentially a part of the Morris Dance, and, therefore, was to be found taking part in the May Day Celebrations, with Robin Hood . . . as well as in the St. George's Day Festivals, and in particular the Rogation Day Beating of the Bounds. These, however, are comparatively modern uses of the Hob-Nob . . ."

Mr. Stevens finds the custom of pagan, probably Scandinavian, origin. " The horse was a frequent victim in sacrifice to Odin, for success in war. . . . It is, therefore, most probable that Hodening (or rather Odening) is a relic of Scandinavian mythology." As early as the seventh century, the practice of clothing one's self in the skins of cattle, and carrying heads of animals was condemned by Archbishop Theodore.[3]

Occasionally, as at Norwich and Salisbury, a pageantic animal became sufficiently characterized to receive a name. We have already spoken of Snap, who is still to be seen in the Castle Museum; the fact that this animal was given a name, is an eloquent sign of its popularity.

---

[1] Says Magnin (1862 ed., pp. 216 f.) "Dans les *May-poles*, le cortège se composait, suivant l'importance des lieux, d'un plus ou moins grand nombre de groupes qui avaient chacun leurs chefs, leurs danses, et leurs chansons à part. D'ordinaire on voyait gambader en avant du cortège soit un Jack ou Jeannot, soit un Fou de ville en costume officiel, c'est-à-dire avec grelots, vessie, marotte et bonnet à oreilles d'âne. Puis, venaient les principaux acteurs des ballades nationales, Robin Hood, frère Tuck, Maid Marian, tous représentés . . . par de jeunes garçons vêtus comme l'exigeait leur rôle. Cette procession devait . . . offrir à l'arrière-garde plusieurs groupes particulièrement aimés du peuple, à savoir des danseurs moresques et certains grands mannequins qu'on appelait *hobby-horses*, chevaux d'osier à tête de carton, que des hommes cachés sous les plis de leurs longues housses faisaient marcher et caracoler."

" At Polebrook, Oundle, the children elect a May Queen and parade the village, the May Queen at the head of the procession, attended by two girls carrying dressed dolls placed in a bower of green and flowers." Ditchfield, p. 109. At Padstow, the first of May is called Hobby-Horse Day: " a hobby-horse is carried through the streets to Traitor's Pool, where it is made to drink." (*Ibid.*, p. 106.)

On Christmas, in Wales, mummers, dressed in all kinds of costumes, at the *Mari Llwyd*, or " Holy Mary," were accompanied by boys dressed as bears, foxes, squirrels, and rabbits (see above, p. 17). The skeleton head and shoulders of a horse were carried in this procession (Trevelyan, p. 32). We shall see, in the next chapter, that Court mummers of the fourteenth century dressed in animals' heads: this custom is evidently a development of the folk habit, an example of which I have just given.

[2] In the Salisbury *Festival Book* (1914), pp. 64 f.

[3] Mr. Stevens cites Kemble's *Saxons*, i, p. 525, on p. 65.

ANIMALS IN ROMANCES

Animals appear frequently in romances, not to mention the beast epics.[1] The relation of these to the animals in pageantry seems to be much like that between the romantic and pageantic giants — where the romantic material is mingled with magic, there is no connection, though perhaps the romantic animals owe something to the folk-customs which give beasts to the pageant. There is, of course, this great difference between the animals and the giants: the former have been the constant companions of man, whereas the latter have not. Probably the romantic animals owe nothing to the mechanical contrivances of folk-custom; but it is possible that, in the cases of legendary beasts like the dragon, the pageant has drawn on the romance.

THE ELEPHANT AND CASTLE

A clear case of this borrowing is shown in the Elephant and Castle, which is probably an importation — direct or indirect — from the metrical romance. We have already seen this pageant in the Chester Midsummer Show;[2] we shall see it again at Henry VII's reception at Bristol in 1486.[3] Of an undoubtedly Indian origin, this figure appears in metrical romances;[4] and the actual life of the

---

[1] Animals do the black giant homage, as vassals to their lord, in Kynon's Tale, *The Lady of the Fountain*, in the *Mabinogion*. King Diderick helps a lion and fights a dragon (Prior's *Ancient Danish Ballads* x (i, p. 114). Cf. the dragons in *Beowulf*, and the combat of the Red-Cross Knight with Error (*F. Q.*, i, 13 f) where the romance is developed into allegory. It is unnecessary to give more instances of a common feature of the romances.

[2] See above, p. 45, n. 5, and p. 46.   [3] See below, p. 160.

[4] I am indebted to Dr. R. W. Pettengill for the following references: Ulrich von Eschenbach, *Alexander* (ed. W. Toischer, Tübingen, 1888), lines 19890 f.:

> " ich hân vernomen alsô
> und vür die wârheit hoeren sagen
> wie daz vil helfande tragen
> vil bercvride und daz die sîn wol beriht
> mit geschozze . . .''

Cf. *Daniel von dem bluhenden Tal;* ein Artusroman von dem Stricker (ed. G. Rosenhagen, Breslau, 1894), lines 585 f.:

> " ein tier daz heizet helfant,
> daz enist dir niht wol erkant,
> des kraft ist so stæte,
> swer kunde mit geræte
> einen berc daruf geladen,
> daz enmöhte im niht geschaden
> ez enwurde niemer müede . . .''

And lines 6500 f.:

> " dar brâhten helfande getragen
> rehte vier und zweinzic hûs
> daz der Künec Artûs
> noch dehein manne nie gesach . . .''

East, embalmed in these romances, is probably the source of these English pageants of castles on the backs of elephants.[1] As Sir George Forrest has reminded
me, the *castle* in chess (the only one of our pieces which does not represent a living
figure) is a survival of an earlier *elephant and castle*, a recognized force in Indian

---

Lamprecht's *Alexander* (ed. K. Kinzel, Halle a. S., 1884), lines 4327 f.:

> " Si brâhten manich elefent
> von den wil ih û sagen,
> wiliche sterke si haben
> si ne hânt in ir gebeine
> nu merket waz ih meine,
> neiren nehein marc.
> si sint ûzer mâze stark
> man mach ûf si bûwen,
> willit irs getrûwen,
> turme unde berchfride
> vil stark sind in die lide . . .
> daz ist ein michil wunder."

and lines 4371 f.:

> " iz treget wol âne zwîbel
> in strîte und in sturme
> berhfriden unde turme
> und riter dar inne."

Cf. the Latin passage (*ibid.*, pp. 270 f.): "habebat enim quatuordecim milia quadrigas omnes
falcatas exceptis equitibus et peditibus et quadrigentos elephantes in quorum dorsis turres
lignee elevate et per unamquamque turrim triginta homines existebant."

Cf. also Wirnt von Gravenberg, *Wigalois* (ed. G. F. Benecke, Berlin, 1819), lines 10498 f.:

> " sehs helfande fûrte er;
> Die trûgen nach des heldes ger
> Wichus unde berchfrit."

and lines 10982 f.:

> " Die helfande volgten mite
> Dem her in ir gelerten site
> Gegen den vienden uf den graben,
> Diu wichus waren dar uf erhaben."

Cf. Heinrich von Neustadt, *Apollonius von Tyrland* (ed. S. Singer, Berlin, 1906) lines 3866 f.:

> " Tausent grosse helffant . . .
> Di waren herleich geladen
> Si trugen castell und gaden
> Und manigen reichen sawm schrein."

and lines 17817 f.:

> " Di helffant waren nit zu schnell
> Si trugen auff in vier kastell:
> In yedem castell besundert
> Sassen frauwen hundert."

[1] Burckhardt (1896 ed.), ii, p. 136 (Middlemore, ii, p. 182), mentions a Burgundian festival
of 1453 when "Olivier himself, to whom we owe the description of the scene, appeared

armies. This piece is still preserved in Indian chessmen, and may be found in old
European sets; the elephant seems to have disappeared from our boards because
the carvers found it an unnecessary elaboration.[1]

" Cutlers in the last century frequently used the *Elephant and Castle* as their
sign, on account of its being the crest of the Cutlers' Company, who had adopted
it in reference to the ivory used in the trade. Hence the stone bas-relief in Belle
Sauvage Yard, which was the sign of some now forgotten shopkeeper. . . . The
houses in the Yard are the property of the Cutlers' Company. The *Elephant and
Castle* public-house, Newington Butts, was formerly a famous coaching inn." [2]

---

costumed as ' The Church,' in a tower on the back of an elephant, and sang a long elegy on
the victory of the unbelievers." (Burckhardt refers to the *Mémoires* of Olivier de la Marche).
The German text adds a giant; " Olivier selbst kam als ' Kirche ' costumiert in dem Thurme
auf dem Rücken eines Elephanten, den ein Riese führte, und sang . . ."

A passage from the Duke of Newcastle's *Country Captain* (1649), Act v, Sc. 1 (p. 80), is
cited by Fairholt, in the first volume of his scrapbooks, preserved in the library of the Society
of Antiquaries: " Thou fight for a *Ladyes* honour, and disarme a Gentleman ? Thou fence
before the Pageants & make roome for the porters, when like Elephants they carry once a
yeare the Cyttie Castles." This shows that the elephant and castle was, in the seventeenth
century, a popular piece of pageantry. The same scrapbook cites a passage from a sermon by
Bishop Hall, quoted in the Variorum Shakspere, in the notes to *Antony and Cleopatra*, Act iv,
Sc. 12: " I fear that some of you are like the Pageants of your great solemnities, wherein there
is the show of a solid body, whether of a Lion or Elephant or Unicorne, but if they be curiously
look'd into, there is nothing but cloth and sticks and wyre."

Dr. Ing. Martin Hammitzsch, in *Beiträge zur Bauwissenschaft*, Heft 8 (Berlin, 1906), *Der
Moderne Theaterbau* (pp. 50–52, figs. 25–27), gives illustrations of pageants in connection with a
tournament at Bologna, 20 March, 1628. One of the pageants shows an elephant with a castle
on his back. (The illustrations are from drawings by Giovanni Battista Coriolano (1589–
1649). Bodl. MS. 264, fol. 236, shows a fourteenth-century illumination of an elephant and
castle (illustrating Marco Polo's voyages).

I have said that this pageant is an importation — direct or indirect — from the metrical
romance. It is possible that the direct origin is connected with the Cutlers' companies, whose
arms often bore the elephant and castle. If this be a trade-pageant — which is mere surmise
— its ultimate origin is undoubtedly to be found in the romance; I am inclined to believe that
there is a mixture of both influences; it is hard to say whether the pageant, drawn from the
romance, suggested — on account of its similarity to the crest — a trade-signification; or
the crest — originating in the romance — gave birth to the pageant.

[1] " The elephant, in the middle ages, was nearly always represented with a castle on his
back. For instance, in the Latin MS. Bestiarium, Harl. 4751 [fol. 9], a tower is strapped to
him, in which are seen five knights in chain-armour, with swords, battle-axes, and cross-bows
. . . and in the description of the animal, it is said, ' In eorum dorsis P[er]si et Indi ligneis
turribus collocati tamquam de muro jaculis dimicant.' The rook, in Chinese chessboards, still
represents an elephant thus armed." J. Larwood and John C. Hotten, *History of Signboards*,
p. 155.

[2] Larwood and Hotten, p. 156. The Elephant and Castle Inn, on the borderland of Southwark and Newington (which gave its name to the district) is illustrated in Rendle and Norman's *Inns of Old Southwark*, from a drawing of 1786 (p. 380). The building shown was
destroyed in 1824. (The authors refer to illustrations of this inn in the *Mirror*, 11 April, 1840,

SHIPWRIGHTS' ARMS

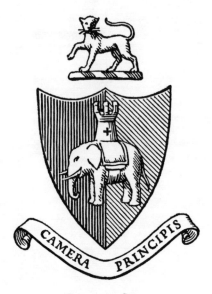

COVENTRY SEAL

If the inn-sign has any connection with pageantry, it is not the only one which shows such influence; — *the Green Man* is probably closely related to the folk figure; perhaps also *The George and Dragon*. It may be to the inn-sign that Mr. Pecksniff referred, when he said, " I remember thinking once myself, in the days of my childhood, that pickled onions grew on trees, and that every elephant was born with an impregnable castle on his back." [1]

We shall see that the pageantic " animal " was borrowed by the masque; there is no need to enlarge on this matter here. As an example, I may refer to the great show at Kenilworth in 1575; [2] Queen Elizabeth " was entertained . . . upon the water, [when] appeared a person in the character of Arion, riding upon a dolphin twenty-four feet in length; and he sung an admirable song accompanied with music performed by six musicians concealed in the belly of the fish. Her majesty, it appears, was much pleased with this exhibition." [3] Says Strutt,[4] " The English are particularized for their partiality to strange sights; uncommon beasts, birds or fishes, are sure to attract their notice, and especially such of them as are of the

---

and in the *Illus. Lond. News*, 8 November, 1879, from a drawing by Richardson). The ground on which it stood was, in 1658, a piece of waste, and was granted for building purposes; the parish wardens' accounts show that in 1673 the original rents were as low as £5 a year; in 1797 they were £190. (*Ibid.*, p. 379. " About this time it was probably first named the Elephant and Castle; at all events on the expiration of the lease in 1818 . . . ' the house called the Elephant and Castle, used as a public house, fell to Jane Fisher for a term of 31 years, at an annual rent of £405 . . . the whole estate realising £623 a year.' " [Cited from *Reports Concerning Charities*, xvi, by Rendle, pp. 379, 380.])

Brewer, in the *Dictionary of Phrase and Fable*, p. 412, says that the sign is " said to derive its name from the skeleton of an elephant dug up near Battle Bridge in 1714. A flint-headed spear lay by the remains, whence it is conjectured that the creature was killed by the British in a fight with the Romans." Rendle (p. 378, n.) echoes Larwood in suggesting that the sign probably is due to the Cutlers' crest. Wheatley and Cunningham, *London Past, and Present*, ii, p. 9, cite Rendle. The inn-sign was not uncommon in England — it is even now seen often — and this suggests an early origin, perhaps from metrical romances and pageantry, in some cases *via* the Cutlers.

A clever suggestion has been made that the inn-sign is a corruption of *Infanta of Castile*. This is not impossible, but is, I think, unlikely; the " picture-signboard " makes the metamorphosis improbable.

The Sheffield Cutlers have an elephant-head as crest; and it should be remarked that the city arms of Coventry are an elephant and castle; it is due to this fact that the 1862 Lady Godiva procession included this pageant. " It happened that Wombwell's Show was at the fair, so the elephant was borrowed and a pasteboard castle put upon his back." (*Morning Star*, 25 June, 1862, p. 6, col. 6.)

[1] *Martin Chuzzlewit*, chapter vi. Cf. *ibid.*, chapter xxxi: " Tom would have helped him with the box; but he made no more of it, though it was a heavy one, than an elephant would have made of a castle, just swinging it on his back, and bowling downstairs as if . . . he could carry a box infinitely better than he could go alone."

[2] See below, p. 209.

[3] Strutt, *Sports*, pp. xxxii f., referring to Laneham's account, in Nichols, *Prog. Q. E.*

[4] *Sports*, § xxviii.

monstrous kind." This accounts for the survival of folk-animals — even of those which are not connected with history or legend [1] (as so many are on the Continent) or given an allegorical or trade signification by the Guilds.

§ 7. THE " JACK–IN–THE–GREEN " AND " WHIFFLER "

A popular figure in the May Day celebrations of England, and one seen in pageants today, is the " Jack-in-the-Green." Its origin may, perhaps, be similar to that of the " wild-man " whom we shall discuss in the next section of this chapter; he may go back to ivy-wreathed Summer in the pre-Christian Spring festival. A " Jack-in-the-Green " heads the May Day processions of sweeps at Oxford,[2] at Cheltenham; [3] and sweeps at Cambridge " evidently used to have a similar festival, as the children still go around with a doll, hung in the midst of a hoop wreathed with flowers, singing the ditty —

> ' The first of May is garland day
> And chimney-sweepers dancing day.' " [4]

At Bampton [5] and at Witney [6] they still have a Jack-in-the-Green, accompanied by various attendants. A " Jack o' the Green " was one of the characters in the Chester pageant of 1908; he also appeared in the Lichfield Bower of 1913, and I saw one at Knutsford on May Day, 1914. " This piece of pageantry," says Strutt, in an excellent description, " consists of a hollow frame of wood, or wickerwork, made in the form of a sugar-loaf, but open at the bottom, and sufficiently large to receive a man. The frame is covered with green leaves and bunches of flowers interwoven with each other, so that the man within may be completely concealed, who dances with his companions, and the populace are mightily pleased with the oddity of the moving pyramid." [7] This kind of thing combines features of the " giant " with those of the " wild-man," perhaps drawing from both.

---

[1] Snap — which is illustrated in Ewing — may, perhaps, be considered in this group, as he accompanied St. George, the patron saint of Norwich. But such animals as the Tarasque are not common in England. At Salisbury, Hob-Nob is preserved, together with the giant, in the Museum. Writes Mr. Frank Stevens in a letter to me: " The Hob-Nob suffers [from rough usage], and last time (1911) he tore open a boy's hand with his teeth, and a doctor had to be called in to stitch up the wound. Two noted Hob-Nob bearers in the city were 'Fiddler' Gibbs and ' Boosey ' Hibberd. The names indicate the class of man." A postcard illustrating the Salisbury giant and Hob-Nob, is in the Harvard Library: see also the Salisbury *Festival Book* (opp. p. 59.)

[2] Ditchfield, p. 97.   [5] P. 99.

[3] P. 98.   [6] P. 100.

[4] Pp. 98–99.

[7] *Sports*, p. 267 and note 1. In the " Jack " which I saw at Knutsford, there was a window made in the frame, so that the man could see where he was going, and the people could see his face. He waddled down the street from curb to curb, rather than danced; and he amused the people greatly with his antics.

THE " WHIFFLER "

The *whiffler*, whom we have already mentioned [1] deserves a few words; he seems to have been a figure used sometimes to clear the way for the procession, and sometimes as a henchman, or attendant. " As there was always a multitude of people to see the Procession, it was necessary to have several Persons to keep them from coming too near, or break the Procession. For this purpose there were six Whifflers, somewhat like the Roman Gladiators, who were neatly dressed, and had the art of brandishing their very sharp Swords in the greatest Crowds with such dexterity as to do harm to none; and of a sudden they would dart them up many yards into the air, and never failed catching them by their Hilts.

" To this purpose also a man or two in painted canvass Coats and ridiculous red and yellow Cloth Caps, adorned with Cats' Tails and small Bells, went up and down to clear the way, whose weapons were only small wands. These were called or known by the name of Dick-Fools: even these had their admirers, but it was amongst the Children and the Mobility." [2]

Whifflers appeared in a London muster on 8 May, 1539: " they that numbered them can report what pains the wyffelers took to keep the soldiers in array . . ." [3] In the Duke of Newcastle's comedy, *The Country Captain*,[4] we read: " Hee that expects my favor . . . must bee none of my Lord Mayors whiffelers; he must be valiant in Armes." These two passages show the change which had come over the word in little more than a century.[5] Whifflers were common enough in the Lord Mayor's Shows; I need only make a few references here. In 1566 there were twenty-eight " wifelers ";[6] and in 1575 the procession included " certayne wyfflers in velvet cotes and chaynes, with white staves." [7] To jump to 1913, in the Lord Mayor's Show of that year rode " groups of young citizens in green and white accompanied by ' wyfflers ' (which interpreted meant ' ushers ')." [8]

---

[1] Cf. above, p. 26, n. 3, where four whifflers escorted Snap at Norwich; p. 28 for the amount paid to the whifflers in 1698 at the same town; — in 1729 there were five (see p. 28, n. 3). Whifflers' costumes are preserved in the Castle Museum at Norwich (p. 28 and n. 6). In 1570–71 there were two " wyfflers " who attended the Cresset-bearers at London (see above, p. 38, n. 5). See the correspondence on the *Whiffler* in the *Gentleman's Magazine*, especially the illustrated article in the issue of February, 1852, pp. 151 f. On p. 153 this figure is identified with the " wild-man."

[2] From Mackerell's MS. *History of Norwich*, printed in Ewing, p. 21. The whiffler and the Dick Fool are illustrated in Ewing's volume; the drawings are preserved in a case in the Castle Museum at Norwich.

[3] *Letters and Papers of Henry VIII*, xvi, entry 940 (pt. i, p. 440).   [4] Act iii, Sc. 1 (p. 49).

[5] The word is derived from *whiffle* [freq. of *whiff*, perh. confused with D. *weifelen*, to waver] + *er* (*Century Dict.*). It means, primarily, a piper or whistler; (2) a herald or usher — a person who leads or prepares the way, because pipers usually led the procession. (*Ibid.*) Webster gives the word only in the sense of " one who whiffles or frequently changes his opinion or course . . . an idle talker, . . . a trifler."

[6] See below, chapter vi. Cf. Fairholt, *Lord Mayor's Pageants*, pt. i, p. 14, n. 4, for remarks on this figure.

[7] See below, chapter vi.   [8] London *Daily Chronicle* for 11 November, 1913.

§ 8. THE " WILD–MAN " IN PAGEANT, MASQUE,
AND ROMANCE

Another important character in the pageant is the " wild-man " or " green man "; his duty was to clear the street for the procession " that the kyng and his trayne might pass with ease." [1] The question of the origin of this figure is not an easy one to settle; but I am inclined to think his wildness was assumed after he came into pageantry. Strutt refers to a stage direction in the *Historie of Promos and Cassandra*,[2] which " requires the entry of ' two men apparelled lyke *greene men* at the mayor's feast with clubbs of fireworks ' "; apparently their method of clearing the way was to turn the fireworks into the crowd.

The wild-men were dressed up to excite the interest which is provoked by a combination of terror and amusement. The figures were not handsome; and to the merriment which their grotesque appearance must have caused, was probably added a kind of fear, due to childhood memories of brandished torches.[3]

From earliest times, cressets have been a part of the Midsummer Watch; [4] and when it became necessary to clear the way for the procession, a couple of men with torches were sent ahead. As ingenuity brought forth fireworks, these were substituted for the more subdued torches.

It will be recalled that, in the " fight between winter and summer " [5] he who symbolized summer was dressed in leaves and flowers. The mock execution of the tree-spirit, personified in the leaf-and-flower-dressed boy of Bavarian folk-festival, as well as that of the " wild man " in Saxony and Bohemia, has been noted; [6]

---

[1] Strutt, *Sports*, p. xxv. For illustrations of this figure see Strutt, *op. cit.*, plate xxxii, opp. p. 291; Unwin, p. 275; Nicholl, p. 223 — this last taken from John Bate, *The Mysteries of Nature and Art* (3d ed.), London, 1635. The woodcut facing p. 13 of Dupuys's contemporary account of Charles V's entry into Bruges (18 April, 1515) shows a wild-man or forester.

[2] By George Whetstone; printed 1578.

[3] The 1522 king of the Moors carried wild fire (see above, p. 40) and may, perhaps, have taken the place of the wild-man on this occasion.

[4] See above, pp. 37 f.; Sharp, p. 184 and plate 9.

[5] See above, pp. 4 f. These fights may go back to older sacrifices, which degenerated into mock-sacrifices and so to mumming. Whether or not this be so, the ivy-clad figure appears to have existed in folk-custom for a long time. The question of its origin cannot be settled here. A bronze head of Silenus was found at Colchester in 1845 (*Archæologia*, xxxi, pp. 443 f.) and among the antiquities found at Caister, near Norwich, was a figure of Bacchus (described and illustrated in *Norf. Arch.* v (1859), p. 200). It may " have been one of a series of ornaments occupying the front or side of a box or casket," says Mr. Fitch (*loc. cit.*). I mention these merely as signs that Bacchus and Silenus were known in very early England; and there is a possibility that the figure of the wild-man or green-man may be descended from early Bacchic rites. Menestrier, p. 26, describes Bacchantes following a car, some dressed in leaves, in a triumph of Ptolemy at Alexandria. I have already mentioned 2 *Maccabees*, vi, 7 (see above, p. 5) and the possibility that Bacchic rites influenced the costume of leaves and flowers.

[6] See above, p. 51, n. 2.

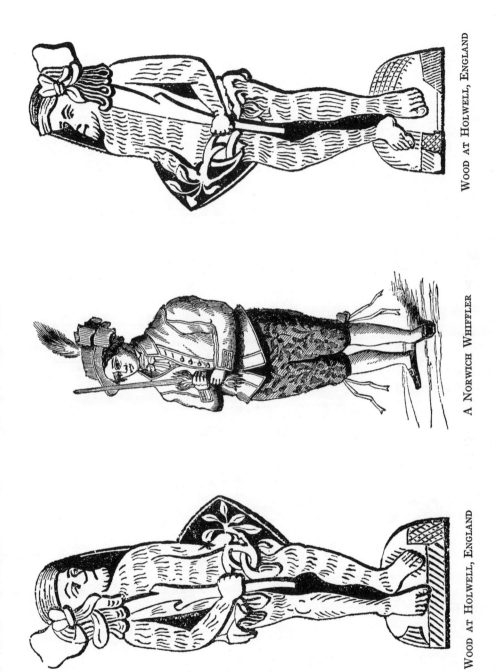

WOOD AT HOLWELL, ENGLAND

A NORWICH WHIFFLER

WOOD AT HOLWELL, ENGLAND

the mock-execution and revival remind us of the St. George plays, and the other sword- and morris-dances which developed " grotesques." It will be recalled that the Fool was an important character in these dances.[1]

At Norwich the riding of the George was established in 1408; here the saint had his club-bearer and henchmen, and as the fight with the dragon seems to have taken place in a wood outside the city, the metamorphosis of the club-bearer to a wild-man with a club, is not difficult.[2]

The term " wodeman," often applied to these characters, seems to point to " wood man "; but it may have been confused with the old word for *mad*, and have caused these characters to color their behaviour accordingly. They must have borne a certain resemblance to insane people, as they brandished their flaming fireworks at the crowd.[3]

When the torch-bearers who cleared the way for the Midsummer Show began to partake of the growing pageantic aspect of this celebration, they were changed, in various ways, from mere marching men into " fancy-dress " characters. At times they appear to be made into Moors; at other times into wild-men.[4] In the popular processions this figure remains nameless; in the masque — where he is more of a forester than an antic — he sometimes is called Sylvanus.[5] This may

---

[1] An interesting connection between St. George and wild-men is found at Chester in 1610. I shall treat this in detail later; here it is enough to point out that the St. George procession was headed by two men " in green evies [ivy] . . . with black heare and black beards, very owgly to behould, and garlands upon their heads, with great clubbs in their hands, with firr works to scatter abroad, to maintain way for the rest of the showe." (Harl. MS. 2150, fol. 356 [pencilled numbering, 186], printed by Ormerod, i, p. 381, n. Cf. also Chambers, i, p. 224, n. 2. This show is indexed in Harl. MS. 2150, fol. 3 b, as " Mr. Amory's new shew invented by him.")

Beatty, p. 291, notes, " The constant use of leaves or green branches has an important bearing on the dress of the actors in some of the St. George plays; " and (*ibid.*, p. 276) " The costumes of the players frequently consist of *masks* and *armor* like leaves." While this performance at Chester is not a St. George " play," it shows a connection — probably a conscious one — between the St. George material and the " wild-man."

[2] It is impossible to prove that this figure was influenced by any of the characters in the folk-dances; I am only suggesting the possibility of the wild-man's coming into pageantry with St. George, or his prototype. It is not likely that St. George received the wild-man from another procession.

[3] There may also have been an element of the Fool of the folk-dance. Says Walker, in *Trans. Royal Irish Academy* (1788), ii, p. 78, n. 1: " Our [i. e., the Irish] mummers are always accompanied by a Buffoon, whose dress and antic manners answer the description of the Vice of the old English comedies, the precursor of the modern Punch. This character likewise appears in the pageant [*i. e., masque ?*] with which the Irish rustics celebrate the first of May." We may compare the *devil* of the mid-sixteenth-century Lord Mayor's Shows of London — (see below, chapter vi); he appears with the wild-man, and may be — presumably is — borrowed from the miracle play. There were " wodmen " at Aberdeen (cf. above, p. 33.)

[4] There is merely a suggested resemblance, based on the " wild-fire."

[5] Cf. the Hombre Salvagio of Kenilworth in 1575, and Sylvanus at Bisham in 1592 (below,

be due to the softening of a figure borrowed by the court from folk celebrations, or he may have come to the court independently from literature. I am inclined to think the former explanation the correct one.

In 1348, " xij capita de wodewose " appear in the *Accounts of the Expenses of the Great Wardrobe of King Edward III*,[1] among the items relating to the Christmas mumming at Ottford. These seem to have been rather fauns or satyrs than the pageantic wild-man who has an element of the miracle-play devil in his make-up.[2]

The relation between wild-men, green-men, foresters, Robin Hood, the Moors and the devil is very difficult to clear up. A great many cross-influences must exist; and it seems obvious that all these figures are connected. There may, however, be little direct connection — except as the figure in Court mumming may have drawn on literature — between these and the " giant herdsmen " of *Ywain* and *Aucassin*.[3]

---

chapter iv). Cf. also the " wild-men " who appeared in the 1511 " jousts of honor " held by Henry VIII (see below, pp. 115 f.)

The name more commonly applied to the figure in the masque is *wodewose* (also spelt *wodwoos, woodwys, wodwos*, etc.) Cf. *The Century Dictionary, s. v. woodwose* (the word is corrupted sometimes to *woodhouse*). It comes from AS. *wudewāsa, a man of the woods*, a *faun* or *satyr*, < *wudu, wood*, and **wasa*, prob. *a being* < *wesan*, dial. *wosan, to be*. The word means " a wild man of the woods, a satyr or faun. Representations of woodwoses often appear in heraldry as supporters "; *The Century Dictionary* gives some citations of the word from metrical romances.

The heraldic wodewose is probably that referred to in the accounts in *Archæologia*, xxxi (temp. Edw. III, 1347). On p. 41: " Et ad fac iij hnes p Rege quoz duo de velutto alb opaī cū garteriis de blu & diasprez p totam campedinē cū wodewoses . . ."; (cf. p. 122: "For making three Harnesses for the King, two of which were of white velvet, worked with *blue Garters*, and diapered throughout with ' wodewoses ' . . . .").

In 1393 Charles VI of France, dressed in flax as a " wild-man " was nearly burned to death at a court masquerade. Torches dropped on the inflammable material the dancers wore, and all but the king died. Froissart's vivid account of this incident may be found in Johnes's (1805) edition, iv, pp. 372 f.; a beautiful colored illumination in Harl. MS. 4380, fol. 1, is reproduced in Johnes's Froissart, iv, p. 374. This dance was the precursor of the masque (cf. Chambers, i, p. 393: on early court mummings and disguisings, see Reyher, pp. 2 f.). We shall return to this subject in the next chapter.

I may add that the form *woodwardes* (cited in Clode, *Early Hist. Merch. Tailors*, ii, p. 263, from the records of the Merchant-Taylors, 1556) suggests the origin of the family name Woodward.

[1] See *Archæologia*, xxxi, pp. 43 and 122. Cf. Chambers, i, p. 392, n. 3.

[2] As early as 1553, wild-men or " wodyn " appeared in the London Lord Mayor's Show, " with . . . grett clubes all in grene, and with skwybes borning." (See below, chapter vi.) In this show, as in those of following years, we find devil and wild-man side by side. These figures are akin to the Norwich " Dick-Fool " (see above, p. 28); there are " green-men " in the Lord Mayor's Shows of 1686 and 1687. At Ripon, in 1886, the millenary procession included " wild-men " (see below, chapter vii); but these were probably meant to represent the primitive inhabitant of Britain.

[3] The " savage " of the romance appears in *Don Quixote* (cf. chapter lxxiv — on pp. 583 f.

WILD MEN

In 1309, Edward II being king, there was a great tournament at Stepney,[1] "de quo dominus Egedius Argentein dicebatur rex de Vertbois; et ipse, cum suis complicibus, fuit contra omnes venientes."[2] Just what *rex de Vertbois* means, I do not know; it suggests masquerading, and recalls the "Green Knight" of the romances. I think we may assume that there was some kind of "dressing up" here: *vertbois* means more than green accoutrements. Even if the costume were in the smallest way symbolical of the greenwood, it is significant; perhaps a forest-tree was figured on the knight's shield; perhaps in place of a plume he wore a green bough.[3] Unfortunately we have no clue as to the reason for the name; but the name we have, and it seems possible to find the reason for it in the knight's costume. How far the symbolism was carried out, is unimportant.

Chivalric and folk elements seem to be linked in the festivals at Lille of the Roi de l'Épinette.[4] The wild-man here is not so much pageantic as chivalric —

---

of the translation published by T. Nelson and Sons [1902]); when the Knight of the Lions is engaged in the Adventure of the Afflicted Duenna, " lo, on a sudden, four savages entered the garden, all clad in green ivy, and bearing on their shoulders a large wooden horse! " Such a comprehensive satire on knight-errantry could not omit mention of an important element of the romance.

[1] See *Annales Lond.* (*Chron. Edw. I and II*), i, p. 157, and *Annales Paulini* (*ibid.*), i, p. 267. (Rolls Series.)

[2] *Ann. Lond., loc. cit.* This passage appears in the *Annales Paulini* as " . . . Egidio de Argentein, qui dicebatur rex de viridi bosco . . ."

[3] I may mention the array of squires and virgins dressed in green at the tournament where Clariodus defeated Sir Brown, Amador, Palexis and others — though this seems to have no allegorical significance. (See the romance *Clariodus*, Book ii.) There were many "green knights," of whom the most famous is probably Gawain's friend.

In history one example will suffice: Earl Richard of Warwick sent challenges to the Court of the French king in 1416 under the name of the Green Knight and the Chevalier Vert. The historical account of these combats is given (with illustrations) by Strutt; the Earl defeats a red knight, a white knight, and one whose color is not given. See also G. L. Kittredge, *Who was Sir Thomas Malory?* in Harvard *Studies and Notes in Philology and Literature.*

[4] That of 27 May, 1438, is described from MSS. of Valenciennes and Cambrai by Rosny, *L'Epervier d'Or* (1839), pp. 29 f. On that date "les Valencenois firent à Lille leur entrée triomphale de la manière suivante: Ils furent accoustrez en hommes sauvages portant leurs escus et gros bastons; leurs chevaux furent tous déguisez de peaux de bestes étrangères, ce qui fut fort étrange à veoyr. . . .

"Entre les dits jousteurs de cheval il y avoit plusieurs hommes vestus en sauvaiges qui marchoient à pied, portant des tours forts estranges. Il y avoit une ville sur un charriot, avec sept tours et cresteaux et une damoiselle à chascune tour, portant leurs armes et banierolles; et sur l'esparguette [*i. e.*, la place supérieure du charriot, la partie la plus élevée] estoit Jehan Grébert, fille de Jehan, portant la bannière de Valenchiennes. . . .

"Le Roy de l'Espinette sortit de la ville de Lille à moult grande compaignie à cheval et à pied; et estoit le dit Roy vestu de peaux et de plumes de cygnes, son cheval harnaché de miroirs et de plumes de paon; et ses pages et laquais aussy accoustrés de plumes de paon; et allèrent ainsi au-devant des jousteurs de Valenchiennes . . ." Cf. plate v (from the MS. of Valenciennes) in Rosny.

he suggests the forester rather than the buffoon, the knight rather than the whiffler.

When Henry VI entered Paris in 1431 there was " au poncelet Saint-Denis ung eschaffault sur lequel estoit comme une manière de bois, où estoient trois hommes sauvages et une femme, qui ne cessèrent de combatre l' un contre l'aultre, tant que le roy et les seigneurs furent." [1] When Charles V entered Bruges in 1515, a pageant connected the wild-man with history; here he was clearly a " forester " of noble origin.[2]

It will not be necessary to gather together many more instances of the wild-man in masque and pageant. The reader will find mention of them in the consideration of the royal-entry, the early masque and the Lord Mayor's Show. That the character was well known to the audiences which attended the sixteenth-century drama may be seen by such passages as the dumb show prefacing the first act of *Gorboduc*,[3] where six wild-men clothed in leaves, act out a symbolical incident;[4] and the character of Bremo in *Mucedorus*.[5] Grotesque as he may have been, he is not comic; he may be due to the literary woodsman, and may even have a dash of the " giant herdsman." If not influenced by pageantry, these

---

[1] Monstrelet, *Chronique* (ed. Douët-d'Arcq, 1857–62), v, p. 3; cf. Delpit, *Coll. gén. doc. franç. en Angleterre* (1847), p. 242: " . . . hommes et femmes sauvages jouans des escus tres gentilment . . ." and the *Journal d'un Bourgeois de Paris* (ed. A. Tuetey, 1881), p. 275. Harl. MS. 540, fols. 41 f. gives a full account of this entry; it mentions " thre woodwases plainge vpon the top of the conduite, and other woodwases benethe." These suggest the " drolls " of the seventeenth-century Lord Mayor's Show, and may forecast the acrobats of 1547 and 1553. (See chapter iii.)

[2] At the rue du Poyure, " fut ung gorgias escharfault sur lequel estoit vne forest moult proprement assise qui souuroit à deulx hayons dont le premier ouurit vne homme sauuage et au dehors du quel furent escript deux vers en latin dont la substance est telle:

' De Lideric forestier de grante age
Ganymedes eust Bruges pour partage.'

" Et au dedans fut à plain figure par personnages tressumptueusement aournez pour demonstrer la source et commencement de la ville de Bruges, comment Liederic premier forestier en son viuant diuisa son pays de Flandres entre ses enfans et fit partaige à son filz Ganymedes de la ville de Bruges. . . .

" Lautre hayon ouurit vne femme sauuaige au dehors duquel estoit escript en latin: Josue viel et ia sur eage departit la terre en nouuelle possession des ligueurs Disrael: et audedant fut representé pour similitude et conformité de la premiere figure comment Josue departit la terre de promission aux enfans d Hisrael, car à chascune ou la plus part des histoires faisant monstre des advenues en la ville de Bruges fut enioinct ung semblable mistere du viel testament . . ." Dupuys, *Entrée de Charles Quint en Bruges* (1850), p. 13. With this contemporary account are woodcuts illustrating various pageants produced on this occasion; one of a wild-man or forester faces p. 13.

[3] See Manly, ii, p. 215.

[4] These men suggest the early Britons.

[5] See Hazlitt's Dodsley's *Old English Plays* (London, 1874), vii, pp. 221 f. This reference was suggested by Professor Kittredge.

figures may have influenced pageantry, and may have helped to determine the character of those who went ahead to clear the way for folk and civic processions.[1]

An interesting combination of forester and " wood-man " occurs in the 1663 Lord Mayor's Show written by Tatham.[2] Faunus sat in an arbor, " the upper part of his body habited like a Forrester in Green; his nether part like a Wood-man in Russet. . . . His attendants are three *Satyres*, habited accordingly, who are in continual Motion, playing on several rude Instruments, singing and dancing . . ."[3] These suggest the " drolls " which were common enough in the seventeenth century shows. In 1553 there were two " wodyn " in the Lord Mayor's Show — these are defined by J. G. Nichols [4] as " wood-men or savage men of the wood." I doubt if there is any connection between these figures and the name Odin; in his account of the Show of 1554, Machyn spells the word *wodys*. They were armed with clubs, and dressed " all in grene." [5]

§ 9. CHARACTERS IN THE PAGEANT: BIBLICAL — HISTORICAL —ROMANTIC—ALLEGORICAL—MYTHOLOGICAL—SYMBOLIC

BIBLICAL AND LEGENDARY

When, in a procession, a person (or an image) represents some famous character, an element of pageantry enters in. The saints' images of religious festivals only continued an earlier, pre-Christian, practice. As soon as pagan gods had become identified with folk-images, pageantry entered the religious procession.

In time, living representatives of the legendary figures replaced their prototypes, and with them Biblical characters came from the miracle-play. We shall see that often, especially in provincial towns, the characters of the miracle-plays,

---

[1] The " green-man " gave his name to a public-house sign, still common in England (see J. G. Nichols in the text which accompanies Shaw's plates of Munday's 1616 Show.) When George IV started on his trip to Edinburgh in 1822, " At the Green Man, in the Kent road, the broad pennant was hoisted and suspended across the road, on which was inscribed ' God save the King.' " (*Historical Account of his Majesty's Visit to Scotland*, p. 76.)

Among the other inn-signs which seem to have their origin in pageantry we have mentioned *The George and Dragon* and *The Elephant and Castle*. Various inn-signs were personified in the " Entrée Magnifique de Bacchus avec Madame Dimanche Grasse, sa femme, faicte en la Ville de Lyon, le 14 februrier 1627." (Described in a book with the above title, now in the Fairholt collection in the library of the Society of Antiquaries.) Here we find *les Trois Roys, les trois Mores, les quatre fils Aymon, l'Arbre Sec* and *le Sauvage*. This seems to have been a carnival rather than a serious pageant, for *Le Mont de Parnasse* was represented by " neuf Lavandières au lieu des neuf Muses," and they spoke in *patois*. Undoubtedly the presence of the *sauvage* is due to his having been an inn-sign; and this in turn is, perhaps, a development of the pageantic figure.

[2] See below, chapter vi.   [3] I quote from Tatham's descriptive pamphlet, p. 6.

[4] In his edition of Machyn's *Diary*. (See below chapter vi.)

[5] I have referred to the wild-man and devil of the early Lord Mayor's Shows above (p. 74, n. 2.).

standing on the pageant-cars used by the crafts, welcomed the visiting sovereigns. Music was furnished by choirs representing angels; the clergy themselves took part in the welcome of the king, and choruses of patriarchs sang extracts from the mass. In 1522 one of the city giants of London was appropriately called Samson; and St. George lasted at Norwich until the eighteenth century.

It was natural that the guilds should keep up a suggestion of the religious element by representing their patrons. From the pageantic welcome of 1298, in which St. Magnus rode with the Fishmongers, until the Lord Mayor's Show passed into pantomime in 1702, we shall see many patron saints. In the closing years of the seventeenth century, we find the Virgin and St. Dunstan; in 1553 and 1554 we find St. John the Baptist. God and the doctors appear in the Chester Mid-summer Show of the sixteenth century; in 1534 the Ironmongers of London exhibited St. Elizabeth; and in 1802 Adam and Eve marched at Preston.

It is useless here to multiply instances of the Biblical and legendary material which permeates the pageant. Closely allied to it is the historical material. Indeed, in the Middle Ages, the Bible was regarded as history; and who shall say Abraham has not as much right to be so considered as Brute ?

HISTORICAL

In 1486 Ebrauk welcomed Henry VII to York; he is the founder of the city, according to Geoffrey of Monmouth.[1] In the same year, when the king went to

---

[1] In the second book of Geoffrey's *Hist. Reg. Brit.*, we learn that Ebraucus, founder of York, is the great-grandson of Locrine, Brute's son, who married Gwendolen, daughter of Corineus; and that he lived when Saul was king. Ebrauk's grandson, Leil, founded Carlisle; and Leil's son, Hudibras, founded Canterbury, Winchester and Shaftsbury. Hudibras was the father of Bladud, who founded Bath; and Bladud's son, Lear, founded Leicester.

Perhaps Evrawc, the father of Peredur, who held — we are told in the *Mabinogion* — the " earldom of the North," is the same figure. Rev. Professor Sayce, in an article entitled *The Legend of King Bladud* (in *Y Cymmrodor*, x, pp. 207 f.), to which Professor E. D. Snyder has called my attention, notes that of all the twenty sons of Ebrauk named by Geoffrey, there is none whose name suggests Peredur; and that Evrawc had only seven sons (p. 219, n. 9). Ebrauk's son Bladud must not be confused with the founder of Bath.

It is interesting to observe that Lud, son of Hely and brother of Cassibelaunus, does not figure in the London pageants. He it was, who, in the time of Cæsar, rebuilt the walls of Troy-novant; and having repaired and beautified the city, he gave it his name. *Caerlud* was later, according to the mythical history, corrupted to *London*; *Ludgate* preserves the memory of this king to the present day. He was the grandfather of Cymbeline, and is mentioned in the fourth book of Geoffrey's history.

The *Chronica* of Thomas Sprott repeats much of this history: cf. p. 85 for reference to " Ebrancus [son of Menpricius] qui ædificavit Eboracum." He mentions " Kayn, qui fundavit Kayrlil. Post hunc Rudhudibras, qui condidit Cantuariam & Wyntoniam. Deinde Bradul (*sic*) filius ejus, qui fecit Batoniam. Post eum filius ejus Leyr qui fecit Leycestriam." Sprott records " Casobilanus " as the son, not the brother, of Lud (p. 87). Drake, *Eboracum*, p. 2, is one of the many who have rehearsed the legendary history of Geoffrey; but he does not hold himself responsible for its authenticity.

Bristol, King Bremmius spoke.[1] Gurgunt, the fabled king who built the castle of Norwich and founded the city, welcomed Queen Elizabeth to the place in 1578.[2]

Real history — though the other was not felt to be unreal — appeared in pageantry in 1460, when William the Conqueror greeted Edward IV at Bristol; in 1511 we find Bruce, " the giant emperor," at Aberdeen. After that date, the historical character is common; in 1522, for instance, we find Henry VIII and Charles V themselves represented in a pageant to welcome these two sovereigns. Charlemagne, Roland, and Oliver were also impersonated. In 1534 William the Conqueror appeared in the London Ironmongers' Midsummer Show.[3]

The Seven Liberal Arts were, in 1432, illustrated by appropriate historical figures. Cicero represented Rhetoric; Aristotle, Logic, and Euclid, Geometry. The Nine Worthies appeared not infrequently — as at Coventry in 1456 and 1498.[4] Some of these last are historical, some Biblical, and some romantic.

ROMANTIC

Much of the material that I have considered historical might as well have been recorded under this heading. The mythical rulers of England, the giants Corineus and Gogmagog, Roland and Oliver are really as romantic as they are historical. King Arthur, who appeared at Coventry in 1498 — to honor Prince Arthur[5] — may be a chivalric development of the " armed-man " similar to the religious development of this figure into St. George.

The Emperor and Empress of the Dublin St. George procession,[6] suggest the romances; although — not being named — it is hard to be sure. The champion-giant of 1432 shows a union of the folk-figure and the romantic element, though he is not named. Among the characters who welcomed Edward VI on his way to his coronation in 1547 were Valentine and Orson.[7]

Bladud appeared as a character in the Bath pageant of 1909. Corineus and Gogmagog — whom we have already mentioned — belong to this fiction, which used to be regarded as history.

[1] He was also a " mythical founder." Bran or Bryn (*Lat.* Brennus), son of Dyfnwal, was one of the founders of Bristol. [Cf. J. F. Nicholls and J. Taylor, *Bristol Past and Present.*] *Bremmius* is a scribal or printer's error for Brennus, obviously. A Brennius is mentioned in Geoffrey of Monmouth's third book. He was the son of Dunwallo and the grandson of Cloten, King of Cornwall; but Geoffrey does not mention the fact that he founded Bristol; he says (Bk. iii, ch. i) that in the partition of the kingdom after Dunwallo's death, Brennius should hold Northumbria from the Humber as far as Caithness.

[2] On these " royal-entries," see chapters iii and iv, infra.

[3] See above, p. 41 and n. 1.

[4] They appeared at Paris in 1431: see below, chapter iii.

[5] See below, chapter iii. He was evidently not considered one of the Nine Worthies on this occasion.

[6] Cf. above, p. 31. The King and Queen of Dele, and their attendants, all " entirely clad in black apparel " may also be romantic.

[7] Possibly Orson is a development of the " wild-man," or forester; Browning, in *The Flight*

Perhaps the nine worthies — who appeared at Paris in 1431, and often in England thereafter — may be considered romantic rather than historic. They probably came to pageantry from romantic literature; we may note that in 1553 they included Henry VIII and Edward VI — out of compliment to Mary.

ALLEGORICAL

Allegory was common in mediæval poetry. As early as B.C. 20, the Scriptures were explained allegorically when Greeks and Jews met in Alexandria, and applied the principles of Plato's philosophy to Hebrew theology. Sarah (Devotion) bore Isaac (Virtue); Hagar (Learning) bore Ishmael (the Sophist). " If learning will not serve Virtue, what says the Scripture ? ' Cast forth the handmaiden and her son.' " [1]

This is not the place to sketch the history of allegory. We shall see, in later chapters, that Lydgate played a considerable part in both pageant and mumming; by 1432 he had brought allegory to the former; and allegory was in the latter even before this year. Here it will be enough to remark that allegory was already in literature; the Castle of Care in *Piers Plowman* shows a combination of religious and chivalric allegory in one of the earliest examples of an allegorical poem composed in English; beside the scholastic allegory, the chivalric, already " masquized " in 1330, developed.

Débats were an early form of literature — I need only mention the debate which Zorobabel won, in 1 *Esdras*. From them grew the *débats d'amour*, a type very familiar in the fourteenth century. Grosseteste's thirteenth-century *Chasteau d'Amour* combines amorous with religious allegory: Mercy, Soothfastness, Right-eousness and Peace are characters in the poem.[2] We shall discuss later the rela-tion of allegory in such poems as this to the visualized allegory of pageant and morality. Here it is enough to indicate certain elements in the pageant which have an affinity with the allegory in literature. In 1377 there was a castle; in 1432 Lydgate gave allegorical names to the personages in a royal-entry;[3] but it is doubtful whether in every case these elements come directly to the pageant from literature. That there were subtle influences from the life of the times on literary productions seems certain; we find them photographed, and preserved, in these shows.

The allegorical element is an important one, as we shall see; in modern American pageants it holds a prominent place. " There is," says Courthope, " a

---

of the Duchess (l. 910) calls him " Orson, the wood-knight "; and it is likely that he is a roman-tic adaptation — as Sylvanus is a classical adaptation — of the folk-figure which also developed into the " green-man."

[1] Courthope, *Hist. Eng. Poetry* (1895–1910), i, p. 343.

[2] In this poem, Christ entered a castle, of which the Virgin was the lady; the rock on which it was built, is her heart; the four towers of it were her four virtues; the castle was her body.

[3] See below, chapter iii.

close and intimate connection between the progress of allegory and the rise of the drama in England." [1]

MYTHOLOGICAL

Mythological characters do not appear in English pageants before the sixteenth century, and then — to use a Celticism — they are found in Scotland. *The Judgment of Paris* welcomed the daughter of Henry VII to Edinburgh in 1503; [2] and twenty years later Udall used the same theme in welcoming Anne Boleyn to London. [3] We shall see that this became a very important element in pageantry; I suggest it came to England from France, through Scotland. [4] In 1522 the London Drapers showed a trade-pageant of the Golden Fleece at Midsummer; [5] in 1802 Vulcan was represented at Preston by an armed knight. [6] These examples show how quickly and how permanently the guilds combined mythology with trade-symbolism.

SYMBOLICAL

The growth of symbolism in pageantry is due to two causes. Since the Fishmongers' welcomed Edward I in 1298, few pageants have been without some kind of symbolism; the fishes on that occasion had a trade significance — they symbolized, one might say, the guild which conducted the festivities. In 1486 Ebrauk welcomed Henry VII to York; as the " mythical founder," he may be said to symbolize the town. In 1438 Jehan Grébert carried the banner of Valenciennes at Lille, [7] showing an earlier step in the direction of symbolical personification.

The " decayed Commonweal " and the " flourishing Commonweal " of 1559 [8] show the connection between allegory and personification. At Bristol in 1574 the city is personified, and in Peele's London Lord Mayor's Show of 1585 a female character [9] represented London. We do not know the sex of the personification of Bristol; but we may assume that allegory, working on the " mythical founder " material, attracted it into the feminine; and that the " genius of the city," developing from the choir-boy angels of earlier shows, remained masculine until the " genius " was absorbed by the personified city. It should be noted that at Norwich in 1578 there appeared, in the same show, Gurgunt, the founder, the

---

[1] Courthope, i, p. 393. The *débat* is closer to the masque than to the pageant; we shall return to the subject in chapter ii below (see p. 111).

[2] See below, p. 169.   [3] See below, p. 180.   [4] See below, p. 111.

[5] See above, p. 40. This undoubtedly was the same as that shown in the entry of Charles V, 6 June, 1522.

[6] See above, p. 34.

[7] See above, p. 75, n. 4. Cf. the city of Corinth and other cities represented by a nymph and images at Alexandria (above, p. 17, n. 6, on p. 18.).

[8] See below, p. 202.

[9] Probably a boy dressed up as a woman. See below, chapter vi.

boy " genius," or spirit of the city, and a feminine personification of the city, who was attended by Deborah, Judith, Esther, and Martia.[1] One cannot chart such a growth accurately, for there are probably a great many cross-influences; but it seems clear that the personification of cities, so common in our own day, is probably a development of the " mythical founder," changed to the feminine through the influence of allegory. We shall see later that personification plays a large part in the Lord Mayor's Show.[2]

§ 10. A NOTE ON " SUBTLETIES "

Many writers refer to a " play of St. George " at Windsor in 1416, when the Emperor Sigismund was entertained by Henry V.[3] " The performance described by Collier . . . turns out on examination of [his] authority (Cotton. MS. Calig. B. ii) to be really a ' soteltie,' a cake or raised pie of elaborate form." [4]

The description of these " subtleties " often reads like that of a pageant; and for this reason I feel justified in adding a note on these " curious devices of cookery or confectionery common at the banquets of the fifteenth and sixteenth centuries." [5] For descriptions of those at the inthronization of Archbishop Warham (of Canterbury) on 9 March, 1504, see the contemporary account of the ceremony in Leland's *Collectanea* (vi, pp. 23 f.). At the end of the account, among the items of expense, we find: " In pictura Throni & operatione de le Sotilties in saccharo & cera, xvi li." [6] There were " sotelties " at the coronation of Queen Anne in 1421;[7] and at the coronation of Henry VI there were subtleties with scriptures.[8] After the king was crowned in Paris, in 1431, there was a banquet, " auquel disner furent présentés par devant la table quatre entremès.[9] Est

---

[1] See below, p. 210.

[2] I may here refer in passing to " the genious of the citie of London " who delivered a long Latin speech when James I and Christian IV of Denmark traversed London in 1606; the genius of the city in Heywood's Lord Mayor's Show of 1639; London, or Augusta, in 1689; Augusta in 1700; London, with " New Troyes Tree of Honor " in Dekker's 1628 show; Augusta, or London, in 1694; Chester in 1610; the genius of London, with Walworth, in 1616; Britannia and Genius Urbis in 1604; Albion, Germania, Hispania and Batavia in 1691; Britannia, Leogria, Cambria and Albania with Troia Nova, or London, in 1605. " Europe, a proper man-like woman; Asia, a majestick person; Africa a tall person; America, a strait stout person," appeared in 1674; Asia and Africa in 1658; the four Quarters of the Globe in 1694; a European, an Egyptian and a Persian in 1659; and Africa — represented by a " female negra " — in 1671. It is needless to add more examples here; see chapter vi below.

[3] See Kelly, *Notices*, p. 40; Ward, *Hist. Dram. Lit.* (1899), i, p. 143; Collier, i, p. 29, etc.

[4] Chambers, i, p. 224; cf. Beatty, p. 277. Tyrrell, *Chron. Lond.* (1827), p. 159, reprints the account of the entertainment of the emperor from the Cottonian MS.

[5] Nichols, *Prog. Q. E.*, i, p. 18 and n. 1.

[6] P. 31.   [7] Tyrrell, p. 164.   [8] *Ibid.*, p. 168.

[9] Johnes's translation (iii, p. 26) runs: " During the dinner, four pageants were introduced." This is either the same error that Collier made — and from which, I may confess, I

assavoir, le premier d'une ymage de Nostre-Dame et ung petit roy couronné emprès; le second fut une fleur de lis d'or couronné, tenue de deux angles; le tiers une dame et ung paon, et le quart, une dame et ung cisne [cygne]." [1]

At a "ryal ffest" *temp.* Henry IV there were various "sotelties" — a "Ceruus" "homo" and "arbor." [2] There were "soltelties" at the coronation banquet of Elizabeth, wife of Henry VII; [3] also at that of Henry IV in 1399. [4] In 1517 when Sir Richard Torkington of Norfolk was about to leave Venice; ". . . we went all in to the fforseyd Shippe. Ther they mad vs goodly Chere wt Diverse Sotylties as Comfytes and Marche Panys, And Swete Wynes." [5] At the banquet following the entry of Margaret, sister of Edward IV, into Bruges, where she married the Duke of Burgundy on 6 July, 1469, there entered "Sir Olifaunt bering his castell wt a subtiltee." [6] It adds to the confusion between pageant and subtlety to find that the subjects treated are often the same.

Descriptions and illustrations of some very elaborate cakes, which appeared at a banquet at the Hague in 1746, may be found in a volume the French title of which is: *Description des Principales Réjouissances faites à la Haye, à l'Occasion du Couronnement de Sa Majesté Imperiale, François I.* [7] At this dinner the confections included allegorical figures, temples and chariots.

----

had a narrow escape; or else *pageants* were once synonymous with *elaborate cakes* or "entremets" as well as with *platforms*. And this is unlikely.

Sharp, p. 217, gives from the Cappers' accounts of Coventry, record of "soteltys" in 1527; his paragraph on page 218, referring to other occasions when subtleties appeared, suggests that perhaps he made Collier's error in thinking them entertainments.

[1] Monstrelet, v, p. 6.

[2] Harl. MS. 279, fol. 48 b.

[3] See Ives, *Select Papers* (1773), pp. 141 f., printing from a MS. in his possession; also Leland, *Collect.* iv, p. 226, whose MS. reads *sotelties*. With one of them was "Writing of Balads (Ives, p. 141, reads *Bales*) whiche as yet I have not."

At a Roman feast in 1473 was a cake made like a mountain, out of which stepped a man who recited verses. (Middlemore, (1904 ed.) p. 416, n.: not in Burckhardt.)

[4] See Harl. MS. 279, fol 45. *Ibid.*, fol. 45 b, tells of those at the king's wedding-banquet. At the "Conuiuium Iohannis Stafford (qui successit Nicholao Bubbewith præfato) in inducto suo ad Episcopatum [of Bath and Wells] die 16 Sept A° D° 1425" there were many elaborate subtleties. One was a "docter of lawe," another an "egle" and a third "sent Andrewe." (MS. *cit.* fol. 48 *et seq.*)

[5] Addl. MS. 28,561 fol. 11 b; Loftie's ed. of the *Diary*, p. 7. Cf. p. 8 (MS., fol. 12 *et seq.* "At the Archinale (qy.: *arsenal*) ther we saw in makyng iii xx (ed. notes *three score*) new galyes and galye Bastards. And galye Sotyltes, besyd they that be in viage in the haven." Here *sotyltes* does not, evidently, mean *cakes*.

[6] Addl. MS. 6113, fol. 99.

[7] This volume, which is in the Fairholt collection in the Library of the Society of Antiquaries, was published at the Hague in 1747. Opposite page 7 is a plate illustrating the confections, which are described, in Dutch and French, on pages 8 f. Dignity stood in "een Tempel van gegooten Suiker" and Fame rode in a Chariot. The dinner was given by the Baron de Reischach, Imperial Minister at the Hague.

Wriothesley mentions " sotteltes " at a wedding in 1536;[1] at the banquet in Westminster Hall, which followed the coronation of Anne Boleyn, in 1533, there were the usual " suttelties." [2] It is needless to give any more examples of these elaborate cakes. Strutt [3] defines subtlety as a figure " made with jellies and confectionary to be set in the middle of the table for shew."   I see no reason to believe it was not eaten, at least in part.

§ 11.   CONCLUSION

In this chapter I have treated various elements found in pageantry. Originating in the mists of pre-Christian folk-custom, some of these elements were modified by Church observance, and all of them were adapted to occasions of public celebration. From earliest times there were processions, in which figures of pagan divinities, perhaps survivals of human sacrifices, were carried round; these became saints' images and folk-giants. Animals were given a trade or heraldic significance, or attached to some historical or legendary story, appropriate to the royal guest or civic host. Like all dramatic, or semi-dramatic, forms, the pageant is a growth, deriving its various elements from different sources. Utilized by the Church, developed by the guilds, this form of entertainment grew with more and more elaboration, until the pageant, as we now know it, came into existence.

During the centuries from Edward I to Elizabeth this kind of entertainment was developing in London under the stimulus of the " royal-entry." Without the hampering tradition of folk-custom, and with the conscious planning of poets and engineers, pageantry developed rapidly, drawing from folk, from history, from romance, the Bible, saint's legend and the tournament — in short from all possible sources. In 1432 Lydgate gave it allegory, and soon — as a result of history and allegory — we find personification. Symbolism is almost inseparable from it; and with the necessity of explaining symbolism, speech appeared.

Before turning to the " royal-entry," however, the pageantic elements in tournament and early masque claim our attention.

---

[1] Wriothesley, i, pp. 50 and 51.

[2] Harl. MS. 41, fol. 7 b.

[3] *Manners and Customs*, ii, pp. 100 f. He quotes, from the Harl. MS. 279, mention of the " sotelties " at the wedding of Henry IV and Jane of Navarre in 1403.

CHAPTER II

REMARKS ON THE TOURNAMENT AND EARLY MASQUE: TOGETHER WITH A DISCUSSION OF THE INFLUENCE OF THE MORALITY, AND OTHER MATTERS

IN order to understand the contributions of chivalry to pageantry, as well as the gifts of the latter to the descendants of the tournament — such as the Elizabethan " barrier " — we shall have to glance, somewhat cursorily, it is true, at the tournament, the " disguising " and the early masque. We shall see that, as the tournament became less serious, an element of disguising crept into it; and that, later still, the knights dressed up as characters in chivalric literature and the " Court of Love." This attempt to dramatize romance, as one is tempted to call it, led to the construction of such castles as that which moved " par engien moult richement " at Valenciennes in 1330; and it is probable that the Goldsmiths' castle of 1377 owed its existence to similar contrivances.

The habit of disguising in tournaments led to, or at any rate stimulated, the court masquerade, which became the ancestor of the masque. Perhaps this influence was strengthened by the folk-mumming, which came into contact with the court on such occasions as that of the Sunday night before Candlemas, 1377. There was, to be sure, court masking long before that date; and one must be very careful not to confuse similarities with proof of influence: but even if we admit that folk-mumming had no effect on that of the court, as far as disguising itself goes, we may, I think, safely assume an influence from the morris dance and the Robin Hood plays on several figures in the mummeries of Henry VIII.

With the habit of " dressing up " came various representations of historical or symbolical characters. Here we get the " soul " of pageantry; the " body " is represented by the car, the introduction of which, in " disguisings," at the Court of Henry VII, prepared the way for modern theatrical scenery. The " technique " of the masque differs greatly from that of the pageant; for the dance is the foundation of this form of art, and the fact that it is performed on a " fixed stage," brings it technically into closer relations with the modern pageant than with the earlier. The popular " spirit " of pageantry is not to be found in the masque, which — like its forerunners — appealed to a select group of people. We may, then, expect to find the cross-influences between masque and pageant confined to what, for want of better terms, I have called " soul " and " body "; each form of expression keeps its " spirit " and " technique " to itself; indeed, it is the latter which differentiates the two.

The pageant-car is the most important gift of pageantry to the " disguising " — as the ancestor of the masque is called. I shall, however, note one or two other gifts. Much has been written about the masque,[1] and I shall not repeat what has been already said. We are concerned with the masque only as it is related to pageantry, and shall not follow its development after the early years of Henry VIII's reign; nor shall we treat the direct descendant of the tournament — the Tudor and Stuart " barrier " — in any detail.

With the exception of a few pages on folk-mumming, we are dealing in this chapter with forms of sport and art which affect a limited circle — that of the court. Hitherto, we have discussed the folk-origins of pageantry, and the next chapter will deal with the development of the " royal-entry " in the hands of the guilds. These shows always retained their " popular " character: their background is always the people. This is a fundamental principle of pageantry — even of the new form of it we have today.

A strict line keeps courtier and folk apart; on the one side is the masque — on the other, the pageant. There were, however, influences which crossed this line in both directions; these form the subject matter of this chapter.

§ 1. THE TOURNAMENT

The Tournament: A Brief Survey of its Origin and Growth

The tournament has been traced back to classical times; it may almost be said to be the expression of an innate desire for supremacy, in terms of the centuries when achievement meant prowess in arms.[2] Strutt derives the practice from the Roman " Troy game," and believes that it " arose by slow degrees from the exercises appointed for the instruction of the military tyros in using their arms." Says de Vulson, " le mot *Tourneamentum*, que nous appellons Tournoy, a tiré son origine de ce mot Grec, Τορνύειν, qui signifie tourner: Quelques autres ont dit que ce mot *Torneamentum*, vient à *Troiano ludo*, des jeux Troyens. . . . Les Tournois furent ainsi appellez (disent quelques autres Autheurs) pource qu'ils se faisoient dans les lieux ronds, ou à cause de certains tournoyemens & carrcols que les Cheualiers y faisoient en combattant, ce qui a aussi donné origine à ce mot d'Estour: On nomma aussi les Tournois *Hastiludia*, comme qui diroit les jeux de la lance, pource qu'au premier choc ils rompoiēt leurs lances les vns

---

[1] See Sörgel, Evans, Chambers, Brotanek, and Reyher. Schelling, *Eliz. Drama*, ii, pp. 93 f. [ch. xv] gives a short history of this form of the drama.

[2] On the whole matter see Strutt, *Sports*, pp. 97 f.; Marc de Vulson, *Le Vray Théâtre d'Honneur et de Chevalerie* (2 vols. Paris, 1648); Menestrier, *Traité des Tournois, Ioustes, Carrousels, et Autres Spectacles Publiques* (Lyons, 1669); de Rosny, *L'Epervier d'Or, ou description historique des Joûtes et des Tournois célébrés à Lille au Moyen-Age* . . . (Paris and Lille, 1839); on tournaments in Italy, see Burckhardt, ii, pp. 157 f. (appendix to § 5), xiv, and references. (This appendix is translated as a note in Middlemore, ii, p. 120). For further mention of English tournaments, see Davey, *The Pageant of London* (1906), i, pp. 262–264; 291–292; 308–314; 391–392; Besant, *Mediæval London* (1906), i, pp. 324 f.; Strutt, *Sports*, p. xi and Book III (pp. 88 f.). For accounts of tournaments, see also the various mediæval historians.

contre les autres, auparauant que de se seruir de l'espée & de la masse, comme ie l'ay colligé des plus anciens Tournois d'Allemagne & de France." [1] Menestrier remarks that " le Tournoy des Anciens estoit vne simple course de Chevaux, qui se mesloient en tournoyant." [2]

Strutt derives *tournoy*, the French original of *tourney*, from the practice of the knights " running *par tour*, that is, *by turns*, at the quintain, and wheeling about successively in a circle to repeat their course." He continues,[3] " In process of time, they improved upon their pastime, and to make it more respectable ran at one another, which certainly bore a much greater similitude to a real engagement; especially when they were divided into large parties, and meeting together, combated with clubs or maces, beating each other soundly, without any favour or paying the least respect to rank or dignity. In one of these encounters, Robert, Earl of Cleremont, son of Saint Louis, and head of the house of Bourbon, was so severely bruised by the blows he received from his antagonist, that he was never well afterwards. And this, says Fauchet, was possibly the cause of the ordinance that kings and princes should not afterwards enter the lists as combatants at these tournaments; which law indeed, continues he, has been ill observed by the succeeding kings, and in our time by Henry the Second, who, unfortunately for France, was killed at the justs he made in honour of his daughter's marriage."

Tournaments were forbidden in the Decreta Lateranensis Concilii — at the third Lateran Council, 5–9 March, 1179.[4] The combatants were often killed or seriously wounded during the tournaments, but such contests formed a part of many a royal entertainment, and the rewards were often large.[5]

Both French and Germans claim to be the originators of the tournament, which seems to have been known in France and Normandy before the Conquest.[6] Says Lochner: " . . . Schon 1197, als Kaiser Heinrich VI in Nürnberg gewesen, die Nürnberger Geschlechter ihm zu Ehren ein Turnier und einen Tanz auf dem Rathhaus gegeben haben." But this is " eine auf jeden Fall erst später ausgebildete und niedergeschriebene Fabel." [7] Warlike amusements existed at Lille before the thirteenth century; Rosny [8] draws attention to the " fameux tournoi

---

[1] *Op. cit.*, i, pp. 27, 28.   [2] *Op. cit.*, pp. 266 f.

[3] Citing Fauchet, *Origines des Chevaliers*, etc., fol. 9.

[4] See *Historia Rerum Anglicarum* Guilielmi Neubrigensis (ed. Richard Howlett [R. S.], London, 1884), i, pp. 219 f.

[5] Strutt, *Sports*, p. 101, quotes a passage " from an ancient romance called *Ipomedon* " (Harl. MS. 2252, fol. 61) wherein the hero " promiscuously encountering " many combatants, and alone remaining unhorsed, won the " gree," or reward, of £1000. We shall return to the romantic tournament anon.

[6] Strutt, *Sports*, p. 103.

[7] *Das Nürnberger Gesellenstechen vom Jahre 1446 nach der im obern Gange des Rathhauses befindlichen Stukko-Abbildung* . . . mit einer geschichtlichen Erläuterung von G. W. K. Lochner (2 ed., Nürnberg, 1853), p. 5.

[8] *Op. cit.*, p. 6.

d'Anchin célébré si près d'elle [Lille] en 1096 ''; he thinks that tournaments at Lille may be traced back to 1226 — under Philip the Good, Count of Flanders, the *fête des Syres de la Joye* was already ancient;[1] it apparently was " remise en vigueur " in 1282. As early as the thirteenth century there were tournaments in Chauvenci, which were described in verse by Jacques Brétex in 1285.[2]

LE ROI DE L'ÉPINETTE

Rosny describes the feast of the " roi de l'Épinette " at the time of Philip the Good (1436). " Le . . . vendredi (troisième jour de carême) le Roi de l'Épinette, entouré de sa suite et de dames vêtues en amazones, allaient à Templemars, afin de prier Monsieur Saint Georges de lui obtenir un règne heureux. . . .[3]

" Le samedi, veille du Béhourt, autre repas, après lequel le *Syre de la Joye*, avec toute sa suite revêtue ' de robes pareilles,' assistait à une représentation de mystères, qui se faisait pour l'édification et pour l'amusement des bourgeois de Lille; et s'il faut en croire Tiroux[4] — ' le roi et les dames de sa connaissance en estoient les principaux acteurs et actrices.' "

The feast began with a banquet, to which knights, squires, and ladies of distinction in the neighborhood were asked. Then followed the jousts, over which the Count of Flanders always presided as *premier juge*.[5] The *roi du Béhourt* wore usually *samy blanc*.[6]

" Erst 1441 hatte Markgraf Albrecht Achilles einen Turnierhof nach Nürnberg gelegt," records Lochner; and his tournament was given " nachdem er vorher bei dem Rath um Geleit und Schutz dazu hatte anhalten lassen."[7] Whatever country may claim to be the originator of the tournament, it is clear that by the fifteenth century in both Germany and France its ancient glories had departed.

THE TOURNAMENT IN ENGLAND, TEMP. RICHARD I

Richard I saw that the tournament made the French more expert in the use of their arms than were the English; so he permitted the reëstablishment of these martial sports in his dominions. He imposed, however, a tax — according to their quality — upon such as engaged in them. An earl had to pay twenty marks

---

[1] Pp. 11 f. Rosny notes (p. 6, n. 2) that the Olympic games "avaient de grands rapports de ressemblance avec les joûtes et tournois du moyen âge." Chivalry, dying, left traces at Lille longer than anywhere else (p. 8).

[2] These verses were edited by Philibert Delmotte: *Les Tournois de Chauvenci*, donnés vers la fin du triezième siècle, decrits par Jacques Brétex. 1285. Annotés par feu Philibert Delmotte . . . Valenciennes, 1835.

[3] Rosny, pp. 23 f.

[4] Toujours oublieux de citer ses autorités. Pourtant il est généralement de bonne foi. — (Rosny's note.)

[5] P. 27.   [6] P. 25. The last *roi de l'Épinette* was elected in 1488 (*ibid.*, p. 8, n. 2.)

[7] Lochner, p. 5.

Richard, Earl of Warwick, at the Christmas Jousts

— a knight, without landed estates, but two; all foreigners were particularly excluded. Richard also appointed five places for the holding of tournaments in England: namely, between Sarum and Wilton; between Warwick and Kenil-worth; between Stamford and Wallingford; between Brakely and Mixelburgh, and between Blie and Tykehill. The act also specified that the peace should not be broken, nor justice hindered, nor damage done to the royal forests.[1]

A FEW WORDS ON THE TOURNAMENT IN ROMANCE

Before we consider the course of the tournament in England subsequent to the time of Edward I, let us glance at the tournament in the metrical romances. Everyone is aware how common a form of celebrating festivals the tourney was; it must be borne in mind that the romances, like the modern novel, reflected, with more or less imagination, contemporary life. The tournaments were held sometimes for glory, sometimes for a more solid reward; one, or more, of the combatants was often disguised — and in tournaments lasting several days, he was very likely to change his armor more than once. Thus Sir Gareth, in a tourney held at King Arthur's Court, appeared in different colored armor;[2] Ipomedon, the hero of the romance which bears his name, was victor in a three-day tournament, appearing in three disguises — red, white, and black armor;[3] Sir Gowther, the hero of another romance, also fights at a three-day tournament in black, red, and white armor, with a horse to match. In the romance of *Lancelot du Lac*, Lancelot appears as a white, red, and black knight; and Richard I fights in black, red and white armor, in the romance which bears his name.[4] I have mentioned an interesting historical parallel to this romantic custom, in the knights whom Richard, Earl of Warwick, under the name of the Green Knight, defeated in the early fifteenth century.[5]

THE " TABLE ROUND "

One of the most famous " properties " of romance was the Round Table of King Arthur; and this was made actual by 1252, when Ernald de Munteinni was killed, " non ut in hastiludio, quod Torneamentum dicitur, sed potius in illo ludo

---

[1] Cf. Harl. MS. 69, fol. 61 f.—which is cited by Strutt, *Sports*, p. 104, n. 1. He reproduces, from Royal MS. 14 E. III, fol. 3, an illustration of the two chief barons entering the lists at the beginning of a tournament (see p. 106). Cf. the illustrations of knights and " barriers " in Harl. MS. 69, fol. 19, *et seq.*; those in the Johnes (1804) edition of Froissart's *English Chronicles;* and in Besant's *Mediæval London*, i, pp. 63, 321, and 324, from Strutt, *Manners and Customs.*

[2] Malory, vii, chs. 28, 29.   [3] *Ipomedon*, ll. 643 f. (Weber's ed. ii, p. 304).

[4] *Richard Coer de Lion*, (ed. H. Weber [3 vols. Edinburgh, 1810], ii, pp. 14 f.) ll. 267 f. It is useless to give more examples of this; see Schofield, *Eng. Lit. from the Conquest to Chaucer*, p. 188 — he notes the custom as " of frequent occurrence." I may end by referring to the shepherd boy who, in steel, silver and gold armor, wins a tourney for a princess; see Cosquin, *Contes Lorrains*, no. 43 — [cited by Ward].

[5] See above, p. 75, n. 3.

militari qui Mensa Rotunda dicitur." [1] Here we see real life borrowing from the romance, as the latter had, in its turn, reflected the former. In 1280, Edward I being king, a Round Table was founded at Kenilworth by " Rogerus de Mortuo Mari " — Roger Mortimer.[2] One hundred knights, and as many ladies, composed it; and the fame thereof attracted many foreigners from abroad.

No word is said of possible masquerading at the Falkirk " round-table " in January, 1302,[3] at the " great tournament " of 26 July, 1305,[4] or at the tournament at Stepney, the same year.[5] We have already discussed the " rex de Vertbois " who appeared in 1309, and who may be the first symbolically disguised figure in a tourney.[6]

Rich prizes were awarded at the " round-table " held by Roger Mortimer of Wigmore in 1328, and this festival of arms lasted several days; [7] but again there is no suggestion of " disguise."

TOURNAMENTS IN THE REIGN OF EDWARD III

In 1330, on 2 May, a great tournament was held at Dartford, in which King Edward III took part, and where he had a narrow escape.[8] He was a king who " turneamenta et hastiludia frequentavit "; [9] he was " in hastiludia validissimus,"[10] and in his reign the sport became highly developed. In 1331, on 16 June, there was another tournament at Stepney, where Robert de Morle, with twenty-five knights, stood against all comers. The tournament lasted for three days; and it is important to note that knights and squires alike were masked.[11] The same year, on 22 September, " fuit celeberrimum hastiludium " in Cheap, kept by William of Montacute. The king visited it with some chosen knights, all of whom were disguised as Tatars.[12] There was a procession of knights and ladies

---

[1] Matthew Paris, *Historia Minor*, iii, p. 124, cited by Strutt, *Sports*, p. 109, n. w.

[2] Walsingham, *Hist. Angl.* (ed. H. T. Riley [R. S.], 1863), i, p. 19, cited by Strutt (note y).

[3] *Annales Lond.*, in *Chron. Ed. I. and II.*, i, p. 104.

[4] *Ibid.*, i, p. 138.   [5] *Ibid.*, i, p. 142.

[6] See above, p. 75. " King of the Greenwood " suggests Robin Hood; unfortunately details are too meager to allow us to be sure what he represented.

[7] Robert Avesbury, *Chronica* (ed. E. M. Thompson [R. S.] 1889) p. 284. The occasion of this celebration seems to have been Mortimer's elevation to the Earldom of March (" factus fuit et nominatus comes de la Marche "). Cf. also Knighton, *Chronicles* (ed. J. R. Lumby [R. S.], 1895), i, p. 449.

These tournaments were very common in the fourteenth century. In 1308–09 Piers Gaveston proclaimed a tournament at Wallingford, and offended the nobles there; see Walsingham, *Hist. Angl.*, i, p. 122.

[8] *Annales Paulini*, in *Chron. Edw. I and II* (ed. W. Stubbs [R. S.], 1882–83), p. 352.

[9] Avesbury, p. 286.   [10] *Commendatio Lamentabilis* (ed. Stubbs), ii, p. 12.

[11] *Annales Paulini*, p. 353: " omnes erant larvati tam milites quam armigeri." The equipment of the knights is given in detail; they were dressed in tunics and mantles, and they carried golden arrows.

[12] *Annales Paulini*, p. 354 (cited by Chambers); Avesbury, p. 285; Walsingham, *Hist.*

through Cheap, preceded by squires, and followed by minstrels; the nobles were dressed in velvet cloaks, and led the ladies at the end of silver chains.[1] On the three following days, there was fighting; an accident — the collapse of the "grandstand" — endangered the lives of the Queen and other feminine spectators, as well as of the knights.[2] There was a three days' tournament in Smithfield in 1334, but the *Annales Paulini* makes no mention of disguises.[3]

The king issued a proclamation in February, 1341 forbidding jousts or tourneys without his special order — "except the jousts which are proclaimed at Norwich."[4] Both Edward and Philippa went to Norwich to see this tournament, which Blomefield notes, making, however, no mention of any pageantic features.[5] The tournament at Northampton, at Easter, 1432, seems to have been more in earnest than in sport.[6] A second one was held at Eltham *circa festum Ascensionis*, in honor of the Count of Hainault's visit to his sister's court.[7] On neither of these occasions does there seem to have been any masking.

A manuscript in the Bodleian records that "in the xvij yere of his Reigne aboute the convercioun of seint Poule kyng Edwarde whan he hadde ben in Scotland and the Scottes were fledde he com ageyn in to Englond and made a turnement at Dunstable to the which turnement come all the newe Bachilers of Englond and also the Chiualrie with Erles Baronns & all oþere Lordes atte ye which turnement the kyng himself was ther presente."[8]

Angl. (ed. H. T. Riley [R. S.], 1863), i, p. 193; Murimuth, *Continuatio Chron.* (ed. E. M. Thompson [R. S.], 1889), p. 63. *Ann. Paul., loc. cit.*, ". . . omnes splendido apparatu vestiti et ad similitudinem Tartarorum larvati."

[1] *Ann. Paul.*, pp. 354 f. "The element of the semi-dramatic *spectacle* was already getting into the fourteenth-century tournament," says Chambers, i, p. 392, n. 4. On *viseres* in tournaments, see *Archæologia*, xxxi, pp. 29, 30 and 118 (cited by Chambers).

[2] "Accidit autem primo die hastiludii mirabile infortunium; solarium namque quod fuerat in transversum, in quo residebant regina et omnes aliæ dominæ ad spectaculum intuendum, subito cecidit solotenus; unde multi tam dominæ quam milites graviter fuerunt læsi et vix periculum mortis evaserunt." *Ann. Paul.*, p. 355. Cf. also *Gesta Edwardi Tertii* (in *Chron. Edw. I and II*), ii, p. 102; Murimuth, p. 63.   [3] *Ann. Paul.*, i, p. 361.

[4] *Calendar of Close Rolls* (Edw. III, vol. vi, p. 100), under date of 5 Feb. 15 Edw. III [1541]. This is cited by Blomefield (1806), iii, p. 86. (His note 8, referring to the *City Domesday Book*, fol. 33, should be attached to the name of Spynk, not to the Priory accounts.)

Mr. Frederic Schenck (whose unpublished work is mentioned in the bibliography) says, on pages 130 f. of his manuscript: "Edward took part in chivalrous festivals arranged by his barons; he soon arrogated to himself the exclusive right of holding such functions, and repeatedly issued orders forbidding any one except himself to hold tournaments." Mr. Schenck refers to Rymer, ii, pp. 732, 749, 808, etc.   [5] *Hist. Norf.*, iii, p. 86.

[6] Which may be said of our football games, some centuries hence! Murimuth, p. 124: "multi nobiles fuerunt graviter læsi, et aliqui mutilati, et perditi multi equi, et dominus J[ohannes] de Bello monte occisus." (Cf. *ibid.*, p. 223.)

[7] Murimuth, p. 124 and p. 224.

[8] Ashm. MS. 793, fol. 105. Cf. Murimuth, p. 123 (where the engagements with the Scots are called *hastiludia*); and p. 223.

Murimuth notes many tournaments in 1343;[1] at Smithfield, "papa et duo-decim cardinales per tres dies contra quoscumque tirocinium habuerunt."

Wives of the London citizens were invited to the tournament of 19 January, 1344, at Windsor.[2] A banquet was given in the great hall of the castle on the Sunday; and jousting followed for three days. After this tournament, a "round-table" was founded. "In the xix yere of his Reigne . . . the same Kyng Edwarde lete make full noble Justes festes and royalte were ij Kynges ij Queenys & þe Prince of Walys and the Duke of Cornewaile x Erles . . . and also of diuerse Londes as by yonde the see were many strau-ngers. And at that tyme whan the justes were done Kyng Edwarde made a grete soper In the which he ordeyned and biganne firste his rounde table, and ordeyned stedefastly ye day of the for-said table to be holde ther atte Wyndesore in ye Whitsonweke euermore after yerely."[3]

The king built a fine house,[4] and the institution became an annual affair. The King of France founded a similar one, "ut sic sibi attraheret militiam Alemanniæ et Italiæ ne ad Regis Angliæ Tabulam properarent."[5]

The king's invitation to the wives of the London citizens recalls the interest of burghers in tournaments referred to in the *Chestre Launfal*:

"Upon a day of the trinitè
A feste of great solempnitè
In Carlyoun was holde
Erles and barones of that countrè
Ladyes and borjaes of that citè
Thyder come bothe yongh and old."[6]

Perhaps this point is not important; but we may note that, just as nobles crossed the line separating court from folk, and assisted at pageants,[7] so the citizens occasionally returned the visit.

---

[1] Murimuth, p. 146. The passage concerning the pope and the cardinals is quoted by Chambers. Cf. Murimuth, p. 230: "ad proclamationem domini Roberti de Morlee, [perhaps him who led the twenty-five knights in 1331] fuerunt facta hastiludia pulcherrima juxta Lon-donias apud Smythefeld, ita quod papa cum xij cardinalibus suis, qui omnes consimili modo erant vestiti, fovebant partem interiorem, deliberantes universaliter de tribus cursibus contra quoscumque equitare volentes," etc. The prince of Wales took part in this tournament.

[2] On this, see Murimuth pp. 155, 156 and 237 f.; Walsingham, i, p. 263; (perhaps this is the one mentioned in the *Chronica de Melsa* (ed. E. A. Bond [R. S.] 1866–68) iii, p. 52). The mayor and aldermen were invited in 34 Edw. III (see below, p. 95).

[3] Ashm. MS. 793, fol. 105b. Cf. Murimuth, pp. 155 f. and 232; *Chron. de Melsa*, iii, p. 73.

[4] Murimuth, pp. 155 f. Walsingham, i, p. 263, gives its dimensions — two hundred feet in diameter — and records the foundation of a similar institution by Philip of Valois, King of France.　　　　　　　　　　[5] Walsingham, *loc. cit.*

[6] Thomas Chester (c. 1350): *Chestre Launfal* (Ritson's ed.) ll. 181 f. I am indebted to Mr. Frederic Schenck for this reference. *Borjaes* is, of course, *bourgeois* (our *burghers*.)

[7] Cf. the nobles who took part in the "fight" at Bristol in 1574 (chapter iv below); Henry VIII's visits to the Midsummer Watch; and the frequency with which royalty assisted at the Lord Mayor's Shows of the seventeenth century.

THE 1344 " ROUND-TABLE " AND THE ORDER OF THE GARTER

The king formed this " round-table " " eodem modo et statu quo eam dimisit dominus Arthurus quondam rex Angliæ, scilicet ad numerum trecentorum militum ";[1] " et præfixit diem rotundæ tabulæ tenendæ ibidem in festo Pentecostes proxime tunc futuro, et omnibus præsentibus dedit licentiam cum gratiarum actionibus ad propria remeandi."[2]

It has been stated that the Order of the Garter was founded upon this institution;[3] but Sir Nicholas Harris Nicolas, who discusses Froissart's statements at some length,[4] observes: " It is . . . highly probable that the ' Society of the Garter ' (as it was long called) arose out of some celebrated Tournament or Jousts, at which the king and ' his ' twelve knights, and the Prince of Wales and ' his ' knights tilted, each having *a Garter* round his left knee in the Lists. . . .

" Many facts concur in fixing *Windsor* as the place where, and the *24th of June*, 1348, as the date when, the Hastiludes which gave rise to the Order occurred, though the Symbol seems to have been worn some months before."[5] Sir Nicholas points out that " the Device of *the Garter* was not adopted before the year 1346; because no notice of a Garter occurs in Accounts of precisely the same kind . . . before 1346."[6]

We are here only concerned with the Order of the Garter as a development of the " round-table " of Edward III, which became an annual affair; and this, in turn, owed its existence to the jousts and tournaments which were common accompaniments of feasts and other occasions of royal entertainment.[7]

---

[1] Murimuth, p. 232. [2] *Ibid.*, p. 156.

[3] See Johnes' Froissart (1803) i, p. 245: " King Edward . . . determined to establish an order of Knighthood. . . . He ordered it to be denominated ' Knights of the blue garter.' . . . The celebration of this order was fixed for St. George's Day . . . 1344 . . . . " Cf. *Chron. de Melsa*, iii, p. 52, " in die Sancti Georgii renovari," cited by Schenck; and Chambers, i, pp. 221 f.: " St. George was the patron saint of England, and his day was honoured as one of the greater feasts, notably at Court, where the chivalric order of the Garter was under his protection." (Chambers refers to Dyer, p. 193; Anstis, *Register of the Garter*, ii, p. 38; E. Ashmole, *History of the Garter*.)

[4] See *Archæologia*, xxxi, pp. 2 and 104 f. On p. 107 Sir Nicholas expresses his doubts as to the founding of the Order at the Round Table of 1344, maintaining (p. 112) that it could not have been founded before 1346 or 12 October, 1347. Cf. *ibid.*, pp. 40, 41, and 121 for the appearance of the Garter at the king's " Hastilude " at Eltham in 21 Edw. III (1347–48).

[5] *Archæologia*, xxxi, p. 125.

[6] *Ibid.*, p. 129.

[7] Says Strutt, *Sports*, p. xi: " Tournaments and jousts were usually exhibited at coronations, royal marriages and other occasions of solemnity where pomp and pageantry were thought to be requisite. Our histories abound with details of these celebrated pastimes." In *Chron. de Melsa*, iii, p. 69, we read: " . . . in diversis civitatibus et villis torniamenta et hastiludia componebant, vocatis ad hæc dominabus, matronis et aliis mulieribus generosis." (Cf. iii, p. 72.)

HASTILUDIA TEMP. EDWARD III SUGGESTING DISGUISED PARTICIPANTS

Entries, which suggest disguising of the participants in *hastiludia*, may be found in *Archæologia*, xxxi.[1] One, " is of fourteen tunics, and Hoods of blue cloth, against the *Hastiludes at Bury*; which is followed . . . by entries of ' glauchus,' i. e., grey or sea-green velvet, and blue velvet, for a Doublet for Lionel the king's son (afterwards Duke of Clarence) against the *Hastiludes at Windsor*. . . . Then occurs an account of the red and mixed cloth . . . and vizards of red sheep skins, for the *Hastiludes at Reading*, ' anno Regis xxj^{mo} ' ";[2] and entries for " hastiludes " at Lichfield, Eltham and other places follow. A " hastilude " at Canterbury (22 Edw. III) at which twelve ladies wore masks, is also mentioned.[3]

The elaboration of the tournament in the reign of Edward III is undoubtedly due to influences from Hainault, the home of Queen Philippa. Mr. Frederic Schenck notes[4] that the elaborateness of these " chivalric pageants " was developed in England after the king's marriage; he suggests the possibility of their origin in Hainault, where in 1326 we find nobles and burghers taking part in the same festival; at this tourney nine citizens represented the Nine Worthies. As early as 1330 the *bourgeois* of Paris held a " round-table "; and in the same year, at Valenciennes, a feast was held in the market-place, and a peacock prize offered for " la plus belle compagnie." [5] Pageantic features of interest occur in connection with this occasion: "sy y vinrent moult noblement ceulx de la Lor-merye à cheval et beaulx paremens et demoiselles avoec eulx qui les menoyent chascun à ung fil d'or [6] et ung grant chasteau devant eulx allant par engien moult richement; et par dessus y avoit quatre angels de quatre josnes enfans et pa deseuse le dieu d'amours.

" Et ceulx de la cauchye y vinrent aussy moult noblement à pied à ung chastel devant eulx dont il yssoit ung hermite et sept feés à ung engien desseue le chastel qui gettoit oyseaux tous vifs. . . ." [7]

---

[1] Cf. *Archæologia*, xxxi, pp. 120 f.

[2] This should be 22 Edward III (1348) — see *ibid.*, p. 115.

[3] Pp. 42 and 122. It is hard to say whether the " certain accoutrements of India silk " bestowed on Thomas de Gray of Codmore by the king at this tourney (see Dugdale, *Baronage*, i, pp. 231 and 711; cited by Edward Hasted, *Hist. and Top. Survey of Kent* (Canterbury, 1800), xi, p. 129) indicate disguising, or a reward.

A tournament at Smithfield in 1357 was reproduced in *The Festival of Empire*, given at London in 1911 (see the *Book* of that Pageant, p. 31.)

[4] In his manuscript before alluded to.

[5] Mr. Schenck refers to the *Récit d'un Bourgeois de Valenciennes* (ed. Baron Kervin de Lettinver, Louvain, 1877), pp. 48–52.

[6] Cf. the tournament in Cheap in 1331 (above, p. 91); and those of 1375 and 1494 (below, pp. 95 and 96).

[7] Cf. the birds of the 1415 entry of Henry V and the 1432 entry of his son (below, chapter iii). See Neilson, *Court of Love*, p. 253, for mention of the " Feste du Prince de Plaisance " at Valenciennes in 1348, and the " Jeux de la Fête Dieu " instituted at Aix-en-Provence in 1474.

The speed with which the influence of these French " chivalric pageants " appeared in England indicates that Queen Philippa's suite may have suggested these models to the English king; that the court was ready to adopt any pageantic suggestions, is shown by the start toward disguising made by the " rex de Vertbois."

Considering the fact that chroniclers and romance writers often pictured contemporary life in their treatment of Arthurian material, it is not inconceivable that when Wace introduced a Round Table into his *Roman de Brut*,[1] he was drawing on the life of his time. I should, however, add that I have not found descriptions of historical " round-tables " as early as the twelfth century.

LATER EXAMPLES OF PAGEANTIC TOURNEYS

It is not my intention to consider the later history of the tournament; but we may glance hastily at some subsequent examples of this pastime, before we pass on to other matters.

In 34 Edw. III " were ordeyned Justes atte London iij daies of Rogacionns, that is to saye þe maire of London with his xxiiij Aldermen ayens all those that wolde come: In whose name & stede the kyng prively with his iiij sonnes Edwarde Lyonell John & Edmonde and xix othre grete Lordes helden ye felde with grete worship."[2]

In 1375 " rood dame Alice Perrers as lady of the sune, fro the tour of London through Chepe; and alwey a lady ledynge a lordys brydell. And thanne begun the grete justes in Smythefeld."[3] " These ridings," says Chambers, " closely resemble the ' mummings ' proper. But they were a prelude to *hastiludia* which from the fourteen to the sixteenth century constantly grew less actual and more mimetic."[4]

Richard II, " being aduertised, with what magnificence and pompe the Queene *Isabella* of *France* had made her entry into *Paris*, thought good to appoint a militarie triumph at *London*, wherin appeared sixty Knights, and so many faire young Ladies of his Court sumptuously apparelled."[5] On the second day of the jousting, the king himself took part; and each day's fighting was followed by an elaborate supper.

---

[1] Cf. Schofield, *Norman Conquest to Chaucer* (1906), pp. 120 f.; Maynadier, *The Arthur of the English Poets* (1907), p. 51. Professor Schofield notes that Wace " seems to have lived most of his life in Normandy " (where " round tables " may have been a feature of court life earlier than in England), and comments on Wace's vivid style.

[2] Ashm. MS., 793, fol. 111 b.

[3] Which " endured vij night." Contemporary documents in the *London Chronicle* (ed. E. Tyrrell), p. 70; cited by Chambers, i, p. 392, n. 4.

[4] Chambers. Cf. the tournament of 1494 (mentioned below, p. 96); those at Hainault in 1330 (above, p. 94), and at London in 1331 (above, p. 90).

[5] Sir William Segar, *Honor, Military, and Ciuill* (London, 1602), iii, ch. 29 (p. 154). Also quoted as ch. 3, by H. Walpole, in *Miscellaneous Antiquities, or a Collection of Curious*

After the Paris coronation of Henry VI in 1431 " furent faites belles joustes en l'ostel de Saint-Pol, desquelles emportèrent le cry et eurent la voix des dames, le conte d'Arondel et messire Jehan, bastard de Saint-Pol, comme les mieulx joustans." [1]

" The Account of William Combes and Richard Ryche for putting-up Lists and Scaffolds for Jousts in West Smithfield on Jan. 30, 1442, between Don Philip Boyl of Aragon and John Asteley, Esq.," [2] records an elaborate, if not a pageantic, tourney, the cost for which was £51, 3s. 1d.

After a three days' tournament in 1494, the knights " were brought in to the palays wt iiij fayre ladyes, which ladde their Bridellis wt iiij silkyn laces of white and blewe, which said ladyes rode vpon iiij white palfrays in gounys of white satyn slevid, wt cremysen satyn in ther her, which was a goodly sight to behold." [3]

Jousts followed the entry of Louis XII into Paris in 1498,[4] and there were many such entertainments in England during the next century.[5]

When Margaret was on her way to meet her Scottish husband, in 1503, she was entertained by a tournament [6] which has an element of disguising. One knight is robbed of his Lady Paramour by another, and challenges him. So is enacted a scene common in the old romances: the two knights " maid a varey fayr Torney " and " did well ther Devor " until the king and queen stopped them. Sir Patrick Hamilton and Patrick Sinclair were the participants; " and ther was com grett multitude of People for to se thys."

At the coronation of Henry VIII a very elaborate tournament was given, in which castles, running wine, and such characters as Pallas with her " scholars " and the knights who were servants to Diana, all show how the mimetic side had

---

Papers, either republished from scarce tracts, or now first printed from original MSS. Number 1, (Strawberry Hill, 1772), p. 8. Both volumes are in the Brit. Mus.

Segar gives other instances of jousting from the time of Darius to the time of Elizabeth; and of knightly customs of many lands.

[1] Monstrelet, *Chronique*, v, p. 6; cf. a reference to the " petites joustes "on this day after the coronation, in the *Journal d'un Bourgeois de Paris*, p. 279. The account may not be impartial: " Mais, pour certain, maintes foys on a veu à Paris enfans de bourgoys, que quant ilz se marioient, tous mestiers, comme orfebvres, orbateurs, brief gens de tous joieux mestiers en amendoient plus que ilz n' ont fait du sacre du roy et de ses joustes et de tous ses Angloys, mais espoir c' est pour ce que on ne les entend point [parler et que ilz ne nous entendent point]; je m'en rapporte à ce qui en est, car pour ce qu'il faisoit trop grant froit en celui temps et que les jours estoient cours, ilz firent ainsi pou de largesse."

[2] Edited by F. J. Furnivall and R. E. G. Kirk for the Chaucer Society (second series, 36, London, 1903). Other accounts for jousts in Smithfield are noted on p. 31 of this volume; most of them are temp. Henry VI, but one dates back to 37 Edw. III. The original MSS. are in the Public Record Office.

[3] Cotton MS. Vit. A. xiv, fol. 150 b, *et seq.*; printed in Kingsford, *Chron. London* (1905), p. 202.

[4] Godefroy, *Le Cérémonial de France* (1619), pp. 64 f.

[5] Cf. Hall and Holinshed *passim*.

[6] Described, from a contemp. MS. in Leland, *Collect.* iv, p. 288.

developed.[1] The pageantry on this occasion was elaborate, but the fighting was not serious. The cars — such as Diana's park and the castle of Pallas — show a debt to the pageant; and the whole thing points the way to such an Elizabethan "barrier" as the siege of the "Fortress of Perfect Beauty" by the "Four Foster-children of Desire," in which Sir Philip Sidney took part in 1581.[2]

Henry VIII and the Pageantic Tournament

Henry VIII was very fond of pageantic tournaments, and we shall have something to say of them when we treat, later, the development of the pageant-car in the hands of the masque. Here it will be enough to refer to the jousts in honor of the queen which Henry held in 1511; he took the name of Cure loial, and three knights assumed those of Bon voloire, Bon espoir and Valiaunt desire. They were called "les quatre Chiualers de la Forrest saluigne."[3] This suggests a chivalric influence; indeed Bonvaleir is the varlet of Meliades, a character in one of the famous romances.[4] Undoubtedly such characters as these are descended directly from the "rex de Vertbois" and other disguised knights of the fourteenth century.

On the occasion of the visit of the Emperor Charles V to the Court of King Henry VIII in 1522, ". . . a tournament and a pageant were held, which must have been gorgeous in the extreme, to judge from the description of the dresses preserved in an account of Richard Gibson, the master of the revels. Two bards, perhaps those worn by the chargers of the king and the emperor, were made of russet velvet, ' with knyghtes un hors bake rydyng up un mowntens of golld, with brokyn speres in their handes, and ladyes cummyng oute of clooudes castyng dartes at the knyghtes and all the upper parte of the saam bardes powdyrd with clowdes purfylled and wroght with venys golld and venys syllver.' "[5] This, in itself, is not, of course, pageantic; but it shows the raw material of pageantry pictured on the bards. There was, however, a pageant at the masquerade in the evening, following this tourney.[6]

On the Monday following the coronation of Anne Boleyn " were the Justs att the tylte before the Kyngs grace where the Mayre and his brethren had a goodly standyng, butt there were very few speres broken by reason the horsses wolde not couple."[7]

---

[1] See Hall, p. 511 (cited by Chambers).

[2] Chambers, i, p. 392, n. 4. (On this "barrier," see chapter iv.)

[3] Hall, p. 517, referred to by Chambers, Wallace, [*The Evolution of the English Drama up to Shakspere* (Schriften der Deutschen Shakespeare-Gesellschaft, IV. 1912)], Reyher, etc.

[4] *Clariodus*, Book ii, l. 202.

[5] Brewer, *Letters and Papers of Henry VIII*, iii, 2305, cited by C. T. Martin in *Archæologia*, xlvii, p. 315.

[6] Cf. Brewer, iii, 2305 (pt. ii, p. 976).

[7] Harl. MS. 41, fol. 11 b; Holinshed, iii, p. 786.

On 29 June, 1536, there was a great " jousting and triumph " at Westminster, " where were ordained two Lighters made like Ships to fight upon the water, one of which brast in the midst, whereby one Gates, gentleman, a servant of Master Kneuets was drowned in his harnesse. In the other, a gunne brast her chamber, and maimed two of the mariners." [1]

1539. — A Water " Triumph " with Disguising of a Political Nature

On 17 June, 1539 there was a " triumphe " on the Thames " before the kinges pallace at Westminster, where were two barges prepared with ordinance of warre . . . one for the Bishop of Rome and his cardinalles, and the other for the Kinges Grace . . . and the Pope [and his cardinals] made their defyance against England and shot their ordinaunce one at another, and so had three courses up and downe the water . . . but at last the Pope and his cardinalles were overcome, and all his men cast over the borde into the Thames; howbeyt there was none drowned, for they were persons chosen which could swimme, and the kinges barge lay by hoveringe to take them upp . . . which was a goodly pastime." [2] The result of this water fight seems to have been decided on beforehand; it is, of course, in no sense a tournament, but was apparently derived from such martial sports.

Mary of Scotland Weds the Dauphin at Rouen

At the wedding of Mary, Queen of Scots to the Dauphin of France at Rouen, there were " douze cheuaulx artificielz, tous parez de drap d'or & t'oille d'argent, conduictz & menez artificiellement, cheminans & allans de telle sorte, qu'on eust dict iceulx estre viuās. Sur lesquelz estoiēt montez monsieur d'Orleans, monsieur d'Angoulesme, les enfans petitz de mōsieur de Guise & d'Aumalle, accompagnez d'autres petitz & jeunes princes, menans dans des coches vn grād nombres de pelerins, tous vestuz de toille d'argent & drap d'or, auec pierreries & ioyalux en grand abundance, chātans melodieusemēt auec instrumens en toute perfectiō de musique, hymnes, & cantiques à la louenges des mariez & du mariage." [3] There were also six ships on this occasion, " si ingenieusement faictes, & conduictes de si grand' dexterité, que l'on eust dict iceux flotter en l'eau & estre menez par les vages & vndes de mer, car en entrant en la salle comme dedans la mer . . . ." [4] These were also guided by young princes.

---

[1] Harl. MS. 540, fol. 9 b (in Stow's hand); Stow, Annals, p. 573, cited by Holinshed, iii, p. 798. On these " boat-jousts " in general, see Strutt, Sports, p. 113, and plate xv (from the fourteenth-century Royal MS. i, B. vii).

[2] Wriothesley, i, p. 100.

[3] Ceremonial at the Marriage of Mary Queen of Scots with the Dauphin of France (ed. by Sir Henry Ellis for the Roxburghe Club [London, 1818]), p. 12. The pamphlet is a reprint of a Discourse, etc., published at Rouen in 1558.

[4] Ibid.

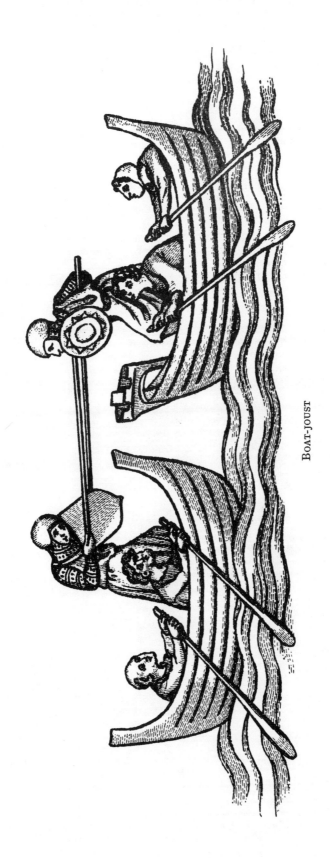

BOAT-JOUST

The artificial horses, rather than the ships, suggest the tournament; but the prancing children show us that we are getting near the time of Don Quixote.[1]

1609 — A Tournament at Stuttgart

By 1609 — at a time when the tournament was dying out in England — we find in Germany a strong current from the pageant to the tournament; a *mélange* of pageantic characters appeared in the great cavalcade and tournament held by John Frederick, Duke of Württemberg, in the city of Stuttgart, on the occasion of his marriage, 6 November, of this year.[2]

There were such figures as Julius Cæsar, Alexander, and Hector (pl. 99); Prudence, Justice, and Fortitude (pl. 67); three men who look like Turks (pl. 45); Abundance, Peace, and " Policia " (on an unnumbered plate); Venator, Amicus, and three headless beings, with faces on their chests (on the last sheet of vol. i, of this collection). What look like " wild-men," and some figures not unlike " whifflers," appear on the first sheet of this volume; Moors and Fame — a female figure, blowing a trumpet — may also be found pictured in this collection. It is hard to tell just who took part in the tourney; but the influence of pageantry is marked.

We shall defer to a later chapter our account of the 1610 tournament, held in honor of Prince Henry;[3] and shall close our survey of these sports with mention of a tournament at Madrid in 1623 when Charles of England went to Spain to marry the Infanta. " On luy donna vn divertissement de cette sorte le 21. Aoust," says Menestrier;[4] and he notes that some of the *estassiers* were dressed *à la turque*.

---

[1] On the tournaments, and the caricatures of them, in Italy, see Burckhardt, ii, pp. 91 f. (§ 5); or Middlemore, ii, pp. 117 f. "Die Sache (*i. e.*, tournaments) wurde gerade in Florenz förmlich populär; der Bürger fing an, sein Turnier — ohne Zweifel in einer weniger gefährlichen Form — als eine Art von regelrechtem Vergnügen zu betrachten, und Franco Sacchetti hat uns das unendlich komische Bild eines solchen Sonntagsturnierers, eines siebzigjährigen Notars, aufbehalten. . . . . Endlich nehmen die ersten Medici sich des Turnierwesens mit einer wahren Leidenschaft an, als wollten sie, die unadligen Privatleute, gerade hierin zeigen, dass ihr gefelliger Kreis jedem Hofe gleich stehe. Schon unter Cosimo (1459), dann unter Pietro dem ältern fanden weitberühmte grosse Turniere in Florenz statt . . . ." Cf. Burckhardt, ii, p. 94, n. 1, for mention of the *Eselturnier* held at the palace of Jacques Cœur, at Bourges (c. 1540).

[2] See the collection of engravings, made by Bathazar Küchler, which was formed by Baron Taylor of Paris, bought at his sale by Mr. Fairholt, and bequeathed by him to the Society of Antiquaries.

[3] Besant, *Mediæval London*, i, p. 326, calls this the last held in England. There have been revivals of this sport in the nineteenth and twentieth centuries, which we shall notice in chapter vii below.

[4] P. 273.

Conclusion

Perhaps this glance at tournaments is enough to show that, as the current bore knights away from serious fighting, and the emphasis was placed more on splendid display than on strenuous exercise, a tendency to " dress up " was followed by " dressing up " in character. Just as the sword dance of the folk gave way to mumming, so the tournament of the court became a " soft and silken war." Before 1330 the Nine Worthies and the god of love had appeared in French tourneys; they were followed closely by Tatars and the Pope with his Cardinals in England. More than twenty years before, a mysterious " rex de Vertbois " suggests a disguised character in a tournament at Stepney.

It is important to note that there was this element of disguising in the tournament, and that later it developed into symbolism. The characters would naturally be, at first, those appropriate to battle. In the middle ages, one party might well disguise themselves as Tatars; and most of the Nine Worthies had won their fame on the fields of war.

As Strutt points out, " the tournament and the joust . . . afforded to those who were engaged in them an opportunity of appearing before the ladies to the greatest advantage; [1] they might at once display their taste and opulence by the costliness and elegancy of their apparel, and their prowess as soldiers; therefore these pastimes became fashionable among the nobility, and probably for the same reason they were prohibited to the commoners." [2] With the presence of the ladies the thoughts of the warriors turned from Mars to Cupid. The strife of love was symbolized, replacing more bloody exercises. Castles, from the literary allegories of the time, appeared upon the scene; the warriors took allegorical names; in short, symbolism absorbed these wars of love,[3] the allegory became tangible, so to speak. Chivalric literature had embalmed the life of a past age, and transmitted the dead spirit to a time no longer chivalrous. Pageant and masque drew

---

[1] Cf. Milton, *L'Allegro*;

> " Where throngs of knights and barons bold
> In weeds of peace high triumphs hold
> With store of ladies, whose bright eyes
> Rain influence . . ."

[2] *Sports*, p. 112. The " musters," or parades of citizen-soldiers, were, of course, of a popular character. (For a description of that of 1539, see Holinshed, iii, p. 809.) Probably such a fight as that at Bristol in 1574 is nearer the " muster " than the " barrier." (See chapter iv.)

[3] Cf. Neilson, *Court of Love*, p. 251, for an account of a " Cour Amoureuse " which was founded in France in 1400. " If this Cour Amoureuse," says Mr. Neilson, " shows us how close the institution of the Court of Love could come to some forms of the allegory, it suggests also how easily it becomes mere pageantry. Even the allegories are often constructed and described in such a way as to be easily enough transformed into spectacles; and in an age that delighted in that kind of exhibition, it was unlikely that the opportunity would be missed." (P. 253.)

from it certain characters; and it gave the pageant its castles " allant par engien moult richement."

It should be noted that the castle at Valenciennes in 1330 antedated the first castle in an English pageant — that of the Goldsmiths in 1377 — by forty-seven years. Castles are not common in English tournaments, until these have a large element of the masque in them; so that it looks as if the pageant in England, receiving the castle from France or Hainault, in turn gave it to the English masque.[1]

In so far as the later tournament strengthened the custom of disguising among the courtiers, to that extent is it important in considering the masque. It is one of the elements which lie at the foundation of this dramatic form.

§ 2. THE DISGUISING

ANOTHER ANCESTOR OF THE MASQUE

Closely related to the habit of " dressing-up " which we have noted in connection with the tournament, is the *disguising*. It is clear that in the days of chivalry, a knight fully armed, and ready for the fray, could be recognized only by his shield. Many, hiding their escutcheons, fought unknown. The custom of " dressing-up," which later came into the tournament, was but a development of the habit many knights had of travelling *incognito*; and this habit, in turn, stimulated the disguises which, later combining with allegory, led to such figures as Cure loial, Bon voloire, Bon espoir, and Valiaunt desire in 1511,[2] and the foster children of Desire in 1581.

But there was another source for the masque. As Chambers points out,[3] *masking* shows the legacy to Christmas of the Kalends celebrations in their *bourgeois* forms. *Larvæ*, or masks, were prominent in the records and prohibitions of the Feast of Fools,[4] from the decretal of Innocent III in 1207 to the letter of the Paris theologians in 1445. We have already spoken of folk-mumming; [5] here let us note that the custom was shared by the courtiers.

Viseres appear in court documents about the middle of the fourteenth century; they were used not only for *hastiludia*, as we have seen, but at the Yuletide celebrations of the court. Disguises of men, women, various animals and " wild-

---

[1] We must remember the possibility that the word *castle* was loosely used, and that the structure erected by the Goldsmiths had little save splendor to connect it with the abode of chivalry.

[2] See above, p. 97.

[3] *Med. Stage*, i, p. 391. As this material lies somewhat outside our field, I shall rely largely on his excellent chapter on *Masks and Misrule* (*op. cit.*, i, pp. 390 f.).

[4] See Chambers, i, p. 391, and his list of references. Schelling, *Eliz. Drama*, ii, p. 96, n. 2, refers to Chambers " on the early connection of the masque with the Feast of Fools and the *exuviæ* . . . ."

[5] See above, chapter i, pp. 4 ff.

men," or *wodewoses*, are common [1] in the lists of stuffs issued for Christmas and Epiphany of 1347 and 1348. In 1388 the wardrobe provided linen coifs for twenty-one counterfeit men of the law in the *ludus regis*.[2]

PRIMITIVE MASQUES

These celebrations, or " plays," seem to be really primitive masques. " The sets of costumes supplied for all these *ludi* would most naturally be used by groups of performers in something of the nature of a dance; and they point to some primitive form of masque, such as Froissart describes in contemporary France,[3] the precursor of a long line of development which, traceable from the end of the following century, culminates in the glories of Ben Jonson." [4] In the fourteenth century, however, there is no trace of the masque as we know it; and these occasions seem rather to be revels or masquerades.

Mask meaning *visor* comes from *mask*, an *entertainment*.[5] At first, says Evans, the masquers invited the spectators to join in one or two dances, and this later

---

[1] Cf. *Archæologia*, xxxi, pp. 5 f.: *Accounts of the Expenses of the Great Wardrobe of King Edward III* (29 Sept., 1344, to 1 Aug., 1345), esp. pp. 37 f.: " xlij viseres . . . xiiij capita draconum . . . xiiij capita pauonum," etc. Also p. 43: " viseres " representing heads of men surmounted by those of lions, elephants, etc.; " xvij capita virginum," are noted. [Cf. *ibid.*, p. 120: " The next entries (those on p. 37) relate to tunics, vizards, and other things for the King's Plays at Guildford, at Christmas, ' in anno xxj°,' 1347."] Cf. Chambers, i, pp. 391 f., 392, n. 2; he cites Strutt, *Sports*, plate xvi, for a reproduction of an illumination from a MS. in the Bodleian Library. Cf. also above, p. 74.

This Bodl. MS. 264 (which contains, among other things, the *Alexander* romance, in Old French) was illuminated by Jehan de Grise who finished his work on 18 April, 1344. Although it is thought that he worked in Flanders, and perhaps at Bruges, the marginal figures seem to be Anglo-Norman in style: they show occupations and incidents of real life; such animal head-dresses as those on folios 110, 117 b, and 181 b picture the kind of thing which is described in various English accounts. It may be that de Grise had visited England; or that the same kind of masking was customary on the Continent.

[2] *Compotus Magn. Garderobæ*, 14 Richard II., fol. 198 b: " pro xxj coifs de tela linea pro hominibus de lege contrafactis pro ludo regis tempore natalis domini anno xii." Printed in Warton, *Hist. Eng. Poetry* (1871), ii, p. 220, and by Chambers from this latter source.

[3] This has already been alluded to (see above, p. 73, n. 5). At the wedding-feast of a young squire of Vermandois and a damsel of the queen, in 1393, the king and some nobles, disguised as " wild-men " broke into the room where the rest of the court were dancing. The dancers, who failed to recognize them, stopped, and watched — as spectators — the dancing wild-men. The late arrival of the Duc d'Orléans with torchbearers resulted in a fatal accident, vividly described by Froissart (Johnes's ed., iv, p. 372; the illustration reproduced (p. 374) is from Harl. MS. 4380, fol. 1).

[4] Chambers, i, p. 393.

[5] Cf. Skeat, *Etym. Dict.* (Oxford, 1882), p. 356, and his *Concise Etym. Dict.* (Oxford, 1901), p. 317. The true sense of the word is *entertainment*; *disguise* is secondary. Cf. Evans, *Eng. Masque*, p. xx, n. 2.

Evans (p. xii) makes a technical distinction between *mask* and *masque*, using the first spelling to denote the entertainment prior to the end of the sixteenth century, when the French

Wild-Men Burning

became an established practice in the masques, which were not introduced from Italy or anywhere else. They grew up as a combination of the old-fashioned masquerade with the dance of everyday life.

Apparently there were disguisings in Scotland as early as 1285; for at the marriage feast of Alexander III and Joleta, daughter of the Count of Dreux, at Jedburgh Abbey in that year, Death, in the form of a skeleton, joined a band of masquers who were dancing before the king and queen.[1] This seems to have made such an impression on the chroniclers — in view of subsequent events — that it was recorded. Professor Neilson is probably right in suggesting that it is only one of many such performances; it is, however, the only one we know of, due to the fact that the death of the king followed after it so quickly.

It is not necessary to assume that on this occasion the other dancers were in costume. Indeed, it is probable that they were not. A solemn procession, preceded by minstrels, might well begin a stately dance at court. The performers seem to have been taken as much by surprise as anyone; the musicians were overcome. Thus " the earliest instance of the pageant on record " resolves itself into the appearance of a man, disguised as a skeleton, before a group of frightened dancers at a wedding feast. Whether it were a practical joke, or a political plot, or even a ghostly reminder that " in the midst of life we are in death," it is interesting as giving us an early example of disguising at a courtly feast. An attempt to connect it with the literary " dance of death," well known in mediæval England, might — or might not — be successful.

Prohibition of Visors, Mumming, etc., by the Authorities

We have already treated folk-mumming to some extent, but we shall have to recall that masquerading is not confined to the court circle. It has always been a popular custom, and still is practiced at Carnival time. As early as 1334 [2] orders of the city of London forbid a practice of going about the streets at Christmas

---

spelling came into vogue; the word later took on the meaning of *visor*, while that of *entertainment* was expressed by *masque*.

[1] Johannis de Fordun, *Scottichronicon* (Edinburgh, 1759), ii, p. 128. This is mentioned by Peter Hume Brown, *Hist. Scot.* (1899), i, p. 129; in a note he says, " This appears to be the earliest instance of the pageant on record."

[2] Chambers collects much material on this matter of folk-masquerading. (See i, pp. 393 f. and his authorities.) Cf. *Liber Albus*, i, pp. 644, 645, 647, 673, and 676; *Letter-Book G*, folios 2, 262; *Letter-Book H*, fol. 54, for prohibitions of masks; *Memorials of London*, pp. 658, 659, for prohibitions of Christmas mumming in 1417 and 1418. I may add that various broadsides in the Taylor collection in the Guildhall library preserve more recent regulations aimed against the practice. Nos. 78 and 79, dated respectively 1671 and 1721, forbid men to go with " painted visages " (article 38 of the *Wardmote Charges*); precepts of mayors to the aldermen from 1721 to the reign of William IV forbid " visards " (see the Taylor collection of Broadsides, nos. 73, 74, 75, and 76). It is worthy of note that the precepts of early Victorian mayors of London do not contain this order.

with a visor or false face; these are repeated in 1393 and 1405. In 1479 the mayor and sheriffs of Bristol forbade Christmas mumming with masks; and the London authorities continued to issue prohibitions against visors to the time of Victoria.

The entering of citizens' houses to play at dice is also forbidden; and in 1417 " mummyng " is specifically included in a like prohibition.[1] In 1418 " mommyng " is classed with " playes " and " enterludes " as a variety of " disgisyng." [2] These prohibitions were due to the fact that mumming, or masquerading, was used to cloak sedition; partisans of Richard II tried to seize Henry IV on Twelfth Night in 1400; in 1414 Sir John Oldcastle and his Lollards were accused of cloaking sedition in a mumming.[3] I have already referred to Gladman's insurrection at Norwich, which took place in 1443,[4] and may mention Snatch's speech in the third scene of *The Marriage between Wit and Wisdom*:

> " Where I lay last night, I stole away a sheete:
> We will take this, and tie it to his head
> And soe we will blind him;
> And, sirra, I charge you, when you here any body comming
> If they aske you any question, say you goe a-mumming." [5]

which shows that certain misdemeanors went then — as they do now — unpunished in cities where a large part of the population disguises itself, as at Carnival time.

1377 — THE VISIT OF THE MUMMERS TO THE KING

Before these prohibitions went into effect, mumming was very common. Stow tells of a visit paid by " one hundred and thirty citizens, disguised and wellhorsed " to Richard II on the Sunday before Candlemas, 1377. They came in the evening with many minstrels, and they carried torches. One was arrayed like an emperor; one " stately tyred " like a Pope, " who was followed by 24. Cardinals, and after them eight or ten with blacke visors, not amiable, as if they had bin Legates from some forraine Princes." The maskers played dice with the king, so that he " did alwaies winne when he cast at them." They gave him valuable gifts; and afterwards " the Prince and Lords daunced on the one part with the Mummers, who did also daunce: which iolity being ended, they were againe made to drinke, and then departed in order as they came." [6]

---

[1] Chambers, i, p. 394; cf. Besant, *Med. Lond.*, i, p. 228.

[2] Chambers, *loc. cit.*

[3] Chambers, i, p. 395.

[4] See above, p. 8.

[5] See Tudor Facsimile Texts, *A Contract of Marriage between Wit and Wisdom* [ed. John S. Farmer (London and Edinburgh, 1909)], p. 15. The play was printed by J. O. Halliwell, in the second volume of *A Supplement to Dodsley's Old Plays* (London, 1853.) The ms. is dated c. 1579 by Mr. Farmer.

[6] Stow, *Survey* (1618) pp. 148 f.; cf. Reyher, p. 3.

" Behind the accretions of literature and pageantry in the ' mummings ' or ' disguisings ' early in the fourteenth century," says Chambers,[1] " may be seen a nucleus of folk-custom in the entry of the band of worshippers with their sacrificial *exuviæ*, to bring the house good luck. The mummers are masked and disguised folk who come into the hall uninvited and call upon the company there to dice and dance . . ."

It would not be surprising to learn that the masque — given by trained dancers — owed much to the dances of the folk-mummers; but I shall not here attempt to prove that it does. Both tournament and folk-play show the same tendency to become less strenuous; in the latter the dancing is much more important than the fighting, of which, indeed, only a shadowy trace is left; and in the tournament, the fighting — originally a combination of sport and exercise — became a mere excuse for show.

Such entertainments as the Robin Hood plays, the Revesby sword-play and the Christmas St. George plays,[2] combine dancing, mock-fighting and speech. The characters that take part in them are drawn from a large field with a catholicity which reminds us of the pageant. If these plays gave nothing to the masque, at least they share with it an essential — the dance. And it is not impossible to imagine that this folk-dancing stimulated, if it did not inspire, court disguises. Such plays as these, combining dancing with disguising, are almost — if not quite — masques themselves; we may, if there is no contradiction in terms, call them " folk-masques." They combine the " spirit " of pageantry with the technique of the masque — being a dance with a great popular appeal — in much the same way that the modern " festival " combines the " spirit " of the masque with the technique of the modern pageant.[3]

The mummers who visited Richard II in 1377 may have helped carry the influence of folk-dancing to the court, though dancing in disguise was known there long before. It is probable that a connection between folk- and court-dancing could be found; and — as the court emerged from the folk — it is likely that folk-dancing was the source of the other, unless we may assume that both developed spontaneously and independently. The disguise, or " dressing-up," is demanded of an actor in the folk-play; at court, it is the result of elaborate costumes, and it leads to the development of allegory. In other words, literature was drawn upon to furnish appropriate names for the disguised figures which had developed from elegantly dressed knights and ladies; while the characters in the folk-play " dressed the parts " they were to give.

The terms *mumming* and *disguising* are used indifferently until the reign of Henry VIII.[4] Chambers points out that in documents of Henry VII the word

---

[1] *Med. Stage*, i, p. 400.

[2] For examples see Manly, *Specimens of pre-Shaksperian Drama*, i, pp. 278–311 (Part III).

[3] We shall have more to say of the so-called " festival " in our second volume.

[4] Chambers, i, p. 396, n. 2, quotes Skeat's etymology: he derives the word *mummer* from Dutch through Old French. He explains it by Low German *Mumme*, a " mask," and adds:

mumming does not occur; and if there is any difference between the two words in those of Henry VIII, *disguising* is used of the more elaborate shows, while both are properly distinct from *interlude*.[1]

LYDGATE AND THE MUMMING

The first step away from a masquerade toward the kind of thing we have come to consider as " masque," was made early in the fifteenth century. John Lydgate's is the first name we can attach to pageantry; it comes into the history of the masque as well. At first, as we might expect, the mumming was a dance without speech; one who hid his face would not want to betray himself by his voice. But gradually, as the emphasis was shifted from the character representing to the character represented, speech crept in; and, as Chambers suggests, " the development of the mumming in a literary direction may very likely have been due to the multifarious activity of John Lydgate." [2] We shall see that he brought allegory to the pageant; [3] Chambers has noted that his poems " show pretty clearly the way in which verses got into the disguisings." He places them all in " the reign of Henry VI, and probably [between] 1427–30." [4]

" The word is imitative, from the sound *mum* or *mom*, used by nurses to frighten or amuse children, at the same time pretending to cover their faces."

[1] Chambers, i, p. 400; cf. Schelling, i, pp. 73 f.

[2] Chambers, i, p. 396.

[3] Cf. chapter iii, below.

[4] *Op. cit.*, i, p. 397. Cf. Brotanek, *Die Engl. Maskenspiele* (1902), pp. 305 f. Reyher, *Les Masques anglais* (1909), p. 109, agrees with these dates.

On Lydgate's mummings, see also MacCracken, *Minor Poems of John Lydgate* (EETS., ES. 107), p. xxi; Hammond, *Lydgate's Mumming at Hertford*, in *Anglia*, xxii, pp. 364 f.; Sieper, *Lydgate's 'Reson and Sensuallyte'* (EETS., ES. 84, 89), i, pp. xvi f.; Tyrrell's *Chronicle of London*, pp. 257 f., contains a poem for a Sheriff's May-day festival written by Lydgate. Reyher, p. 4, says, " Les documents . . . ne sont ni des comptes, ni des relations, mais une série de tirades en vers composées pour des mascarades et peut-être d'autres spectacles. Ces poèmes sont fort curieux parce qu'ils sont les premiers du genre; ils sont en outre précieux, parce qu'ils ont été composés par le plus grand poète de l'époque, le moine de Bury. . . . Ce sont des pièces de vers destinées soit à presenter des personnages déguisés, un à un, ou en troupe, soit encore à esquisser à l'avance les grandes lignes d'un spectacle sans doute mimé; . . ."

Sieper notes that in Addl. MS. 29729 — one of Stow's — are copies, on fol. 132 b, *et seq.*, of " A letar made in wyse of balad by daun John Lydgat / brought by A pursyvaunt in wyse of momers dysguysyd to fore þe mayre of london estfeld vpon the twelffthe nyght of cristmasse," etc.

" A lettar made by John lidgat for a mommynge whiche þe gold smythes of london shewyd before Eestfyld þe mayr on candylmas day at nyght this letar was presentyd by an Harold callyd fortune." (Fol. 134.)

" a balade made by daun John Lidgate at elltham in cristmasse ffor amomyng to fore the Kynge and the Quene." (Fol. 135 b.)

(Other verses by Lydgate follow.) In the margin of this MS. (fol. 132 b) is written "William Estfeld mereser mayre anno domini 1430 also ye second tyme mayre anno 1438." Both Cham-

Bacchus, Juno, and Ceres send gifts to the king and queen in a 1427 mumming; " cette ballade a pour objet de présenter les momeurs, d'expliquer leur venue, ainsi que la raison d'être et le sens de leurs présents. Elle fournit aussi au poète l'occasion d'offrir au roi et à sa mère les vœux traditionelles du joyeux temps du Noël." [1] It is to be noted that the classical element appears here almost a century before we find it in the pageant.

" Lo here foloweth the deuyse of a desguysinge to fore the grete estates of this land than being at london made by lidgate daun John the monke of bury / of dame *fortune* dame *prudence* / dame *rightwysnesse* / and dame *ffortitudo* / behold it for it is morall plesaunt and notabell / lo first cometh in dame *fortune*." [2] This masque, unlike the last — which dealt with the presents carried by the merchants, the divinities who sent them, and the meaning of the wine, oil and wheat, rather than with the dancers themselves — is concerned with the persons which it introduces. They are not the gods of fable, but personified moral abstractions: is not Lydgate's aim to give a disguising " morall plesaunt and notabell " ? The abstractions " n'en sont pas moins pleines de vie, et Lydgate a décrit d'une manière très pittoresque leurs costumes, leurs emblèmes . . . ." [3] The two " devyses " for mummings at London and Windsor were probably recited by a " presenter," as Chambers points out; [4] and the Hertford disguising [5] seems to have resembled an interlude very strongly.

Whether or not Lydgate were the author of an innovation, says Chambers, " the introduction of speeches, songs, and dialogues was common enough in the fully developed mummings. For these we must look to the sumptuous courts of the early Tudors. Lydgate died about 1451, and the Wars of the Roses did not encourage revelry." [6]

It would not be surprising if future investigators should find that Lydgate, in his contributions to pageantry and masque (or its early ancestor) was a more important figure than is generally supposed. " It is," says Sir Adolphus Ward, " clearly erroneous to suppose that the English moralities . . . grew gradually out of the mysteries and miracles, under the coöperating influence of the pageantry which had become a public custom in the English towns in the latter part of the Middle Ages. The love of allegory from a very early period onwards, domesticated itself in the English mind, to which there seems to be nothing

---

bers (i, p. 396, n. 3) and Hammond (p. 366) note that Addl. MS. 29729 is copied from (Shirley's) Trin. Coll. (Camb.) MS. R. iii, 20. Cf. the verses printed by Brotanek, p. 306; Mac-Cracken, p. xxi, gives a list of Lydgate's mummings, which includes those at Bishopswood, Eltham, Hertford, London, and Windsor, besides those for the Mercers and the Goldsmiths.

[1] Reyher, p. 110. Cf., on this mumming, *ibid.*, pp. 109 f.; Chambers, i, p. 397, n. 2; Brotanek, pp. 306 f.

[2] Addl. MS. 29729, fol. 140.   [3] Reyher, p. 112.   [4] *Med. Stage*, i, p. 397.

[5] Dated 1430 or 1431 (p. 398, n. 1). Cf. Brotanek, p. 306; Reyher, pp. 113 f.; it is reprinted by Miss Hammond in *Anglia*, xxii, pp. 367 f.

[6] Chambers, i, p. 398.

intrinsically congenial in this species of composition . . ." [1] Lydgate brought allegory to the pageant; and we may surmise that, being an author of allegorical poems, he did not draw upon the morality, but went straight to literary sources. Allegory and speech he seems to have given to the masque at about the same time.[2] Ward points out that " in England the soil was peculiarly favourable for the cultivation of moral allegory in any and every form ";[3] the morality play grew up in the " second quarter of the fifteenth century; *i. e.*, the reign of Henry VI." [4] This was just the period when we find allegory in mumming and " royal-entry." President MacCracken [5] recalls that allegory was Lydgate's " stock-in-trade poetically," and admits that he may have been responsible for its introduction into the 1432 " royal-entry "; if so, it comes not from the morality but from literature.

Allegory

It is not inconceivable that the personified " moral abstractions " which appear in masque and on pageant-car about 1430, and which owe their presence in these forms of dramatic expression to the monk of Bury, were not without influence on the moralities. It is, however, possible that the latter show an independent development of the same tendencies which brought allegory into pageantry and mumming.

On the other hand, perhaps the author of *The Temple of Glass* (whose place in the history of allegory [6] is not affected by what we may term his " dramatic writings ") derived the allegory he brought to these entertainments from the morality plays. But the chances are that if the moralities did not get their allegory, at least in part, from the mumming and " royal-entry," both drew independently on non-dramatic literature.

Such figures as Lechery, Sensuality, Mundus, and King of the Flesh, which appear in *Mary Magdalene*, are undoubtedly from such literature; but the Seven — or Four — Virtues appeared in pageantry. It is true that we have no instance of their appearance before the visit of Queen Margaret to Coventry in 1456; and

---

[1] *Camb. Hist. Eng. Lit.*, v, p. 23. Cf. Creizenach, in the same history, v, pp. 56 f. Dr. H. R. Patch thinks that " the pageant is not much indebted to the morality. . . . In general the morality would serve rather to make more familiar symbolic figures which were already generally known in the Church, the masque and tournament, and in literature."

[2] We must not stress the matter of dates too much. Even supposing that his first masque was written in 1427, and his first pageant in 1432, it is possible that he conceived the idea of adding allegory to the " royal-entry " before he had a chance to put it into effect; just as Mr. Louis Parker dreamed of giving an historical play at Sherborne a quarter of a century before the opportunity came to him to realize his project.

[3] *Hist. Eng. Dram. Lit.* (1875), i, p. 56.

[4] *Ibid.*, i, p. 58.

[5] Herrig's *Archiv*, cxxvi, p. 99.

[6] Cf. Courthope, i, p. 352, etc. (His ninth chapter is on *The Progress of Allegory*.)

this reception may show an influence from the moralities. I do not agree with Chambers as to the source of the allegorical figures of the 1432 welcome to Henry VI;[1] Lydgate did not need to draw from the moralities (which are more likely to have drawn on the vital abstractions of mumming and pageantry); though it is, of course, possible that Lydgate included allegory in the 1432 show, because he saw that it was a popular feature of contemporary drama.

Evans believes that allegory came into the " disguising " from the morality, with which it was often combined.[2] Does he forget the " mummings " of John Lydgate, where allegory appeared without any such connection ? The whole subject of the relations between mumming, morality and " royal-entry " is a large one; and this is not the place to try to settle it definitely — if that can ever be done.

---

[1] " Such scriptural subjects as John the Baptist of 1392 or the Prophets and Apostles of 1415 pretty obviously come from the miracle-plays. The groups of allegorical figures which greeted Henry VI in 1432 are in no less close a relation to the moralities, which were at that very moment beginning to outstrip the miracle-plays in popularity." Chambers ii, p. 173. It must not be forgotten that, as the guilds gave the later miracle-plays, the properties and characters were at hand for the " royal-entry "; it would not be so natural for them to draw on the moralities. Chambers may be right — it would be hard to prove him wrong; but if Lydgate put the allegorical figures in the 1432 show, as I think he did, he did not, I feel sure, draw on the moralities. There were allegorical figures in the miracle-plays, and it is possible that these contributed their influence. On the general subject of moralities, see Ward, *Hist. Eng. Dram. Lit.* (1899), i, pp. 99 f.; Schelling, *Eliz. Drama*, i, pp. 45 f.; Chambers, ch. xxiii, etc. Schelling (p. 51) says that the earliest references to the morality have been traced to the end of the fourteenth century; but he points out that there were allegorical figures in the *Antichristus* of the twelfth century; that Contemplacio, Mors, and Sapientia appeared in the Hegge plays [he refers to Hohlfeld in *Anglia*, xi, p. 278]; and there were others in the *Play of the Paternoster* acted at York in 1378, as well as in a similar play at Beverley where there were eight pageants, one assigned to Vicious, and the other seven to the Deadly Sins. Ward (p. 101) shows that Hrosvitha gives to some of her characters " names corresponding to the qualities which the behaviour of these characters illustrates," *e. g.*, Fides, Spes, Charitas; that allegory had flourished in England — especially moral allegory — since Cædmon's *Paraphrase* and Gynewulf's *Christ* (where the allegory is close to reminiscences of native mythology). Cf. also Courthope, ch. ix and ch. x (esp. i, pp. 414 f.) where he mentions several miracle-plays which have allegorical characters. Cf. Schelling i p. 73, for remarks on the contribution of earlier pageantry and masking to the drama; on allegory in masque and ballet, see Reyher, pp. 129 f.

[2] Evans, p. xxii; in n. 1 he quotes Collier, ii, p. 237: " The title-page of the interlude of *The Nature of the Four Elements* (1519), after giving directions for the shortening of the piece if desired, provides that ' also yf ye lyst ye may brynge in a dysgysinge.' " Evans notes that disguisings commonly followed moralities or interludes, and that sometimes the masque was brought on in the middle of the performance. As a reward for relieving the tediousness, says he, the masque was imbued with the allegorical character, which remained one of its permanent attributes. Beneath this irony, we see Evans's unfortunate assumption that its contemporary audiences shared his own opinions of the morality; he seems also to forget that the Londoners liked Lydgate's work so well, that they employed him more than once.

An interesting combination of allegory from chivalric literature with morality material may be found in *The Castle of Perseverance*.[1] Humanum Genus, with his companions, the Seven Cardinal Virtues, is besieged by the Seven Deadly Sins under the command of Mundus, Belial, and Caro in the Castle of Perseverance. Whether or no this play came from France is, for us, unimportant. We cannot be sure that the castle did not come straight from the romances — or *via* the " pageantized " Court of Love; but we may note a possible influence of pageantry on this play, since there was a castle in the royal-entry of 1377. If the play came from France, the chances are that the " Court of Love " influence was more direct.

Another early morality, *Mary Magdalene*,[2] has a castle, which also suggests chivalrous literature; and romances undoubtedly fathered such strongholds as the House of Unity, built by Piers Plowman, attacked by Pride and besieged by seven giants representing the Seven Deadly Sins.[3] Both the castle of Magdala and the castle of Perseverance were besieged. I have already[4] referred to Grossteste's castle — where the four towers are the four virtues of the Virgin.

We have noted allegorical and symbolical characters in the tournament; they belong rather to love than to religious allegory. I think we may safely say that this love-allegory came directly from the literature of chivalry to the tournament, whence it may have been taken, and adapted, by these moralities; but perhaps they borrowed it directly from the romances. Mention has been made of the coating of religious significance given to this material in *Piers Plowman*; I may add a reference to the Castle of Care, in this, one of the earliest examples of an allegorical poem composed in English.

Courthope distinguishes between " the chivalrous form of allegory " — such as that which Lydgate wrote (" it was developed by Lydgate," are Courthope's words) — and " two opposite modes in which the monastic form of allegory can be used as an instrument of religious thought."[5] The castle of Perseverance shows a combination of the chivalrous and monastic allegory, which are often found combined in pageant and masque as well.

---

[1] MS., c. 1425. See *The Macro Plays* (ed. Farmer), no. 3; and *English Miracle Plays, Moralities and Interludes* (ed. Pollard). Cf. also Collier, ii, p. 279, and Ward, *Hist. Eng. Dram. Lit.* (1875), i, p. 61. The play may belong to an earlier period, for Mr. Pollard (p. xxxii) thinks the scribe who copied the MS. in the first half of the fifteenth century copied it from an earlier MS., "at such an interval that it was no longer possible to get at any alternative source in order to correct obvious blunders." Ward suggests a possible French origin of this play, for the castle is described as "strenger thanne any in Fraunce," and there is a French morality of 1506 which treats the same subject less elaborately.

[2] Cf. Courthope, i, p. 416; Chambers, ii, p. 155.

[3] Cf. Courthope, i, p. 225. These giants seem to be "allegorized" early inhabitants, imported from the romance directly.

[4] Above, p. 80.

[5] Courthope, i, p. 351.

THE DÉBAT

From earliest times the *débat* has appeared in the masque, especially when the latter tended toward the interlude. I need here refer to but two occasions — the dialogue which Lydgate wrote, telling the complaint of the " rude uplandish people," and their wives' " boisterous answer," [1] and the 1528 dialogue which framed a mock tourney.[2] But the *débat* exerted little influence on pageantry. This is due chiefly to the circumstances of presentation. Few of the multitude could hear what was spoken from each platform; the speakers addressed king or mayor directly. The nearest approach to a *débat* in pageantry is the *Judgment of Paris*,[3] which is almost a play. Rarely does dialogue intrude into the pageant, and when it does, it is primitive. The strife between Envy and Virtue in Dekker's 1612 Show, as well as that between Error and Truth in Middleton's Show for the next year,[4] remind us more of the " barrier." The dialogues called " interludes," which were sometimes sung at the Lord Mayor's banquets toward the end of the seventeenth century,[5] are not unlike the *débat*; but they took place in the hall during the feast, and cannot be considered part of the pageant. The reason why *débat*, interlude, and play were rarely utilized by pageantry is obvious.[6]

§ 3. GROWTH OF THE MASQUE

Informal dancing at court seems to be an old tradition, as it was in many country houses.[7] We read in the *Record of Bluemantle Pursuivant*,[8] that in September, 1472, " the Kynge dyd to be impareled on the far syde of the quadrant ij chambers richeley hanged wᵗ clothes of Arras, and wᵗ Beddes of astate; and when he [9] had spoken wᵗ the Kinges good grace and the quene, he was accompanied to

---

[1] See below, p. 112.   [2] See below, p. 116.

[3] At Edinburgh in 1503, and at London in 1533. (See below, chapter iii.)

[4] Cf. ch. vi. Envy's " forlorn castle " is reminiscent of earlier structures.

[5] See ch. vi, below.

[6] Occasionally, as we shall see, there are short dialogues in the Lord Mayor's Shows — but they are rare, and have no element of the *débat*.

[7] Cf. *The Paston Letters* (ed. Gairdner), iii, p. 314 (cited by Reyher, p. 5). Under date of 24 December, (?) 1484, Margery Paston wrote to her husband John: "Plese it you to wete that I sent your eldest sunne to my Lady Morlee to have knolage wat sports wer husyd in her hows in Kyrstemesse next folloyng aftyr the decysse of my lord, her husbond; and sche seyd that ther wer non dysgysyngs, ner harpyng, ner lutyng, ner syngyn, ner non lowde dysports, but pleyng at the tabyllys, and schesse, and cards. Sweche dysports sche gave her folkys leve to play and non odyr." [If, as Gairdner says in a note, the lady died 4 November, 1484, perhaps this letter should be dated 1483. Chambers, i, p. 398, refers to this, and says that Lady Morley forbade disguisings in her house at Christmas after her husband's death in 1476.]

[8] Reprinted from Cotton MS. Julius C. vi, folios 255–259, collated with Addl. MS. 6113, folios 101–107, by Kingsford, *Eng. Hist. Lit.*, pp. 379 f.

[9] The ambassador of the Duke of Burgundy, Lord Gruthuse. The king is, of course, Edward IV.

his chamber by me lorde Chamberlein. . . . When they had sopte, my lord chamberleyn had hym againe to ye Kinges chamber, and incontinent the Kinge had hym to ye quenes chamber, where she sat plainge w^t her ladyes . . . and Daunsing. . . . Also ye kinge daunsed w^t my lady Elizabethe, his eldest doughter . . . ."[1]

Another dance followed a banquet the next evening, " and aboute ix of the clocke the king and the quene w^t her ladies and gentlewomen brought ye sayde lorde Grutehuse to iij chambers of Pleasance . . ."[2] — his apartments. In the morning he left Windsor for Westminster.

From dancing, to dancing in character, to allegory, the development was easy; from the early " presenter," who explained the allegorical significance of the characters, to the " rude vpplandishe people complayninge on their wyves with the boystrus answere of ther wyues deuysed by lidgate," was not a hard step. The masque, which soon developed singing and dialogue, at times approached the *débat* and the interlude.[3]

In 3 Henry VII, " on New Yeres daye at nyght there was a goodly disguysinge & also this cristmas ther wer many & dyvers Playes."[4] It was in the reign of this king that the mumming grew into the masque. In 1494 pageant-car and disguising were united: " . . . and that nyght in Westm halle was a great bankett & wasshall of lx dysshes for the Kinge & as many for the Quene. Where there was a playe wth a pageant of St George w^t a castle. And also xij Lords, Knights, Esquires w^t xij Ladies dysguysed wch daunced after the wasshall wch beinge endyd & the voyde [5] & all was don by x of the clocke."[6] Another account of this event differs in some details, and fails to mention the pageant or castle.[7]

---

[1] See Kingsford, p. 386.   [2] P. 387.

[3] Cf. Chambers, ii, p. 201 and n. 2. On the *débat* in masque and ballet, see Reyher, pp. 130 f.

[4] Cotton MS. Julius B. xii, fol. 46 b, copied in Addl. MS. 7048, fol. 254 b.

[5] Halliwell's *Dictionary of Archaic and Provincial Words* (*s. v. voide*) defines this word as *last course*. Cf. Addl. MS. 4712, fol. 20: " . . . and also they that woll supe in the seyd vygill [of St. George] schall wer the same [mantles] at super and the order also vnto the woyde. . . ."

[6] Addl. MS. 6113, fol. 169, cited (as Harl. MS.) by Reyher, p. 349, who also refers to Kingsford, *Chron. Lond.*, p. 200.

[7] Cotton MS. Vitellius A. xiv, fol. 148 b (printed in Kingsford, *Chron. Lond.*, p. 200), records: " And this yere [1494] was a Roiall feste kept at Westmynster by the Kyng, on the Twelvith day, where dyned the Mayr and his brethir, and at nyght was a disgysyng of xij ladyes and xij gentilmen. And all the greate hall was hanged w^t Arras, and staged Round abowte w^t Tymber, that the people myght easely behold. And after the disgysyng was doon, the Kyng was serued with lx disshes of dyuers confeccions . . . ." (This seems to be a contemporary record of events narrated — see Kingsford, p. ix.)

There is mention of what seems to be a pageant of some sort accompanying a dance in Olaus Magnus, Book xv, ch. vii, where he notes "another kind of dance or play, where, upon a woodden Engine men are carried in the ayr by the motion of wheels: or else they sport otherwise, being very nimble of body: as with spears, about which they will turn themselves . . . ."

Cf. on the early court festivals, C. W. Wallace, *Evolution Eng. Drama* (1912). He mentions (from Harl. MS. 69, fol. 34 b) that children, as mermaids, sang in Christmas "disports" in

After his progress through Paris in 1498, Louis XII held a splendid banquet: " en la dicte salle auoit trois grands escharfaults, sur lesquels estoyent trompetes, clairons, & haults menestriers, lesquels faisoit si bel ouyr que sembloit vn Paradis." [1] These scaffolds seem to have been only platforms for the musicians.

1501 — THE WEDDING MASQUE OF ARTHUR AND THE PRINCESS OF SPAIN

Although it is called a " disguising," the celebration following the wedding of Prince Arthur and Katherine of Spain contains the chief characteristics of a masque.

" Item that Jaques Hault and Wm Pawne to bee appointed . . . to devise and prepare disguisings and some morisques after the best manner they can whereof they shall haue warninge by my L Chamberlein." [2]

When the king and queen were seated in the hall, " then began and entered this most goodly and pleasant disguising, convayed and showed in pageants proper and subtile, of whom the first was a Castle right cunningly devised, sett upon certaine wheeles and drawne into the said great hall of fower great beasts with chaines of gold . . . which every each of the which foure beastes were two men, one in the fore part, and another in the hinder part. . . . And thus this castle was . . . convayed from the nether part of the hall. . . . There were within the same Castle disguised viij goodly and fresh ladyes, looking out of the windowes of the same, and in the foure corners of this Castle were iiii turretts . . . in the which . . . was a little child apparelled like a maiden." [3] The children sang as this pageant moved up the hall.

Then came a ship, with masts, sail, and tackle all complete. The maskers who were aboard, " in their countenances, speaches and demeanor, used and behaved

---

1490 — but it is not clear whether there was, on this occasion, a pageantic background. The disguise is enough, however, to suggest pageantry.

[1] Godefroy, p. 63.

[2] Cotton MS. Vitellius, c. xi, fol. 125 b; Harl. MS. 69, fol. 43 b. Cf. the expenses for this occasion in Egerton MS. 2358, cited by Reyher, p. 333, n. 2; he also refers to the preparations at Westminster Hall recorded in Cotton MS. Vit., c. xi, fol. 124 b, et seq.

The description of this disguising may be found in Harl. MS. 69, fol. 29 b, et seq. (printed in the Shaks. Soc. Papers [ed. Goodwin, 1844], i, pp. 47 f., and in Reyher, pp. 500 f.). A contemporary account is also printed in Antiq. Rep., ii, pp. 296 f. Cf., for mention of this occasion, Collier, i, p. 58, cited by Chambers, i, pp. 398 f.; Brotanek, pp. 26 f.; Reyher, pp. 17 and 351 f.; Evans, p. xvi; Schelling, i, pp. 74 f.; etc.

This affair is not to be confused with the " royal-entry " which took place on the princess's arrival. (See chapter iii.)

A song, in parts, sung like dialogue, is reprinted by Reyher, pp. 116 f., from Padelford's Early Sixteenth Century Lyrics; he suggests (p. 118) that it was rendered at this disguising.

[3] It is, perhaps, not worth noting that Chambers, in his résumé of this disguising, places the lady who is dressed like the Princess of Spain in this castle, rather than in the ship where she belongs. (Cf. Chambers, i, p. 398, and Goodwin, p. 49.)

themselves after the manner and guise of mariners, and there cast their anchors somewhat besides the said castle; in the which shippe there was a goodly and a faire ladye in her, apparelled like unto the Princesse of Spain "; two ambassadors " calling themselves Hope and Desire " left the ship and went to the castle with their banners, " from knights of the Mount of Love unto the ladyes within the Castle, making a great instance in the behalfe of the said knights for the intent to attaine the favour of the said ladyes present; . . . the said ladyes gave their small answer of utterly refuse, and knowledge of any such company . . ." The ambassadors, therewith angry, threatened an assault on the castle.

" Incontinent came in the third Pageant, in likeness of a great hill or moun-taine in whom there were inclosed viij goodly knights, naming themselves Knights of the Mount of Love, the which passed through the said Hall towards the King's grace, and there they took their standing upon the other side of the shippe." The two ambassadors reported the disdain and refusal with which the ladies had met them; the knights assaulted the castle, and captured it; the ladies yielded themselves, and descended, " and submitted themselves to the power grace and will of those noble knights, being right freshly disguised and the ladyes also, fower of them after the English fashion, and the other foure after the manner of Spaine, daunced together divers and many goodly daunces, and in the time of their dauncing the three Pageants, the Castle, the Shippe and the Mountaine moved and departed. The same wise the disguisers rehersed, as well the knights as the ladyes after certaine leasure of their solace and disport avoyded and vanished out of their sight and presence," whereupon the royal party themselves fell to dancing. " This disguising royall thus ended, beganne the voydee to enter in the manner of a bankett . . ."

This masque — for masque it is — shows an obvious debt to the " Court of Love "; the pageants recall the Fishmongers' ship of 1313, the Goldsmiths' castle of 1377, and the " wilderness " of John the Baptist in 1392, all of which had numerous descendants.

1503 — REVELS AT THE BETROTHAL OF MARGARET

Margaret was betrothed to James IV of Scotland (for whom the Earl of Both-well acted as proxy) at Richmond in January, 1502–03. On the day after the ceremony, after the prizes for the jousts had been given, " there was in the Hall a goodly pageant curiously wrought with Fenestrallis, having many Lights bren-ning in the same, in manner of a Lantron, out of wich sorted divers Sortes of Morisks. Also a very goodly Disguising of six Gentlemen and six Gentlewomen which danced divers Dances." [1]

We shall not collect here the many instances of the disguising, or early form of the masque, with which Brewer, Hall, and Holinshed abound. Suffice it for us

---

[1] A contemporary account, in Leland, *Collectanea*, iv, p. 263.

to notice that even before 1501 the masque had drawn on the pageant for its cars; and the seed was planted which led to the elaborate court-festivals of the Tudor century. " For justs, and tourneys, and barriers," writes Bacon, " the glories of them are chiefly in the chariots, wherein the challengers make their entry; especially if they be drawn with strange beasts, as lions, bears, camels, and the like; or in the devices of their entrance; or in the bravery of their liveries; ... " [1]

The 1501 disguising shows the " Court of Love " theme complete; the tournament is recalled by the storming of the castle; that the castle represents the ladies' hearts is suggested by the names of the two ambassadors, Hope and Desire. The ladies will not yield without some pressure, but they fall before the determined attack of the cavaliers.

Evans distinguishes between the *entertainment*, the nucleus of which was a speech of welcome; the *masque*, the nucleus of which was a dance; and *barriers*, the nucleus of which was a sham tournament.[2] In 1501 we find elements of all three at a court disguising; above all, for us, is the importance of the pageant-cars, which form a background against which the symbolic love-allegory is acted out.[3]

1511 — ALLEGORICAL PAGEANTS IN THE EARLY YEARS OF HENRY VIII

In the early years of the reign of Henry VIII we find a number of allegorical pageants which suggest the symbolism of the spectacles — diversified with dance and song — described by the chroniclers.[4]

At a joust of honor held by Henry at Whitehall, 12 and 13 February, 1511, was constructed " a forest . . . 26 feet long, 16 feet broad, 19 feet high, garnished with artificial ' hawthorns, oaks, maples, hazels, birches . . . with beasts and birds embossed of sundry fashion, with foresters sitting and going on the top of the same, and a castle on the said forest, with a maiden sitting thereby with a garland, and a lion of great stature and bigness, with an antelope of like proportion after his kind [5] drawing the said pageant or forest, conducted with men in wodwoos' [6] apparel, and two maidens sitting on the same two beasts; in the

---

[1] Bacon, Essay xxxvii, *Of Masques and Triumphs.*

[2] Evans, p. xii, n. 1. Cf. Schelling, ii, p. 94.

[3] On the " Minneburg " see Brotanek, pp. 27 f., 325 f. " Durch den Rosenroman gelangte die Vorstellung bald nach Italien. Die *Castelli d'Amore* waren in Venedig, Padua, Treviso (1314) und Ferrara ,beliebte Schauspiele." (P. 325.) We have already noted how this kind of thing came into England from France.

[4] Cf. Hall, *passim*; Brewer, ii, 1495, 1497, 1499, 1501, 1509; iii, 1558 (cited by Chambers, i, p. 400). Cf. also C. W. Wallace, *Evol. Eng. Drama* (1912), pp. 41 ff., and Reyher and Brotanek for mention of these pageant-cars in masques; many of them were prepared by Richard Gibson.

[5] Cf. the lion and the antelope of the 1415 entry of Henry V into London (chapter iii).

[6] Wild-men's; cf. above, p. 74.

which forest were four men of arms, riding, that issued out at times appointed; and on every one of the 4 quarters of the forest were the arms of the four knights challengers . . .' " [1]

" Thys forrest or pagent after the ewsans had into Westminster Gret Hall, and by the king's gard and other gentyllmen rent, brokyn, and by fors karryed away." [2]

One of the knights who took part in this joust was the king himself, who assumed the name, Cure loial; the other three " chiualers de la Forrest saluigne " were Bon espoir, Bon voloire and Valiaunt desire. [3] These names, as well as those given various pageants, show the influence of chivalric allegory, as exerted through the tournament on these entertainments: the " Dangerus Fortrees " was shown at Greenwich, 9 March, 1511; the " Golldyn Arber in the Arche-yerde of Plesyer " appeared at Whitehall on 13 February of the same year. The " Ryche Mount " — " a rock or mountain of gold and precious stones . . . planted with broom to signify Plantagenet, and also with red and white roses " [4] — was exhibited at Greenwich, 6 January, 1513; the " Pavilion of the Parlous Place " was provided for the revels of 6 January, 1515, at Greenwich; the " Garden of Hope," or " de Esperance," for those of 6 January, 1516. [5]

1528 — A MASQUE WITH DÉBAT, TOURNEY, AND PAGEANT-CAR

In 1528 there was an entertainment at court, whereat " two persones plaied a dialog theffect wherof was whether riches were better thē loue, and when they could not agre vpon a conclusion eche called in thre knightes, all armed, thre of them woulde haue entred the gate of the Arche in the middel of the chambre & the other iii resisted, & sodēly betweene the six knightes, out of the Arche fell doune a bar all gilte, at the whiche barre the six knightes fought a fair battail, and then thai were departed, and so went out of the place: then came in an olde man with a siluer berd, and he concluded that loue & riches both be necessarie for princes (that is to saie) by loue to be obeied and serued, and with riches to rewarde his louers and frendes and with this conclusion the dialogue ended." [6]

---

[1] Brewer, iv, 1494. It may be noted that in the account of expenses for this occasion (*ibid.*, 1495) the companion of the lion is sometimes called " antelope," sometimes " olyvant."

[2] Brewer, iv, 1495. Says Hall, p. 519: " In the meane season the pagiaunt was conueyed to the ende of the place, there to tary till the daunces were finished, and so to have receyued the lordes and ladies againe, but sodanly the rude people ranne to the pagent, and rent, tare and spoyled the pagent, so that the lord Stuard nor the head officers could not cause them to abstaine, excepte they shoulde haue foughten and drawen bloude, and so was this pagent broken."

[3] Hall, p. 517.

[4] Brewer, iv, 1499.

[5] On these see Brewer. (Hall, p. 526, mentions the Fortress Dangerous; for a " Rich Mount " at Richmond on Twelfth Night, 1511, see pp. 516 f.)

[6] Hall, p. 723; (Strutt, *Sports*, p. 121, quotes it from Hall).

Immediately after the dialogue, " a rich mount " in the shape of a fortress was discovered; on it sat eight lords, richly apparelled, who descended, chose partners " and danced divers dances." Princess Mary with seven ladies then emerged from a cave; they were all " apparelled after the romayne fashion." They danced with the eight lords of the mount; then suddenly entered six more masquers dressed " after the fashion of Iseland, and these persons had visers with syluer berdes, so that they were not knowne: these Maskers tooke Ladies and daunsed lustely about the place." Then the King and the Viscount of Touraine joined the revellers, dressing with six others after the Venetian fashion; they danced long with the ladies, and afterwards the queen plucked off the king's masque, and so did the ladies the visors of the lords; and the king gave the viscount his own masking apparel, as well as that which the viscount himself had worn, " which were very riche, for the whiche he thanked hym." A banquet followed, and the gaiety lasted till sunrise.

1572 — A MASQUE AT WHITEHALL

In June, 1572, there was a masque at Whitehall which will serve us as an example of the continued use of pageant-cars in these entertainments. " Apollo, the Nine Muses (in a chariot), Lady Peace, Argus, and Discord were presented. . . . The castle for Lady Peace or Lady Plenty, and the prison in which Discord is watched by Argus, are mentioned in the list of properties in 1572." [1] This was given in honor of the Duke of Montmorencie.

1634 — A PAGEANTIC MASQUE BY SHIRLEY FOR THE INNS OF COURT

Preceding Shirley's *The Triumph of Peace*, which was performed at Whitehall on 3 February, 1633–34, by the Inns of Court, was a procession; it started early in the evening from Ely House, Holborn, and went to Whitehall *via* Chancery Lane.[2] " It consisted for the most part of a number of mounted cavaliers, attended by pages and torchbearers, and followed by trumpeters and truncheon men. At the rear of the procession came four triumphal chariots, each drawn by four horses." [3] In them " were mounted the grand Masquers, one of the foure

---

[1] Fleay, *Hist. Stage*, p. 19. Cf. Cunningham, *The Revels at Court*, pp. 18 f. (Fleay considers this a modified form of a 1562 masque.) Cf. *Prog. Q. Eliz.*, i, pp. 305 f., for the entertainments in honor of the Duke of Montmorencie; there were barriers at Whitehall on 14 June; on the 18th he was stalled Knight of the Garter, and on the 28th returned to France.

[2] On this masque, see especially Bulstrode Whitelocke, *Memorials* (London, 1732), pp. 19 f.; W. J. Lawrence, *The Mounting of the Stuart Masques* in the *English Illustrated Magazine* for November, 1903, pp. 174 f.; James Shirley, *The Triumph of Peace*, A masque presented by the Foure Honourable Houses, or Innes of Court . . . at White Hall, February the third, 1633. . . . (London, 1633.) Mr. Lawrence's article, above cited, was revised and reprinted as *The Mounting of the Carolan Masques*, in *The Elizabethan Playhouse and Other Studies* (1912).

[3] Lawrence, *op. cit.* On p. 176, he identifies Inigo Jones's drawing of a chariot, in the Salvin collection at the Royal Institute of British Architects, as one of those belonging to this masque.

Houses in every Chariot, seated within an halfe Ovall, with a glorious Canopy over their heads, all bordered with silver Fringe, and beautified with Plumes of Feathers on the top . . . "   The four great chariots were " all after the Romane forme, adorned with much embossed and carved workes, and each of them wrought with Silver, and his seuerall colour. They were mounted on carriages, the Spring-trees, Pole and Axle-trees, the Charioter's seate and standers, wheeles, with the fellyes, spokes and naves all wrought with Silver and their severall colour." [1]

The following characters in masque and antimasque took part in the procession: Fancy, Opinion and Confidence, Jollity and Laughter, six " Proiectors," — the first a Jockey, the second a country fellow, the third, " a grimme Philosophicall fac'd fellow," the fifth a " Physition," and the sixth a seaman. After forty on foot, and a hundred cavaliers, came the cars. [2]

Whitelocke and Mr. Edward Hyde were the members of the committee on the masque chosen from the Middle Temple. Mr. Simon Ivy and Mr. Laws were selected to write the music for the masque, [3] and their success was marked; for " the Queen . . . was so taken with this Show and Masque, that she desired to see it acted over again: whereupon an Intimation being given to the Lord Mayor of *London*, he invited the King and Queen, and the Inns of Court Masquers to the City, and entertained them with all State and Magnificence, at *Merchant-Taylors* Hall. Thither marched through the City the same Show that went before to *Whitehall* . . ." and the masque was repeated. Some of the " musicke " got £100 apiece, " so that the whole Charge of the Musick came to about a thousand Pounds ": one hundred suits at £100 apiece came to £10,000: " the Charge of the whole *Masque* which was born by the Societies, and by the particular Members of it, was accounted to be above one hundred and twenty thousand Pounds." [4]

1662 — A Pageantic Masque at Munich

A gigantic Atlas-like figure, a huge car drawn by lions, a polycephalic dragon spouting flames, various animals upright and bearing torches, Centaurs blowing trumpets, knights, etc., are on a plate in the second volume of Baron Taylor's collection presented by Fairholt to the Society of Antiquaries. Before the print the donor has written: " This and the following plates are from an Italian Drama acted at Munich in 1662 and entitled ' Antiopa Justificata,' by P. P. Bissari. It was performed at the feast held to commemorate the birth of a son to the Elector Ferdinand." The plates show castles, cars, giants, animals, torch-

---

[1] Shirley's pamphlet, pp. 4 and 5, cited by Lawrence.

[2] See Shirley's pamphlet.

[3] Full details of masque and procession are given by Whitelocke. Shirley, it may be recalled, was a member of Grays Inn.

[4] B. Whitelocke, *Memorials*, pp. 21 and 22.

bearers, knights and other pageantic material; and if it is a "drama" it shows clearly that it has absorbed much pageantry. The arrangement of the figures in the plates is processional; *drama* is probably less exact a word for this entertainment than *masque*.

PAGEANT AND MASQUE

With the advent of dancers who represent allegorical or symbolical figures, such as Hope and Desire in 1501, the "soul" of pageantry comes into the masque. At first, the masque was a meaningless masquerade — the "raw-material" of a soul, if you will, but not a soul. Once allegory, symbolism, and mythology — represented by living persons — were admitted to the masque, it began its development, reaching the heights which it attained in the days of Ben Jonson. But the poet was not the only important figure; there was also the engineer. Inigo Jones was quite as necessary a personage as Ben Jonson in the success of these masques; hence a quarrel.[1] Very little, comparatively, of the enormous sums spent on masques in the Jacobean and Carolian times, went to the poet; the cost was due to the costumes and setting.

When the pageant-car was borrowed by the disguising, the seed was planted from which grew the elaborate background of the later masque under Jones, just as the parleyings between ladies and ambassadors, and the "sweet and harmonious" singing of the children, lie at the roots of the speeches and lyrics of the Jonsonian productions.[2]

When, with Charles II, the drama was also restored, the elaborate masques of earlier Stuart reigns were remembered by the court circle; many of the plays — under the new name, "opera" — bore a close resemblance to the older masques.[3] It is not surprising that scenery was demanded; and scenery came.[4]

---

[1] Evans, p. xlvi.

[2] "The word *Pageant*, which came finally to mean a spectacle or show, such as the Lord Mayor's, originally signified a scaffold . . . and it was only necessary to convert the pageant into a castle, a mountain or a ship, and wheel it into the hall, in order to furnish a practicable scene for the disguising." (Evans, p. xvii.)

At the Christmas revels at Greenwich in 1515, the gentlemen of the chapel, who accompanied the children on the "Pavyllyon un the Plas Parlous," "first declared the intent of the pageant by process of speech." (Brewer, iv, 1501.)

"Ainsi, au début du xvie siècle, les mascarades de la cour ont quelquefois un sujet emprunté à la littérature de l'époque. Il détermine ou explique le choix des costumes et des machines, sert à relier entre eux les divers éléments du divertissement et en fait un tout. . . . Il n'est pas encore question d'un dialogue à proprement parler; mais l'influence du drame se fait d'ores et déjà nettement sentir. Le sujet est, en outre, parfois adapté aux circonstances. Enfin il y a un élément lyrique, de petits poèmes chantés, qui sont d'ordinaire des compliments ou des vœux adressés aux souverains." (Reyher, p. 118; cf. Evans, p. xxii, for the growth of speech in the masque, and the influence of the contemporary drama on it.)

[3] Cf. Reyher, p. 473, etc., for the history of the early opera in England: esp. n. 1: "A la Restauration, quand les décors furent définitivement adoptés, il fallut rebâtir les théâtres."

[4] On this whole subject, see Reyher, ch. v (pp. 332–383) where it is treated in more detail

" Il ne semble pas qu'il y ait eu de décoration à proprement parler," says Reyher, speaking of the theatre; " elle se réduisait à des accessoires, à des ' practicables,' et il n'en est pas en Angleterre comme en France, où l'Hôtel de Bourgogne hérite de la mise en scène du théâtre du Moyen-Age." [1] Again: " Il serait . . . exact de dire que les ' Pageants ' et la décoration des ballets marquent, dans l'histoire de la mise en scène, la transition du Moyen-Age à l'adoption des décors dans les théâtres publics. Ce sont les fêtes de la cour, les ' masques,' bien plus encore que les représentations dramatiques, qui continuent et perfectionnent cette mise en scène, et cela est si vrai que les auteurs de la Restauration font remonter l'origine de leur décoration aux ballets. ' Quant aux décors et aux machines, dit Richard Flecknoe, peu après 1660, ce ne sont pas des inventions nouvelles; notre ' masque ' et quelques unes de nos pièces (quoique ce fût alors l'exception) en avaient eu jadis d'aussi beaux et même de plus beaux que ceux d'aujourd'hui . . .' " [2]

" There can be little doubt that the later Stuart masques, remote as they were by nature from the ordinary run of dramatic performances, had a certain measure of influence upon the scenic system of the Restoration theatres," says Mr. Lawrence.[3] Mr. Blomefield remarks, " on historical grounds, Inigo Jones's designs for masques are nearly as important as his architectural work, for he completely revolutionized the scenery of the stage." [4] He notes performances of Heywood's *Love's Mistake* at court in 1636 when Jones changed the scenery for every act; and of Cartwright's *Royal Slave*, produced before the king and queen at Oxford, in 1637, where Jones provided eight sets.[5] Everyone admits the strong influence

---

than we need to give here. He deals with masque as well as with the drama proper. Cf. also George F. Reynolds, *Some Principles in Elizabethan Staging*, in *Mod. Philol.* for April and June, 1905; and W. J. Lawrence, *The Elizabethan Playhouse and Other Studies* (1912).

[1] Reyher, p. 382.

[2] Reyher, p, 382, citing Richard Flecknoe, *A Discourse of the English Stage* (at the end of *Love's Kingdom, a Pastoral Tragi-Comedy*); he also quotes Davenant, *The Playhouse to be Let* (c. 1663), act i:

" We'll let this theatre and build another where At a cheaper rate, we may have room for Scenes." Pepys (*Diary*, 15 August, 1661, cited by Reyher, p. 383) records: " To the Opera, which begins again today with ' The Witts,' never acted yet with scenes . . . and indeed it is a most excellent play, and admirable scenes."

[3] W. J. Lawrence, *The Mounting of the Stuart Masques*, in *the English Illustrated Magazine*, for November, 1903 (illustrated), p. 174.

[4] Reginald T. Blomefield, M.A., writing in *The Portfolio* for May, 1889 on *Inigo Jones* (see pp. 88 f.; a second part, which concerns us less, appeared in June, 1889, pp. 113 f.—both are illustrated).

[5] Blomefield, p. 91. He discusses Jones's stage machinery, and notes that in the Lansdown MSS. in the Brit. Mus. are eight authentic drawings by Inigo Jones, which throw a valuable light on how he managed his scenery. Until after the Restoration, scenery was confined to masques and court performances; " the use of movable scenery was the most important improvement introduced by Inigo Jones, but there can be little doubt that he greatly developed the mechanical resources of the stage all round."

of Italian pageantry on Jones; but the interesting thing for us to note is that a foundation already existed in England, upon which he could build. The development from the 1494 pageant-car to Inigo Jones and Gordon Craig, Max Reinhardt, Granville Barker, and Sam Hume, is unbroken.

The pageant-car was not the only gift of pageantry to the masque. Animals[1] — especially the lion and the antelope — and " wild-men " appear in the early disguisings. Undoubtedly heraldry influenced both " royal-entry " and masque to a large extent — not in presenting animals, which were a gift of folk-custom, but in suggesting which animals to present. Romance also played its part here, as we have seen; undoubtedly animals often came directly to the masque from the romances. But the stimulation and suggestion of the pageant seem to be underneath all.

In 1522 Henry VIII gave a masquerade for Charles V at which appeared foresters and " woodwos " or savage men.[2] The " meskeler and revels " on this occasion were devised by William Kornyche, gentleman of the chapel; and there were used " 240 ells of canvas from the king's store, for wodwos' garments, covering the pageant, and a stuffed body." [3] Does this " stuffed body " refer, perhaps, to a giant ?

I have already mentioned [4] the embroidered knights and ladies on the bards of the sovereigns' chargers at the tournament preceding this mumming; I may recall here the embroidered figures of " wodewoses " on the " harnesses " of Edward III.[5] The royal-entry must have had some influence on the indoor revels of the court; and, as we should expect, these borrowings from civic shows are adapted to their courtly surroundings. Instead of symbolizing trade, animals realize the romance; Bible, folk-tradition and moral-allegory give way to the love-allegory of the " Court of Love." The wild-man is softened to a forester, or metamorphosed into a wood-spirit, just as the " wilderness " of John the Baptist was changed to a " royal mount."

§ 4. CONCLUSION

I have elsewhere reviewed [6] the discussion of Hall's famous passage which led many writers to assume that the masque came to England from Italy. Chambers, Brotanek, Evans, Sörgel, Reyher, and Scherm have dealt with the matter in some detail. Just what " after the maner of Italie " may mean, is still obscure; but one thing is plain: that the masque is little indebted to Italy for its ingredients; all the elements — masquerade, disguising, pageant-car, song —

---

[1] On animals in Italian masques, see Burckhardt, ii, p. 143.

[2] " A favourite character at revels " notes Martin in *Archæologia*, xlvii, p. 315.

[3] Brewer, iii, 2305 [pt. 2, pp. 976 and 977] cited in *Archæologia*, xlvii, p. 315.

[4] See above, p. 97.   [5] *Archæologia*, xxxi, pp. 41 and 122.

[6] See my paper entitled " After the manner of Italy " in *Journ. Eng. Germ. Philol.* for July, 1916.

which go to make up the form of art so popular at the courts of Elizabeth and the earlier Stuart kings, were in existence — had even been combined — before Hall's famous passage was written. It used to be thought that England owed the masque to Italy; and undoubtedly, even before the time of Inigo Jones, there were Italian influences which made for elaboration of music, dance, and scenery. But the seed had been planted — had even begun to sprout — before the warm Italian sun shone upon it.[1]

There is no need of tracing the development of the tournament into the " barrier " — or of following the progress of the masque any farther than we have done.[2] Whatever developments there were during the sixteenth century, come from materials already gathered together early in the reign of Henry VIII.

We have seen how the tournament became a " soft and silken war " — how the " rex de Vertbois," Tatars, Pope, and Cardinals originated a long line of disguised characters that led to the Bon voloire, Bon espoir, Valiaunt desire and Cure loial of the 1511 jousts, and to the four Foster-children of Desire in 1581. Disguising in the tournament gave way to a " dressing-up in character," and the characters chosen were drawn largely from the allegory of the " Court of Love " — perhaps through an influence from Hainault.

We have also seen how the " disguising " developed at the Christmas celebrations of the Court in the reign of Edward III;[3] how this gradually became a dance of masked courtiers, which may have been influenced by folk-mumming. The more formal occasions, for which preparations had been made, and in which the participants remained distinct from the spectators, were called " disguisings "; the word " mumming " was kept for the less formal dances, for which cavaliers entered masked, and chose their partners from among the court ladies.

Lydgate seems to have introduced verse into the disguisings; and he also contributed allegorical symbolism to these festivals. Although it is possible that this allegory may be due — at least in part — to the morality-plays, it seems unnecessary to suppose that Lydgate drew on them. The allegorical castle came into the " royal-entry " in 1377, from the " Court of Love," — probably under French influence; it is found in France as early as 1330. It seems to have been borrowed by the morality-play (which may have absorbed it direct from such literature as

---

[1] On the masque in Italy, see Symonds, *Shakspere's Predecessors*, ch. ix (pp. 317 f.); cf. also Ward, i, pp. 145 f.; Burckhardt, § 5, esp. ch. viii (ii, pp. 132–156). The masque itself is outside our field.

[2] Tournaments, tilts, citizens' musters, and " barriers " were common enough through the reigns of the Tudor sovereigns. The interested reader is referred to Hall and Holinshed, *passim*; and (for those of Elizabeth's reign) to *Prog. Q. Eliz.*, i, pp. 63, 71, 73, 80, 82, 276, 296; ii, pp. 312, 330, 411; iii, pp. 41, 195, 214, 262, 309, 318, 355, 364, 371, 389, 498, 570, 586, etc. One or two, of particular pageantic interest, will be noticed in chapter iv (*Elizabethan Pageantry*), infra.

[3] There is at least one example of a disguised — possibly an allegorical or symbolical — figure in Scotland as early as 1285. Cf. above, p. 103.

the *Chasteau d'Amour* of Grosseteste); and latter still by the "disguising." When this latter borrowing was made, the seed was planted for the elaborate scenic background of the masque, which, in Restoration days, was adopted by the theatre.

Animals and "wild-men" appear in the early masquerades, and seem to indicate further borrowings from pageantry. One must remember, however, that the "wild-man" is rather a forester than a buffoon in these dances; and this suggests the possibility of a literary, rather than a pageantic, origin. Occasionally, however, a car is dragged into the hall by "wild-men," so that we may assume that the pageant contributed something toward the figure in the masque; and it is not impossible that the masque exerted an influence on the character in the pageant. Romantic literature may have influenced both.

Whatever Hall meant by his oft-quoted and much-discussed passage, it seems clear that England owes little to Italy for her masque. The native product was later polished as a result of Italian influence; and Inigo Jones brought as much from contemporary Italy to enrich the masque scenically as did Ben Jonson — from an earlier Italy — to enrich its lines. But the foundation of the masque was English, and all the elements which compose it were united in the time of Henry VII.

Music, of course, is a necessary adjunct of the dance; and it is unlikely that the "disguising" took muscians from the pageant.

By the time of "bluff King Hal," we find an elaborately developed form of entertainment drawing material from masquerade, tournament, and pageant. It is noteworthy that the tournament had, at times, a processional feature;[1] but this is probably an independent development of the same causes which underlie pageantic processions. With the car, however, the pageant gave a processional feature to the "disguising," in that one group of figures surrounding a car danced, and then gave way to the next[2] — or, as in 1501, more than one car entered the hall. It is probable that the development of this in English and Italian masques was independent — in Italy it arose from the Florentine carnival processions and the Venetian water parades; in England, from the folk-pageants of Midsummer Eve, the miracle-plays, and the civic triumphs which attended the "royal-entries," to which we shall turn in the next chapter.

---

[1] Cf. *e. g.*, that of 1375.

[2] Symonds notes chariots introduced into ballets at Urbino in 1513; they gave a processional character to the masques, making them equivalent to triumphs. "Each interlude," says Symonds, "had its car attended by a choir of dancers." Is it possible that England made this gift to Italy?

CHAPTER III

THE "ROYAL–ENTRY," 1298–1558

FROM the early years of the thirteenth century to the accession of Queen Elizabeth, the most notable development of pageantry was seen in the "royal-entry." The splendor surrounding these events was great long before 1200;[1] but pageantry, in the proper sense, does not appear until the Fishmongers' celebration of the victory which Edward I gained at Falkirk. I have elsewhere[2] treated the "royal-entry" of the thirteenth century in some detail; suffice it here to repeat that Stow's authority for pageantry in 1236, when Eleanor of Provence was received at London, is doubtful[3] — and that there is no clear case of real pageantry before 1298.

Whether or not Edward I saw the Fishmongers' celebration in this year, is uncertain. " The Cytezyns of London hearyng tell of this great Victorye made great solempnyty euery one accordyng to his crafte & in especyall the fyshmongers which wth solempne processyon passed through the cytye havyng fyrst 4 storions[4] gylded caryed on 4 horses and after 4 horses caryed 3 samons[5] of sylver and after xlvi knyghtis all armed vppon luces of the water and St. Magnus among the rest wth a thowsand horsemen passed to leaden hall And this they dyd on St Magnus Day in honor of the Kyngis Victorye."[6] This show is interesting, in that we have here the first " triumph " in which animals — or, to be more exact, fishes — are used with a trade-significance. The reason for St. Magnus's presence is obvious; and though we cannot tell whether he was impersonated by a living rider, or was an image borne by horsemen, this point is unimportant — if the former, we see probably a development of the latter.

Before 1300 we find much splendor in the royal-entry; but — with this exception — no pageantry in the strict sense. The " knights " who rode on the " luces

---

[1] See Wendover's account of the coronation of Richard I in 1189 (*Flores Historiarum*, i, pp. 164 f.) copied by Matthew Paris (*Historia Minor*, ii, pp. 6 f.; *Chronica Majora*, ii, p. 348); cf. Strutt, *Manners and Customs*, ii, p. 59. There is much splendor — but no pageantry — before 1298.

[2] See *The Early "Royal-Entry"* in *Publ. Mod. Lang. Assoc.*, for December 1917, pp. 616 f.

[3] Matthew Paris, *Chron. Maj.*, iii, p. 336; " quibusdam prodigiosis ingeniis et portentis " is at best ambiguous — Stow, *Survey* (1618), p. 147, translates: " besides many Pageants and strange deuices there presented." Had there been real pageantry on this occasion, we should expect to find established instances of it in other royal-entries before 1298 — there were plenty of opportunities for its use.

[4] Sturgeon.   [5] Salmon.

[6] *The Chronicle of Dunmow*, in Harl. MS. 530, fols. 2–13; this paragraph is on fol. 7 b.

of the water " were probably guild-members — perhaps members of the marching watch — whose knighthood was ephemeral. If the king himself were not present, the celebration was held in his honor, and may be considered the equivalent of a " royal-entry." The pageantic growth of this institution was marked during the centuries which follow.

§ 1 — THE FOURTEENTH CENTURY

1300 — The Citizens Welcome Queen Margaret

Stow records the citizens' welcome of Queen Margaret of France, the second wife of Edward I, in 1300. Six hundred met the new mother as she came up from Yorkshire; they were dressed in " one livery of red and white, with the cognizance of their mysteries broidered upon their sleeves," but were not accompanied by any sort of pageantry.[1]

1308 — The Coronation of Edward II

The joyful reception of Edward II by the citizens, when he came to London with his French bride, is described in the *Annales Londonienses*.[2] The city was decorated, and looked — says the enthusiastic chronicler — like the new Jerusalem. Mayor and citizens took part in the coronation which followed this reception, two weeks later; but no pageants appear to have graced either occasion.[3] It is worth noting that the citizens broke forth into spontaneous dancing — *coram rege et regina karolantes* — a natural folk-procedure on occasions of great joy. This link with the kind of thing which later, through " mumming " and " disguising " developed into the masque, is stronger in the earlier entries when pageant-cars and set speeches had not done their part toward making the jubilation less spontaneous, if none the less sincere.

---

[1] Stow, *Annals*, p. 208; cf. J. G. Nichols, *Lond. Pag.* (1831), p. 10 (freely quoting Stow). I cannot find Stow's source, which may be " W. Packington," a chronicler not mentioned in Gross.

This event is not narrated by Walsingham (cf. *Hist. Angl.*, i, p. 81) nor in *Flor. Hist.* (cf. iii, p. 109) where the birth of Thomas at Brotherton is recorded. The *Ann. Lond.* has a break between 1293 and 1301 (i, p. 102).

[2] *Ann. Lond.*, i, pp. 152 f.: "Tandem Londoniam venerunt, cui copiosa civium turba obviabant, et per regales vicos tapetos aureos dependebant, et tunc visa est Londonia quasi nova Jerusalem monilibus ornata." Cf. Walsingham, i, p. 121, and *Flores Historiarum*, iii, p. 141. The latter chronicle places this event in February, 1307, while the editors of the other two agree in dating it 1308. The marginal date in the *Ann. Lond.* does not agree with that in the text; (apparently the year 1308 begins on p. 153 — perhaps because the editor uses the new style, beginning each year on 1 January).

[3] *Ann. Lond.*: " Ad quam coronationem major aldermanni et cives Londoniarum induti samiteis et sericeis vestimentis et ex armis Angliæ et Franciæ depictis, coram rege et regina karolantes, et servi civium ad illud festum, ut moris est, de cupa servientes, omnibus intuentibus inauditum proviserunt gaudium . . ." etc.

1313 — Fishmongers' Pageantry on the Birth of Edward III

Much the same kind of dancing is seen in 1313 — this time as a part of a real pageant — when, on 4 February, the Fishmongers escorted the queen from Westminster on her way to Eltham, after the birth of Edward III.[1] With them they carried a ship ingeniously contrived,[2] which had a trade-symbolism as had the fishes exhibited by the same guild in 1298. It is interesting to note the folk-dancing, which we saw accompanying the coronation of Edward II, here linked with a " pageant." This combination on the London streets may be indirectly responsible for the later union of pageant-car and masquers; at all events, we find dancing and pageantry united in the procession of 1313.[3]

The troubled state of the kingdom in the reign of Edward II was not conducive to elaborate and expensive shows; but it is important to remember that folk-custom had given birth to pageantry by the early years of the fourteenth century, and that Edward's troubled reign only retarded its growth.[4]

1327 — January: Queen Isabella in London. December: Philippa of Hainault at London

In 1326 Queen Isabella kept Christmas at Wallingford, and early the following January came to London. The citizens met her, and escorted her to Westminster,

---

[1] " Cum rumor ejusdem nativitatis civibus Londoniensibus pervenisset, major cum aldermannis per totam civitatem, diebus et noctibus continuis choream duxerunt, et quælibet contubernia civium catervatim præ nimio gaudio hoc idem fecerunt: sed et piscenarii, contra adventum dominæ reginæ Westmonasterio se præparantes, inæstimabilem ordinaverunt choream . . . rege et regina Westmonasterium pervenientibus, dicti piscenarii induti sindone depicta ex auro, de armis regum Angliæ et Franciæ, per medium civitatis equitabant versus Westmonasterium; coram quibus præibat quædam navis, quodam mirabili ingenio operata cum malo et velo erectis, et depictis de supradictis armis et varietate plurima; et sic coram regina karolantes, et per medium prædictæ civitatis ante reginam equitantes, conducendo ipsam versus Heltham omnibus intuentibus inauditum præmonstraverunt solatium." *Ann. Lond.*, i, p. 221. Cf. Chambers, ii, p. 167, referring to Riley, *Memorials of London*, p. 107, from *Corp. Letter Book D*, fol. 168 (p. 310); cf. also G. J. Augier, *Chroniques de Londres depuis l'an 44 Hen III jusqu'à l'an 17 Edw. III* (ed. [from Cotton MS. Cleop. A. vi, fol. 54, *et seq.*] for the Camd. Soc. (xxviii), London, 1844), p. 37, *sub anno* 6 Edward II: " En mesme l'an fu née sire Edward de Wyndesore, fitz le roy de dame Isabele la reyne, qe fu la fille le roy de Fraunce, le lundi en la feste seint Bryce. . . . En cele an, le dimeigne après la chaundelure, firent les pessoners de Loundres une nief siglaunt par my chepe jeske à Weimouster."

It is, perhaps, worth noting that the mayor at this time was not a Fishmonger, but a Goldsmith, Nicholas Farringdon. (See Stow, *Survey* (1618), p. 925.)

[2] Cf. the " folk-ships " mentioned above, p. 12, and n. 3.

[3] Chambers, ii, p. 172, notes that " the functions carried out by the fishmongers in 1298 and 1313 are much of the nature of masked ridings or ' disguisings ' and must be held to have a folk-origin." Cf. *ibid.*, ii, p. 167.

[4] On the citizens' attitude towards the queen's cause, see Walsingham, *Hist. Angl.*, i, pp. 181 f.

but we find no mention of pageants.[1] In December of the same year, Philippa of Hainault was received at London by the mayor and citizens; edibles, and more lasting gifts, to the value of three hundred marks, were given her by the civic authorities; then she continued her journey to York, where she was married to Edward III.[2] Neither at this time, nor at her coronation, three years later, do the celebrations include pageantry.[3]

1330 — EDWARD III BECOMES A FATHER. A NOTE ON TOURNAMENTS

The unorganized folk-celebration which we saw in 1308 and in 1313 broke out again in 1330 when the citizens of London heard of the birth of a son to their king and queen. This event happened on 16 June, 1330, and the public joy in London lasted several days.[4] On the birthday of the young prince began a three-day tournament at Stepney, in which the king took part.[5] In this year, and the following one, were several elaborate tournaments, which we have considered; we have seen that the custom of holding tournaments in masquerade may have come into England from Hainault with Philippa. Long a chivalric pastime, the tourney was beginning to become a " soft and silken war " in the early years of the fourteenth century; like the sword-dance, it degenerated into mumming.

1332 — CHRISTMAS KEPT WITH SPLENDOR BY THE COURT

As we have observed, the authors of the metrical romances probably drew their pictures of the splendor of court festivals from real life. Although the fourteenth-century chroniclers speak of these celebrations only in general terms — as an illustration I cite the entry under Christmas, 1332, in the *Annales Paulini*: " . . . tenuit dominus rex sollempniter Natale apud Welles usque Epiphaniam; ubi fiebant multa mirabilia sumptuosa "[6] — they show us that the early kings, when favored by fortune, celebrated Christmas in no niggardly fashion. It is well to note, in passing, that Tudor and Stuart sovereigns had a tradition of splendor at Christmas which came down to them from the times when folk-pageantry was beginning to touch the court.

1357 — NO PAGEANTS TO GREET JOHN OF FRANCE

In 1357, Edward the Black Prince entered London with his prisoner, King John of France; they were greeted by a large crowd, but there seems to have been no pageantry, although several writers — without giving any authority —

---

[1] *Ann. Paul.*, i, p. 319; Stow, *Annals*, p. 224.

[2] *Ann. Paul.*, i, pp. 338 f.   [3] *Ibid.*, p. 349.   [4] *Ibid.*, p. 349.

[5] *Ibid.*, p. 353. There had been one at Dartford on the 2 May preceding, in which the king had had a narrow escape. (i, pp. 352 f. Cf. above, p. 90.)

[6] *Ann. Paul.*, i, p. 356.

say that there was.[1] In 1363 three kings visited London; gifts were given — but this, while often a part of pageantry, does not in itself, obviously, constitute a pageant.[2]

1377 — RICHARD II CROWNED — AN IMPORTANT PAGEANT

Important in the annals of pageantry is the date 1377; for when, in that year, Richard II was crowned, an elaborate castle was erected by the Goldsmiths' Company at the head of Cheapside.[3] Walsingham's description of this castle is very detailed,[4] and from it I take the essentials. It had four towers, on each of which stood a beautiful virgin,[5] who blew leaves of gold on the king, and threw counterfeit gold florins before him and his horse. Wine ran forth in abundance from two sides of this structure, which was surmounted by a gold angel; this stood between the towers, and was so contrived that when the king came, it bowed down and offered him a crown. The mechanical device, the elaborate structure, the giving of gifts, the flowing wine and the damsels — who later were given allegorical names — are all characteristic of later pageants.

It has been suggested [6] that castles such as this came from the " Court of

---

[1] Ashm. MS. 793, fol. 111 b: " And in the xxiiij daie of Maye [32 Edw. III] aboute iij aftir none they [Prince Edward with King John and his son Philip] come to london Brigge. And so wente forthe vn to the Kynges Palois of Westmynster." A great crowd pressed about them so that " vnnethes from midday vn to nyght, they myght not come vn to Westmynster." Walsingham, i, p. 283, and Stow, *Annals*, p. 263, do not mention pageants in telling of this entry; but Gough, *Brit. Top.* (1768), p. 338, says, " the first pageants we meet with in London were exhibited when the Black Prince made his entry with his royal prisoners, 1357." He gives neither authorities not details; Hone, *Anc. Mys.*, p. 234, quoting Jones, *Biog. Dram.*, art. *pageant*, says there were pageants on this occasion; see Jones (1812), iii, p. 114 — he gives no authority for his statement.

[2] On this visit, see Walsingham, i, p. 299. The three kings were those of France, Cyprus, and Scotland; the first died at London — the second, while travelling in England shortly after, was robbed. (Walsingham.)

[3] The 1913 castle — which was historic, rather than chivalric — cannot be connected with the descendants of this " romantic " castle. (See below, chapter vi.)

[4] *Hist. Angl.*, i, p. 331. Fairholt, pt. i, p. 3 (referring to Walsingham) calls his, " the first detailed account of a ' pageant.' " Cf. also on this, Chambers, ii, p. 167; J. G. Nichols, p. 11; Davidson, p. 85 (referring to Herbert, ii, p. 217); Strutt, *Manners and Customs*, ii, p. 49, quoting Fabyan. Herbert, *Hist. Liv. Cos.*, *loc. cit.*, says that the books of the Goldsmiths' Company have no account of this pageant, and that he takes his own account from "historians."

The mumming of 1377, recorded by Stow (*Survey* (1618), p. 148) has been considered. See above, p. 104.

[5] As far as we can tell, these damsels were alive; the gold angel was, of course, a mechanical device.

[6] By Dr. H. R. Patch, who quotes from Grossteste:

> " þe foure smale toures abouten
> þat [witeþ] þe heiȝe tour wᵗ-outen
> Foure had þewes þᵗ aboute hire i-seoþ
> Foure virtues cardinals [þat] beoþ,"

Love " literature, possibly by way of the tournament. We have already noted the fact that in the reign of Edward III, the tournament showed signs of softening to a masquerade; and it is not at all unlikely that various features of the Court of Love were reproduced in reality.[1] If this took place, it is not surprising to find a guild borrowing the castle from the tournament when it wanted an elaborate structure to cover up a conduit, and to suggest its trade.

1382 — Anne of Bohemia Comes to London

When the crafts welcomed the new queen, Anne of Bohemia, in the sixth year of Richard II, the Goldsmiths had a pageant in Cheapside similar to that of 1377.[2] Herbert says that there were on this occasion only three female characters, but that probably the machinery of five years before was used again. The woodwork of this machine cost £2, 4s.; the silver skins, or leather, for covering it, 8s., $10\frac{1}{2}d.$; a sum of £13, 5s. was spent for black and red cloth, but Herbert says it is not noted whether this was for the castle or the liveries. Among other items enumerated was a sword, which cost 6s., 8d. The total expense to the Goldsmiths on this occasion — including the charge for the minstrels — amounted to £35, $9\frac{1}{2}d.$[3]

1392 — Richard Restores the Rights of the Citizens

Because in 1392 the citizens refused a loan to the king, he deprived mayor, sheriffs, aldermen, and chief citizens of London of their offices;[4] " And þan þe Kyng and his counsaile for grete malice of þe cite of London & for dispite removed all his courtes from Westmynstre vn to the cite of York þat is to saye the Chaunc'ye the Cheker & the Kynges benche & also þe comune place [pleas] and ther they helde all his courtes of lawe from mydsomer þat is to saye þe feste of seint John Baptiste vn to þe feste of cristenmasse next comyng after. And þan þe Kyng & his counsaille sawe it not so prophitable there as he was atte London: than anone he remeved it ageyn vn to London and so to Westmynster for grete ese of his officers and avauntage for the Kyng & all the comunes of ye Reame. And when the people of London sawe & knewe that these courtes weren come ageyn & ye Kyng & his people also, than the mayre & the Aldremen with the chief comoners lete gadre a grete some of golde of all the comons of ye cite and ordeyned and made a grete Rialte ayens his comyng to London and for to haue his grace & his gode Lordeship & also hir libertees & fraunchises graunted vn to hem

---

and says: " It is extremely doubtful whether the Castle carried any special significance with it when it left the Court of Love." (From an unpublished paper.) Cf. also Neilson, *Court of Love*, p. 136.

[1] On this, see chapter ii above.

[2] Herbert, ii, pp. 217 and 218. He gives the dress of the craft from the Goldsmiths' books, and remarks that it " must have had a very splendid effect."

[3] Herbert, ii, p. 218.

[4] Walsingham, ii, pp. 207 f.; Knighton, *Chron.* (ed. J. R. Lumby [R. S.], 1895), ii, p. 319.

ageyn as they afore tymes hadde. And bi grete instaunce and praier of Queene
Anne and of other Lordes & ladyes the Kyng graunted hem grace and this was
done atte Shene in Sotheraye. And than the Kyng withynne ij daies after come to
London. And than ye mayre of London shirriefs Aldermen & all the worthy cite
afterwarde riden ayens the Kyng in goode arraye vn to the heth on this side the
maner of Shene submyttyng hym. . . . And þus they brought the Kyng & the
Queene to London. And whan þe Kyng come to the Gate of the brigge of London
ther they presented him with a mylke white stede sadiled & brideled and trapped
with white clothe of golde and rede parted togidre, and the Queene had a palfrey
all whyte and in the same arraye trapped with white & rede and all þer condytes
in London ronnen with wyne, and redy for all maner people to drynke of and
betwene seynte Poules & the crosse in chepe þere was made a stage," whereon
" wer many Aungells with diuerse melodies and songen. And an Aungell come a
downe from þe stage on hye bi a vyse [1] and sette a croune of golde and precious
stones and perles vpon ye Kynges hede and a noþer croune vpon the Queenys
hede and so the citezeins brought the Kyng & the Queene vn to Westmynster in
to his palois.[2] And than on the morne aftir the mayre & the Shirriefs and the
Aldremen of London come vn to the Kyng in his palois atte Westmynster presentyng hym with ij Basyns of siluer and ouer gilte full of coyned gold sum of
xx. m. li. prayng hym of his heigh mercy & Lordship & speciall grace: that they
myght haue his goode love & libertees & fraunchises like as they haue hadde
before tymes and bi his lettres & patentes and hir chartir confermed. And the
Queene and other worthy lordes and ladies felle on knees and bisought the Kyng of
grace to conferme this: than the Kyng tooke vp the Queene & graunted hir all
her askyng. And than they þanked the Kyng and the Queene and wente home
ageyne." [3]

---

[1] Cf. Maidstone, *De Concordia inter Regem Ric. II et Civitatem London*, in *Political Poems
and Songs* (ed. T. Wright [R. S.], 1859–61), i, pp. 282 f. P. 291 —

> " Descendunt ab ea juvenis simul ipsaque virgo
> Nulla fuit scala, nec patuere gradus.
> Nubibus inclusi veniunt, et in æthere pendunt,
> Quo tamen ingenio nescio, crede mihi."

[2] The speech of the maiden who gave the crowns to the king and queen may be found in
Maidstone, p. 292. Other gifts — a golden picture of the Trinity to the king, and one of
St. Anne to her royal namesake — were given (Walsingham, ii, p. 210; Knighton, ii, p. 320);
Maidstone records the speeches which accompanied the gifts, and the replies of the sovereigns
on accepting them (p. 296).

[3] Bodl. MS. Ashm. 793, fols. 128 b and 129. (This is a *History of Britain from Brutus to
Henry V*, written in the fifteenth century.)

Cf. on this entry Strutt, *Manners and Customs*, ii, pp. 49 f. (quoting Fabyan); Hone,
Anc. Mys., p. 234; Chambers, ii, p. 168; J. G. Nichols, pp. 12 f. (referring to Knighton and
Fabyan); Thomson, *Chron. Lond. Bridge*, p. 206 (referring to Walsingham, Fabyan, Knighton,
Stow, and Maitland).

Other accounts of this entry tell of a second ornamental conduit at the door of St. Paul's which held a chorus of angels of both sexes, and God himself was represented.[1] Songs and musical instruments welcomed the king and queen, who dismounted and entered the Cathedral.

Continuing their progress towards Westminster, they came to a platform built at Temple Bar, representing a " desert " where stood St. John the Baptist surrounded by all kinds of trees and a menagerie of strange beasts.[2] We may observe that the mayor of this year was a Grocer — William Stondon;[3] this combination of Biblical material and trade-symbolism points both backwards and forwards. It is nothing new to find a union of the two; as Chambers points out, we see here the influence of the miracle plays.[4] The angelic hosts and God suggest a further influence of these plays. Here the sacred element is strong; we shall find, in later shows, that the emphasis is on trade-symbolism. The castle recalls that of 1377, and may show a chivalric influence. Speeches appropriate to the occasion accompanied the presentation of the gifts — Maidstone probably does not give the exact words spoken; for while the donors may have addressed the king and queen in Latin verse, it is not likely that the sovereigns, who probably spoke without preparation, adapted their speeches to the language and meter of the poet.[5]

By 1392 we have a pageant which shows the influence of the miracle-play; which combines elements of trade-symbolism and tournament, and which includes appropriate speeches. Clergy and citizens joined to honor the king and queen; and both classes are reflected in the resulting show. We must, however, bear in mind Chambers's warning in regard to exaggerating the influence of the miracle and morality plays on these pageants. London, he points out, was not a very great dramatic center at this time, and what plays there were, were not in the hands of the guilds, as were the receptions we are now considering.[6]

---

[1] " Supra sedebat eos juvenis, quasi sit Deus ipse,
    Lux radiosa sibi solis ad instar inest.
    Flammigerum vultum gerit hic, niveas quoque vestes,
    Supra hierarchias cœlicas ille sedet."
(Maidstone, p. 293.)

[2] Maidstone, p. 294; Chambers, ii, p. 173; Cf. the Norwich Grocers' tree, above, p. 35; and note that in 1553 the Merchant-Tailors had a mayoralty pageant of St. John (see below, chapter vi).

[3] Stow, *Survey* (1618), p. 932. Cf. below, chapter vi.

[4] Chambers, ii, p. 173.

[5] The queen's speech was short and to the point:
    " Illa refert grates nimias pro munere tanto:
    ' In me, si quid erit, perficietur,' ait." Maidstone, p. 297.

[6] Cf. Chambers, ii, p. 173. (The " ridings " of the trade-guilds were very common in the fourteenth century: but we are here concerned only with those which have pageantic features.)

1399 — The Duke of Lancaster and Henry IV of England

When the Duke of Lancaster entered London in 1399, he was received with great pomp by the civic authorities, but no pageantry in the stricter sense accompanied the reception.[1] The same year he was crowned King Henry IV, and Froissart narrates the procession and coronation service. " Thus the duke rode through London with a great nombre of lordes, euery lordes seruaunt in their maysters lyuerey. All the burgesses and lombardes merchauntes in London, and euery craft with their lyuerey and deuyse. . . . He was in nombre a syxe thousãde horse, and the streates hanged as he passed by: and the same day and the next there were in London rynnynge seuen cundyttes with wyne, whyte and reed." [2] It is small wonder that Perkin Revelour could not resist the temptation offered by such a " riding "!

Perhaps the troublous times account for the absence of pageantic features at this royal-entry — but pageantry is well established before the end of the fourteenth century.[3]

§ 2.   THE FIFTEENTH CENTURY

1415 — Henry V Returns from Agincourt

When Henry V returned from Agincourt in 1415 there was a very fine show indeed. We have several contemporary accounts of the pageant;[4] that which I follow is printed in Strutt's *Manners and Customs*. The king was welcomed by Mayor, Aldermen, and twenty thousand citizens, who met him at Blackheath, and brought him to the city. Here he was " riolly receyvet with procession and

---

[1] J. G. Nichols, p. 13, quoting from Tyrrell's *History of England from MSS. in Lambeth Library*, gives an account of the entry.

[2] Froissart, *Chronicles* (J. Bourchier's transl. [1812] ii, p. 752). Cf. also. J. G. Nichols, pp. 13 and 14; Herbert, i, p. 90; Strutt, *Manners and Customs*, ii, p. 60, all of whom go back to Froissart. The conduits running wine was a common accompaniment of pageants to the time of Charles II; cf. Fustigo in 1 *Honest Whore*, iii, i, 202: " This should be a coronation day; for my head runs claret lustily."

[3] For an account of the entry of Charles VI and Isabella of Bavaria into Paris, 20 June, 1399, see Froissart, ii, pp. 429 f.

[4] Harl. MS. 53, fol. 157 b (in Strutt, *Manners and Customs*, ii, pp. 50 f.); Harl. MS. 565, fol. 111 b — where *Passus Tertius* begins — (in Nicolas, *Agincourt* (1832), pp. 325 f.; Tyrrell, *Chron. Lond. 1089–1483* (1827), pp. 229 f.); Cotton MS. Julius E. iv, fol. 113 (in B. Williams, *Gesta Henrici Quinti* (1850), pp. 61 f.); Sloane MS. 1776 — a careless copy of the Cotton MS.: " the author was, as he himself tells us, one of the chaplains (*clericalis militiæ*)of Henry's army," and his chronicle was written before 1418 (*Gesta*, pp. vi and vii). See Ashm. MS. 793, fol. 144, for a brief mention of this entry.

Cf. also Kingsford, *Henry V* (1901), pp. 156 f.; Nicolas, *Agincourt*, pp. 149 f., 292 f. (a translation of *Gesta*), and appendix, pp. 67 f.; Tyrrell, pp. 103 f. (for a brief notice); Walsingham, ii, p. 314; Elmham's *Vita Henrici Quinti* (ed. T. Hearne, 1727), pp. 71 f.; Holinshed (1808), iii,

song (stiling him Lord of England! Flower of the World! and Soldier of Christ!).[1]
And when he was come to London brigge, wher as were two turrettes on the draw
brigge, & a gret geaunt [2] and on the turretts stondyng a lyon and a antelope,

----

p. 84; Chambers, ii, pp. 168 f.; J. G. Nichols, p. 15; Fairholt, pt. i, p. 6; Herbert, i, pp. 91 f.;
Fabyan, *New Chron. Eng. and France* (ed. H. Ellis, 1811), p. 581; Grafton, *Chronicle* (1809), i,
p. 520, for mention — more or less detailed — of this occasion. This 1415 reception is dated
23 November in *Gesta*, Kingsford, *Henry V*, and Nicolas, *Agincourt*.

Thomson, *Chron. Lond. Bridge*, pp. 221 f., refers to Stow's *Annals*, Harl. MS. 565, and
Cotton MS. Julius E. iv. Of the former MS. he quotes from fol. 76 b: ". . . and ayens his [the
king's] comynge was ordeyned moche ryalte in London; that is to weten, at London Bregge,
at ye Conduyt in Cornhill, at the grete Conduyt in Chepe; and at ye Crosse in Chepe was
mad a Ryall Castell with Angells and Virgynes, syngynge there inne . . ." Of the Cotton
MS. he translates considerable.

A detailed account of the king's arrival may be found in C. A. Cole's edition of *Elmhami
Liber Metricus de Henrico Quinto* (*Memorials of Henry V* [R. S.]), pp. 125 f. The entry is described in the following chapters: xliii — *De Adventu Regis Londonias;* xliv — *De Adventu
Regis ad Pontem Londoniarum;* xlv — *De Transitu Regis per Aquœductum de Cornhil;* xlvi —
De Transitu Regis ad Introitum de Chepe; xlvii — *De Transitu Regis ad Crucem in Chepe;*
xlviii — *De Transitu Regis ad Aquœductum prope portam Sancti Pauli;* xlix — *De concursu
populorum in plateis Civitatis;* l — *De gestu Regis maturo in equitando;* et quod intravit in
ecclesiam Sancti Pauli;* li — *Quod Dominus Rex iter arripuit versus Westmonasterium.*

This entry of Henry V was reproduced in *The Festival of Empire*—the London Pageant of
1911. The giant and various pageants were reconstructed; see the *Book* of this pageant, pp. 49 f.
In some " pageantic " productions of Shakspere's *Henry V*, this entry has been staged —
without any attempt at historical accuracy.

[1] Cf. Tyrrell, p. 231:   " To London brigge thanne rood oure kyng,
        The processions there they mette hym ryght,
        ' Ave Rex Anglor ' thei gan syng,
        ' Flos Mundi,' thei seyde, Goddys knyght.
        To London brigge whan he com ryght,
        Upon the gate ther stod on hy,
        A gyaunt that was full grym of syght
        To teche the Frensshmen curtesye."

That this poem was not written by an eye-witness, is implied on the same page:
        " Men and women for joye they alle
        Of hys comyn thei weren so fayn
        That the Condyd bothe grete and smalle
        Ran wyn ich on as y herde sayn."

But this may be a mere conventional utterance.

Strutt translates the titles of the songs, which the MS. gives in Latin.

[2] Accounts vary as to the number of giants. *Gesta Henrici Quinti* notes two: " in cujus
dextro latere stetit effigies non multum minoris magnitudinis, muliebus . . . quasi vir et
uxor." (p. 62). Of these figures, Kingsford, *Henry V*, p. 156, n. 2, says: " No doubt they are
the mediæval ancestors of the modern Gog and Magog." Cf. Nicolas, *Agincourt*, pp. 150 and
293 (translating the *Gesta*); the *Elmhami Liber Metricus*, Thomson, Chambers, and J. G.
Nichols, also note two giants.

Some accounts include mention of St. George. *Gesta*, p. 63, says that he was an image:
" sub uno tabernaculo splendido stetit imago formosissima Sancti Georgii, armata." He held a

with many angeles [1] syngyng, Blessed is he who cometh in the name of the Lord;
& so he rode forth into London, & the stretes were riolly hanget with rich clothes,
& in Cornhylle was made a riol toure full of patriarches [2] syngyng, Sing unto the
Lord a new song, praise his name in the Holy Church: & they kest down quyk
briddes which flawe thikke about the kyng: & when he came into Chepe the
condites ranne wyne, & on the gret condit ware 12 aposteles [3] syngyng, Have
mercy on my soul, Oh, Lord! and 12 kynges knelyng, castyng doune oblays,
and welcomet hym home.[4]   And the cros in the Chepe was riolly arrayet like a
castell with toures pight full of baners,[5] and therein angeles syngyng Nobell,

---

scroll with the inscription — *Soli Deo honor et gloria*. Cf. also Kingsford, *Henry V*, p. 157;
Nicolas, *Agincourt*, pp. 151 and 294 (translating *Gesta*). The account given in Tyrrell mentions
only one giant, but includes St. George.

These figures show the adoption of the folk-giant and saint's image by the royal-entry; it
is hard to say whether the giant or St. George partook of the " champion " aspect of the 1432
giant—who may be a result of both giant and sacred knight. I may refer here to "St. George's
bar " mentioned in 1522 (see below, p. 175).

[1] Kingsford, *Henry V*, p. 157, n., reprints the first stanza of the welcoming song, sung by
boys " who represented the hierarchy of angels "; the whole of the song — as he notes — may
be found in Nicolas, *Agincourt*, appendix, pp. 67 and 68. Nicolas takes it from Percy's
Reliques of Ancient Poetry. The first stanza runs:

> " Deo gratias Anglia redde pro victoria!
> Owre Kynge went forth to Normandy,
> With grace and might of chivalry;
> The God for hym wrought marvelously,
> Wherefore Englonde may calle, and cry
>   Deo gratias, &c."

[2] On the patriarchs or prophets, see *Gesta*, p. 64; Nicolas, pp. 152 and 295; Kingsford,
Henry V, p. 157. All accounts mention the birds and the anthem sung — " Cantate Domino
canticum novum, Alleluia! Quia mirabilia fecit, Alleluia! Salvavit, &c."

[3] On the apostles and kings see *Gesta*, pp. 64 and 65; Nicolas, *Agincourt*, pp. 152 and 296;
Kingsford, *Henry V*, p. 158. The *Gesta* says that the kings represented the martyrs and
confessors of the succession of England.

[4] (I have here substituted the MS. reading for Strutt's). The poem in Tyrrell (p. 232)
records " xii kynges . . . obles aboughte oure kyng gan throwe " — which is rendered in the
Latin: " Et emiserunt ei argenti folia rotunda intermixtis panibus ejusdem tenuitatis et
rotundatis. . . ." (*Gesta*, p. 65; this is translated (Nicolas, *Agincourt*, p. 296): " And they
sent forth upon him round leaves of silver mixed with wafers, equally thin and round.")

The bread and wine represented — or recalled — Melchisedec's reception of Abraham,
returning victorious from the slaughter of the four kings. *Gesta*, p. 65; Kingsford, *Henry V*,
p. 158; Nicolas, *Agincourt*, pp. 152, 296.

[5] On this castle, *Gesta*, p. 65, notes " erat scriptum in frontibus januarum ex utrâque parte:
Gloriosa dicta sunt de te, civitas Dei. (Cf. Kingsford, p. 158; Nicolas, pp. 153, 297.) The arms of
St. George, as well as the king's were on the castle. (*Gesta*, p. 65; Nicolas, pp. 153, 297). A
chorus of beautiful virgins sang from the castle, in English, *Welcome Henry the Fifte, Kynge of
Englond and of Fraunce!* " velut alteri David de cædo Goliathe, qui in Gallorum superbiâ
congruè designari poterit." (*Gesta*, p. 66; cf. Nicolas, pp. 154, 298). This may have suggested
to Lydgate the possibility of visualizing qualities, and so led to the 1432 allegory.

nobell;[1] gyvyng besandes[2] of golde to the kynge, & so he rode forth to Paules[3] where as mette hym 14 bisshopes and al ye belles ronge agaynes hym;[4] & there he alight and went to the hye awter & ther thei song Te Deum Laudamus; & from thense he rode forth to his palice at Westminstre."

---

[1] Cf. Rosny, p. 23 (à propos of the creation of a new Roi de l'Épinette on mardi gras at Lille in the time of Philip the Good): " Puis, comme d'ordinaire en pareille occurrence, la foule des spectateurs criait Noël! . . . et les applaudissemens ou joyeuses acclamations retentissaient de toutes parts." Cf. also Le Journal d'un Bourgeois de Paris, p. 274 (à propos of the entry into Paris of Henry VI, 1431), " et aussi tost que le roy entra dedens la ville ilz lui mirent ung grant ciel d'azur sur la teste . . . et le porterent sur lui les IIII eschevins tout en la fourme et maniere c'om fait à nostre Seigneur à la Feste-Dieu, et plus, car chascun crioit: Nouel! par où il passoit." Cf. Gesta, p. 67, n. 2. " Lydgate states that the virgins . . . greeted the king with the accustomed welcome, Nowell! Nowell! Henry was in like manner greeted with this acclamation after the capture of Rouen (Archœol. xxii, p. 383)." [Lydgate did not write the verses in Tyrrell.]

[2] Strutt suggests basons. It is rather besant or bezant — a coin of Byzantium. The poem printed by Tyrrell mentions (p. 232) that the angels " strowed oure kyng on euery syde " with " besaunts." The Latin reads: " emiserunt in caput regis subgredientis minas aureas " (Gesta, p. 66) and the editor notes, " margin — id est talenta." (Ibid., n. 2.) Nicolas fails to translate, writing minœ (Agincourt, pp. 154 and 298); he notes (p. 154) " They were probably small pieces of coin." Williams (Gesta, p. 66, n. 2) errs in saying " Lydgate calls them ' oboles ' "; but he is right in saying they were " probably small pieces of money."

[3] The Elmhami Liber describes an elaborate " aquæductum prope portam Sancti Pauli " where a virgin scattered gold lightly in the air; a golden Archangel (presumably artificial) stood on the highest point, and " angelus ad postem quemlibet unus erat." The throne of angels and archangels resounded with hymns; " hæc scriptura datur, gratia grata Deo: ' O Pater alme, Deum te laudamus modulando; Hæc omnis terra te veneratur ita.' "

The poet cannot, perhaps, be held to describe accurately in such enthusiastic outbursts as this:

" Turris amicta fuit stellis: sapphirica nubes
Fulsit tectura: splendor ubique nitet."

The last phrase is probably true: but we cannot tell just how far the rest of it is. The Latin account in the Gesta (p. 67) and its translation in Nicolas (p. 299), are equally enthusiastic. Whether or not these attain veracity, there must be some foundation for them; the germ of the achievements of Inigo Jones and Gerard Christmas is here.

The mechanical angel may be a resurrection of that used in 1377; it is, however, more likely a new one.

Gesta, pp. 66 f.; Nicolas, pp. 154 f. and 298 f., and Kingsford, Henry V, p. 158, mention (after the angels who threw besants of gold and sang Te Deum) that, having come to the tower of the conduit at the end of Cheap, towards St. Paul's, the king found many artificial pavilions (tabernacula) in each of which a beautiful virgin, " ad modum imaginis " — after the manner of an image — elegantly dressed and crowned with laurel, stood with a gold cup in her hand, from which she blew leaves of gold upon the king. And the tower was covered with a canopy, the color of the sky, with clouds; and on top was the image of an archangel, " quasi in auro lucidissimo. . . ." And angels " shone with celestial gracefulness, chaunting sweetly with all sorts of music . . ."

[4] Here again I adopt the MS. text, in which Strutt's interpolation after bisshopes does not appear.

Clergy and burghers united to honor their victorious sovereign. In this celebration, a folk-element appears with the giants — to whom a poet's patriotism assigns the task of teaching " the Frensshmen curtesye." A boy-choir, representing the heavenly host, sang an anthem, as did a company of patriarchs; twelve apostles and twelve kings sang sacred music — more or less appropriate to the occasion — and offered gifts; wine flowed from a castle built on the conduit in Chepe, and maidens issued forth, dancing, and sang " Nowell," as they scattered golden leaves into the air.

This " triumph " has been attributed to Lydgate, but Dr. MacCracken does not include it in his list of the genuine poems of the monk of Bury.[1] Whether there were speeches in this show, aside from the sacred selections I have noted, is not clear.[2] There were " scriptures " on the castle and on the conduit near the door of St. Paul's — these we shall see again in 1432. Chambers notes that Warton says speeches seem to be admitted into pageants about the reign of Henry VI; there were songs, and perhaps speeches, in 1415, 1392, and 1377.

These songs, it is worthy of note, are for the most part taken, or adapted, from the ritual of the Church. We have already recorded the popular joy in 1308, 1313, and 1330; and while such expressions as " karolantes " and " choreas facientes " do not prove that the singing was more than a spontaneous outburst of music on the part of the people, yet they link music to the royal-entry early in the fourteenth century. Verses such as those which Lydgate wrote for the 1432 " triumph " were often fastened on the pageants, and read, even if not aloud, when the royal guest approached.[3] The choirs of children dressed as angels recall choirs perched on the battlements of churches in Palm Sunday processions.[4] It is easy to see how speech in pageants resulted, when it became necessary to explain the " scriptures " — not always easily read — especially since choirs had been dressed in appropriate costume to sing sacred anthems. Gifts could not be

---

[1] See *The Minor Poems of Lydgate*, i, pp. xi f., and *King Henry's Triumphal Entry into London*, in Herrig's *Archiv.*, cxxvi (1911), p. 100, n. 1.

It is noteworthy that until we have a pageant definitely by Lydgate, we do not find the allegorical element which became so important in later shows. I am not sure that we shall ever know the relations between allegory in the pageant, and in the morality play; I have suggested that Lydgate introduced allegory from literature into the pageant, and that the morality play received a certain amount of stimulus from the allegorical element in pageantry. It is impossible to prove this; anyone else may make other suggestions with an equal chance of being right. Both forms of expression exerted more or less influence on each other, in all likelihood; and he would be daring who should assert that the morality play was founded on pageantry — but he would be braver who should claim that there was no relation between the two.

[2] The virgins sang from the castle, " Welcome Henry the Fifth, King of England and of France " (cf. above, p. 134, n. 5).

[3] Chambers, ii, p. 173, n. 1. Devices of heraldry were worked into the pageants very often — and their meaning needed no explanation.

[4] Cf. Chambers, ii, p. 5.

silently handed to the recipient; mayors could not greet their royal guests in pantomime. The joy of the citizens had long been voiced; it needs no great argument to show that a less spontaneous, and more clear, expression of their pleasure was bound to develop.

Hitherto, it will be remarked, save for the Fishmongers' animals and St. Magnus in 1298, and the ship which the same guild exhibited in 1313, the pageantry of the " royal-entry " has been stationary. Instead of moving platforms — or wagons which remain fixed for the while — we find in London castles built on conduits, filled with prophets, angels and fair damsels, who may be considered the " raw material " of the later allegory. We have seen John the Baptist standing in a " desert " at Temple Bar; and the vegetation which surrounded him may have had as close a connection with the Grocers as the 1377 castle had with the Goldsmiths. It is to be noted that the stationary pageantry of the early royal-entry is as characteristic as the moving pageantry of folk-celebrations.

Yet there is a processional element in these entries. The king and his suite go from one platform to another, and see everything prepared for their entertainment. This is but the reverse of the modern method of putting the distinguished guests on a stage whence they may review the procession of floats. In the Lord Mayor's Shows of the seventeenth century, the mayor rides; sometimes the cars attend him, and sometimes they are fixed. In the nineteenth century " pageants " both spectators and performers remain in one place.[1]

1416 — SIGISMUND IN LONDON

In 1416 the Emperor Sigismund came to London, and was much honored by Henry V.[2] As we have mentioned, the " dumb-show " on this occasion was an elaborate cake.[3] No other pageantry during his stay has been suggested, though Grafton records " iustes, tourneyes, and other martiall feates." The same year came the Duke of Holland " cum apparatu maximo." [4]

1421 — RETURN OF HENRY V AND KATHARINE

In 1420 Henry V married Katharine of France,[5] and the next year, returning with his queen, " a clero et populo ludicis et vario apparatu, ut decuit, cum maximo gaudio receptus fuit." [6] Elmham records giants; " immensæ staturæ

---

[1] The Parkerian pageant usually has a " Final March " across the stage; and the episodes may be said to follow each other in a " procession of events."

[2] See Cotton MS., Calig. B. ii. Also Harl. MS. 53, fol. 157 b; Harl. MS. 565, fol. 77 b for mention of this visit — without record of pageantry. Cf. also Walsingham, ii, pp. 315 f.; Grafton, i, p. 521; Kingsford, *Henry V*, pp. 169 f.; Elmham, *Vita Henrici Quinti*, cap. xxxi, p. 76; Williams, *Gesta Henrici Quinti*, pp. 77–78. (It may be noted in passing, that there are slight differences between dates in Kingsford and Williams.)

[3] See above, p. 82.   [4] Walsingham, ii, p. 316.   [5] Ibid., ii, p. 335.

[6] Ibid., ii, p. 336; cf. also *Gesta*, p. 147. Kingsford, *Henry V*, p. 344, citing Elmham, *Vita*, pp. 297, 298, says that " the pageants and decorations in the streets rivalled those of

gigantes, artificii mirabilis," who were made to bow as the queen passed; there were lions, whose eyes could roll — " leoninas effigies, oculorum motibus "; the apostles, martyrs, and confessors reappeared; there were choruses of virgins, who sang beautiful songs; the conduits ran wine; boys were dressed up as angels; and there were pageants. One recalls the last one of the 1415 entry — " illac tronos, cœlum simulantes emperium angelorum psallencium ierarchiis, fulgore mirabili radiare stuperes." [1]

1431 — Paris Coronation of Henry VI

Ten years after this entry of Henry V and his bride, Henry VI was crowned at Paris.[2] He entered the city 2 December, 1431, and was met on his way from St. Denis by the civic officials of Paris. Just outside the city, Fame, "une deesse," on horseback,[3] accompanied by nine male and nine female worthies (" ix preux et ix preuses ")[4] bade him welcome. A herald " lui presenta icelle deesse et

---

five years previous." Hearne's Elmham (1727), cap. cx (pp. 297–298), gives full details "de adventu reginæ usque Londoniam & de honorifica receptione ejusdem." Herbert, i, p. 92, gives — from the books of the Brewers' Company — an account of the preparations for the reception; Fabyan, p. 586, passes over " the great and curious ordinance provided by the citizens for the receiving of the king and queen . . ." and Grafton, i, p. 543, simply says they were received " most joyfully and honorably " by the citizens of London. (Chambers, ii, p. 169, says the details of this reception are not preserved.)

[1] " . . . triumphal arches and castles, bands of singing boys and maidens, fountains running with wine, giants of a huge stature ingeniously constructed to bow at the right moment, lions which could roll their eyes and make other appropriate gestures were all prepared for the welcome of Catherine to the capital of her husband's kingdom." Kingsford, *Henry V*, p. 344, from Elmham, *Vita*.

[2] See on this, C. L. Kingsford, *Eng. Hist. Lit.*, p. 92; *Letter-Book K*, pp. 135–137; Monstrelet, *Chronique*, v, pp. 1–7; *Journal d'un Bourgeois de Paris*, ed. Tuetey (1881), pp. 274 f.; Delpit, *Collection générale des documents français qui se trouvent en Angleterre*, (1847), pp. 244 f. Sharpe, in *Letter-Book K*, gives merely an outline of the MS. (Archives de la Mairie de Londres; reg. K. fol. 101vo) which Delpit prints; he refers to Delpit, Monstrelet, and Hall, pp. 160–162. Kingsford (*Eng. Hist. Lit.*) says that " the long account of the reception of Henry VI at Paris in December, 1431 " which is to be found in Harl. MS. 540, " confirms the narratives of Monstrelet and the *Journal d'un Bourgeois de Paris*, but is independent of them; probably it is derived from the narrative inserted in ' Letter-book K ' . . ." which has been described by Delpit " as surpassing all other accounts in its wealth of detail." Delpit (introduction, p. clx) says this account was " écrite probablement par un membre de l'Université de Paris, et peut-être par l'ordonnateur lui-même des cérémonies qui y furent faites."

Harl. MS. 540, fols. 41 f., gives a full account of this entry into Paris; it tells of " the 9 worthy emperours," a " shippe " at the gate of St. Denis, with people on it; and, as the king approached, of " whit doves and other birds " which were let loose. There also " was a conduite and thre mare maydens swiminge above the watar, and out of the condiote cam renninge divers wynes. . . ." In the same street was a scaffold, whereon was played the wedding of Our Lady, and the Birth of Christ. Many other details are mentioned.

[3] Monstrelet, v, p. 2, and the *Journal*, p. 274 do not mention Fame.

[4] The worthies, given in Delpit, p. 240, are: Hector, Alexander, Cæsar, Joshua, David,

preux " with an eight-verse speech.[1] " En la bastide Saint Denis . . . avoit une
nef d'argent envoillés " in which were twelve[2] persons, " en trois estas, distingans
ses estas de la dicte ville," who gave the king three hearts, " lesquelz a la vue
dicelui, se ouvrirent et de l'un d'iceulx yssy deux coulons blans, de l'autre oyseles
volans[3] et de l'autre fleurs violettes et verdurez odorans, en signe que les cuers des
estas dicelle ville se ouvrirent de joye . . . et dessoubz icelui escu estoit escript
en un tableau en bien grosse lettre ce qui sensuit:

> " Les estas de ceste cite,
>   Vous offeront d'un còntentement
>   Leurs cuers, par vray humilite:
>   Recevez les benignement.

" Et quant le dit Roy od bien veu et regardé ce que dit est, il entra dedens la
bonne ville de Paris." [4]

At the " poncelet Saint-Denis " was a scaffold, " sur lequel estoit comme une
manière de bois, où estoient trois hommes sauvages et une femme, qui ne cessèrent de combatre l'un contre l'aultre, tant que le roy et les seigneurs furent.[5]
Et avoit desoubz ledit eschaffault une fontaine jettant ypocras,[6] et trois seraines
dedens; et estoit ledit ypocras habandonné à chascun. Et depuis ledit poncelet,
en tirant vers la seconde porte de la rue Saint-Denis, avoit personnage, sans parler,[7]

Judas Maccabæus, Charlemagne, Arthur and Godfrey of " Billon "; " les preuses " are: " La
royne Penthasillée, la preuse Deiphille, la royne Synope, la vieille Semiramis de Babilone, la
belle Menalippe, la sage Ypolite, la royne Lampheto, la vierge Thenca, la royne Thamaris."

The *Journal* mentions the eighteen worthies — " et après foison chevaliers et escuiers, et
entre les autres estoit Guillaume qui se disoit le Berger, qui avoit monstré ses plaies comme
sainct Françoys . . . mais il ne povoit avoir joie, car il estoit fort lié de bonnes cordes comme
ung larron " (p. 274).

[1] Delpit, p. 241.

[2] Monstrelet says there were six; one was dressed like a bishop; one like a citizen; one
represented the university — and the other three were dressed as " sergeants."

[3] So Delpit: cf. Monstrelet, v, p. 3: " . . . dont ou premier avoit deux coulons blancs et
ou second des petis oyseletz, qu'ilz laissièrent voler par desus le chief du roy . . . et le tiers
cuer estoit plain de violettes et autres fleurs . . ." Cf. on this, the 1415 and 1432 entries at
London.

[4] Delpit, p. 241.

[5] So Monstrelet: cf. Delpit, p. 242: " . . . hommes et femmes sauvages jouans des escus
tres gentilment." Cf. also *Journal d'un Bourgeois*, p. 275. We have already mentioned these
" wild-men '" above, p. 76. They suggest the " drolls" of the seventeenth-century Lord
Mayor's Shows.

[6] Wine ran forth in England, in 1377.

[7] " C'est-à-dire," notes the editor of Monstrelet (v, p. 4, n. 1) " une pantomime." Sharpe
(in *Letter-Book K*, p. 136) calls these " live but motionless figures." In the *Journal* they are
called " mistere " (p. 275). Cf. Delpit, p. 242: " figures de personnaiges vifs . . . lesqueles
personnes aucunement ne se mouvoient et apparoient estre ymages et estoient bien huit vins
personnaiges."

de la Nativité Nostre-Dame, de son mariage, et l'Annunciacion, des Trois Rois, des Innocens, et du bon homme qui semoit son bled. Et furent ces personnages très bien joués.[1] Et sur la porte fut jouée la légende de Saint Denis; et fut voulentiers veue des Anglois. En oultre, devant les Innocens avoit une manière de forest en la rue, dedens laquelle estoit ung cerf vif, et quand le roy passa devant, on fist coure ledit cerf et des chiens et veneurs après fut grand pièce chacié à force, et se vint rendre emprès les piés du cheval du roy . . .[2] Et à l'entrée de la Porte de Chastelet avoit encore ung eschafault sur lequel avoit en personnage ung petit enfant en samblance du roy . . . deux couronnes sur son chef."[3] Various French and English nobles were represented about the king.

Delpit[4] records another scaffold whereon " estoit represente par figure le prevost de Paris, tenant un escript en sa main et le presentoit au dit Roy . . ." and a scripture explained the living-picture.

Before the " ostel des dames de Saint Antoine avoit une petit chastel d'or," on one tower of which was a peacock. And there was a " scripture " — *Filie Syon exultent in Rege suo, laudent nomen ejus* — rendered into French:

> " Les dames de religion
> Comme les filles de Syon,
> Se rejouissent pour leur roy
> Qui est venu en noble arroy."

And at the corner of the rue de Jouy, the goddess Fame and the worthies met the king again, " rengiez en moult belle ordonnance." And so the king rode to the hôtel des Tournelles where he was received by the Duchess of Bedford and other ladies.[5]

It is possible that Lydgate was present at this show, and that the figure of the " deesse " Fame suggested the allegory which appears in his 1432 show, as Dr. MacCracken suggests.[6] But I see no reason for assuming that this was the case.

---

[1] Delpit, p. 242, notes the subjects as " la nativité de notre (Sr.) Jeshus Crist; . . . trois histoires de Saint Denis " explained by written verses.

[2] Delpit, p. 244, notes that this had a trade-signification. " Et a l'entree du grant pont presenterent les bouchers de la dite ville, une serf tout vif, comme de huit cors, vestu et couvert des armez de France et d'Angleterre, et le menerent depuis la jusques a l'ostel des Tournelles."

[3] Monstrelet, v, pp. 3 f. Cf. Sharpe, pp. 136 f., and 137, n. 1. The *Journal*, p. 276, notes " deux couronnes pendans qui estoient tres riches à veoir à ung chascun, sur sa teste . . ."

[4] P. 243; around the representation of the Parisan prevost " estoient autres gens en grant nombre, representans les prevost des marchands, eschevins, bourgois, laboureurs, gens de mestiers et habitans d'icelle ville . . . et si estoient tous iceulx personnages, sans mouvoir, samblans estre ymages, et au dessoubz et a l'endroit d'un chacun ystoire, estoit escript en grosse lettre, ce qui s'ensuit."

[5] Delpit, p. 244.

[6] See MacCracken in Herrig's *Archiv.*, cxxvi, p. 99: " Lydgate may have seen the Paris show and brought over suggestions."

Fame is the only allegorical character in a royal-entry where the emphasis is strongly Biblical; some accounts do not mention her presence. The living-pictures representing Biblical and legendary material are more prominent, per-haps, and more popular,[1] than the same element in England; yet Biblical material was far from unknown in English pageants before 1431. The " wild-men " were common figures in England, as well as on the Continent; and while it is possible that the nine Worthies were imported into England from France, this seems to me unlikely. I imagine that they came into English pageantry, as they probably did into French, directly from literature — Biblical, historical and romantic.

1432—Henry VI Returns from his Coronation in Paris—Lydgate

The most elaborate show that we have yet encountered — and one of the most important historically — was that which greeted Henry VI on his return from his Paris coronation. For the first time in the history of pageantry we can connect a name with a form of entertainment which, in Elizabethan times and since, has attracted many a well-known writer. The descriptive verses which John Lydgate wrote of this royal-entry do not, it is true, prove him to be the author of this " triumph "; but I think he may safely be so considered.[2]

---

[1] The Biblical " beaux misteres " were produced again in 1437 when Charles VII was received in Paris. He, too, had " un ciel sur sa teste comme on a à la Saincte Sauveur à Porter Nostre Seigneur " (*Journal d'un Bourgeois*, pp. 335 f. On that carried by members of various guilds over Henry VI, see *ibid.*, p. 276). " A la Porte des Champs avoit angles chantans, à la fontaine du Ponceau-Sainct-Denis moult de belles choses qui moult longues seroient à raconter, devant la Trinité la maniere de la Passion, comme on fist pour le petit roy Henry, quant il fut sacré à Paris . . ." (p. 336).

[2] Delpit (introduction, p. clx, n. 1) suggests that Carpenter's narration of this entry of Henry VI " fut trouvée si belle, qu'un de poëtes les plus célèbres de cette époque, Jean Lyd-gate, la mit en vers anglais. Son amplification poétique a été publié à la suite de la *Chronique de Londres*." It is quite possible that Carpenter described the show that Lydgate planned and also described. Even if he did not plan the whole, he may have made suggestions, even without having seen the Paris show of two months before. That the descriptive poem is genuinely Lydgate's there can be no doubt (see MacCracken, *Minor Poems of Lydgate*, i, p. xvi); and I may add that later it became a common custom for the author of a show to describe it, not only for his contemporaries, but for posterity.

Dr. MacCracken, in Herrig, *Archiv.*, cxxvi, pp. 76 f., says that these verses are Lydgate's; but that he was guided by a " source " — which source is John Carpenter, Town Clerk. A letter by the latter is preserved in the letter-files in the Guildhall; it is in Latin, and describes the royal-entry to one who had, thinks Dr. MacCracken (p. 77), seen it himself. After com-paring Carpenter's letter with Lydgate's verses, he comes to the conclusion that while some suggestions may have come from Lydgate, the selection of the " deviser " of the pageants cannot be narrowed to him. " And we may be sure that Lydgate did not write the songs of welcome, nor in any other detail is it certain that he depended on his own information " (p. 100). In a note on the same page MacCracken remarks " some of the pageants, we happen to know, were due to devices and images that had been left over from former pageants; which the economical citizens furbished up and changed about a bit." He points out that in the 1415

The king, Henry VI, landed at Dover on 9 February, " and so com forth tyll he com to ye Blake heth, wher he was mett with the maier Jhon Welles, with all the craftes of london clad all in white and so yei brought hym to london ye xxj day of the same moneth." [1] The mayor was clad in red velvet, while the sheriffs

---

show there is the original of the giant at London Bridge — though I may add there is some doubt as to whether this was the same giant — the angels, conduit running wine, the doves, the castle in Cheap with virgins singing therefrom. The Latin songs and scriptures are not, it is true, new; but Dr. MacCracken forgets that it is no proof against pageantic authorship to point out that the same properties were used. As we shall see, later Lord Mayor's Shows utilized often the same properties under different authors — this is one of the handicaps under which the originality of the seventeenth-century authors was placed.

The novelty in 1432 is found in the genealogical trees, and above all, in the allegory — the last of which " was his stock-in-trade, poetically," and " may have been Lydgate's suggestions," as Dr. MacCracken (p. 100, n. 1) admits. That there is not much new in technique need not trouble us; one great step in advance — the introduction of allegory — seems to be due to Lydgate; though we have seen that the " raw material " of allegory was in pageantry before. In all forms of art, a new element is based on elements already existing; the perfecter is never the innovator. It is natural that one pageant-writer should borrow much from earlier ones, even as he uses earlier " properties." And here there is no servile borrowing, but a step in advance.

Kingsford, in *Eng. Hist. Lit.*, pp. 92 f., says: "The . . . description of the London pageant for Henry's return in February, 1432 [in Harl. MS. 540] seems also to be the work of an eye-witness, and to be independent of Lydgate's verses; ' Letter-book K ' may again be the source; the narrative given there was written by John Carpenter, the town clerk." If it were written by an eye-witness, there is no need to suppose he went back to Carpenter's letter.

Allegory appeared in " disguisings " as early as 1427, as we have seen; this also seems to be due to Lydgate. While admitting the possibility of an influence from the morality-plays here, I think it is unlikely that Lydgate drew upon this source; it is even possible that — although there were allegorical figures in the miracle-plays — the moralities may owe a stimulation to the allegorical figures of pageantry.

[1] Harl. MS. 3730, fol. 110 b (*Chronicle of Brute* — imperfect). No details of the entry are given here; this passage is reprinted in Halliwell, *Lydgate's Minor Poems*, p. 2. Harl. MS. 540, fol. 41 b records "The xxj of february he came from Eltham towards London and ye maior and Aldermen . . . rode agaynst the kynge on horsebacke." Halliwell refers " to the minute account of the ceremony given in Fabyan's Chronicle. . . . Another curious account of it is preserved in a manuscript at Lambeth Palace, and will be included in a volume I am now (1840) editing for the Camden Society . . ."

The chief sources for information on this entry are: Cotton MS. Cleop. C. iv, fols. 38 f.; Cotton MS. Julius B. ii, fols. 89 f.; Harl. MS. 540, fols. 41 b f.; and Harl. MS. 565, fol. 114 b (fol. 77 for a brief mention). On the relation of these various MSS. see Kingsford, *Chron. Lond.*, pp. ix f. The MSS. are variously reprinted by Halliwell-Phillipps, *Lydgate's Minor Poems* — (Percy Soc.), ii, pp. 2 f.; Kingsford, *Chron. Lond.*, pp. 97 f.; Tyrrell, *Lond. Chron.*, pp. 235 f.; Thomson, *Chron. Lond. Bridge*, pp. 239 f.; etc. Cf. also MacCracken, *King Henry's Triumphal Entry into London; Lydgate's Poem, and Carpenter's Letter* in Herrig's *Archiv.*, cxxvi, pp. 75 f., already referred to. My attention was called to this by Professor Kittredge. A bibliography of the entry is given, pp. 101 f.

Cf. also Fabyan, p. 603; Strutt, *Manners and Customs*, ii, pp. 51 f., and J. G. Nichols, p. 18 — both citing Fabyan. Nichols says that Lydgate " was the author of speeches in the pag-

and aldermen wore " ffurred clokys, the colour scarlett. . . . Eche oone welle horsed . . ." [1] The citizens were dressed in white " to shew the trouthe that they did mene, Toward the Kyng." [2] Foreign merchants resident in London, dressed in the fashion of their countries, took part in the procession; they were chiefly Genoese, Venetians, Florentines and " Easterlings."

And when the citizens got to Blackheath, the mayor —

> Made hem hove in rengis twayne
> A strete betwene eche party lyke a walle,
> Alle clad in whyt, and the most principalle,
> Afforne in reed, withe thaire mayre riding,
> Till tyme that he saughe [the kyng] komyng.[3]

And when the king came, the mayor greeted him (in a prose welcome) full of loyalty; [4] then were " noble devices, divers ordinances " shown, " conveyed be scripture withe fulle grete excellense." [5] First —

> . . . whan he whas passid the Fabor,
> Enteryng the brygge of this noble cité,
> Ther whas a piler reysed lyke a toure,
> And thereon stood a sturdy champion,
> Of looke and chere sterne as a lyon;
> His swerd upreryd, proudly gave menace
> Alle foren enmyes from the king to enchase.

> And in defence of his state rialle,
> The geaunt wold abyde eche aventure,
> And all assautis that were martialle
> For his sake he proudly wold endure;
> In tokyn whereof he had a scripture
> On outher side declaryng his entent. . . .[6]

---

eant " — a statement I cannot find in Fabyan. Malcolm, in *Lond. Rediv.*, (1803–07), ii, pp. 397 f., prints part of the poem; but he modernizes the spelling and omits the most interesting descriptions. Collier, ii, p. 244, and Herbert, i, pp. 92 f., (the latter quotes Stow and Lydgate,) also mention this pageant.

Chambers, ii, p. 169, n. 4, and Kingsford, *Eng. Hist. Lit.*, p. 93, n. 1, refer to the contemporary account by John Carpenter, printed from *Letter-Book K*, by H. T. Riley in *Liber Albus*, iii, pp. 457 f. (appendix 3). Carpenter's letter is printed also in Delpit.

[1] Halliwell-Phillipps, *Lydgate's Minor Poems*, p. 3 (printed from Cotton MS. Cleop. C. iv).

[2] Herbert, i, p. 93, says: "Lydgate . . . supposes they [*i. e.*, the crafts] adopted it [their white clothing] as expressing the *purity* of their loyalty." Did it occur to Herbert that perhaps Lydgate may have planned this bit of symbolism ?

[3] *Lydgate's Minor Poems* (Halliwell-Phillipps), p. 4.

[4] Cf. *Liber Albus*, iii, p. 458.

[5] Halliwell-Phillipps, p. 5.

[6] Harl. MS. 540, fol. 41 b records that on London Bridge " stode a gyant in a towr, with his sworde drawne in his hand to manas [*menace*] forren enemyes to yr [*their*] deathe." This giant appears to have some of the qualities of the " champion " who takes part in English coronations to this day. The speech of the giant is given on p. 5 of Halliwell-Phillipps' edition; it

Two antelopes stood on either side of the entrance to the bridge, bearing the arms of France and England,

> In tokenyng that God schalle for him provide
> As he hath title be juste enheritaunce,
> To regne in pees, plenté, and plesaunce.[1]

And as the king began to ride on, three empresses issued forth from a " toure " arrayed with soft velvets, cloth of gold, silk and tapestry, built in the middle of the bridge. The first was called Nature; the second was her sister Grace, and lastly came Fortune. Each of them gave the king " gostly giftes ": Grace gave "science" and "cunning"; Nature, strength and "fayreness"; Fortune, prosperity and wealth. Then a " scripture " appeared:

> " First understond and willfully procede
> And long to reigne," the scripture sayd indede.[2]

On the right of these " empresses " were seven celestial maidens, beautiful and bright, with angelic faces, " alle clad in white in tokyn of clennes." [3] They presented more " gostly gyftes " to the king, " outeward ffigured " by seven white doves [4] — " gyfftes callyd of the Holy Goste." And as they gave them, they said, " lyke as clerkes wryghte," " God fill thee with intelligence and wisdom, preserve thee from heaviness, give thee a spirit of cunning, dread, pity and humility." [5]

At the left of the empresses were seven other pure virgins, all clad in white " smytt fulle of sterris schene." And they gave " thre gifftes shortly in sentence " — that the king might have glory, clemency,[6] and pity, might and victory, pru-

---

was written — whether also spoken is not clear. By comparing Fabyan's account with Lydgate's poem, we see that many speeches supplemented the " scriptures."

This giant shows a blending of the folk- and chivalric-elements. He seems to be a folk-giant turned knight.

[1] In Carpenter's letter (see MacCracken in Herrig, cxxvi, p. 81; Riley, *Liber Albus*, iii, p. 459 and Delpit, p. 245) these stood on the same pageant. "Ex utroque quidem latere ipsius gigantis in eadem pagina (machina) erigebantur duo animalia vocata: Antelops que regnorum Anglie et Ffrancie arma vexillatim fulgentia patule supportabant." Chambers, ii, p. 169, n. 5, observes — " Carpenter uses the term *pagina*, which here occurs for the first time in connection with these London receptions. Mr. Riley quite unnecessarily proposes to read *machina*."

[2] Halliwell-Phillipps, p. 7.

[3] P. 8. Cf. Carpenter's letter in *Liber Albus*, iii, p. 459: " A dextro latere dictæ fabricæ stabant septem deificæ Virtutes in puellaribus effigiebus . . . quæ . . . septem dona Sancti Spiritus per emissionem septem albarum columbarum sibi figuraliter exhibentes . . ."

[4] Cf. the 1415 and 1431 entries, and the 1330 festival at Valenciennes.

[5] Halliwell-Phillipps, p. 9.

[6] Halliwell-Phillipps prints " cleanness "; the Cotton MSS. Julius B. ii (fol. 93, l. 19, *clennesse*) and Cleop. C. iv (fol. 41 b, l. 16, *clennes*) read the same. But both show *clemencie* in red ink in the margin. Cf. Kingsford, *Chron. Lond.*, p. 104, " And with septre of clennesse and pytee," and Malcolm, ii, p. 403: *sceptro clemencie* (l. 1 — cf. Harl. MS. 565, fol. 118, l. 8.) —

TOWER OF LEARNING

RHETORIC

PTOLEMY AND ASTRONOMY

dence and faith, health, love, and peace. Having spoken, the maidens sang a roundelay welcoming the king.[1]

Henry then entered the city, and rode to Cornhill, where he found a " tabernacle " richly arrayed: it was made for Dame Sapience, before whose face were the Seven Liberal Sciences — Grammar, " which had afore her old Precyane "; Logic, before whom stood Aristotle, " most clerkly disputing "; Rhetoric had in her presence Tully, called " Mirror of Eloquence "; Music had " Boece, her clerk," with his scholars playing many instruments. " Arsmetryk " with " Pyktegoras "; Geometry with Euclid, and Astronomy with Albmusard ended the list.[2] Before Sapience was a " scripture " telling that kings reign by her, and prosper with her help.[3]

And so progressing, the king came to the conduit, " made in cercle wise " where a child sat " middes aboue " on a throne, arrayed like a king. Mercy and

"And with a sceptre of cleanness and price " (l. 5). — [*Price* is an error for *pity* — cf. Harl. MS. 565, fol. 118, l. 12.] The Latin verses (printed by Malcolm with no difference of type) presumably represent " scriptures."

MacCracken, in Herrig, cxxvi, p. 85, n. 1, notes that cleanness here is " of course for clemence." Carpenter's letter (Riley, iii, p. 460) mentions the " sceptrum clementiæ."

[1] This is printed in full by Halliwell-Phillipps, p. 10; by Fabyan, p. 604, and Riley, iii, p. 460.

[2] Cf. the fresco, in the Spanish Chapel of S. Maria Novella at Florence, of the school of Giotto, attributed to Simon Memmi by Ruskin. (See *Mornings in Florence*, v, *The Strait Gate*.) The painting is reproduced opposite page 56 in the *Book of Words* of the Oxford Pageant of 1907.

The Seven Liberal Arts appeared in the *Masque of the Mediæval Curriculum* — an interlude in the Oxford Pageant; in the Lord Mayor's Shows of 1676, 1687, and 1612; and in the royal-entry of 1547.

Professor Kittredge has called my attention to *The Tower of Learning*, a wood-cut in Gregory Reisch's *Margarita Philosophica* (Heidelberg, 1496) opposite page 3, where the Liberal Sciences are illustrated. The figures in the Florentine picture are not exactly those of Lydgate's pageant; Tubal Cain represents the musician, and Ptolemy the astronomer; the others are the same.

[3] Even when speech was an important part of the pageant, "these scriptures" occasionally appeared. In Heywood's Lord Mayor's Show for 1631 (see Fairholt, *L. M. Pag.*, pt. i, p. 55) the first land-pageant was a tree "amongst the leaves and fruits" whereof were inserted " divine labels with several sentences expressing the causes which make cities to flourish and prosper, as — *the feare of God — religious zeale — a wise magistrate — obedience to rulers — unity — plaine and faithfull dealing* — with others of a like nature." In Settle's 1691 show there was a "Theatre of Victory"; "among the Ornaments of the several Columes, are intersprinkled these proper Mottos— *Victrix Fortuna; Triumphans Causa*"; and over Neptune: " Imperium Oceano, sed Famam terminet Astris " — Over Mars: " Vltricibus Armis." (Descriptive pamphlet of the show.) The descriptive pamphlet of Dekker's show for 1628 records " scriptures " on the second pageant.

These " scriptures " were simply explanatory sentences affixed to the pageants — sometimes supplemented by speech. Those of the 1431 entry into Paris were not at all Biblical — and while sometimes a Biblical text was used as a " scripture," there is nothing in the word itself to limit its meaning to *text*.

Truth sat on either side, and Clemency [1] " aloft did abyde." Before the boy stood two judges and eight sergeants, each presenting this scripture in every man's sight:

> Honor of kyng, wiche I schalle expresse
> Of comyn custome, lovithe equité and righte.

The king forth riding entered into Chepe, and when he came to the conduit, the water was turned into wine, " lyke to the watyr of Archideclyne." [2]

Three virgins — Mercy, Grace [3] and Pity — drew up wine at three wells: Mercy, of temperance; Grace, of good governance, and Pity, of comfort and consolation — which they gave to the king.[4]

And there were eke trees, with fresh leaves, laden with fruit — oranges, almonds, and pomegranates; lemons, dates, and quinces. And beside this glorious Paradise [5] were two old men, " ffull circumspecte and wise." One was Enoch and the other Elias; and they prayed for the king, wishing him joy, and blessing him.[6]

And the king rode on to a castle [7] built of green jasper, on whose towers the sun shone full bright. Two green trees grew upright, showing the king's arms and ancestry: one line led back to St. Edward, and one to St. Louis, showing the king's right to France, and his descent. On the other side of this castle was a tree " wiche sprang ouȝt of Jessé " — David crowned first for his humility: the branches conveyed lineally to Jesus, son of Mary — and this device was set on the side next to Paul's.[8]

And the king went on toward the Cathedral, and at the Conduit there was a " lykenes Indivisable made of the trinité "; and a multitude of heavenly angels

---

[1] The lady Clemens (Cotton MS. Julius B. ii — Kingsford, *Chron. Lond.*, p. 107; Harl. MS. 565, fol. 119 b; cf. *clementia* in the scripture introducing the verse. Kingsford, n. 3, points out that Cotton MS. Cleop. C. iv, and Fabyan, read *cleanness*, as does Halliwell-Phillipps, p. 13).

[2] Cf. the pageant at Bruges in 1468 — below, p. 152.

[3] What seems like a lack of invention on the part of the poet may be due to the novelty of allegory in the pageant. I do not think that these are the same characters as the earlier Grace and Mercy.

[4] The mayor was John Wells, a Grocer; hence the appropriateness of the wells. Lydgate himself points out that they were " devised notably indede For to accordyne with the Maier's name."

[5] Cf. the 1392 pageant, where John the Baptist " stood in a desert surrounded by all kinds of trees and a menagerie of strange beasts." This is obviously a trade pageant.

Chambers, ii, p. 170 compares this with the Norwich Grocers' tree, of which we have already spoken; I may add a reference to the " lemon tree " prepared in 1616, when Munday wrote the inaguration show for Mr. John Leman, Fishmonger. This is rather a pun than a trade-pageant. (See Fairholt, *L. M. Pag.*, pt. i, pp. 40 f. — and below, chapter vi.)

[6] Cf. the patriarchs in the 1415 entry.

[7] Cf. the castles in 1377, 1392, 1415, 1431, etc. This was at the conduit in Chepe. — See Carpenter's letter, cited by MacCracken in Herrig, *Archiv.*, cxxvi, p. 92.

[8] Halliwell-Phillipps, p. 17.

stood about, to whom was given a precept in scripture. When the king arrived at St. Paul's, he dismounted and entered the church: and there to meet him was a procession, and the archbishops and chancellors of Lincoln, Salisbury, Norwich and Ely; the Bishop of Rochester and the Dean of St. Paul's.

After the service, the mayor and citizens escorted Henry to Westminster, where the Abbot and all the convent, in rich copes, met him and brought to him the sceptre of St. Edward. There was a *Te Deum* in Westminster Abbey, and the people rejoiced. Then the king went home, and rested in his palace; the mayor and the citizens returned to London.[1]

This show has been described in detail, because we find in it not only much which attaches it to the past, but also almost every element seen in later pageantry. For the first time we see allegory in the royal-entry; but the " raw material " stood ready at hand. Trade-symbolism as shown in the " gracious Paradise," we have seen before; the Biblical element: Enoch and Elias, and — by extension — the angels, with the " romantic " material — the castle — we have also met. The giant, we saw in 1415; the coats-of-arms, the displayed genealogies, the prose welcome, the gratulatory writings and the moral epigrams we have met, and shall meet again. Sacred music is giving way to roundelays; but the wine flows from conduits as it has in the past, and will in the future. The lion and antelope are rather heraldic than trade animals; and they do not seem to have been carried through the streets as were the animals of the Fishmongers in 1298. The one element which later, under the influence of the Renaissance, plays such a large part in these triumphs, and which has not — until now — suggested itself, is the classical; and that, in the figures representing the Liberal Sciences, may be said to have appeared in this entry. It is probably not a matter of chance that allegory first appears in the first pageant to which we can assign an author.

In 1433 Henry VI spent Christmas at the Abbey of Bury St. Edmunds. Although there was some splendor on this occasion, there seems to have been no pageantry.[2]

---

[1] Halliwell-Phillipps, p. 20. Though the king received " gostly giftes " from the damsels in this entry, he was given something more substantial the next Saturday, when the mayor, aldermen, and sheriffs took him £1000 for which he thanked them heartily. For the mayor's prose presentation speech, see Halliwell-Phillipps, p. 21.

[2] The account of the king's arrival and stay, taken from " the Register Curteys of the Abbey, so-called from the Abbot of that name who was elected in 1429 and died 1445," is printed in *Archæologia*, xv, pp. 65 f. Welcomed by "aldermannus, burgenses et communitas" of the city, who escorted him to his ecclesiastical hosts, the king arrived with ceremony, but without pageantry in the strict sense.

In 1443 when Alfonso the Great entered Naples, there were the seven Virtues, Fortune, her " genius," a Julius Cæsar, who explained the allegories to the king, and Catalaus, on lay figures of horses, who had a mock fight with a body of Turks; and last of all, a gigantic tower, with the four Virtues, each of whom addressed the king with a song. See on this, Burckhardt, ii, pp. 147 f.

1443 — Henry VI Expresses his Gratitude for 1432

On 30 November, 1443, the Goldsmiths' Company received a special letter from King Henry, desiring them to prepare themselves to meet his Queen, Margaret of Anjou, in company with the mayor, aldermen and crafts of the city. The king's gratitude for the 1432 show is expressed in his letter: " as we ben enfourmed your crafte have at all times notably acquited them, — and in especiall at our comynge home from oure coronacion at *Parys*, whereof we con you right singular esp'all thanks." [1]

1445 — Margaret of Anjou Enters London

Lydgate is the reputed author of the pageant welcoming Queen Margaret, the wife of Henry VI, on 28 May, 1445. His verses exist in two MSS., one of which is not complete.[2] The queen was met on Blackheath by the civic authorities who escorted her to the town. The first pageant was erected at the foot of London Bridge; it was an allegorical representation of Peace and Plenty. Upon the bridge itself appeared a pageant representing Noah's Ark,[3] before which a second speech was delivered. At the Tun in Cornhill stood St. Margaret and angels; at the Conduit in Chepe, the Wise and Foolish Virgins; at the Cross in Chepe, appears to have been the " Heavenly Jerusalem," and at St. Michaels in Querne, the Resurrection and the Judgment. The character of the pageants and speakers must be guessed from the speeches; only one is mentioned — " at Leadenhall was a speech by Madame Grace, who is styled the ' Chauncelor de Dieu.' " Fabyan records " sumptuous and costly pagentes, and resemblaunce of dyverse olde hystoryes." [4]

---

[1] This letter is printed by Herbert, ii, p. 133, from the Goldsmiths' Wardens' accounts of that date; Herbert notes " the costume adopted by the Goldsmiths, in attending the ceremony, justified the royal compliment, and suitably accorded with the splendor of the company."

[2] Harl. MS. 3869 — the complete version — is reprinted by Carleton F. Brown in the *Modern Language Review*, vii, pp. 225–234; Harl. MS. 542 — the incomplete version — I have printed in *Modern Philology* for May, 1915, pp. 53 f. Thomson, *Chron. Lond. Bridge*, pp. 275 f., prints lines 1–32 of this MS. which is in Stow's hand. (Cf. *Cat. Harl. MSS.*, 1808, i, p. 346.)

Cf. for mention of this 1445 show, Stow, *Annals*, p. 385; Fabyan, p. 617; Davidson, p. 87; J. G. Nichols, p. 21; Chambers, ii, p. 170; Taylor, *Glory of Regality*, p. 268; Hone, *Anc. Mys.*, p. 235.

[3] Probably another example of the common union of Biblical and trade material. The Ark is the crest of the Shipwrights' Company, and figures in their arms; its trade-significance is very likely due to the miracle-play. Cf. the Grocers' " Paradise."

[4] Fabyan, p. 617. I may note here that at Reggio in 1453 an elaborate pageant or " machine " greeted Duke Borso. On it the patron of the town, St. Prospero, appeared to float, surrounded by cherubim and angels. Justice, attended by a genius, also appeared on this occasion; a car drawn by a unicorn followed a car in the form of a ship; the clergy furnished religious allegory in the lay-figure of Idolatry and the personification of Faith. When the girl representing the latter had addressed the duke, the column supporting the former broke in

1456 — QUEEN MARGARET AT COVENTRY

Eleven years after her reception at London, the queen was received at Coventry by the municipal authorities. The account of this occasion in the Leet Book is detailed.[1] John Wedurby was paid twenty-five shillings for preparing the pageants, and perhaps writing the verses.[2]

First, " at Bablake there was made a Jesse on the yate right well [arayed] and there were shewed too speeches " by " Ysay " and " Jeremy." The first prophecied ". . . like as mankynde was gladdid by the birght of Jhūs, So shall þis empyre joy the birthe of yor bodye," and the other — " I Jeremy þe prophete trew þies wordes of you wyll say: this reme shall joye þe blessyd tyme of yor nativyte."

" Afturward with inne the yate at the est yende of the chirche was sette a pagent right well arayed & þerin was shewed ij speches on of seynt Edward & the other of Seynt John Evñgl as foloweth:

" S. Edward: ' . . . I Kyng Edward welcū you wᵗ affeccion right cordiall . . .' "

after which he prays for the queen's weal, and for that of the king, with St. John.

" Afturward the Cundit yn the Smithforde strete was right well arayed & there was shewed iiij speches of iiij cardynall virtues as foloweth." The Virtues were Righteousness, Temperance, Strength, and Prudence.[3]

" Afturward at the Crosse yn the croschepyng there were ordeyned diverse angels sensyng a high on the crosse & there ranne out wyne at mony places along while.

---

pieces. Cæsar, accompanied by the seven Virtues (personified by women) also addressed the duke, and after the service at the Cathedral all the *paginæ persones* rendered homage to him, while three angels flew down from an adjacent building. For an account of this entry, see Burckhardt, ii, pp. 144 f. I mention this rather elaborate reception merely to show there is nothing here that we did not find in England in 1432.

[1] See *Coventry Leet-Book* (ed. Mary D. Harris (EETS.), 1907–09), ii, pp. 285 f.; T. Sharp, *Dissertation on Pageants at Coventry* (1825), pp. 145 f. Cf. Miss Harris's *Life in an Old English Town*, pp. 160 f.; Chambers, ii, p. 174, and Hone, *Anc. Mys.*, p. 235.

[2] " Memorandum, that . . . the Meyre payd to Joh Wedurby of Leycetur for þe provicion and makyng of these premisses of the welcomyng of oure Souerayn lady the quene & for his labour Inne & out xxv s," *Leet-Book* (fol. 170 b), ii, p. 292. Miss Harris in *Life in an Old English Town*, p. 162, calls Wedurby " an indifferent poet."

[3] These characters appeared in Lydgate's masque (cf. p. 107 above) and often in later shows. I may refer here to a masque — or the verses for a masque — by Lod. Lloyd, printed at London in 1607, where these four characters were the speakers. They are called *Iusticia*, *Temperantia*, *Fortitudo*, and *Prudentia*; the speeches are in iambic heptameter.

There is a considerable classic element in Lloyd's volume, which is dedicated to the king. The author has " presumed . . . to write these fewe Verses, to honour this our Tryumphant and Sacred Feast, *Hilaria*, the fift of August . . ." Though there is nothing in the pamphlet to prove that the qualities were meant to be living, one may assume a masque, either planned or produced, behind the verses.

" Afturward betwix the seyde crosse & the cundit bene þᵉ that were sette ix pagentes right well arayed & yn every pageant was shewed a speche [1] of the ix conqueroures: yn the furst was shewed of Hector . . ." The other Worthies were Alexander, Joshua, David, Judas Maccabeus, Arthur, Charles, Cæsar, and God-frey of Bouillon. All bow to the Queen in reverence and fealty.[2]

"Afturward & last the Cundit yn the Croschepyng was arayed right well with as mony virgyns as myght be þʳuppon and there was made a grete Dragon & Seynt Marḡet sleyng hym be myracull & there was shewed full well this speche that foloweth." St. Margaret [3] bids the queen welcome, will pray that she come to no harm, will protect her, adding, " when ye be yn any dredefull cace Call on me boldly . . . and trist to me feythefully. . . ."

A large part of this entertainment is drawn from Biblical or sacred subjects. Saint, or King, Edward — together with the Worthies — may be regarded as historical; but, as Chambers points out, " in many provincial towns the pageants used at royal-entries had a far closer affinity to the miracle-plays proper than was the case in London." [4] It is more likely that the Worthies came from romantic literature directly, than that we have here an echo of the Paris entry of Henry VI in 1431.

1461 — EDWARD IV IN LONDON AND COVENTRY.

The books of the Carpenters' Company show that in 1 Edward IV — perhaps at the king's coronation — there was a royal-entry. " Paide to Edward Stone for Riding ayenst the Kynge, iiij s." [5] After his coronation, the king visited

---

[1] This phrase may mean that there was a " scripture " fastened on each pageant, which may have been read aloud by the character; we may assume, I think, that oral speech played an important part in this show.

[2] The Nine Worthies — which, with nine female worthies, appeared in Paris in 1431 — appear again at Coventry in 1498. It may be remarked that what has wrongly been called a " pageant " of these Worthies may be found in *Love's Labours' Lost* (v, 2); this scene is rather an " interlude " (if we may stretch that word to cover a " play " within a play) in which the cast of characters take more or less important parts. Of course one Worthy appearing after another, introducing himself, and uttering what is on his mind, is not very dramatic; but there is little " pageantry " about the scene! Cf. Magnin's error in calling the masque in Jonson's *Tale of a Tub* a " pageant " (1862 ed., p. 228): " . . . . une action muette, expliquée par une exposition verbale ou une cantilène narrative, ce que les Anglais appellent une *pageant*. . . . Le *masque*, dans *the Tale of a Tub*, se compose de cinq *motions* ou tableaux." See Jonson's *Tale of a Tub* (Gifford's ed., ii, pp. 480 f.) act. v, sc. 5. In the introduction, the fifth "motion," and the epilogue, Jonson calls this a *masque*; nowhere does he call it a *pageant*.

[3] It is obvious that St. Margaret was substituted for St. George out of honor to Queen Margaret.

[4] Chambers, ii, p. 174.

[5] Jupp, *Hist. Account of the Carpenters* (1887), p. 32, from the books of the Carpenters' Company. He gives no date.

In 1459–60 eight men of the Pewterers' craft rode to meet the king, and were paid 4s. 4d.

Coventry,[1] but — as Sharp informs us — " the MS. Annals are silent as to the reception of the king, and the Leet book makes no mention of Pageants or any particular ceremony used on the occasion; whence it may be conjectured that there was no display at the City charge." That the companies were called upon to exhibit a pageant seems evident from the Smiths' accounts.[2] The pageant dealt with Samson, and " we may imagine from the usual tenor of these complimentary shews that Samson promised to use his strength in supporting the claim and just right of Edward IV to his newly-acquired sovereignty." [3]

It is worth noting that here we have a union of trade-symbolism, miracle-play, and royal-entry. The first two elements were often combined, and — as has been noticed in connection with the 1456 show — the last two were commonly found together in provincial towns.[4] Coventry was often honored by royal visitors, and availed herself of the many opportunities of using the Corpus Christi pageant-cars to receive them.

1461 — THE KING AT BRISTOL

When Edward visited Bristol, this same year, he was welcomed by William the Conqueror, and three lords. A " greet Gyaunt " delivered the keys of the city to the king; Saint George " on horsebakke " fought with a dragon, while

---

(Welch, *Hist. Pewterers* (1902), i, p. 26); in 1460–61, the same number rode to meet the king and received 6s. 4d. (p. 27); in 1462–63 the guild met the king coming to Parliament, with a barge and a boat (p. 28). [There seem to have been no pageants connected with these "ridings" — see *ibid.*, i, pp. 55, 56, 58, etc. Welch's use of the word *pageant* in his index is the free use of it, as meaning a splendid show, rather than the stricter sense of a show with pageants.]

Arundell, *Hist. Reminiscences of London* (1869), p. 297, Humpherus, *Hist. Origin and Progress of the Company of Watermen and Lightermen* (n. d.), i, pp. 54 and 60, and Jupp, pp. 32, 34, and 35 gives various extracts from companies' records relative to barge-hire in 1470, 1483, 1485, and 1490, to meet various kings. These are not in the field of pageantry, but we should remember that at the end of the fifteenth century water-processions of the guilds were not uncommon.

[1] For mention of this visit see Sharp, p. 151; Chambers, ii, p. 174; H. Craig, *Two Coventry Corpus Christi Plays* (EETS. ES. 87), p. 114; *Coventry Leet-Book*, ii, p. 316, n. 4. Fabyan, p. 652, dates the king's coronation 1460, and mentions his journey through the realm after it, though he does not mention Coventry as one of the towns visited. Most authorities place the king's coronation in 1461 — cf. *e. g.*, Polydore Virgil (Royal MS. 18 C. viii–ix, fol. 29; ed. Camden Soc., xxix by Sir Henry Ellis, 1844, p. 113) and Stow, *Annals*, p. 416.

[2] See the items extracted by Sharp, p. 152. Pageants were ordered in 1460; for what purpose is not clear. See *Leet-Book*, ii, p. 312.

[3] As Chambers points out, this pageant was probably that used by the Smiths at Corpus Christi. The king received £100 and a cup on this visit.

[4] On the lack of plays by the craft-guilds of London, see Davidson's suggestion (p. 88) that the cost of the frequent pageants necessary for royal-entries made the guilds reluctant to build moving pageants for Corpus Christi and other feasts. It must be added, however, that they had their pageants at Midsummer.

a king and queen " on hygh in a castelle " looked down on their daughter, who stood beneath with a lamb. Great melody of angels was there, when the dragon was slain.[1]

1468 — A PAGEANT AT BRUGES

On 6 July, 8 Edward IV, the king's sister was married to the Duke of Burgundy at Bruges, and there were pageants. When Margaret entered the city " those that bare the torches were clothed in Blew And that were marchaunts were clothed in Cramoyssey velvett." [2] A pageant " made by subtyll crafte after the fforme of A castell gate " showed the creation of Adam and Eve, and their marriage; " and other pageauntes of diuers histories after the same forme." [3] There was one of " Alexander the great conqueror how he marryed the Doughter of the Kinge of egipt," and the fourth pageant, " of Archideclyne that of water made wyn [4] . . . the vjth Pageaunte was of the crucifying of our lorde Jhu Christe . . . the vij th Pageannte " showed Moses wedding " Tharbis the Kinges Doughter of Egipt." The eighth pageant " was a mayden settinge Betwene A lyon and A leopard beringe the Armes of Burgoyne the whiche hercules conquered from the Bestes. And aboue the maydyns hed there was a greate flouredelice . . ."[5] The pageants on this occasion had explanatory Latin " scriptures."

It will be observed that some of these pageants were appropriate to a wedding — that of the Crucifixion, however, hardly seems to fall into this category. Besides the Biblical pageants, was one heraldic; what we ought particularly to notice, is that there seems to have been nothing here which we have not already found in England.

1469 — QUEEN ELIZABETH AT NORWICH

From the Norwich Chamberlains' Accounts for 9 and 10 Edward IV, Mr. Harrod recounts the queen's visit to that city in 1469.[6] When she arrived, the Corporate Body received her at the Westwyk Gates, where also " a stage had been constructed covered with red and green worstead, adorned with figures of angels, and with scutcheons. . . . Here were also two giants made of wood and

---

[1] From MS. Lambeth, 306, fol. 132 (not dated), printed by F. J. Furnivall, in *Political Religious and Love Poems* (EETS., orig. series 15, London 1866, reëdited 1903), p. 5. Cf. Chambers, ii, p. 176, n. 1. This bears a striking resemblance to the St. George pageant at Coventry in 1474 — see next page.

On the visit of Edward IV to Bristol in " the summer of the year 1461 " see *Archæologia*, xxix, p. 131; this is presumably that for which the above arrangements were made.

[2] Addl. MS. 6113, fol. 95 b.

[3] Fol. 96.

[4] Cf. the 1432 entry of Henry VI — above, p. 146.

[5] Fol. 96 b.

[6] Henry Harrod, *Queen Elizabeth Woodville's Visit to Norwich in 1469* in *Norfolk Archæology*, (1859) v, pp. 32 f.

hungry (Hungary) leather, their bodies stuffed with hay, and their crests glittering in all the grandeur of gold and silver leaf. There were also two patriarchs, twelve apostles, and sixteen virgins in mantles with hoods. A certain friar played Gabriel. John Mumford's son assisted in this performance; and Gilbert Spirling exhibited a pageant of the Salutation of Mary and Elizabeth, which required a speech from him in explanation. There were many clerks singing finely, accompanied upon the organs. From thence she proceeded to the gates of the Friars Preachers and here . . . another stage had been erected, similarly decorated. . . . The entertainment offered to the queen at this point was limited to a vocal performance by one ' Fakke ' and his boys. More was probably provided, but the shows and pageants terminated abruptly by reason of the great and continuous rain. . . . Very much damage was done . . . and thus ominously did this reception, which was to rival that of ' any queen that was afore her,' end."

1474 — PRINCE EDWARD VISITS COVENTRY

The Coventry *Leet-Book* gives a detailed account of the reception of Prince Edward at that city on 28 April, 1474.[1] After making the prince a gift of a hundred marks and a " gilt coppe of xv Ounces w^t a Kerchyff of Pleasaunce upon the said coppe," the corporation welcomed him into the city. where " at Babulake ȝate ther ordeyned a stacion therein beyng Kyng Richard w^t xiij other arrayed lyke as Dukes Mark'es Erles Vicouns and Barons & lordis w^t mynstrallcy of the Wayts of the Citie and Kyng Richard ther " spoke. He welcomed the prince and prayed that he might always be kept in good health, and have perpetual joy.

" Also at the Condite afore Richard Braytoft the Elder [2] a nother stacion w^t iij P'riarkes [3] ther stondyng upon the said condite w^t Jacobus xij sonnes w^t my[n]stralcy of harpe and Dowsemeris & ther Rennyng Wyne in oñ place . . ." and one of the patriarchs spoke.

" Also at the Brodeyate a Pagiont and seint Edward beyng therein w^t x a states with hym w^t mynstralcy of harpe and lute. . . ." Here the saint spoke.

" Also at the Crosse in the Cros-chepyng were iij prophets standyng at the crosse sensyng and upon the Crosse a boven were Childer of Issarell syngyng and casting out whete obles [4] & ffloures and iiij pypis rennyng wyne.

" Also in the Croschepyng a fore the Panyer [5] a Pagent and iij Kyngs of Colen therein w^t other divers arraied and ij knyghts armed w^t mynstralsy of smal pypis " and one of the kings spoke the eulogy.[6]

---

[1] See Harris's ed., ii, pp. 390 f.; Sharp, p. 152; H. Craig, p. 114. (Miss Harris, in *Life in an old English Town*, pp. 189–190, refers to this visit, citing the *Leet-Book*.)

[2] The mayor's father [Sharp's note].　　[4] Sweet cakes [Sharp's note].

[3] Patriarchs [Sharp's note].　　　　　[5] An inn very near to the cross [Sharp's note].

[6] In Miss Harris's edition of the *Leet-Book*, ii, p. 393, n. 1., Craig, p. 115, n. 4, is referred to, as suggesting that the three kings of Cologne here were those of the shearmen and tailors'

"Also upon the condite in the Crosse Chepyng was seint George armed, and kynges dought⟨r⟩ knelyng a fore hym w⟨t⟩ a lambe, and the fadyr and the moder beyng in a toure a boven beholdyng seint George savyng their dought⟨r⟩ from the dragon. And the Condite rennyng wyne in iiij place₃ and mynstralcy of Orgonpleyinge "; [1] and St. George spoke, calling himself the protector of the prince, and praying the Lord to preserve him, as he himself defended the maiden here. The companies were called upon to take part in this reception.

The crafts escorted the king through London on 30 May, 15 Edward IV (1475) but there seems to have been no pageantry.[2] Nor was there in 1478 when Edward visited York.[3]

ACTIVITY OF THE LONDON GUILDS

In 1483 and the following years there was considerable activity among the London guilds, which were called upon often to meet various monarchs. An examination of the expenditures of the various companies, as recorded in Herbert [4] shows preparations for meeting Edward V, Richard III, and Henry VII; but on none of these occasions is there any mention of pageantry in the technical sense.[5]

The London coronation of Richard III was unaccompanied by pageants, but there was a certain amount of symbolism on this occasion — as is the case with every coronation.[6]

Grafton records: " . . . the Erle of Northumberland . . . with the poyntlesse sword naked in his hand, which signified mercy . . . and the Lord Lisle

---

pageant. "They would have the necessary costumes for the Magi." As we have remarked, it was common enough to draw upon the guild-plays on the occasion of a royal-entry in the provinces.

[1] Cf. the St. George at Bristol in 1461.

[2] W. M. Williams, *Annals of Founders* (1867), p. 212, referring to the city records. On this date "a watch was made by the Aldermen and Mysteries when the King went through the Citie by night from the palace of the Bishop of London through Chepe to the Bridge and from thence to Greenwich. The standing of the Founders was in the 'Pultry' where were also placed the 'Armurers, Talugh Chandlrs, Paten Makers and Poulters.'"

[3] Cf. R. Davies, *Extracts from the Municipal Records of the City of York* (1843), pp. 68 and 78 f., citing town records.

[4] See Herbert, i, pp. 95, 405; ii, pp. 134, 535, etc.

[5] Hall, *Chron.* (1809), p. 359, narrating events in the reign of Edward V, says: "Wherevpon the lorde protectour caused a counsaille to be set at the tower on the fridaye the thirtene day of Iune, where was muche commonyng for the honourable solemnite of the coronacion, of the whiche the tyme appoincted aproched so nere, that the pageauntes were a makyng daye & night at Westminster, and vitaile killed which afterwarde was caste awaye." Here *pageant* seems to mean nothing more than *grandstand*, or *scaffolding*.

[6] See Hall, p. 375; Grafton, ii, pp. 113 f.; J. G. Nichols, p. 22 (going back to Buck, whose authorities are Moore, Grafton, Polidore, Hall, Croyland, Holinshed, Stow; cf. Cotton MS. Tib. E. x, fol. 41 b [Buck's MS.]); Buck, p. 26.

Viscount bare the rod with the doffe, which signifieth innocencie," were of the procession. This symbolism is not explained by Hall; but Buck notes in the margin that the *curtana* symbolizes mercy, and that the " second Sword naked with a poynt," borne by Viscount Lovel, and another, borne by the Earl of Kent, signified Justice to the Temporality and to the Clergy. The Ball and Cross, carried by the Earl of Lincoln on this occasion, signified Peace, and the other regal emblems indicated Monarchy.[1]

1483 — RICHARD III AT YORK

In 1483, Richard III was entertained at York, and there were pageants, together with a performance of the Creed Play. In August, John Kendale, secretary to the king, wrote to the York Corporation as follows:

" Ryght Worshipfull Sirs, I recomaunde me unto you as hertly as I can and thanked be Ihu the Kinges grace is in good helth, and in lyke wyse the Quenys grace and in all þeir progresse have been worshipfully ressayved wᵗ pageants . . ."[2] The letter goes on to ask the York authorities " as honorably as yor wisdomes can imagyne, to ressayve him [the King] & the Quene at þeir comyng dispose you to do, as well pageantes wᵗ soch good speches as can goodly, thys short warnyng considered, be devised and under suche forme as Mr. Lancaster of the Kynges counsell, thys brynger, shall sumwhat advertise you of my mynd in that behalve, as in hangyng the streites thorough wich the Kinges grace shall come wᵗ clothes of arras, tapistre werk. . . . Me nedeth not thus to advise you, for I doubte not ye have provided þerefore better þan I can advyse you. Writtn in hast þe xxiij day of August at Not[tingham]."[3]

On 16 August, 1 Ric. III, it was agreed that the city authorities of York in " skarlet gownys " should meet the king.[4] On 6 September it " was agreed that for the honor of this Cite that all my maisters the Aldermen & all the xxiiij shalbe

---

[1] Cf. the 1547 pageant (below, p. 186); and the *Handbook of Ceremonials* for London officials (1906), p. 133, where an extract from the London *Gazette* of 28 October, 1902, is reprinted, which describes the coronation of Edward VII. The *curtana* on this occasion was borne by the Duke of Grafton.

On the costume worn by Richard III on " the vigil afore the day of his moost noble Coronation, for to ride in from his Toure of London, unto his Palays of Westminster," see Dean Milles, citing the Wardrobe Account for 1483 in *Archæologia*, i, pp. 367 f.

[2] Davies, pp. 163 f. Cf. also Francis Drake, *Eboracum* (1736), pp. 116 f.; Chambers, ii, p. 175.

[3] I have been unable to find the original of this letter in the MS. *House-Books* of York for 1483; nor do the *House-Books* give the details of the king's reception on the 7th September printed by Davies, pp. 173 f.

[4] Cf. *House-Books* ii, iii, and iv (bound together), fol. 96 (in the red numbering); Davies, p. 163. Davies, p. 162, dates this entry, 16 August, 1 Ric. III. In his volume (p. 164) Kendale's letter is dated the 23ᵈ; it was evidently added to the records, the next date in Davies being the 26ᵗʰ.

wᵗ my lord the mair to atend apon the Kyngs gude grace to morow at seyng of the Creed play." [1] And then is crossed out " and [th]at a steward shalbe made emong tham to p've for them & every man shal pay elyk,[2] that is to say, as moch he þt is away as he þt is thar." [3]

Other accounts of this visit to York, and the king's coronation, make only general mention of pageants. Beside the Creed play, we do not know what characters appeared, or what scenes were exhibited. Hall [4] records this visit of the king to York " where the citizens received him with great pomp and triumph . . . and made divers days plays and pageants in token of joy and solace."

It is possible that the king visited Norwich on this same progress; Blomefield believes he did, " for at an assembly held on the Nativity of the Blessed Virgin, Sept. 8, it was agreed that £160 should be cessed on the citizens, against the first coming of the king to this city, and that there should be grand pageants [5] made against his coming in the same manner as those were, at the first coming of King Edward IV." [6]

---

[1] Fol. 99 b, printed in Davies, p. 173. He does not indicate that anything is crossed out.

[2] Alike.

[3] The names of those who contributed to the king's gift on this occasion are recorded in the same *House-Book*, fol. 98. On fol. 97 b is a record of the vote to give both king and queen golden gifts.

On 2 September, i Ric. III, " it was agreed that the Creed play shall be playd afore or suffreyn lord the kyng of Sunday next cumyng apon the cost of the most onest men of every parish in this cite." (Fol. 98 b, printed by Davies, pp. 171 f., and cited from Davies by L. T. Smith, p. xxx, n. 4.) In a note on p. 172, Davies remarks: " The selection of the Creed play for the special entertainment of the royal visitors, is a proof that it was the favourite drama of the day. An allusion to the pageants exhibited on the occasion of the king's visit is found in the minutes of the proceedings of the council at a meeting held in March, 1484 . . ." See the same *House-Book*, under date of 27 March, 1 Ric. III, fol. 116; it was agreed that " Thomas Gray, maister of Saint Xrofers gyld shall have the canvas yt lys in the Chamber yt remaynyd of the shew made late to the king to make hallyngs of in the common hall to be stend (stained) and paynted of the cost of the Mr. of the gyld."

[4] *Chronicle*, p. 380. About the same account may be found in Grafton, ii, p. 120. Cf. Cotton, MS. Tib. E. x, fol. 44 b *et seq.*, where this much-mutilated MS. (the " History of King Richard III, written by Sir George Buc, Knt, master of the king's office of the Revels " — *Catalogue of the Cotton MSS.* (1802), p. 41) relates the festivities of the York coronation. In Buck's printed volume, *The History of the Life and Reigne of Richard the Third* (1646), p. 28, we read: " And indeed it was a day of great state; for (as *Polidore* saith) There was then three Princes in Yorke wearing Crownes, the King, Queene, and Prince; In acclamation whereof, there was Stage-Playes, Turneaments, and other Triumphall sports, as Sir *Thomas Moore* relates." The Cotton MS. is cited by Drake, *Eboracum*, p. 117.

I can find no mention of these in Sir Thomas More's *Life and Reign of Richard III*. The Prior of Croyland, as quoted by Buck, says: " Eodem die quo Richardus coronatus est Rex in Ecclesia Metropolitana Eboracensi, mox Filium Edwardum in Principatum Walliæ cum insigniis virgæ, aureæ &c evexit, & Pomposa & sumptuosa festa & convivia ibi fecit."

[5] Blomefield notes " triumphal arches."

[6] F. Blomefield, *Hist. Norf.* (1745), ii, p. 124; (his authority is *Lib. Conq.*, 1 Ric. III).

1485 — HENRY VII WELCOMED AFTER THE BATTLE OF BOSWORTH FIELD

The triumphal progress of Henry VII from the Battle of Bosworth Field is recounted in much the same fashion by Grafton and Hall. The common people, assembled along the road in great numbers and hailed the king with eager shouts. As he drew near London, the mayor and magistrates, " being all clothed in violet," met him at Shoreditch, and the people crowded around him joyfully.[1] " And with great pomp and triumph he rode through the city to the cathedral church of St. Paul. . . . After his prayers said, and *Te Deum* sung, he departed to the Bishops Palace, and there sojourned a season, during which time plays, pastimes and pleasures were shewed in every part of the city." [2]

1486 — HENRY'S PROVINCIAL TOUR

After his coronation, the king made a journey through the provinces, visiting some of the more important towns. A contemporary MS., printed in Leland's *Collectanea*, gives us an account of this trip;[3] it is entitled: " A shorte and brief Memory by Licence and Corveccon of the First Progresse of our Souveraigne Lord King Henry the VII. after his noble Coronacon . . . towards the North Parties." At York, the king and his train were met by the mayor three miles out of the town; the Recorder welcomed the royal visitor, recommending the place and its inhabitants to his good grace. Half a mile from the gate of the city, processions of the clergy met the king, and — with an immense multitude — attended him to the gate, where " was ordeyned a Pajannt with dyvers Personages

---

[1] The entry of Henry VII on 3 September, 1485, was reproduced in the London Pageant of 1911 — see the *Book* of the *Festival of Empire*, p. 62.

[2] Grafton, ii, pp. 157 f.; Hall, p. 423. Neither historian specifies the plays, pastimes, and pleasures in detail. Arundell, p. 297, notes that the Carpenters' Company paid for " barge at metyng of the kyng on the water, vij*s*., vij*d*." (from the books of the Company); and Humpherus, i, p. 60, tells of the great rejoicing with which Henry VII was received on his accession; he also quotes from the books of the Carpenters' Company, showing barge hire " to reseyve the king on the water."

Taylor, *Glory of Regality*, p. 274, n. 119, says that the device of the ceremonial of Henry VII's coronation " was printed (very incorrectly indeed) by the late John Ives, Esq., Suffolk herald extraordinary, in his *Select Papers* . . ." This volume — published in 1773 — is in the Brit. Mus. and the Soc. Antiq.; the coronation of Henry VII is described on pp. 93 f.

[3] Cotton MS. Julius B. xii, fols. 8 b–66, printed in Leland, iv, pp. 185 f. The king's visit to York is to be found in MS. *cit.*, fols. 8b–21b; another account, from *House-Book*, vi, fols. 15–18, is printed in *A Volume of English Miscellanies* (Surtees Society, lxxxv [1890]) by James Raine, Jr., pp. 53 f. Cf. also Chambers, ii, p. 175; Hone, *Anc. Mys.*, p. 236.

Harris, *Leet-Book*, ii, pp. 529 f., records the collection made for King Henry's present from the town of Coventry; but there seems to have been no pageantic accompaniment.

and Mynstrelsyez, and thereby stode a king coronede, whiche had his Speche that foloweth whos Name was Ebraucus." [1]

The pageant, which showed a heaven, and beneath it " a world desolaite full of treys and floures," suggests a guild pageant-car with a trade-symbolism, like the Norwich Grocers' " Paradise," or the 1392 " wilderness " in which St. John stood at Temple Bar. It is important to observe that in Ebraucus, or Ebraut, we have not a personification of the city, but an historical — or pseudo-historical — personage in the shape of its founder.[2] It is quite likely that this figure, and others like him,[3] had an important influence on the later personification of cities, common in the Lord Mayor's Shows, and in our modern pageants; they may also have affected the chronicle-history of the Elizabethan stage.

After Ebrauk's speech, the king passed on to the " hider Ende of House Brigge," or the bridge over the Ouse,[4] where was a pageant from which Solomon spoke, giving Henry a sceptre as a token that in him was wisdom and justice.[5]

---

[1] Leland, iv, p. 187. This pageant is also described in Raine, p. 54; the latter account says his speech was " in prose " and that he gave the keys of the city to the king. In the York MS. the speech of Ebrauc is in four seven-line stanzas; the third verse of the second stanza—"To you henrie I submitt my citie key," shows that Ebrauc's duties were not unlike those of the " great giant " who welcomed Edward IV to Bristol.

[2] *Chronica* Thomæ Sprotti (1719), p. 85: " [Menpricio] mortuo regnavit filius ejus Ebrancus, qui ædificavit Eboracum, & regnavit xxx annis." I have already mentioned the possibility of a "romantic" element in this figure, who may be the same as Evrawk, the father of Peredur. (Cf. above, p. 78, n. 1.) Ebrauc appeared in the first episode of the York Pageant of 1909—(see the *Book* of that pageant, pp. 10 f.)—when he and his followers were represented as Trojans.

In 1588–89, at Chester, " also a play was playd at hye crosse called the storey of King Ebrauk w[t] all his sonne but such rayne fell it was hindred much." — Harl. MS. 2125, fol. 43, (Randle Holmes, *Chronicle of Chester*), cited by R. H. Morris, p. 322. It is interesting to note that a character in pageantry appears more than a century later in the early days of the chronicle-play. The connection between the historical characters in pageantry and those in the drama has yet to be studied; that there is one, seems clear.

[3] Cf. Bremmius at Bristol this same year (below, p. 160) and Gurgunt at Norwich in 1578, (below, p. 210).

[4] See Raine, p. 55. Leland's MS. mentions the decorated houses provided by the corporation, which also planned " a convenient thing divisid whereby, if the weder be fair, of the lordes before and othrene before the king schall rayne rose water." The York *House-Book*, vi, fol. 15 b records: " a certaine nowmbre of Childrine as shalbe gaddard togeddre aboute sanct James chappell calling Joyfully King Henrie after the maner of children."

[5] Solomon's speech in Leland is longer than the version given by Raine. *House-Book*, vi, fol. 16 b tells of six Henries with Solomon; Leland does not mention them. This may point to a change of plans — for the *House-Book* account is more likely to give what was prepared, and Leland's MS. what the king saw. In Raine, this pageant is described as a " rioall troyne "; in Leland, as " garynshede with Shippes and Botes in every side, in Tokenyng of the Kings Landing at Milforde Havyn."

At the turning into Conyeux Street — or Conyngstrete — was a Pageant of the Assumption of Our Lady, from which the Virgin addressed the king.[1]

A castle, wherein stood David, armed and crowned, with a naked sword in his hand, was the next pageant.[2] He gave Henry the " sword of Victory," saying:

> When I reynid in Judie, I know and testify
> That Ebraunce the noble which subdewid Fraunce,
> In memorie of his triumph this citie did edify,
> That the name of his noble should have continuance.[3]

The reception ended with a service at the Minister, which the king and queen attended.

The narrator of the events recorded in the Cotton MS. which Leland prints was evidently an eye-witness of what he describes; for he continues: " At Wytsene Even at whiche Tyme I came to the Kinges Grace at Worcester, wher as I understande wer ordeyned certeyn Paiants, and speeches like as ensuen, whiche his Grace at that Tyme harde not." [4]

On the Monday following, Henry went to Hereford, where the mayor with horsemen met him a mile outside the town; and as he entered the gate, " ther was ordeyned a Pageant of seint George, with a speche as ensueth." [5] From a pageant at the Cross in the market-place, of a king and two bishops, King Ethelbert spoke; and at the entrance of the minster, Our Lady addressed the royal visitor from a pageant where she stood surrounded by " many Virgins mervealous and richely besene."

---

[1] There is a slight difference in the order of some lines at the end of the two versions; and Raine's account puts this pageant " at thend of Swynegale joining of Staynegate." The York House-Book, vi, fol. 17, notes that " in thend of a strete Joining on the syde of on strete passing into Conyngstrete shallbe a shew and fro the same shall come haile stones to be maid by viace falling on the lords and others comyng in before the king hailestones to be made by crafts of cumfetts." (Cf. Raine, p. 56) Cotton MS. Jul. B. xii, fol. 12, notes the casting of "obles [cf. the " oblays " of 1415 and 1474] & wafers, & the casting oute of comfetts in great quantitie, as it had been hayle stones, for Joye and Reioysing of the king's comyng." (Cf. Leland, iv, p. 190.)

Conyng, or Conyeux, street, is the modern Coney Street, which runs parallel to the Ouse. The name is a relic of the Danish occupation of York, and is equivalent to King's Street.

[2] David's castle, " appereing of grete force " was " at the Comon Hall " (House-Book, vi, fol. 17).

[3] The two versions of David's speech are essentially the same. Raine's document mentions citizens in this castle, " in clothing of white and greyne, shewing y' trueth and hertly affeccion unto the kinge." The House-Book quoted from, fol. 17 b, makes no mention of the service at the Minster; it places the Virgin at the end of " Swynegale," joining " staynegate." Here " our lady comyng frome hevin " was to welcome the king, " and yrvpon ascend ayene into heven wit angell sang and yr schall it snaw by craft to be made of waffrons in maner of snaw."

[4] Cotton MS. Jul. B. xii, fol. 13 b, et seq.; Leland, iv, pp. 192 f. These speeches—which are rather long — should have represented Henry VI and a Janitor ad Januam.

[5] From the same MS., printed in Leland, iv, p. 197.

The next Friday, Henry went to Gloucester, where he was met by mayor, sheriffs, and many of the people, all on horseback, three miles outside the town. The clergy met him at the gate; but "in that Towne ther was no Pageant nor speche ordeynede." [1]

On the Monday the king went to Bristol, where the civic authorities met him three miles from the city; the Recorder "right conyngly" welcomed him in the name of the citizens. Again a procession of the clergy greeted the king at the gates; and there was a pageant " with great melody and singing." [2] After this, King Bremmius spoke.[3] At the cross, Prudence spoke from a pageant " ful of maydyn childern richely besene "; and from another at St. John's gate, Justice addressed the king. Farther on, " ther was a Pageant made, called *The Ship-wrights Pageannt*, with praty conceyts pleyng in the same, withoute any speche; and a littill further ther was another Pageannte of an Olifaunt with a Castell on his Bakk, curiously wrought. The Resurrection of our Lorde in the highest Tower of the same, with certeyne Imagerie smytyng Bellis, and al went by Veights, merveolously wele done." [4]

It is worth noting that this elephant and castle combines the romantic and the Biblical elements of pageantry. A representation of the Resurrection was not often added to this Eastern animal.

1487 — Coronation of Henry's Queen, Elizabeth

Rules for the conduct of a royal-entry, temp. Henry VII, are printed from a contemporary MS. by the compilers of the *Antiquarian Repertory*.[5] It may have been prepared for the coronation of Elizabeth, which took place in the third year of her husband's reign. " And at the Touyr gate the meyre & the worschipfulle men of the cete of London to mete hir in y^r best arraye, goinge on ffoot ij and ij togedure, till they come to Westm^r: And at the condit in Corynlle ther must be ordined a sight w^t angelles singinge, and freche balettes [6] y^{r}on in latene, engliche, and ffrenche, mad by the wyseste docturs of this realme; and the condyt in Chepe in the same wyse; and the condit must ryn bothe red wyn and whit wyne; and the crosse in Chepe muste be araid in ye most rialle wyse that myght be thought; and the condit next Poules in the same wyse . . ."

---

[1] The same MS., printed in Leland, iv, p. 198.

[2] The same MS., printed in Leland, iv, pp. 199 f.

[3] Like Ebrauc, a " mythical founder." *Bremmius* is probably an error for *Brennus*, the Latin form of *Bran*, or *Bryn*, son of Dyfnwal, one of the founders of Bristol. I have already suggested that there is a connection between this figure and the Brennius of the third book of Geoffrey of Monmouth's *History*. He was the son of Dunwallo, and the grandson of Cloten, King of Cornwall.

[4] Leland, iv, p. 201, printing the same MS. This is cited by Chambers, ii, p. 176.

[5] *Antiq. Rep.*, i, pp. 296 f.

[6] The older " scriptures."

On the Friday before St. Catherine's day, 1487, Queen Elizabeth left Greenwich to go to London for her coronation.[1]

" And at ther commyng fourth from Grenewiche by water, ther was attendyng uppon her ther, the Maire, Shirffs, and Aldremen of the Citie . . . in barges fresshely furnysshed with baners and stremers of silk richely besene[2] . . . and in especiall a barge called the Bachelers Barge, garnysshed and apparellede, passing al other,[3] wherein was ordeynede a great red dragon spowting flamys of fyer into temmys.[4] And many other gentilmanly paiants wele And curiously devysed to do her highnesse sport and pleasure with. . . ." On the morrow her progress through the city to Westminster was accompanied by magnificence; along the streets, from the Tower to St. Paul's, all the crafts of London stood in their liveries; and in diverse parts of the city were ordained " wele singing childerne. Some arrayde like angells, and other like vyrgyns, to singe swete songes as her grace passed by." [5]

1489 — ARTHUR CREATED PRINCE OF WALES

When Arthur was created Prince of Wales, 21 November, 5 Henry VII, there was a royal progress on the Thames, in barges, in which the civic authorities of London took part; and when the Prince landed at the " Kinges Brigge, all the wourshipfulist Craftes of London stode in Ordre on bothe Sides from the Brigge to the Kings Benche in Westmynster Halle, wher abode the Maire and the Aldermen and so forth." [6]

---

[1] My account of this festivity is taken from Cotton MS. Julius B. xii, fols. 30 f. (esp. fols. 34 b, et seq.), printed by Leland, iv, pp. 216 f. Cf. also Ives, *Select Papers* (1773), pp. 120 f.; Taylor, *Glory of Regality*, p. 275; Hone, *Anc. Mys.*, pp. 236 f. Bare mention of this coronation is made by Hall, p. 438, and Stow, *Annals*, p. 473. Jupp, pp. 35 f., prints the accounts in Stow and Leland; Humpherus, i, pp. 61 f., also records this event.

The queen's passage from Greenwich to London is described on pp. 127 f., of Ives's volume. The language, if not the orthography, varies little from the text here quoted; it seems to be taken from another version of the same MS. See Jupp, p. 35, for the Carpenters' barge hire on this occasion: " to receive the king and queen from Greenwich to the Tower, 10s, 5d." Welch, i, p. 65, gives the expenses of the Pewterers on this occasion.

[2] Ives reads: " richely beaton with the Armes and Bagges (badges) of their Craftes " (p. 127). The MS. cited, fol. 35, seems to read *beten*.

[3] Ives, p. 127, punctuates with a semicolon; the MS. has no punctuation here.

[4] Cf. the dragon at Warwick in 1572 (below, p. 205) and that in the Hudson-Fulton Pageant at New York in 1909 (chapter ix, next volume).

The text at this point is corrected from the MS. (fol. 35). Ives, p. 127, reads: " . . . Flames of Fyer into the Thamess, and many other Gentlemanlie Pagiaunts. . . ."

[5] Leland, iv, p. 220. The streets of the city were cleaned and decorated (Ives, p. 129) and the queen rode in a litter much adorned, over which was borne a canopy of cloth of gold. (Ives, pp. 130 f.; Leland, iv, p. 222.) The coronation ceremony is described in detail, Leland, iv, pp. 222 f.

[6] Leland, iv, p. 250. I may note here that in Italy at the end of the fifteenth century there were very splendid shows; but there seems to be little that we have not already found in Eng-

1496 — Henry VII at Salisbury

St. Christopher, the giant of the Merchant-Tailors' Guild of Salisbury, appeared in the Corporation cavalcade which greeted Henry VII and his queen on their visit to Clarendon in 1496; the guild took part in the procession — and their giant was escorted by his Sword-bearer, Mace-bearer, Hob Nob, and Morris Dancers.[1] This is apparently the first mention of a figure who appeared regularly at the Salisbury Midsummer Shows, and continued to appear as lately as 1911.

1497 — Arthur at Chester

On 3 August, 14 Henry VII, Prince Arthur visited Chester; he was then fourteen years old. The Assumption of Our Lady was played before him at the Abbey Gates, and another play at the High Cross. On the 26th, he made Richard Goodman, the mayor, Esquire; and on 9 September he departed.[2]

1498 — Louis XII at Paris

As an example of a French royal-entry, I shall cite the arrival of Louis XII at Paris on Monday, 2 July, 1498.[3]

" L'escharfault de dessus la porte Sainct Denys estoit honnorablement faict & composé par messeigneurs les Preuost & Escheuins de la Ville de Paris. Dessus lequel estoit vn lis triomphant, à sept fleurons. Et an pied du lis estoit habillé vn personnaige richement, en habit Royal, semé de fleurs de lys d'or. Au premier des fleurons d'embas à main dextre estoit Noblesse. . . . Et de l'autre costé estoit vn autre personnaige aussi dedans le lis nommé Humanité. . . . En demonstrant que l'homme noble doibt estre humain.

---

land. The water processions at Venice were marvelous; in 1491, genii with attributes symbolizing the various gods, floated on machines hung in the air; below stood others grouped as Tritons and nymphs, and the Bucentaur was followed by such a crowd of boats that the water could not be seen for a mile around. (Burckhardt, ii, p. 152; Middlemore, ii, pp. 203 f.) The Carnival at Rome included allegorical and mythological figures — but this was rather a masquerade with pageantic suggestions, than a real pageant. For a description of this festival in the fifteenth century, see Burckhardt, ii, pp. 153 f.; Middlemore, ii, pp. 205 f. The one element which we find in Italy, and not yet in England, is the mythological; that does not appear in England until the beginning of the next century.

[1] Corporation Minutes (Ledger B) cited by Mr. Frank Stevens, *The Giant and Hob Nob and their Story*, p. 63.

[2] Harl. MS., 2125, fol. 32, cited by R. H. Morris, p. 322; King's *Vale Royall of England* (1656), p. 190.

A visit of Henry VII to Bath, this same year, was reproduced in Episode IV of the Bath Pageant of 1909; the episode ends with a joust — no pageants are represented.

[3] My account is taken from Godefroy, *Le Cérémonial de France* (1619), pp. 51 f. It is interesting to compare this entry with that of Henry VI in 1431, which we described, above, p. 138.

"Au deuxiesme fleuron du costé dextre estoit vn autre personnaige nommé Richesse. . . . Et de l'autre costé du fleuron vn autre personnaige nommé Liberalité. . . . Demonstrant que l'homme riche doibt estre liberal.

"Au troisiesme fleuron estoit vn autre personnaige nommé Puissance. . . . Et à l'autre costé estoit Fidelité. . . . Demonstrant que vn homme puissant doibt estre feal.

"Au milieu du lys auoit vn fleuron qui montoit depuis la teste du Roy Charles le quint tout outre les autres Fleurons, & paruenoit à vne Couronne qui estoit richement composée. Et estoit au pied de l'escharfault vn personnaige vestu d'escarlate, qui tenoit vn rolle de papier en sa main, Et disoit ce qui s'ensuit.

> "Par noblesse & humanité,
> Richesse, liberalité,
> Puissance, aussi fidelité,
> Le Chef paruient à la Couronne," etc.

"Le Roy passa outre iusques enuiron les filles Dieu, où il rencontra vn grand porc espic, que deux Mores menoient. . . .

"Y avoit à la fontaine du Ponceau vn lis bien ordonné, duquel lis sortoit par quatre fleurons de l'eaüe en grand' abondance, pour rafraischièr ceulx qui estoyent alterez et partroublez de chauld.

"Plvs outre deuant l'Eglise de la Trinité auoyent faict faire les Gouuerneurs & confreres de la Confrairie de la Passion vn escharfault, où esoit Abraham qui sacrifoit à Dieu le pere son fils Ysaac. Et à autre costé de l'escharfault le cruci-fiement de Iesus Christ. . . . Et couroit incessament des playes du crucifix.

"A la porte aux Paintres auoit vn escharfault sur lequel auoit vn monde, de-dans lequel estoyent deux personnaiges, bon temps, & paix, & menestriers qui ioüoient melodieusement. Et autour du dict monde estoyent trois autres per-sonnaiges, le peuple François, resiouyssance, & le bon Pasteur, lesquels disoient

> "Ie suis dehait menant resiouyssance,
> A la venüe du bon Pasteur de France,
> Paix & bon temps il entretient au monde,
> Honneur, loüange, triomphe en luy abonde.
> Dieu le preserue de mal & de souffrance."

"Au dict lieu trouua le dict Seigneur vn Cerf volant, enuiron de vingt six pieds de hauteur, & autant de long. Lequel vne ieune fille nommée bonne volonté menoit en laisse. . . . Et la dicte fille presenta le dict Cerf au Roy, en disant

> "A votre venüe excellente
> Le cerf volant ie vous presente,
> Affin que la Ville desserue
> Vostre amour, à vous se rend serue,
> Et de tous biens obediente."

Before the Châtelet was a large scaffold, where was "vn lis où estoyent figureés empraintes & neuf pourtraictures de Roys" — Louis XII himself, Charles and

Louis, dukes of Orléans, King Charles V, John, Philip of Valois, Charles, duke of Valois, King Philip, and St. Louis. A king sat enthroned on this pageant, with Good Counsel on his right, and Justice on his left; under his feet lay Injustice. He was surrounded by the Church, the People, the Nobility, Power, Union and Peace.

Before the Palais Royal stood " vn autre escharfault que Messeigneurs de la Chambre des Comptes auoyent faict faire." Various animals, and a scripture, saluting the king, were on this pageant. Before Nôtre Dame stood the Rector of the Universities, surrounded by doctors " en leurs beaulx habits," masters and bachelors with other University officials; and before the doors of the Cathedral, which were closed, stood many ecclesiastics, in whose presence the king swore, on the Bible and relics, to keep the liberties of the Church, and to chase heretics out of his kingdom; to uphold the nobles; to do justice to little as well as to great, and to guard his people from their enemies. Whereupon the doors of the Church were opened, and *Te Deum* was chanted.

This, it will be remarked, is much like English pageantry of this time. There is more allegory than we saw at Paris in 1431; there is a Biblical element, and there is history. The French people are personified, as are the three estates; and the clergy take an active part in the ceremony.

Arthur at Coventry

On 17 October of this same year, Prince Arthur of England visited Coventry; [1] " . . . aȝenst whose coming was þe sponstrete ȝate garnysshed with the ix worthys and Kyng Arthur," who gave the speech of welcome.

" And at the turnyng into þe cross-chepyng befor Mr. Thrūptons durr stode þe barkers paiant well appareld in which was the Quene of Fortune [2] with dyvers other virgins . . ." and Fortune spoke.

" And the crosse in the croschepyng was garnysshed & wyne ther rennyng and angels sensyng & syngyng with Orgayns and other melody &c. [3] And at the Cundyt ther was seynt George kyllyng the dragon " [4] — and the saint addressed the prince.

" And this Balet was song at þe Crosse, Vivat le prynce Arthúr." The first of the six stanzas is this —

> Ryall prince Arthur —
> Welcome newe tresur — } to þis yor cite."
> Wᵗ all our hole cur —

---

[1] For the account in the *Leet-Book*, see Harris's edition, iii, pp. 589 f.; Sharp, p. 154. Cf. also H. Craig, pp. 116 f.; Chambers, ii, p. 175; Harris, *Life in an Old English Town*, p. 346.

[2] This is worth noting, as showing the union of allegory and the miracle-play background.

[3] Was this the Tanners' pageant? Cf. at Coventry in 1565 (below, p. 204, n. 1).

[4] The popularity of this subject at Coventry is noteworthy. In 1456, it was, to be sure, St. Margaret who killed the dragon; but that was a compliment to the queen. Again in 1474 we find St. George, (and in 1461, when Edward visited Bristol, we find a similar pageant).

It is sad to compare the tragic events, which too often follow them, with the buoyant, almost fulsome, hopefulness and gratulation of the speeches of these triumphs. The same sad contrast is sometimes seen in the marriage masques of a later generation.

1499 — A CIVIC PAGEANT ON AN UNKNOWN OCCASION

In November, 1499, various persons took part in some kind of a pageant at London, the occasion of which is not stated. "The story on the bridge," those at the great conduit, the conduit in Cornhill, at the standard in Cheap, the little Conduit in Chepe, and "the second station at the Conduit in Gracechurch Street" are not particularized, nor do we know the characters represented.[1]

A RÉSUMÉ

We have now reached 1500 in our survey of the "royal-entry," and may pause to "take account of stock," as it were. All but one of the elements of the pageant, which later years will elaborate, are gathered together. Folk-custom and the miracle-play have contributed their share; speeches have replaced Church canticles, and "scriptures" reinforce the speeches. Historical characters, of national and local importance, seem to foreshadow the chronicle-play of the next century; Saints rub elbows with the Nine Worthies; the Crucifixion appears on a tower in a castle on the back of an elephant; King Arthur, Edward the Confessor, Isaiah, and the kings of Cologne show the catholicity of the pageant. Every element is welcomed by this form of artistic expression, and made to fit the occasion for which it is borrowed. Trade-symbolism is linked to St. John the Baptist; a castle comes from chivalric literature to cover a conduit; Lydgate has turned virgins and angels into Truth, Fortune, Nature, Justice, Mercy, and Grace.

During the wars of the Roses, as Chambers points out,[2] people had but little time or heart for pageants, which begin with Henry VII to grow in splendour; and this growth continues throughout the Tudor century. It reaches its highest point in the reigns of Elizabeth, James, and the first Charles; and in the development to come, but one new element enters. This may be said to have sent pioneers to the 1432 show, when Aristotle, Cicero, Euclid, and other classical figures stood about Dame Sapience. Save for these historical representatives of classical times, which Lydgate introduced, and those included in the number of the Nine Worthies, there is no classical influence until the next century, when mythology comes in with the Renaissance.

---

[1] The real names of the persons taking part, together with the stations specified above, are given in *Repertory* i, fol. 61 b. A list of persons appointed to communicate from time to time with the king's commissioners, regarding the preparations to be made for receiving "them that shall come out of Spain," may be found in the same *Repertory*, fol. 62. (Cf. p. 39, n. 2.)

[2] Chambers, ii, p. 170.

All the other elements are assembled. Fostered by the guilds, they are built into a form of entertainment which appeals at once to king and to apprentice, which gives employment to poet and to engineer.

§ 3. THE EARLY SIXTEENTH CENTURY

1501 — ARTHUR MARRIES KATHERINE OF SPAIN

On the occasion of the marriage of Prince Arthur to Katherine of Spain in 1501, there were many pageants. The civic authorities prepared for the entry long beforehand: " Also this yere in the said moneth of May and the vjth day of the said moneth was graunted by Auctorytie of a Comon Counsell w^t in the Citie of London a Quindecim and an half, for to prepair certeyn pageantes and other charges agayne the comyng of Dame Kateryn, Doughter of the Kyng of Spayn." [1] When the princess was expected for her wedding, " . . . the maior and crafts of London shall meet her in their seuerall barges after their maner accustomed at Deptford and owyt of these barges shall hayle and salute her in the best manner they can and rowe about behind and vppon the sides of her shippe and of this attendance to be given by the maior and other [2] my L. Chamberlaine hath the chardge to give warning vnto them and when they shall come vppon the water then they to be ordred by my L. Steward." [3]

" It is to be remembred that no barge attending vppon the said Princesse take vppon them to land in any place nether vppon the one side nor vppon the other of the thames but always to hover till the Princesse be landed and then depart to their lodgings at their pleasure exccpt the Ladyes, the Duke of Buck [4] and the Earles which shall land with her and convaye her to her lodging and that my L. Steward give vnto them warning and chardge of the same." [5]

When the princess entered the city, on her way to Westminster, " vj goodly beautiful pageauntes " lined the way from London Bridge to Paul's.[6] " At first at

---

[1] Cotton MS. Vitellius A. xvi, fol. 178 b (printed in Kingsford, *Chron. Lond.*, p. 229, *sub anno* 1500.

[2] Qy: *others*: or else *officers* or some such word is omitted in both MSS.

[3] This, and the following paragraphs, are from *Certeine notes taken out of thentertainment of Katherine Dowager*, which may be found in Harl. MS. 69, fols. 37 f., and Cotton MS. Vitellius C. xi, fols. 117 f. (This passage is on fol. 39 b of the Harl. MS., and fol. 118 b of the Cotton MS.)

[4] The Cotton MS. reads *Buckingham*.

[5] Harl. MS., fol. 40; Cotton MS., fol. 119 b.

[6] A full contemporary account of this show is printed in the *Antiq. Rep.*, ii, pp. 248 f.; another is to be found in Cotton MS. Vitellius A. xvi, fol. 184, *et seq.*; this — collated with the text in the *Antiq. Rep.* — is printed by Kingsford in *Chron. Lond.*, pp. 234 f. See also Stow, *Annals*, p. 483; J. G. Nichols, *Lond. Pag.*, pp. 26 f.; Chambers, ii, p. 171; Hone, *Anc. Mys.*, 237; Thomson, *Lond. Bridge*, pp. 305 f.; Jupp, pp. 37 f., reprints an extract of the *Antiq. Rep.* account, and a selection from Stow. Cf. Hall, p. 493, and Grafton, ii, p. 222, for mention of this entry, which is not to be confused with the 1501 " disguising," (see above, p. 113). Welch, i

London Brigge was ordeyned a goodly pagent and costlewe, of karvyn werke paynted and gilt in most costle maner, standyng vpon the Drawe brigge; wherein were set ij personages princypall, that oon representyng Saynt Kateryn, and that other of Saynt Vrsula, wᵗ dyuers livyng virgins . . ." [1] The speeches of both saints follow.[2]

The second pageant, built in Gracechurch Street, was a castle, wherein were two knights,[3] Policy and Nobleness, and a Bishop, Virtue; all of them addressed the " bright sterre of Spayne." [4] The third pageant, in Cornhill, held Raphael, the angel of marriage, Alphonso, Job, and Boethius, all of whom spoke.[5] The fourth pageant, in Cheapside, between the great conduit and the Standard, contained the sun and many angels; there was much symbolism in the construction of this " temple," and many of the angels carried " scriptures." The speech was delivered by the " Father of Heaven." [6]

---

p. 88, gives the expenses of the Pewterers on this occasion; and the entry is referred to by W. S. Simpson, in *The Bishop of London's Palace, near S. Paul's*, in the *Trans. London and Middlesex Arch. Soc.* (London, 1905), n. s. i, pp. 25 f. (Dr. Simpson cites Dugdale's *S. Pauls*, and Stow.)

Chambers notes that Bishop Foxe is said to be the contriver of this ceremony; the editors of the *Antiq. Rep.* assign their account of it to an " officer of arms" who was an eye-witness of what he describes.

The following citations regarding the 1501 entry of Katherine of Spain, are taken from Harl. MS. 69, fol. 41 (also in Cotton MS. Vit. C. xi, fol. 121):

At her passage from the Tower through the city, " Itm. that the Maior, Cittizens and Crafts attend vppon the said Princesse at the Crosse in Cheape in such maner and in such solemne Pageants and Ceremonies as they have deuised for the honnor of the Cittie and of the ffeast where my L. Burgavenny hath the chardge.

" Itm. that the said Princesse be conveyed through the high streets of London in such case accustomed straight to the west dore of Powles where she shalbe receaued with procession by the Archbishoppe of Canterbury in pontificalibus accompanied with a good number of such prelates and in likewise in pontificalibus as he shall call to him and fro the said dore with the Queere of the Church processionally to bring her to the high aultar and there to doe such ceremonies as in such case is accustomed . . ."

[1] Cotton MS. Vit. A. xvi, printed in Kingsford, *op. et loc. cit.*

[2] They are also given in the *Antiq. Rep.*, ii, pp. 261 and 262. This account says that above both saints was a picture of the Trinity.

[3] Cotton MS. Vit. A. xvi, fol. 186 (Kingsford, *Chron. Lond.*, p. 237), gives the speech of Policy who was " Arayed like a Senatour." The other speeches follow.

[4] *Antiq. Rep.*, ii, pp. 264–266.

[5] *Antiq. Rep.*, ii, pp. 268–272. Cf. Cotton MS. Vitellius A. xvi, fol. 188 (Kingsford, *op. cit.*, p. 239): " In Cornhill, where was ordeyned a Costlew pagent wᵗ a volvell by the which the xij signes moved aboute the zodiak, and the mone shewed her course of light and dirknesse. And ouer that voluell Sat, in a stage or pynnacle, Raphaell the Archangell; And vnder the voluell vpon a sate sat iij Astates, Alphons, Job, and Boecius, called Astronomers." All the speeches follow.

[6] *Antiq. Rep.*, ii, pp. 273 f. Cotton MS. Vit. A. xvi, fol. 191 b, in Kingsford, *op. cit.*, p. 244, records that in Cheap, " foragayne Soperlane was set the iiijᵗʰ pagent, In maner of an heven,

In the fifth pageant, at the Standard, was the Godhead.[1] At the four corners stood four prophets, richly dressed; lions, dragons and greyhounds of painted lead decorated this pageant; many angels surrounded God, singing harmoniously, " as it had been in a chirche, w^t a swete and solempne noyse." Many windows, pinnacles, and vanes were at the top of this pageant: and " in every inch's space of this work were pearles of silver counterfeited." God made the first speech, which was followed by that of the Prelate of the Church.[2] The sixth pageant, near the little conduit in Cheap, contained Honor and the Seven Virtues: Faith, Hope, and Charity, Justice, Temperance, Prudence, and Fortitude. The speech was made by Honor.[3]

Mayor, sheriffs, recorder, and aldermen received the princess near this last pageant, and gave her rich gifts of plate and coin. She then attended service in the Cathedral, and the show was over.

Music, wine flowing from the conduits, and speeches, were all part of this triumph, the characters in which, it will be noticed, were allegorical, historical, chivalric, and Biblical; there were saints and angels, and even God himself.

1503 — MARRIAGE OF MARGARET OF ENGLAND TO KING JAMES IV OF SCOTLAND

The reception of Margaret, daughter of Henry VII, at Edinburgh, when, in 1503, she married James IV of Scotland, is described by John Young, Somerset Herald, who accompanied the princess on her journey from England.[4] On her way north from Richmond, Margaret was greeted by civic and religious authorities — and in some towns by the waits and minstrels; many places were decorated, and often the firing of guns welcomed her or sped her on her journey. But there were no pageants until she got to Edinburgh.

---

whereyn was paynted the xij signes, and ouer theym was Arthure, clene armed, in his Golden Chare." He was attended by children, twelve or fourteen years old, also " clene armed." If this be King Arthur, the appropriateness is obvious.

[1] Cf. the 1392 show, above, p. 131. The Cotton MS. cited, fol. 192 b (cf. Kingsford, p. 245) records God in " a right Costlew pagent " against the Standard in Cheap.

[2] *Antiq. Rep.*, ii, pp. 275 f. " In an hous, wheryn than dwellyd William Geffrey, haberdasher, stood the Kyng, the Quene and many grete astates of the Realme." — Cotton MS. Vit. A. xvi, fol. 192 b (Kingsford, *op. cit.*, p. 245); cf. *Antiq. Rep.*, ii, p. 277.

[3] *Antiq. Rep.*, ii, p. 280. The mayor and his brethren met the princess " at the ende of ffriday strete " (Cotton MS. Vit. A. xvi, fol. 193 b; Kingsford, *Chron. Lond.*, p. 246); and then, having received their welcome, Katherine went on to the Little Conduit in Cheap, where were Prelacy and Honour in a goodly pageant; and both spoke (*ibid.*). Prelacy's speech preceded that of Honour; both are given in the Cotton MS., fol. 194; Kingsford, pp. 246 f.

[4] His account is to be found in Leland, *Collectanea*, iv, pp. 258 f. Cf. Chambers, ii, p. 176; Hone, *Anc. Mys.*, pp. 237 f. Young notes that the journey of the princess to Scotland began on 27 June, 1503 (Leland, p. 265).

A painted gate at the entrance of the city, " with two towrells, and a windowe in the midds," greeted her arrival. Angels sang joyfully from the windows, and one of them presented the keys of the town to the new queen. The clergy of St. Giles met the royal party at the city gate; in the middle of the town was a fountain running wine; and near it was a " scarfawst " whereon was represented the Judgment of Paris.[1] There was also represented here the Salutation of Gabriel to the Virgin, " in sayinge *Ave gratia*, and sens after, the Solempnizacion of the varey Maryage betwix the said Vierge and Joseph." The appropriateness of the Biblical subject is obvious.

Further on, upon another new-made gate, were the Four Virtues: — Justice, with scales and sword, trod on Nero; Fortitude, on Holofernes; Temperance, in whose hand was a horse's bit, on Epicurus; while Sardanapalus lay under the feet of Prudence. With these figures were tabrets that played merrily while the noble company passed.

The city of Edinburgh was hung with tapestry, and the church bells rang joyfully.

It is interesting to note that the first appearance of the classical element in pageantry — represented here by Paris, Mercury and the three goddesses — is made in Edinburgh. *Deessys* and *Mercure* may indicate that the idea of this pageant came from France; though these forms may be due to the French training of the Herald who wrote the account.[2] Scotland and France were then, and long had been, on friendly terms; and there was close communication between the two countries. In spite of the fact that there was a large element of French in the language of heraldry, John Young's account does not betray a strong tendency to give many words their French form; and it is possible that his use of *deessys* and *Mercure* may be an indication of the source of this classical material, which has not yet — though it soon will — come to England. The group of the Virtues shows the development of the figures on a pageant into the *tableau vivant*.

1509 — THE CORONATION OF KING HENRY VIII AND KATHERINE

The festivities in honor of Henry VIII and his queen, Katherine, on the day before their coronation, are recorded by Hall.[3] The streets of London were hung with rich draperies; a great part of the south of Cheap, and part of Cornhill, with cloth of gold. The streets were barred on one side from Gracechurch to Bread

---

[1] Leland, iv, p. 289. Paris, Mercury and the three goddesses were represented: " Paris and the Thre Deessys, with Mercure, that gaffe hym th Apyll of Gold, for to gyffe to the most fayre of the thre wiche he gave to Venus." Cf. the entry of Anne Boleyn, in 1533 — below, p. 183.

[2] His use of *vierge* is also noteworthy.

[3] See Hall, pp. 507, 508; J. G. Nichols, pp. 33 f.; Strutt, *Manners and Customs*, iii, p. 129. For the appearance of the Pewterers on this occasion, see Welch, i, p. 98.

Street in Cheapside; and behind the railing stood every occupation in its liveries, beginning with the mean and base trades, and ascending to the worshipful companies. Highest stood the mayor and aldermen; the Goldsmiths' stalls, at the end of Old Change, were filled with maidens in white dresses; priests and clerks in rich copes, with crosses and censers of silver, censed the monarchs as they passed. A procession of noblemen included " the nine children of honour," each of whose horses was "trapped with a trapper of the Kynges title, as of Englande, and Fraunce, Gascoyne, Guyan, Normandy, Angeow, Cornewall, Wales, Irelande, &c." There were no pageant-cars on this occasion; but the personification of colonies is pageantic.

1511 — Henry and Katherine at Coventry

In 1511, there were three pageants for the king and queen at Coventry. One, at Jordan Well, had nine orders of angels; one, at Broad Gate, contained divers beautiful damsels; and on a third, at the Cross, was given " a goodly stage play." [1] This play may well have been a miracle-play, the characters from which we have so often seen used by provincial authorities for royal-entries.

Queen Margaret at Aberdeen

Margaret of Scotland visited, for the first time, the northern counties of her country in May, 1511. Laing notes that the poet Dunbar must have been in her train, for his poem descriptive of her reception at Aberdeen, is evidently the work of an eye-witness of the festivities.[2] The " pleasant padyheanes " included Adam and Eve, the Salutation of the Virgin, the Magi and the Bruce. The latter,

> . . . rydand under crown
> Richt awfull, strang, and large of portratour,
> As nobill, dreidfull, michtie campioun, [3]

suggests earlier heroic " founders " like the Ebrauk of 1486 — or the civic giants. He may, of course, be an image on horseback; if so, he probably goes back to the folk-giants.

After the pageants came twenty-four maidens, singing and " playand on timberallis." The streets were decorated; wine ran abundantly at the Cross; and the city gave the royal guest a costly cup filled with gold.

---

[1] Harl. MS. 6388, fol. 27 b — H. Wanley, *Collections Relating to Coventry*. This is cited by Miss Harris, *Life in an Old English Town*, p. 346. Cf. Sharp, p. 157, (he dates the visit 1510) cited by Chambers, ii, p. 175.

[2] See *Poems* of William Dunbar, ed. Laing (Edinburgh, 1834), i, p. 31. The poem is printed in the same volume, pp. 153 f. Cf. Davidson, p. 89; Chambers, ii, p. 176.

[3] Laing, i, p. 154.

1513 — ENTRY OF LOUIS XII'S QUEEN INTO PARIS

Cocheris, printing contemporary MSS., gives details of the entries of Mary, sister of Henry VIII and wife of Louis XII, into Abbeville and Paris in 1513.[1] The first entry took place on 9 October;[2] the second shows more pageantic features. As it is interesting to see what was going on in France in the early years of the sixteenth century, let us examine this entry, though it is not English.

The streets were decorated from the Porte Saint Denis to Notre Dame; and "a lentree de ladite ville auoit ung grant escharfault sur lequel auoit vne grande nauire dargent sur une mer dedans laquelle estoit le roy bacus tenant vng beau raisin denotant plante de vins & vne royne tenant vne gerbe denotant plante de blez & aux trois matz de ladite nauire au pl. hault estoient trois grosses hunes dorees dedans lesquelles estoient trois personnages les deux armes aux deux boutz tenant chacun vng grant escusson & celuy du meilleu vng escu de france, & aux quatre boutz de ladite mer estoient quatre grans monstres soufflant denotant les quatre vens nommez subsolamus, auster, boreaus & zephirus, & dedans ladite nauire estoient matelotz & autres personnages lesquelz chantoient melodieusement, & aux deux boutz de ladite nauire estoient les armes de lhostel de ladite ville.[3]

"Item deuant la trinite auoit vng escharfault sur lequel estoit le roy dauid[4] & ses chlrs & la royne de saba & cinq ieunes damoiselles, laquelle royne portoit la paix a baiser audict roy, lequel la remercioit humblement & au pied dudit escharfault estoit escript:

> Royne saba dame de renommee
> Est venu veoir salamon le tressage
> Qui la receue dun amoureux courage
> Par sur toutes la prisee & aymee
> Cest le royne par vertu enflammee
> Belle & bonne vertueuse en langaige
> Noble saba . . ."[5]

Other scaffolds were erected, on which stood such characters as "le grant pasteur";[6] five "ieunes pucelles c'est assauoir france, paix, amytie, confederation & angleterre, lesquelles chantoient melodieusement"; the four virtues; dame Peace again, and five representing "bon accord, stella maris, minerue, dyana, phebus."[7] Note the classical element, which we have already met in Scotland.

---

[1] H. Cocheris: *Entrées de Marie d' Angleterre, femme de Louis XII, à Abbeville et à Paris* (Paris, 1859 — in Fairholt's collection at the Society of Antiquaries).

[2] Pp. 6 and 17.　　　　　　　　[3] Pp. 26 ff.

[4] A scribal slip for *Solomon*. *Chlrs* is the scribal abbreviation for *chevaliers*, apparently. This suggests a chivalric element, due, perhaps, to the fact that David was one of the nine worthies.

[5] Pp. 27 f.　　　　　[6] P. 28.　　　　　[7] Pp. 28 and 29.

Various inscriptions appeared on these pageants, explaining them, and referring to the characters on them. The Virgin, saluted by Gabriel, was the subject of one pageant, " et au bas dudict escharfault auoit vng beau iardin nomme le vergier de france seme de plusieurs beaulx lys. Et au dessus dudict iardin estoient vng roy et vne royne & a dextre estoit dame Iustice tenant vne espee en sa main & a senestre estoit dame verite tenant en sa main la paix, & dedans ledict iardin estoient plusieurs bergiers & bergeres lesquelz chantoient melodieusement." [1] Verses, not without a pun, were affixed to this scaffold: the last line of one stanza reads, " Car marie auec nous se marie."

This entry has appropriate Biblical pageants, allegorical figures, and such symbolical personifications as France and England. With the exception of the mythological figures, however, the entry is not unlike those we find at this time across the Channel. Before we return thither, let us note the entry of Charles V into Bruges in 1515.

1515 — AN HISTORICAL PAGEANT AT BRUGES

The contemporary account of the historical pageant at Bruges, when the Emperor visited that city on 18 April, 1515, shows us much that it interesting; for it anticipates, to some extent, the later historical pageant of our own day.[2] The past history of the town was linked with Old Testament stories — which points back to the miracle-play; it is as if we saw here the Middle Ages flowing into modern times.

Liederic, dividing the land among his sons, is paralleled by the division of the Promised Land by Joshua; [3] in the second pageant it was " demonstré par personnages " how the body of Saint Dona was presented to the town by Count Baldwin, first of the name — and before the Church of St. Dona was David, playing before the ark of God " laquelle il menoit en grande solennité et liesse hors de Ebedon pour en douer sa cité." [4] An elaborate pageant represented the coming of the Holy Blood to Bruges; the other scene was " Heraclius victorieux fit don à la ville de Hierusalem de la Saincte Croix." [5] The Latin inscription on the next pageant is thus translated by Dupuys,

> Louis dict de Nevers que Flandres aduoua
> De gens, de droitz, et divers ceste ville doua,

---

[1] P. 30.

[2] The account — by Rémy Dupuys — entitled *La Triomphante et Solennelle Entrée de Charles-Quint en sa ville de Bruges le 18 Avril 1515*, was reprinted from a contemporary volume by the Société d'émulation de Bruges in 1850. This illustrated edition is in the Fairholt collection in the library of the Society of Antiquaries.

[3] Cf. the discussioh concerning the " wild-man," in § 8 of chapter i, above. In a note (p. 76) I have cited from this pageant to show the " forester " connected with history.

[4] Illustrated in the Bruges volume, opp. p. 14.

[5] These are illustrated, opp. p. 15.

and marks the subject shown: the Biblical parallel is Moses, giving the Ten Commandments at the foot of Sinai.[1] Other pageants there were, historical and Biblical — some taking notice of the commerce which played so important a part in the past and contemporary growth of the town. The Aragon merchants furnished two pageants: one, an elaborate tower,[2] was burned, and the royal guests barely escaped injury. Other pageants showed the Emperor surrounded by his Electors; Alexander on Bucephalus, paralleled by Charles and Flanders. A large warship represented the emperor's victories on the enemies of the Christian faith; there were also castle-pageants, and a strong allegorical element permeated the entire show. But for us, the historical element is especially important, in view of its later development.

In 1516, " the Queene of Scottes, sister to the kinge, came porelie out of Scotland to the kinge, and was richlye receaved, and rode thorowe London." [3] I know of no pageants prepared for this reception.[4]

1518 — A CIVIC RECEPTION IN LONDON

An order devised by the mayor and his brethren the aldermen by the king's command, for a triumph to be done in London at the request of the right honorable ambassadors of the King of the Romans, is preserved in the City Archives under date of 10 July, 10 Hen. VIII (1518).[5] Cheapside, Cornhill, Gracechurch Street, and Bishopsgate Street were "to be ffurnyshed w^t cressett lights," and big bonfires — located where the pageants usually stood, namely at St. Magnus corner, Gracechurch Street, Leadenhall, at the Conduit in Cornhill, at St. Thomas of Acres, the Standard in Chepe, the Little Conduit, at the Standard in Fleet Street, and at Bishopsgate Street — were prepared. Men in " harness " were to line the route of the procession; but no pageantry seems to have been planned.

1520 — THE FIELD OF THE CLOTH OF GOLD

What has often — and wrongly — been called a " pageant," took place in 1520, when the kings of England and France met on the " Field of the Cloth of

---

[1] These are illustrated, opp. p. 16.

[2] Illustrated, opp. p. 23.

[3] Wriothesley, *Chron. Eng. during the Reigns of the Tudors* (ed. W. D. Hamilton, 1875–77), i, p. 10.

[4] C. T. Martin, in *Archæologia*, xlvii, p. 304, quotes Grafton's *Chronicle* (ii, p. 288) which — without mentioning pageantry — narrates that " on the third day of May [Margaret] made her entry into London, ridyng on a whyte palfray . . . richely beseene, and with great companie of lordes and ladies. She rode through the citie to Baynardes Castell, and from thence she was conveyed to Grenewich, and there receyved joyously of the king . . . and highly was she feasted . . ."

[5] Cf. *Journal* xii, fols. 9, *et seq.* Mirfin being mayor, the date of this is 1518—see Stow's list of mayors.

Gold." This was simply a splendid show; there were no actors to take the parts of allegorical, symbolical, historical, or mythological characters; the thing was not in any way " popular "; and it can only be a misuse of the term *pageant* to apply it to this famous meeting.[1] The same year Charles V visited London; Henry met him at Dover, and both the king and the newly-elected emperor were received by Wolsey at Canterbury, where Archbishop Warham waited on them. And one night in Whitsun week, " there was a great triumphe made in the great Hall " of the Archepiscopal palace; this appears to have been a " disguising " of some kind.[2]

1522 — CHARLES V AT LONDON

Although the visit of the Emperor Charles V to London in 1522 did not take place until 6 June, the guilds were looking forward to his coming as early as March. At the end of that month, divers Italian merchants came to the aldermen; to them was declared the preparation for the coming of the Emperor's Grace, and they desired that the other merchants, Ragusans, Florentines, etc., be warned to be contributary. Several refused, however, to prepare any pageant.[3] On the 28 March, it was decided that the livery to be given the Lord Mayor's officers against the emperor's coming be provided by Aldermen Rudstone and Skevyngton,[4] and that the sheriffs should give, on the same occasion, coats of ginger-color to their officers; the chamberlain was to provide two coats of red and white damask for two of the mayor's footmen. The Italians undertook to make " the pagent of the Duke of Lancastre to stand at ledyn hall." [5]

That different men had charge of various pageants is clear from the City Archives. On 6 May, " it is agreed by this Court that the pagent deuised by Rastall to stand at the litle conduyte by the stocks shall goo forth and take effect for all days that the charge thereof excede nott xv li." [6]

---

[1] Among the many illustrations of this famous scene may be mentioned no. 1, in a collection of engravings in the British Museum, numbered 3 Table 24. This is " from the original picture . . . preserved in the private apartments of Windsor Castle."

[2] Cf. Leland, *Collectanea*, vi, p. 33, for a contemporary MS. account of this visit, which is referred to by Dr. Sharpe, in *London and the Kingdom* (1894–95), i, p. 364; he notes that " the young emperor did not visit the city on this occasion."

[3] *Repertory* iv, fol. 112 b.

[4] Fol. 114 b.

[5] *Ibid.* Cf. *Repertory* v, fol. 279 b.

[6] Fol. 117 b. Cf. also *Repertory* v, fol. 284. (The " days " is troublesome, unless it allows for a rehearsal of some sort. There was no civic show which would permit us to suppose that more than one " performance " was given.) On 8 May, " it is agreed that the Chamberlain shall give unto the Garter King of Heralds for his pain and labor that he has taken in devising the pageants against the coming of the Emperor to the city, five marks " (*ibid.* Cf. *Repertory* iv, fol. 122, fol. 124, and *Repertory* v, fol. 284 b). On the 13th — " agreed that every alderman who has not brought in money levied within his ward for the pageants, bring it in at the next Court " (*Repertory* iv, fol. 118 b; cf. *Repertory* v, fol. 286). The Wardens of the Skinners'

CRESSET, AND CRESSET BEARER WITH ATTENDANT

" Yt ys agreed," we read in the City Records, " that syr Thomas More vndertresurer of Englande for his labors & paynes that he toke for the citie in makyng of a proposicion at the comyng and receyvyng of thempror " is to have £10 towards a gown of velvet.[1] Mr. Lylly for his labor and diligence in devising speeches for the pageants received £5;[2] and he was asked to bring a copy of his verses " to this court that they may be entered for a precedent hereafter." One Lumnow was paid £15 for the " stuff " on the pageants,[3] and the Chamberlain was to pay to Alderman Brown, for the gilding of the Cross in Cheapside, £100.[4] " It^m yt ys agreed that the Chamberlain shall pay to Rychard Howman aswell for xxvj^s viii^d by hym payd as for other hys busynes & labor by hym sustayned in the makynge of the pageant of thassumpcion of our lady agenst the cumyng of the emperour," four marks.[5]

There are many accounts of the reception of the emperor when he came to London in June, 1522.[6] The city was prepared for his entry " after the manner as is used for a coronation," [7] and the

lorde mayer and the aldyrmen rode iij myles from London almoste to depforde where they mette the emperour and the kyngys grace in most goodly maner doyng the dewty to whom they hadde an oracion in laten in gratulacion off theyr comyng, by the mouth off syr Thomas Moore knyght, and that done they rode before them styll and thorow owte the cytee. And att the entryng of Seynt George barre on the ryght hande as the[y] rode thorow the cytee the clergy stoode in good ordyr and aray all att leyngth contynually wnto the church off Powlys, that is to say all the prelattys, prestys and clerkys off the churchis w^tyn the cytee and suburbys and dyuerse other parysshe churchys in Midilsex . . . in ryche copys and ryche crossys and sensers of silver alway sensyng the emperour and the kyngys grace as they cam by. . . . Also wppon the left hande from the sayd seynt Georges barre contynnally thorow London wnto

---

Company promised to pay the money assessed on the Ward of Dowgate for making the pageants (Rep. iv, fol. 125 b); and they promised to pay 53s. 4d. which their Hall was assessed towards the sum of £9 granted for making the pageants. (Rep. v, fol. 318b.)

[1] Repertory iv, fol. 134 b; under date of 18 November.

[2] Fol. 135. Dr. R. R. Sharpe, London and the Kingdom, i, p. 365, identifies him as " the first high master of Colet's School." (He is not the author of Euphues, it is unnecessary to point out.)

[3] Repertory iv, fol. 154.

[4] Fol. 163.

[5] Fol. 169 b.

[6] One of the fullest is a contemporary MS. in the library of Corpus Christi (Cantab.) entitled: The descrypcion of the pageantes made in the Cyte of London att the recevyng of the most excellent pryncys Charlys the fyfte Emperour & Henry the viij Kyng off englonde. This MS. is that referred to by J. Nichols, Hist. Leicestershire (1795–1811), iv, p. 496, n. 3. (" In Benet college library, No. vii," etc.) — and by Gough, Brit. Topog., p. 339, note q. The entry is also described by Stow, Annals, p. 516; Hall, pp. 637 f., and Grafton, ii, pp. 322 f. (the last two accounts are very similar, and rather detailed; that of Hall is somewhat fuller.) Cf. also J. G. Nichols, p. 3; Chambers, ii, p. 171; Welch, i, p. 105, etc. I follow chiefly the Cambridge MS. referred to; (Corpus Christi (Cantab.) MS., 298 (no. 8), p. 132, et seq.)

[7] Stow, Annals, p. 516.

Poules the Citizens off London stode in aray, euery occupacyon and company by themselff in theyr lyvery and best apparell.

At the Draw bryce off London.

Also att the drawe bryge off London att the enteryng off the gate off the cytee dyd stande ij greate Gyauntys one presentyng the parson of Sampson (*sic*) and the other hercules standyng in ryche apparell holdyng betwen a grete cheyn of yron and a table hangyng in the myddys off the chayne wheryn was wrytyn in goldyn lettyrs sett in byce [1] the namys of all the landys and domynyons where the emperour is Kyng and Lorde in tokennyng thatt the emperour is able to holde all those domynyons by pour and strength as the seyd gyauntys holde the same cheyne by pouer and strengyth. The names of the which domymyons here after folow in wrytyng as was wrytyn wppon the seyd table. . . . Also thes ij versis folowyng were wrytyn wnder the same table —

> Carolus Henricus viuat defensor vteros
> Henricus fidei Carolus ecclesie.

The whiche is to say in englisshe, God graunte that Charlys and Henry may lyve and prosper whiche be both defenders, that is to say Henry defender off th[e] feyth, Charlys defender of the churche.

Att the myddyll off London bryge.

Also att the myddyll off London bryge dyd stande a pagiaunt of the story of Jason and medea wyth the dragon and ij bollys [2] beryng the goldyn flese, by cause the emperowr is lorde and gever of the tewson [*Toison d'Or*] and hedde & maker of all the kynghtys off the tewson, lyke as the kyng of englonde is of the ordyr of the kynghtys off the garter. And a childe in a goodly apparell salutyng the emprowr shewyng thatt his presens and comyng was lyke ioy to the cytee off london as the conqueryng off the golden fleese was wnto the people of Mynius. [3]

[We may note here the beginning of the classical element in English pageantry; this is probably due to Mr. Lyly's classical knowledge, but he may have received the idea of using it in pageantry either from France direct, or through Scotland. As we shall see, Jason (given a trade-appropriateness) became a popular figure in the Lord Mayor's Shows.]

Att the condytt in Gracious strete.

Also att the condytt in Gracyous strete dyd stand a pageaunte rychely arayede in the myddys whereoff Charlemayne the emprowr w[t] Rowlande and Olyuer waytyng wppon hym, stode holdyng in his hande ij swerdys and ij Crowyns imperyall off golde offeryng oon to the emprowr and the other to the kynges grace. On the ryght syde of the stage stode Charlemayne agayn setting the Pope in his see.[4] And on the lefte syde off the stage Charlemayn stode agayn, and the kynge of Constantinople and the patriarke off Jerusalem presentynge to Charlemayne the crowne off thorne whiche he receyved w[t] grete honour. [A scripture explained this pageant.] Also ther stode a chylde in a goodly apparell salutyng the emprowr and shewyng thatt he was descendyd off the seyde Charlemayne.

---

[1] See *NED*, *s. v. bice.*

[2] Bulls. (Cf. Withington, *The Lord Mayor's Show for 1623*, in *Publ. Mod. Lang. Assoc.*, xxx, 1 (March, 1915), p. 113 and n. 2. The story of Jason, which is obviously appropriate to the Drapers, was a favorite subject in the Lord Mayor's Shows a century later).

[3] The MS. is not clear at this point; the word looks like *My'ius*, and I have assumed that the scribe wrote *Mynius* for *Minyas*. The word *Minyae = Argonauts*, which is clearly the sense of this passage.

[4] Note the mixture of romance and history, both made appropriate by the fact that the imperial guest was also a great Charles.

Att the Ledyn Hall.

Also att the Ledyn hall dyd stand a pageaunt off the progeny off the emprowr and off the kynge rychely and costly made w^t pictures and Images off the parsons off Kynges and Quenys and princes all in fyne golde in dyvers setys and stagys and a lyne ascendyng from oon to an other, from the lowyst to the hyest, and in ij the hyest setys ij ymages one of them repre-sentyng the parson off the emprowr and another the kynges grace, and in the lowest off all an ymage representyng the parson off John of Gawnte Duke off Lancaster, shewyng ther by how bothe the emprowr and the kynges grace doo descende and com lynially owt off the howse off englonde from the seide John of gawnte. Whiche John off Gawnte was son to Kynge Edwarde the iij^{de} " . . . [The genealogy of both rulers is then traced in the MS.]

Att the Condytt in Cornhyll.

Also att the Condytt in Cornhyll dyd stande a pageant off a goodly Castell well and rychely garnysshede and arayde where satte the ryght noble and victorious emprowr Kynge Arthur w^t a crowne imperiall in complett harnes and a swerde in hys hande w^t the rounde table before hyme. Whiche was accompanyed w^t all the noble prynces thatt were wnder his obeisaunce that is to say on the ryght hande, Skater Kynge off Scotlande, Aloth Kynge of Denmarke, Walganus Kynge of Gutlande, Guyloin Kynge off Northwalys, Achilles Kynge off Iselande, Cander yerle of Cornwall and Eueraldus yerle of Sarylbury. And wppon the lefte hande of Kynge Arthur sate fyrste Madad Kynge of Irelonde, Cadwar Kynge of Southwalys, Cador Kyng of litill brytyn, Andher Kynge off Orkeney, Gunwado Kynge off Norwey, Morwidus yerle off glocester and Cutsall yerle of Chester. Also ther was a childe goodly apparelde whiche saluted the emprowr in laten versis laudyng & resemblyng hym in noblenes to the seyd Arthur.

Att the Stockys.

Also att the Stockys ther dyd stand a pageaunte off an ylonde betokenyng the Ile off englonde compassede all abowte w^t water made in silver and byce lyke to waves off the see and rockys ionyng thereto watelde (*wattled*) abowte w^t roddys off siluer and golde and wythyn them champion (*campagne*) contrey mountayns and wooddys where were dyuers bestes goyng abowte the mountayns by vyces and dyuers maner off trees herbys and flowres as roses, dayses, gyloflowres, daffadeles and other[s] so craftely made thatt hitt was harde to knowe them from very naturall flowres, and in the mountayns pondys off fressh water w^t fisshe. And att the comyng off the emprowr the bestys dyd move and goo, the fisshes dyd sprynge, the byrdes dyd synge reioysyng [at] the comyng off the ij princes the emprowr and the kynges grace. Also ther were ij goodly ymages one in a castell lyke to the emprowr in visage, and the other in an herbar wyth rosys lyke to the kynges grace with ij swerdys nakyd in ther handys. Which castell, garden, and the ymages dyd Ryse by a Vyce. The ymages dyd beholde eche other, and then cast away ther swerdys by a vyce, and w^t another vyce ioyned eche to other and em-brasede eche other in tokennyng off love and pease, whiche don an ymage off the father off hevyn all in burnyd golde dyd disclose and appere and move in the topp off the pageant wyth thys scripture wrytyn abowte hym —

Beati pacifici qui filij dei vocabuntur.

. . . Also there wer ij children in goodly apparell on (*one*) on the one syde which spake englisshe and the other on the other syde which spake frenche salutyng the emprowr and the kynges grace declaryng and poyntyng every thing in the pageannt off the premisses at the tyme and in ordyr acordyng as hitt was done and playede.

Att the greate Condytt in Chepe.

Also att the grete Condytt in Chepe stode a pageannt which was . . . richely garnysshede and also hanged w^t clothes off golde and had ij gates the east gate & the west gate. And when the emprowr and the kynges grace entryde at the east gate ther apperyd a rose nott fully blowen which openyd by litill & litill, and when hitt was fully blown ther apperyd a goodly yong mayden all arayed in cloth off golde w^t ij rosys in her hande, a whyte rose the which she gave to the emprowr and a red rose the which she gave to the kynges grace. Also att the west gate stode the iiij cardinall vertues, sc$_3$ Justice Prudence, ffortitude and Temperance. And a childe goodly apparelde which in laten salutyd the emprowr besechyng god thatt he myght have grace to defende the trew cristen people agaynst the infidelys. And also to govern them by Justice prudence, Strenghth and Temperance.

Att the Standarde in Chepe.

Also att the standard in chepe dyd stand a pageant off great hyght rychely garnysshed w^t golde & siluer and asure and dyuers setes [and] stages, and in the hyghest stage sate a yong man representyng the parson off the emprowr and another representyng the kynges grace, an[d] a yong mayden representyng the quene and an other the princes[s], and wnde[r] these setes and stages wer dyuers other setes in dyuers degreys one wnder an other, wheryn satte dyuers kynges, quenys and princes, and in the lowest off them all satte one Kyng Alfonsus Kyng of Castell and lyons and a lyne from hym ascendyng by degre to degre of euery kyng, quene, prince, and princes[s] wnto the hyghest stage off the emprowr and off the kynges grace shewyng how they bothe descend and com linially owt of the howse off spayne from the seyd Alfonsus. And the seyd Alfonsus salutyd the emprowr and the kyng att their comyng, expownyng and declaryng to them in laten all their seyd progeny . . . [The list of their ancestors is given in the MS.]

Att the Litill Condytt in Chepe.

Also att the litill Condytt in Chepe dyd stand a pageant representyng hevyn w^t son, mone & sterrys shynyng and w^t angellys and w^t xij apostollys & w^t Seynt George, seynt John baptiste, seynt Edmu[n]de Kyng, seynt Edwarde Kyng and confessor, Kyng Henry the vjth w^t certayn bisshoppes sayntes off englonde, as seynt Dunstane, seynt Thomas off Cantorbury and seynt Erkenwolde w^t the assumpcion off owr lady meruelous goodly conveyde by a vyce and a clowde openyng w^t Michael and Gabriel angellys knelyng and dyuers tymes sensyng w^t sensers and w^t voyces off yonge queretters syngyng psalmys and ympnys (*hymns*) w^t chalmys and organs w^t most swetyst musyke thatt cowed be devysede.

The show ended with the customary service at St. Paul's.

In this royal-entry, the mechanical elaboration may sound more wonderful than it really was; but it is worth noting, because there is no doubt that the pageant had a good deal of influence on the physical stage, and therefore on dramatic technique. This was not felt to any great extent before the days of the Elizabethan theatre and Inigo Jones, save in the court masques; but it is well to remember that the mechanism of the pageants used in the royal-entry had begun to be elaborate in the early sixteenth century. Here is also a tendency to use figures rather than living people, the *tableau* rather than the *tableau vivant*. Just how far this is carried, is hard to determine. There is considerable repetition — notably of genealogies; though one line is traced to John of Gaunt and another to King Alfonso. Representations of the two monarchs occur frequently; and besides the sacred and allegorical elements we have found in earlier pageants — the former of which, through the English saints, is linked to history — we have romantic, classical, and historical elements as well. Charlemagne and Arthur may be considered historical, rather than romantic; but the mechanical castle at the stocks goes back to romance, even though it contains an image of the emperor. A mechanical device in this same pageant permitted the spectators to see an image of God himself. The castle at the conduit in Cornhill, which contained Arthur and his vassals, is even more closely related to the romance.

In the figures of Jason and Medea, we see, for the first time, the classical element which we have already noted at Edinburgh and Paris. Its presence here may be due to Mr. Lyly, who — if he were a schoolmaster — would have been likely to draw on his knowledge of classical stories; the Order of the Golden Fleece suggested an easy adaptation of the material to the occasion.[1] By 1522, all the elements in English pageantry are united; the folk-figures at the drawbridge have received names (though Samson and Hercules were not retained by the giants); and history, romance, allegory, mythology, legend, and the Bible have united with mechanical skill to form a symbolic whole.

1525 — MARY AT COVENTRY

In 1525 the princess Mary visited Coventry. The Mercers' pageant was gallantly trimmed, and stood in the Cross Cheaping. When the royal guest departed, she received a kerchief and a hundred marks.[2]

1528 — THE EARL OF KILDARE ENTERTAINED AT DUBLIN

While the entertainment of the Lord Lieutenant of Ireland, by the crafts of Dublin at Christmas in 1528, can hardly be called a royal-entry, we may mention it here; for it shows an interesting example of the influence of the pageant on the drama.[3]

" Thomas Fitz-Gerald, Earl of Kildare, and Lord Lieutenant of Ireland in the year 1528, was invited to a new play every day in Christmas, Arland Usher being then mayor, and Francis Herbert and John Squire bayliffs, wherein the Taylors acted the part of Adam and Eve; the Shoemakers represented the story of Crispin and Crispianus; the Vintners acted Bachus (sic) and his story; the Carpenters that of Joseph and Mary; Vulcan, and what related to him, was acted by the Smiths; and the comedy of Ceres, the goddess of corn, by the Bakers. Their stage was erected on Hoggin-green (now called College-green), and on it the priors . . . caused two plays to be acted, the one representing the passion of our Saviour, and the other the several deaths which the apostles suffered."

---

[1] It is to be remembered that the Drapers showed the Golden Fleece in their Midsummer Show this year; undoubtedly this same pageant used here.

[2] Sharp, p. 158; cf. also Chambers, ii, p. 175, and Harris, *Life in an Old English Town*, p. 347. There is no mention of this visit in the *Leet-Book*, which may mean that the city did not share the expenses of the reception.

[3] I quote from *An Historical Essay on the Irish Stage* by Joseph C. Walker, in *Trans. Royal Irish Acad. (Antiquities)*, 1788, vol. ii. The author cites an (undated) account preserved among the MSS. of Robert Ware. Cf. Fairholt, *Civic Garland*, p. xxx.

This is clearly not pageantry in its technical sense; the Biblical and legendary material suggests the miracle-play, but the large element of classical mythology shows an influence, perhaps from Continental pageants, which may not have been unfelt in England.

1533 — CORONATION OF ANNE BOLEYN

Many are the accounts of the coronation, in 1533, of the unfortunate queen Anne Boleyn. With this entry, we can bring another name not unknown in the history of English literature into our survey, for Nicholas Udall wrote many of the verses spoken on this occasion. The king was glad to have the citizens join him in honoring Anne; and the fact that this show was a recognition of the revolt from the Pope[1] gives it a peculiar significance.

The importance of the " mob " in these shows is emphasized; we realize here, for the first time, how *impersonal* these exhibitions are. Certain blanks are filled with new names, as the years pass; but the formulæ remain pretty nearly the same. The station, rather than the individual, is of importance — while the crowds in the streets, unchanging from age to age, give these " triumphs " the continuity of an institution. Kings, queens, archbishops, and mayors may come and go; but the companies and the citizens are always there to greet their successors. A new executive may feel the excitement of his installation; a new sovereign may thrill at his first welcome by the populace; but the institution is as unmoved by the individual as is the marriage-service by the emotions of each new bride. The pageant has its formula; and the chief participants are there, not because they are Henry Tudor or John Norman, but because they are King of England and Lord Mayor of London.

The city, when called upon by the king to prepare for the reception of Anne, agreed to furnish three pageants — one at Leadenhall, a second at the Standard in Cheap, and a third at the Little Conduit in Cheap; these to be goodly hanged and garnished with minstralcy and children singing; and at the conduits, and at the Standard was wine to run. The City Council sent to the Duke of Norfolk to know whether the clergy should attend when the queen passed through London, and also to know whether the company of the " stylyards," [2] or any other strangers inhabiting within the city should make any pageant. The authorities also asked Mr. Cromwell that the city might have the king's minstrels for the furnishing of the pageants.[3]

---

[1] Arber, *An Eng. Garner* (1877–96), ii, p. 41, notes: " This was a much greater matter than a simple coronation pageant. It was the official recognition of the Revolt from the Papacy; and all who took a prominent part in it favoured the new Faith."

[2] On " the steleyard " see Kingsford's Stow's *Survey*, ii, pp. 318 f. It was the house of the merchants of Cologne in London; they occupied it before 1320.

[3] *Repertory* ix, fol. 1 b.

The king wrote letters to the city to prepare pageants for the coronation,[1] and on the 19th of May, the crafts with their banners, in good array, filled fifty great barges, " comely besene "; and every barge had minstrels making sweet harmony. Before the mayor's barge was a " foist " full of ordnance, and a dragon spouting fire.[2] The Bachelors' barge led the procession, and every craft followed in its degree and order, to Greenwich. At three o'clock the queen came to her barge; guns were fired, and the citizens accompanied her — surrounded as she was, with nobles — to the Tower wharf, where the king received her, and thanked the citizens for their great kindness.[3]

On Saturday, 31 May, the queen was escorted from the Tower to Westminster. The procession was headed by nobles, judges, and abbots; then came bishops, the archbishops of York and Canterbury, the ambassadors of France and Venice; then the Lord Mayor, the King of Heralds and Master-Garter; then two

---

[1] Hall, p. 798.

[2] On this pageant, see a contemporary account published by Arber in *An English Garner*, ii, pp. 41 f.; Cranmer's account is printed, from Harl. MS. 6148, fol. 26, *et seq.*, in *Archæologia*, xviii, pp. 78 f. Harl. MS. 41 contains a full account of this progress, and the subsequent coronation of the queen; Egerton MS. 2623, fol. 5, contains instructions regarding this entry, and a request for the aid of the king's minstrels in furnishing the pageants, addressed to the Duke of Norfolk. (Cf. above, where I have quoted from *Repertory* ix.)

Other accounts of this ceremony may be found in Hall, pp. 798 f.; Grafton, ii, pp. 447 f.; Wriothesley, i, pp. 18 f.; *Antiq. Rep.*, ii, pp. 232 f.; Stow, *Annals*, p. 564; Maitland, *Hist. Lond.* (1760), pp. 234 f. (from Hall and Stow); J. G. Nichols, pp. 35 f.; Hone, *Anc. Mys.*, p. 238; Fairholt, *L. M. Pag.*, pt. i, pp. 9 f.; etc.

See also *Ballads from Manuscripts* (ed. Furnivall for the Ballad Society), i, pp. 364 f., for the verses devised by John Leland and Nicholas Udall for this occasion, together with a reprint of Hall's account. Some of these verses were " set up," while others were spoken from the pageants (p. 378.) The verses are also printed in Arber, ii, pp. 52 f., and in *Tudor Tracts, 1532–88* (ed. A. F. Pollard [1903]), pp. 20–28.

The Pewterers hired the Duke of Norfolk's barge for this occasion. On their expenses, see Welch, i, pp. 124–125. For the expenses of the Ironmongers on this occasion, see Nicholl, *Some Account of the Ironmongers* (1866), appendix ix.

[3] Cf. Harl. MS. 6148, fol. 26, *et seq.* (printed by Ellis in *Archæologia*, xviii, pp. 78 f.: the editor notes (p. 77) that the MS. is in Cranmer's hand, and that it "appears to have been once archbishop Cranmer's rough Copy-Book of Letters.") I quote from it: " The Thursdaye nexte before the feaste of pentecost the Kyng and the Queene beyng at Grenewyche, all the Craftes of London therevnto well appoynted, in severall bargis deckyd after the most gorgiouse and sumptuous maner, with dyverse pagiantes thereunto belongyng, repayred and wayted all together upon the Mayre of London, and so, well furnysshed, cam all vnto Grenewiche, where they taryed and wayted for the Queenes commyng to her barge; which so done they brought her unto the tower, tromppets, shambes, and other dyverse instrumentes all the wayes playng and makyng greate melodie, which, as ys reported, was as combly donne as neuer was lyke in any tyme nyghe to our rememberaunce: and so her grace cam to the tower on Thursdaye at nyghte abowte v of the clocke, where also was suche a pele of gonnes as hathe not byn harde lyke a great while before. . . ."

" As ys reported " indicates that the archbishop was not an eye-witness of this progress.

knights, " disguised, who did represent the dukes of Normandy and of Guinne, after an old custom." Then came the Lord Constable of England, the Duke of Suffolk and the deputy to the Lord Marshal.[1]

After the queen — who rode in her litter, with a rich canopy, borne by the Lords of the Five Ports, over her head — came the Master of her Horse, leading her palfrey; then twelve Ladies of Estate, followed by the Master of the Guard, with the guard and constables. Four rich chariots with ladies of honor were followed by thirty ladies and gentlemen; " and so the serving men after them." A cannonade saluted the queen as she departed from the Tower.

" Cornehill and graciouse street [2] were hanged with ffyne scarlett Crymsyn and other grayned clothes and in some place[s] with Riche arrays (arras) tapestry and carpetts and the moost parte of chepe was hanged with clothes of Tyssue golde velvett and many riche hangyng[s] which made a goodly shewe." [3] At Fenchurch " was a pageant fair and seemly with certain children [4] who saluted her Grace with great honour and praise, after a goodly fashion." There was at Gracechurch " a right costly pageant of Apollo with the Nine Muses among the mountains, sitting on the mount of Parnassus: and every of them (sic) having their instruments and apparel according to the description of poets, and namely of Virgil; with many goodly verses to her great praise and honour." [5]

" And so " — to continue the account printed by Arber — " she passed through Gracious street unto Leaden Hall where was built a sumptuous and costly pageant in manner of a castle wherein was fashioned a heavenly roof and under it upon a green was a root or a stock, whereout sprang a multitude of white and red roses, curiously wrought. So from the heavenly roof descended a white falcon,[6] and lighted upon the said stock and root: and incontinent descended an

---

[1] Arber, ii, pp. 46 f. Cf. Cranmer's letter (Harl. MS. 6148, already quoted from) where the procession which accompanied the queen is described. The MS. continues: " to [her] also as she came alongeste the Citie was shewid many costely pagients, with diverse other encomyes spoken of chyldren to her, Wyne also runyng at certeyne Condits plentiously. And so procedyng thorowte the streats passid furthe vnto Westminster Hall, where was a certeyn Banket prepared for her. . . ."

[2] Grasschurch, Gracious, and Gracechurch are common forms of the name of this street.

[3] Harl. MS. 41, fol. 4 b.

[4] The accounts in Harl. MS. 41, the Antiq. Rep., and Hall, specify that these children were dressed as merchants, and addressed the queen in English and French. I am quoting Arber's account.

[5] From the account in Arber. Hall, and the account in the Antiq. Rep., add the Fountain of Helicon, runnihg wine. In Harl. MS. 41, fol. 5 b, we read that at " gracyous church corner " was " a costly and a mervelous connyng pagyaunt made by the marchaunts of the Stylliard." On it was Mount Parnassus, with Apollo and the Muses playing instruments; " and att their ffeete epigramynes (sic) and poyses were wrytten in golden letters."

[6] Harl. MS. 41, fol. 5, notes that at Leadenhall the queen's device was in a pageant; and " certeyn ymages and parsonages certeyne virgyns Representyng her name, Right goodly beseene, and oon of theym made a goodly Oracion to the qwene."

angel with goodly harmony, having a close crown between his hands, and set it on the falcon's head. And on the said floor sat Saint Anne in the highest place. And on that one side, her progeny with scripture, that is to wit, the three Maries with their issue . . ." [1] The verses of this pageant were written by Nicholas Udall.[2]

The queen went through Cornhill, and at the Conduit found a sumptuous pageant of the Three Graces. At the coming of the queen's grace, a poet declared the nature of all three, and gave high praise to Anne; then each of the three addressed her majesty; they were called Hearty Gladness (Aglaia), Stable Honour (Thaleia), and Continual Success (Euphrosyne). The verses of this pageant were also written by Udall. [3]

And the queen went on to Cheap, where a costly fountain was made at the great conduit; it ran red and white wine in great plenty all the afternoon. The cross was newly gilt; and there were music and speeches here. The Recorder of London received the queen before the aldermen, as she progressed toward the lesser conduit; with reverence he gave her a thousand marks,[4] for which free gift she gave great thanks.

At the lesser conduit was a rich pageant whereat was goodly harmony of music both instrumental and vocal; and within the pageant were five costly seats, on which sat Juno, Pallas, Venus, Mercury, and Paris; the last named gave the queen a ball of gold. *The Judgment of Paris*, spoken in this pageant, was almost a play; [5] Mercury gave Paris the apple from Jupiter, and Paris announced:

> Jupiter a strange office hath given me,
> To judge which is fairest of these ladies three.

Juno, Pallas, and Venus each plead for it; Paris is about to give it to Venus — but here comes Anne, a fourth more worthy still. The goddesses join him in presenting her with riches, honour, and felicity.[6]

---

[1] Hall, p. 801, notes that one of the children of " Mari Cleoph " made an oration extolling the issue of St. Anne, and hoping the like for her namesake, Anne Boleyn. (This must be the " oracion " mentioned in Harl. MS. 41. Cf. also *Antiq. Rep.*, ii, p. 237.)

[2] I have already mentioned that they may be found in Arber, and have referred to Furnivall's *Ballads from Manuscripts*, and *Tudor Tracts*.

[3] Hall, p. 801, and *Antiq. Rep.*, ii, p. 237, note a spring of grace continually running wine, and the presentation by each lady of a " gift of grace " to the queen.

[4] £666, or about £5000 in present value, notes Arber.

[5] On this see Arber, ii, p. 57; Hall, p. 802; *Antiq. Rep.*, ii, p. 238; cf. also Harl. MS. 41. " The conclusion of this pageant pronounced by a child," writes Udall: here *pageant* is equivalent to *show* or *scene*. The interest of the first part is entirely among the characters in the " play "; it is " intensive," until attention is turned to the queen. For this reason the scene is noteworthy; ordinarily the speeches of those on the platforms are directed at once to the person for whom the show is given. When, however, the same subject was presented at Edinburgh in 1503, it seems to have been given as a play.

[6] An undramatic break in characterization, common in pageantry. In a real play, Udall would have made the goddesses angry at Paris's action: he could not well do so here.

This, and the Edinburgh show in 1503, are examples of the rare *débat* in pageantry. That this form of literature did not take root in triumphs of this sort is due to the fact that the circumstances of presentation were not favorable to it; the pauses which the guest of honor made before each platform were not long; and the voices of the speakers could not be heard far from the stage. The open air, and the noises of the holiday crowd, together with the fact that the guest of honor had to be flattered, militated against " intensive drama "; the interest could not be kept to the scaffolds. The chief attraction was probably in the mechanical devices exhibited on each pageant, rather than in the poetical quality of the speeches, which were all more or less alike, and did not demand too much concentration on the part of anyone.

To return to Queen Anne: at Paul's Gate there " was a proper and sumptuous pageant, that is to wit, there sat three fair ladies, virgins, costly arrayed, with a fair round throne over their heads; whereabout was written, Regina Anna prospere! procede! et regna! " Various other appropriate inscriptions graced the pageant; and as the queen passed, wafers and rose-leaves were cast over her. In Paul's Churchyard, at the east end of the church, against the school, was a great scaffold whereon stood two hundred children " who received her [Anne] with poet's verses to her noble honour." [1]

Ludgate was " costly and sumptuously garnished with gold, colours, and azure; [2] with sweet harmony of ballads to her [the Queen's] great praise and honour; with divers sweet instruments." [3] The conduit in " fletestrete " was " newly paynted " and decorated, and angels sang from it, and it " ranne wyne clarett and Redd all the after none." Temple Bar was repaired and decorated, and singing men and children stood thereon. [4]

And so Queen Anne Boleyn went to Westminster, to begin her short reign.

1536–1546 — At London and Edinburgh

Henry VIII and his new queen made a splendid progress by water on 7 June, 1536, from Greenwich to York Place at Westminster; [5] but the citizens supplied no pageants — possibly because the progress was on the water; perhaps because they were already tired of welcoming the king's wives! On 22 December, of the same

---

[1] Hall, p. 802, and the *Antiq. Rep.*, ii, p. 238, imply that these verses were the work of more than one poet. Both accounts record the queen's approbation.

[2] Harl. MS. 41, notes it was " painted."

[3] Both Hall and Harl. MS. 41, record a choir on St. Martin's Church. I quote from fol. 7 of the MS.: " And on the leeds on Saynct Martens Churche stode a goodly Qwyre of syngyng men and children which sange newe balads made in prayse of her grace."

[4] Harl. MS. 41, fols. 7 and 7b. Hall, and the *Antiq. Rep.*, note the Cardinal Virtues in Fleet Street; and Arber's account mentions a tower with four turrets and vanes, wherein were music and singing children. This must be the conduit.

[5] Wriothesley, i, p. 44.

year, the King, Queen, and Princess Mary crossed London in state, and were welcomed by burgher and priest; but again there seems to have been no pageantry in the strict sense of the word.[1]

When Edinburgh welcomed Queen Mary of Guise in 1538, there was, apparently, no pageantry, although the guilds were to be arrayed, the inhabitants to be dressed in their best, and " it is devysit that Maister Henry Lawder be the persoun to welcum the Quenis grace . . ." [2]

In January, 1540, Anne of Cleves was received in state at London, apparently without pageantry.[3]

On 21 August, 1546, when the French admiral passed through London, the mayor and aldermen welcome him " at the Conduite at Saincte Michaells in the querne," and a French address was spoken.[4] It will be recalled that in 1445 there was a speech delivered " at Seynt Michaeles in Querne," [5] when Queen Margaret of Anjou came to London.

1547 — KING EDWARD VI RECEIVED IN LONDON

On 19 February, 1546–47, King Edward VI went through the city of London in great state to his coronation at Westminster.[6] The procession was very splendid; the houses of the city were gaily decked. Citizens and clergy did honor to the new king; and there were pageants in the customary places.

At the conduit in Cornhill, which ran wine, musicians played and children sang; two of them delivered speeches of welcome. The song contained " expres-

---

[1] Wriothesley, i, p. 59.

[2] *Extracts from the Records of the Burgh of Edinburgh,* ii, pp. 89 f. (The quotation occurs on p. 91.)

[3] Wriothesley, i, pp. 110 f. Under date of 1540 (when "the Company's accounts of receipts and expenditure commence," — though the appendix to Nicholl shows accounts older than 1540) Nicholl gives the expenses of the Ironmongers " at the cōing in off the quene to Greneweche " and " the comyng of the quene from Greneweche to Westemynster." These entries in the Ironmongers' books may refer to the arrival of Anne of Cleves.

[4] Wriothesley, i, p. 172.

[5] Printed, from Harl. MS. 3869, in the *Mod. Lang. Rev.,* vii, pp. 230 f. Cf. above, p. 148.

[6] For accounts of this event, see " a MS. formerly belonging to William Le Neve Norroy, printed in Leland, *Collect.,* iv, pp. 310 f. (which dates the entry 9 February.) Both Hone, *Anc. Mys.,* p. 238, and J. G. Nichols, p. 42, go back to this. There are short accounts of the entry in Stow, *Annals,* p. 594, and in Wriothesley, i, p. 182; both the latter date the progress 19 February; we may note the king was but nine years and three months old. Cf. also on this entry, Chambers, ii, p. 171.

A detailed description of a painting illustrating the entry of Edward VI may be found in *Archæologia,* iii, pp. 267 f.; viii, pp. 406 f. An engraving, "from a coeval painting at Cowdray, in Sussex, the seat of Lord Viscount Montague," of " the procession of King Edward VI from the Tower of London to Westminster Feb. xix, MDXLVII, previous to his coronation " may be found in a Brit. Mus. collection of engravings, press-marked " 3 Table 24 "; none of the pageants appear in this picture, which is no. 4.

sions very like some in the present song of *God Save the King*," as Hone points out.[1] On the pageant at the great conduit in Cheap were persons representing Valentine and Orson, who spoke; the conduit ran wine, and was richly garnished. Near it stood four children, as Grace, Nature, Fortune, and Charity, who spoke; Sapience, with the seven Liberal Sciences,[2] offered her services to the king; and each Science presented herself after the speech. At the end of the conduit towards Cheapside, was a double scaffold, hung with rich cloth; the upper contained a heaven " with the Sunn, Starrs, and Clowdes very naturally." From this cloud there descended a phœnix to a mount of sweet shrubs on the lower scaffold, and there a lion of gold, crowned, made " Semblance of Amyty unto the Bird " by motions of his head. Between which familiarity there came forth a young lion, on whose head two angels from heaven placed an imperial crown. Then the old lion and the phœnix vanished, leaving the young lion crowned, alone.

On the lower scaffold a child, representing the king himself, sat on a throne, supported by four other children — Royalty, with a sceptre; Justice, with a sword; Truth, with a book; and Mercy, with a *curtana*:[3] these four spoke briefly. Beside the throne was the Golden Fleece,[4] kept by two bulls and a serpent, their mouths flaming out fire, " according to the story of Jason." Also there were six children who played upon the " regalles " and sang with great melody divers goodly songs.[5]

The little conduit in Cheap was richly ornamented; and at the top was a tower, with the waits playing upon it; and an old man, representing Edward the Confessor, sat crowned and sceptred on a throne. A lion of gold lay before him, " which moved his Head by Vices." On a stage at the foot of the conduit sat St. George in full armor on horseback; a page carried his spear and shield; and a fair maiden held a lamb " in a string." Near them a child richly apparelled was ready to pronounce a Latin oration, and St. George was to have made one in English; but for lack of time it could not be done, the king made such speed: howbeit, there was a song.[6]

From the battlements of St. Paul's a rope had been stretched to the ground; and as the king approached, " a native of Arragon lying on the same rope, his

---

[1] Both song and speeches are printed in Leland, iv, pp. 313, 314.

[2] The eight who represented Sapience and the seven sciences were " richly apparelled . . . like Ladyes." (Leland, iv, p. 315.)

[3] " The pointless sword carried before the kings of England at their coronations, and emblematically considered as the Sword of Mercy." See *Century Dictionary*, under *curtein*. Cf. above, the progress of Richard III through London on the day before his coronation in 1483 (p. 154).

[4] We saw this in 1522; by 1547 it may have become a trade-pageant. It had a trade-significance in the later Lord Mayor's Shows, and perhaps the classical element, brought by the Renaissance, had influenced trade-pageantry as early as this.

[5] Leland, iv, p. 318; cf. Hone, *Anc. Mys.*, p. 239.

[6] Leland, iv, p. 319 — where St. George's speech is printed: on p. 320 is the " Ballet of the King's Majesty."

head forward, casting his arms and legs abroad, running on his breast on the said rope from the said battlements to the ground, as it had been an arrow out of a bow, and stayed on the ground. Then he came to the king's majesty, and kissed his foot," and after speaking a few words to him, he " went upwards upon the said rope till he was come over the midst of the said churchyard, where he having a rope about him, played certain mysteries on the said rope, as tumbling and casting one leg from another. Then he took the said rope, and tied it to the cable, and tied himself by the right leg a little beneath the wrist of the foot, and hung by the right leg a certain space, and after recovered himself up again with the said rope, and unknit the knot, and came down again, which stayed the king's majesty with all the train a good space of time." [1]

The procession then continued its way to Fleet Street, where on the conduit sat three children, representing Truth, Faith, and Justice, " whose names were before them written in their places." Truth spoke,[2] and after the king had passed, two hogsheads of wine were broached, " take who would." The gate at Temple Bar was painted with battlements and buttresses, richly hung with cloth of arras, and garnished with fourteen standards. Eight French trumpeters blew their trumpets " after the fashion of their country "; and there was a pair of " regalles " to which children sang. And so Edward went to Westminster.[3]

1549 — HENRI II ENTERS PARIS

When Henri II entered Paris, on 16 June, 1549, " pour la somptuosité & magnificence de la dicte entrée, & afin de faire claire & ouuerte demonstration de la ioye & liesse incroyable qu'ils receuoyent de la nouuelle venüe en la dicte Ville de leur souuerain & naturel Seigneur, feirent eriger & dresser aucuns arco de triomphe, & autres manufactures, d'excellent artifice, subtile & loüable invention, tant à la porte de la dicte Ville nommée la Porte Sainct Denys, qu'au dedans d'icelle Ville, ainsi qu'il est cy apres escript." [4] The city was decorated with rich tapestries on this occasion;[5] and much the same ceremony was observed as on the entry of Catherine de Medicis two days later.[6]

No pageantry played a part in Edward's passage through London on 23 July, 1549;[7] nor when he went through the city on the 17 October, 1549 — though on the latter occasion there was music, both vocal and instrumental; and the houses were decorated.[8]

---

[1] Leland, iv, p. 320; cf. Hone, p. 240. The presence of the acrobat in pageantry may be a development of the "wild-man" through such figures as the acrobatic wild-men of the Paris 1431 show (see above, p. 139). Cf. chapter i, § 8, for further remarks on the "wild-man."

[2] The speech is in Leland, iv, p. 321.

[3] He was crowned on Shrove Sunday, 20 February; an account of the ceremony may be found in Leland, iv, pp. 322 f. On the Monday following, there were jousts.

[4] Godefroy, pp. 359 f. [6] Pp. 384 f. [8] Ibid., pp. 28 f.

[5] P. 379. [7] Wriothesley, ii, p. 19.

1553 — Queen Mary's Progress before her Coronation

The coronation of Queen Mary, on 1 October, 1553, was the occasion of pageantic exhibitions.[1] The day before, she rode through the city, as the custom was; and " all the streetes from the Tower to Temple barre were richelye hanged with divers costlye pageantes, &c." [2] As early as 3 August, the City Council prepared for the event: "Itm—All the Companies of Crafte[s] to prepare Raylles for ther Standyngs, and they to stand in ther Lyverys to receyve her Grace, begynnyge (*sic*) wt the meanest Companies firste, at the Well with ij Buckets within Aldgate, and so the Companies in order after other followin, shal as they be of Aunciyetie, so farre as they may stretche." [3]

Edward Underhill witnessed the procession. Says he: " the fyrst daye off october was quene mary crowned . . . and beynge very desyrous to se the qu. pass thorow the cittie gott vppe on horsebak beynge scantt able to sitt gyrdide in a longe nyght gowne . . . thus wentt I fforth . . . to the west ende of polles, and ther placed my selff amoungst others thatt satte on horsebak to se the quene pass by, before her comynge I behelde poles steple bearynge toppe and toppe galantt [yards] [4] lyke a ryall shippe wt many fflags and bannars and a man tryommfyng and daunsynge in the toppe. . . ." [5]

Three pageants on this occasion were contributed by the Genoese, Florentines and Easterlings; that of the Florentines was " very high, on the top whereof there stood four pictures, and in the midst of them and most highest, there stood an angel all in green, with a trumpet in his hand, and when the trumpeter who stood secretly in the pageant did sound his trump, the angel did put his trump to his mouth, as though it had been the same that had sounded, to the great marvelling of many ignorant persons; [6] this pageant was made with three thoroughfares or gates, &c." [7]

The conduit in Cornhill ran wine, and beneath it a pageant was made at the city's expense; another stood at the great conduit in Cheap, and a fountain beside it ran wine. The waits of the city played from the newly painted Standard, and the Cross was new washed and burnished. The aldermen stood in a pageant

---

[1] Cf. on this, Stow's *Annals*, p. 616; Holinshed, (1808), iv, p. 8; Edward Underhill's account, in Harl. MS. 424, fol. 92, *et seq.*, reprinted in Arber, *English Garner*, iv, pp. 84 f. Cf. also J. G. Nichols, pp. 50 f.; Hone, *Anc. Mys.*, pp. 240 f.; Taylor, p. 287; Chambers, ii, p. 172. For the Pewterers' expenses on this occasion, see Welch, i, p. 175; Jupp, p. 50, gives the expenses of the Carpenters at this progress.

[2] Wriothesley, ii, p. 103.

[3] W. M. Williams, *Annals of the Founders*, p. 215, citing from the City Records.

[4] Inserted by Arber.

[5] Harl. MS. 424, fol. 92, *et seq.*

[6] Evidently the angel was mechanical; or the trumpeter himself could have been dressed up to represent one.

[7] Stow, p. 616.

at the little conduit in Cheap, and when the queen came, the recorder welcomed her, and the chamberlain gave her, in the name of the mayor and the city, a thousand gold marks in a purse. In Paul's Churchyard, in a pageant under a vine, sat " one master Heywood," who addressed Mary in Latin and English.[1] One " Peter, a Dutchman " stood on the weathercock of St. Paul's steeple, " holding a streamer in his hand of five yards long, and waving thereof." He stood " sometime on the one foot and shook the other, and then kneeled on his knees, to the great marvel of all people." [2] He had two scaffolds under him; one above the cross, hung with streamers and torches, and the other, likewise hung, over the bowl of the cross; but the wind was so great that the torches would not burn.[3]

The choristers of Paul's furnished vocal and instrumental music from a pageant made against the Dean of Paul's gate; Ludgate, newly repaired, painted and richly hung, housed more minstrels; there was a pageant at the conduit in Fleet Street; and Temple Bar was newly painted, and covered with tapestries. The queen thanked the mayor for his pains, and the city for their cost, as she departed for Westminster.

1554 — THE RECEPTION OF PHILIP OF SPAIN IN HIS WIFE'S CAPITAL CITY

The next year, London was called upon to welcome Mary's husband, King Philip of Spain. It is probably to this show that the arrangements for pageants, to be found in *Repertory* xiii, on folio 118, apply.[4] Pageants were appointed at the conduit in Gracechurch Street; at Leadenhall; at the conduit in Cornhill; at the Stocks; at the great conduit in Cheap; at the Standard, the Cross, and the little conduit; at Ludgate, and at the Conduit in Fleet Street. At the meeting of the city authorities on 22 May, 1554, a committee was appointed to set forth their opinions for such pageants and demonstrations of joy to be made within the city at the coming of the Prince of Spain; [5] and the volume is full of further refer-

---

[1] This is probably John Heywood, the author of *The Foure PP*. In preparing for the reception of Philip, the next year, it was agreed that Nicholas Chyne, haberdasher, should join with Mr. Barthelet and the other devisers of the city pageant in the place of John Heywood, gentleman, who for press of other business could not attend to this matter. See *Repertory* xiii, fol. 166 b.

[2] Stow, p. 617. He is the " man tryommfyng and daunsynge," whom Underhill saw.

[3] Stow. Peter received from the city £16, 13s. 4d. for " his costs and pains and all his stuffe."

[4] The entry is dated 29 January, 1 Mary. This would be after October, 1553; and the entry probably does not refer to the Lord Mayor's Show of that year, which took place on 29 October. The reception of Philip took place in August.

[5] *Repertory* xiii, fol. 162 b. Perhaps the meeting of 29 January had considered only the location of the pageants.

ences to the coming celebration. The gates and conduits were to be trimmed;[1] the Cross in Cheap was to be newly gilded;[2] the devisers of the city pageants were to make the merchant-strangers, who intended to give pageants, privy to the matters of the city pageants; and the wardens of the Painter-Stainers had to take order with their fellowship, that none of them covenant to work with the merchant-strangers at this time of the coming in of the Prince of Spain, until the city was fully furnished;[3] the Company of the Spaniards agreed to make answer whether they would make any pageants; and a day was given to the merchants of the "Styllyarde" touching the setting up of their pageant;[4] the altering of the persons named to survey the pageants was referred to Grafton and others.[5] The merchants of the Stillyard were permitted to set up their pageant in Gracechurch Street;[6] the surveyors of the pageant were to have the necessary free stone for the pageant at London Bridge;[7] the pageant of Orpheus in Soper lane was viewed, and it was decided to go on with it;[8] the merchants of the Stillyard were to stand on the east side of Gracechurch Street, next their pageant, on the coming of the king;[9] the common waits of the city were to serve at the Standard in Cheap.[10] The order for the pageants to be taken down is in the minutes of the meeting held on the 6 August, 1554.[11]

There are two interesting accounts of this royal-entry; my excuse for quoting from both, is that one is friendly and the other unfriendly.[12]

---

[1] *Rep.* xiii, fol 165.
[2] *Ibid.*, and cf. fol. 167.
[3] Fol. 166.
[4] Fol. 166 b.
[5] Fol. 169.
[6] Fol. 170.
[7] Fol. 175.
[8] See fols. 185 b and 187 b.
[9] Fol. 190 b.
[10] Fol. 191.
[11] Fol. 191 b.

[12] The unfriendly one may be found in Foxe's *Acts and Monuments* (1838, vi, pp. 557 f.). His account is followed by Holinshed, iv, p. 62. [This fact is noted by Thomson, *Chron. Lond. Bridge*, p. 581; he quotes Foxe (1610, ii, p. 1338)]. The other account is by John Elder, an eyewitness of the entry, printed in a rare pamphlet in the Guildhall Library, entitled, *The Copie of a Letter sent in to Scotlande, of the ariuall and landynge, and most noble Maryage of the moste Illustre Prynce Philippe, Prynce of Spaine, to the most excellente Princes Marye, Quene of England. . . .* [Black Letter, London, 1555]. The letter is written to Robert Stuart, Bishop of Caithness.

Wriothesley, ii, p. 122, mentions this entry in passing: " Saterdaye the 18 of August, in the after-noone, the King and Queenes Majesties rode throughe Sowthwerke, over the bridge, and so throughe London; where they were with great provision receaved of the citizens, pageants in places accustomed, the crosse in Cheape new gilte, &c."

The expenses of the Carpenters' Company on this occasion, together with an extract from Stow's account, may be found in Jupp, p. 51: " toward ye pageants and gyldyng ye crosse, vij s. vj d." (Jupp mistakenly dates this 1555.) For Stow's short account, see his *Annals* (1600) p. 1057; it resembles Wriothesley's and notes in addition: ". . . passing through *Paules* churchyard, a man came sliding, as it were flying vpon a rope frō Paules steeple down to the deanes wall."

Cf. also on this entry, J. G. Nichols, pp. 52 f.; and Chambers, ii, p. 172. "The Marriage Festivities of Queen Mary and Philip of Spain " is the subject of Episode VII of the Winchester Pageant (1908). See the *Book of Words* of that Pageant, pp. 67 f.

What Foxe calls " vain pageants " greeted the king and queen; " at London-bridge . . . was a vain great spectacle set up, two images representing two giants, the one named Chorinæus, and the other Gogmagog, holding between them certain Latin verses, which for the vain ostentation of flattery I overpass." [1] Elder writes:

"Nowe to begyn and declare their cumming to London, . . . your reuerend Lordship shall vnderstande that bothe their moste excellent Maiesties made their moste noble and Triumphinge entres into the noble Citie of London, furthe of Southwarke place, the next satterdaye, whiche was the .xviii of August, at .ii. of the clocke at after none. Where, after all the lordes of their most honorable priuie counsel, and the ambassadours of all nacyons, with the nobilitie of Englande and Spayne, and divers other noble and ientle mē, as wel English as straunge, wer al on horsebacke, two and two in a rāke, the lord Maior of Londō, as the two Prīces came out at the gate, kneled and delivered a mace, whiche signified his power and authoritie within the citie of London, to the Quenes grace. Whose magestie deliuering the said mace to the lord Maior again, the kinges highnes and she ascended their horses, & so marchyng to wardes London bridge, the quene of the righte hande, and the king of the lefte, with two swerdes of honoure before theym, and before the swerdes the Lord Maior of London bearing the Mace, the Toure of London begynneth to shoote. And when they came to the drawe bridge, there they made the fyrst staye, where there was in the higth thereof, a fayre table, holden up with two greate Giauntes: the one named *Corineus Britannus*, and the other *Gogmagog Albionus*. In which table, in a fielde siluer, with faire Romaine letters of sable these .xii. verses following were wrytten. . . ." The verses, both in Latin and English, are printed in the pamphlet.

" Here also the Toure of London (the signe geuen that the kinge and the Quene were in syghte thereof) shotte suche peales of ordinaunce in & about every quarter thereof, and specially out of the toppe of the whyte toure & of the wharff, as neuer was heard the lyke in Englande heretofore."

To return to Foxe's narrative: he tells us that the conduit in " Gracious-street " was finely painted; " and among other things, the nine worthies, whereof King Henry the Eighth was one.[2] He was painted in harness, having in one hand a sword, and in the other a book whereupon was written ' Verbum Dei '; delivering the same book (as it were) to his son King Edward, who was painted in a corner by him.

" But hereupon was no small matter made: for the bishop of Winchester, lord chancellor, sent for the painter, and not only called him knave, for painting a book in King Henry's hand, and specially for writing thereupon ' Verbum Dei,' but also rank traitor and villain; saying to him that he should rather have put the book into the queen's hand (who was also painted there), for that she had reformed the church and religion . . . according to the pure and sincere word of God indeed: . . . That it was the queen's majesty's will and commandment,

---

[1] Foxe, vi, p. 557. As the king and queen passed over the bridge, ordnance in the Tower was shot off, " such as by old men's report the like hath not been heard or seen these one hundred years."

[2] Note that these are not living figures, as was usually the case. Apparently Edward VI and Mary were included in the list.

that he should send for him: and so, commanding him to wipe out the book and 'Verbum Dei' too, he sent him home. So the painter departed; but, fearing lest he should leave some part either of the book, or of 'Verbum Dei' in King Henry's hand, he wiped away a piece of his fingers withal!"

Elder tells of the progress of the procession

"vntil they came in gracious strete, where in their waye the conduit thereof was finely trimed, whereon was painted verye ingeniouslye the nine worthies with many notable prouerbes and adages, written with fayre Romā letters on euery side thereof. And at the signe of the splaied Egle, they made the second staie where the first pagēt was deuysed [1] and made by the marchaunt straungers of the Stilliarde.

"Where emōgest diuers notable stories there was in the top thereof, the picture of the king sitting on horsse backe, all armed verye gorgeously and richly set out to the quicke. Under which picture were written in field siluer with fayre Romaine letters of sable, these wordes folowinge after this maner.

Diuo Phi. Aug. Max.

` Hispaniarum principi exoptatissimo.

"That is to saye.

"In honour of worthy Philip the fortunate, & most mighty, Prince of Spaine, most earnestly wyshed for.

"And vnder that were wrytten in a field blue, whiche Heroldes call azure, with faire Romaine letters of siluer, these two verses folowinge.

Constantem, fortemque animum, ter magne Philippe,
Nec spes a recto, nec metus acer agit.

"That is to saye.

Most mighty Philip, nether hope nor feare may fright
Thy stronge and valiaunt hart, away from ryghte.

"Which picture & al other notable stories & wrytinges in the saide Pagent pleasing their magesties very wel, they marched forward vntill they came to Cornewall (sic) where the cōduite also there beig (sic) very excellentlye painted, at the west end of the strete was the seconde pagent which was ryghte excellently handled and set out, where their magesties made the thirde staye. In whiche pageante were foure liuely persons, which represented the foure most noble Philips, of whose moste noble actes and doinges we read in auncient stories. That is to saye Philip kyng of Macedonia, Philip the Romayn Emperour, Philip Duke of Burgundy surnamed *Bonus*, and Philip Duke of Burgundy surnamed *Audax* betwixt which foure princes, two beyng of the right side of the pagent, and two of the leaft, there was a fayre table, wherein were written in a fielde azure, wyth Roman letters of siluer, these viii verses folowyng." Both the Latin and the English translation of the verses are printed in the pamphlet.

"This pageante with the stories therein contayned liking the kinges highnes and the quene wonderous well, they passed towardes Chepeside, & at the Easte end thereof, the conduite there also being finely paynted and trimed, they made the fourth staye, where the thirde pagente was made. In ye heigth wherof, was one playing on a harpe, who signified the most Excellente musician *Orpheus*, of whom, and of Amphiō, we reade in the fables of old Poetis. Where also were nyne faire ladyes playing and singing on divers swete instrumentes, signifying the nine muses.

---

[1] The "nine worthies" was evidently not considered a pageant.

" And not farre from them were men, and children decked up like wilde beastes, as Lions, wolfes, foxes, and beares. So that the moste swete strokes, noyse, and soundes of *Orpheus*, with the nyne Musis playing and singinge in the sayd Pageant, and also the counterfeated beastes daunsing and leapinge, with *Orpheus* harpe, and the Musis melodye exhilarated and reioysed their maiesties very much. Under *Orpheus* in a field siluer, with faire romaine letters of sable, were written in a very faire table these .viii. verses followinge." They were in Latin and English; I quote the translation:

> The prince that hath the gift of eloquence
> May bend his subiectes to his most behoue
> Which in old time was shewed by covert sence
> In Orpheus whose song did wilde beastes moue.
> In like case now thy grace of speche so franke
> Doth comfort vs, whose mindes afore wer bleke
> And therefore England geueth the harty thanke
> Whose chiefest ioy is to heare thee Philip speke.

Elder's letter helps us to tell how much of the symbolism in Foxe's account is pageant, and how much is Foxe, who writes: " In another poetry King Philip was resembled by another image representing Orpheus,[1] and all English people resembled to brute and savage beasts following after Orpheus's harp, and dancing after King Philip's pipe . . ." We see that Foxe does not exaggerate things much; and we can imagine his bitterness before he knew that Mary's reign was going to last only five years.

" Their maiesties beig (*sic*) satisfied with the sighte of that pageant," continues Elder, " they marched from thence, and passinge through Chepeside, where they perceuing the crosse thereof, which was with fine gold richely gilded, they staied a litle lokinge thereon, which was (no doute it is) vnto them a right excellent view, where also the kinges highnes perceauing the crucifix in the top thereof, very humblie put off his cap. Thys sene, they marched forwarde, and at the west end of Chepe they made the fyft stay, where was ye fourth and most excellent pageant of al. Wherein was contained, declared and shewed their moste noble Geneology from kinge Edwarde the third, which Geneologie was most exellently (*sic*) & moste ingeniously set out, with a great Arboure or tree: vnder the roote whereof was an olde man liinge on his left side, with a long white beard, a close croune on his head, and a sceptour in his ryght hand and a ball Imperial in his lefte. Which olde man signified kinge Edward the third, of whom both their maiesties are linially desceded, which grene Arboure or tree grewe vp of bothe the sides with braunches, whereon did sit young faire childrē which represēted the persones of such kinges, quenes, Princis, dukes, Earles, lordes & ladies as descēded frō ye said king Edward the .iii. vnto their daies, whose names were writtē aboue their heades in fields azure in faire tables with Roman letters of siluer. Where also in the saied top of the said arbour or tre was a Quene of the right hande, & a king of ye left, which presēted their magesties. Aboue whose heades was written their new stile and title, with fayre Roman letter of sable in a feilde golde. And aboue that, in the heigth of al, wer both their armes. Joined in one vnder one Crown emperial. And finally vnder the old mā whiche lay vnder the rote of the Arbour & signified (as I have said) king Edward the third, were written these vi verses . . ." which follow, both in Latin and English, in the text from which I quote.

" Quhich pageant beynge throughlye vewed and much commēded of their maiesties, they wente hence towardes s. Paules Church. And in their way a skoller of Paules skoole decked vp in cloth of gold, delyuered vnto the kinges highnes a fayre boke, which he receaued verye ientlie. Where also a fellow came slipping upō a corde as an arrow out of a bow, from Paules

---

[1] *Image* may here mean *figure of speech.*

steple to the grownde, & lighted with his heade forwarde on a greate forte of fether beds:
And after he clame vp the corde again, and done certaine feates,[1] their magesties lighted, &
being in Paules church receaued with procession by the Bishop of London, and *Te Deum* songe
& ended, they departed, and marched towards fletestrete, at the condit whereof they made the
sixt and last staye, where was the fift and hindermost pagent of all. Wherein was a Quene & a
king representing their highnes, hauing of their right side *Iusticia* with a swerde in her hande,
and *Equitas* wyth a payre of ballaunce. And of theyr left side *Veritas* wyth a boke in her
hande, whereon was written *Verbum Dei*, & *Misericordia* with a hearte of golde. Where also
from the heigth of the pageant descended one which signified *Sapientia* with a crowne in eche
of her handes, whereof the one she put on ye head of her that presented the quene, and the
other on the head of him that presented the king: vnder which two wer written '' verses which
the pamphlet gives in Latin and English.

"And after yt their magesties had seen the effecte of thys pageant they proceded forward
towardes tēple bar, where they stayed a litle in viewinge a certayn Oracion in Latin which was
in a long table wrytten with Romayne Letters, aboue the porte thereof as they passed and
departed furth of ye Citie. Which oraciō declared, that such triumphes and pagiantes as were
deuised and made in the noble citie of london by the Lord Maior thereof, his brethren, and the
citisens, for theyr entries, whose most happy cumming, they most hertly so long tyme desired,
and wished for, and agayne the running and reioysing of the greate number of people as were
there calling and crying euery where *God saue your graces*, was an evident token, testimonie and
witnes of their faithful, and vnfained hertes to the Quenes highnes & the king. For whose
moste excellente Maiesties they prayed vnto almightye God long to lyue, rule, and reygne ouer
their moste noble Empyre of Englande.

"And now makyng an end here of this theyr most triumphyng entries into ye noble citye of
Lōdon, they departed from Temple Barre towards Yorke place, otherwyse called the whyte
hal . . ." And so "Bloody Mary" led her husband home.[2]

It may be imagined that Mary's reign was not productive of public expressions
of joy: when one thinks what that reign meant to many citizens of London, the
" table " at Temple Bar becomes a pathetic object. Four years later Elizabeth
came to the throne; and with her what has been called " the Augustan age of
pageantry " began.

1558 — THE WEDDING OF THE DAUPHIN AND THE QUEEN OF SCOTS

In 1558 the Queen of Scots married the Dauphin of France. The Edinburgh
authorities paid " to Walter Bynning, painter, for his panting (*sic*) and all his
lawbouris takin be him in the tryumphe maid at our Souerane Ladyis mariage
the sowm of xxv merkis; to William Lauder [3] the sowm of aucht lib., by [4] the

---

[1] This is the man referred to by Foxe, " that came down upon a rope tied to the battlements
[of Paul's] with his head before, neither staying himself with his hand nor foot; which shortly
after cost him his life."

[2] For the queen's letter of thanks for this reception, and the order touching the good
treatment of the Spaniards, see *Repertory* xiii, fol. 191. (The oration " to be made to the king
in the name of the city " is also on that folio.)

[3] Perhaps a connection of the Henry Lawder who welcomed Mary of Guise in 1538.

[4] This evidently means *in addition to*.

fourtie schillingis quhilkis he has ellis ressauit for his travell and lawbour tane
vpone him in setting furth of the play maid at our Souerane Ladyis mariage; . . .
to all the wrychtis quhikis wrocht the play grayth in the play maid at the tryumphe of our Souerane Ladyis mariage for thair tymmer and workmanschip the
sowm of five lib. four s. nyne d . . . to Patrick Dorane for his travell takin on
him for making of certane claythis agane the tryumphe of our Souerane Ladyis
mariage the sowm of four lib. . . . to Adam Smyth, takkisman of Andro Mow-
brayis yarde the sowm of vj s. viij d. for the dampnage and skayth sustenit be
him in tramping down of his gers of the said yard be the convoy and remanent
playeris the tyme of the trumphe (*sic*)." [1]

CONCLUSION

We have seen how the pageant grew from small beginnings into a distinct form
of entertainment. At first, a trade-guild marched with animals symbolic of its
craft; then castles were built on conduits, peopled with angels who discoursed
sweet music, and with virgins whom Lydgate turned into allegorical figures, by
the simple process of giving them allegorical names. John the Baptist, God, and
other Biblical characters appear to have come from the miracle-plays; and the
guilds were not unwilling to combine this sacred element with trade-symbolism.
The folk-figure of the giant appears in the royal-entry as early as 1415; but it
does not receive a name for more than a hundred years. The Aberdeen Bruce
of 1511 suggests the " giant-champion," but may be a living person; in 1522 we
find the London giants called Hercules and Samson; [2] and in 1554 Corineus and
Gogmagog welcomed Philip of Spain.

It is not surprising that saints should join the angelic and Biblical host; they
come early and appropriately to adorn these triumphs, being patrons of the guilds.
The Nine Worthies bring an historical, or — what is the same thing for us — a
pseudo-historical, element, mixed with Biblical and romantic influences. Perhaps
the feeling for history, always more or less prominent in the pageant, is a rem-
nant of the days when Adam and Eve were regarded as historical characters and
every word of the Bible implicitly believed; days not, after all, very distant.

Such romantic figures as King Arthur were probably considered historical;
and it is doubtful whether Charlemagne could be looked upon as anything else.
If it be true that the historical element of pageantry awakened a desire for history

---

[1] *Extracts from the Records of the Burgh of Edinburgh*, iii, p. 26. In 1559, when Charles V
was buried at Brussels, there was a pageant. Pictures of a funeral car exhibited on this occasion — with Faith, Hope, Charity, and banners — are in the Musée Plantin at Antwerp.
The entry of Isabella and Albert (including a Giant, currus Neptuni, state pageants, etc.) is
also illustrated there by contemporary copper plates. In Charles de Coster's charming version
of the *Ulenspiegel* tales, the hero describes pageantic *fêtes* in Belgium, at the time of Philip II.

[2] The Drapers' Midsummer giant was named by 1522, if not earlier. (See above, p. 56,
n. 3, and p. 40.)

which was satisfied by the chronicle-play, we have an interesting parallel between the sixteenth century and our own day. For the Parkerian pageant has much in common with the Elizabethan chronicle-play, to which, indeed, it has been likened; and while it was not inspired directly by the older pageantry, it is quite likely that the historical element in recent Lord Mayor's Shows helped to prepare the public for the new *genre*.[1]

Such characters as Ebrauc, at York in 1486, suggest the development of the personified city (common enough in the seventeenth century, and not less common today) from the historical figure of its founder. These shows encouraged a love of the spectacular, and they may have drawn, as Ward suggests,[2] the popular taste to the national history; at any rate, they helped to familiarize the people with the nation's past.

The pure classical element, unmixed with history, seems to have appeared first at Edinburgh — perhaps having come from Italy *via* France. By 1522 we find Jason in a London royal-entry; and that same year the Drapers grasped the possibility of giving the Golden Fleece a trade-signification, for they used " our newe pageant of the *Goldyn Flees* " at midsummer.[3] The folk-animals were given a trade-signification as early as 1298; they were combined with heraldry — the 1415 lion and antelope, the 1432 antelopes, and the falcon of 1533, are a few examples.[4] The dragon of saints' legend comes into the pageant with St. George and St. Margaret; the animal of chivalric fiction is seen in the elephant and castle, which we have already mentioned.[5] Very soon the animals were mechanically perfected to appeal to the crowds for their own sakes.[6]

Aside from certain characters, who were felt to be historical rather than romantic, and such figures as Valentine and Orson in 1547, the chief contribution of chivalry to the pageant is the castle, which first made its appearance in 1377. The influence of romantic fiction was — as we might expect — much greater in the masque; and as the tournament gave rise to the metrical romances, so they in

---

[1] We shall come back to this point in a later chapter.

[2] *Eng. Dram. Lit.*, i, p. 148. Hone, *Anc. Mys.*, p. 232, quotes Warton (ii, p. 202), who thinks that pageants, which on civic occasions derived a great part of their decorations and actors from historic fact, and which consequently made profane characters the subject of popular exhibition, dictated ideas of a regular drama much sooner than the mysteries. While it is possible that the living allegory in Lydgate's pageants helped to develop the morality, these cross-influences are hard to determine, and were probably not all one way. The pageant received much — especially in the provinces — from the miracle-play; it developed allegory about the same time as the morality; and history was an important part of pageantry long before the chronicle-play arose.

[3] See above, p. 40.

[4] I do not mean that these are descended from folk-animals; rather that folk-animals were responsible for the use of these various kinds of beasts in pageantry. The use of animals with Orpheus, in 1554, shows a further development.

[5] See above, ch. i, § 6.

[6] Cf. *e. g.*, the 1487 dragon who spouted flames.

turn furnished material to the tournament, when it became retrospective. The realism of one age is the romanticism of the next; when Don Quixote's grandfather was alive, chivalric literature made its largest contribution to the masque.

During these two centuries and a half which we have reviewed in tracing the royal-entry to the time of Elizabeth, pageantry grew up around the procession, drawing to itself elements from folk-custom, the miracle-play, historical, allegorical, chivalric, and classical literature, and adapting them to the occasion for which they were borrowed. The mythology of Greece and Rome was given a trade-symbolism, or made to fit the reception of a queen. Elizabeth was fond of show; during her reign, pageantry became very elaborate. But the elements developed by the poets and engineers of her age, are inherited from the triumphs we have been considering.

CHAPTER IV

ELIZABETHAN PAGEANTRY, 1558–1602 [1]

AFTER the dark days of Mary's reign, the people of England turned with hope to their new sovereign. We have seen how eagerly they greeted their rulers in the past; it is a satisfaction to know that their welcome to Elizabeth heralded one of the most glorious reigns of English history.

The progresses of the " Virgin Queen " afforded her people many opportunities to express their ever-increasing love for her; and the young sovereign's fondness for display early directed the people to devote their energies to developing the possibilities of pageantry. A "curious manuscript chronicle"[2] reveals the queen's delight in shows even before she came to the throne; we are told of a masque or " disguising " held at Hatfield House in 1556, in which knights and ladies took part: it included a " devise of a castell of clothe of golde " and other " pageauntes . . . marvellously furnished." Sir Thomas Pope made this " maskinge " for the Lady Elizabeth; " but the Queen percase mysliked these folliries, as by her letters to Sir Thomas Pope hit did appear, and so their disguisinges were ceased." Undoubtedly when Elizabeth became her own mistress, she entered into these pleasures with all the more zest because they had been forbidden by Mary.

The expansion and development of other forms of artistic and literary expression, for which this reign is famous, were shared by pageantry. A queen who could deliver a Latin oration at Cambridge, and reply in Greek to a Greek welcome at Oxford, could appreciate the talents shown by flattering poets, whose work must have found stimulation in the thought that it would not be ignored.[3]

Queen Mary died on 17 November, 1558, and on the 23d Elizabeth went from Hatfield to London.[4] The account of her journey and arrival, printed by Nichols,[5]

---

[1] The main source for much of the material in the chapter is Nichols, *Progresses of Queen Elizabeth* (1823). For remarks on Elizabeth and her influence on pageants and masques, see Schelling, *Elizabethan Drama* (1908), i, p. 99.

[2] Printed by Nichols, *Prog. Q. Eliz.*, i, p. 16.

[3] Davey, *The Pageant of London* (1906), i, p. 103, remarks that " in Elizabeth's day, after the suppression of the religious processions, the great queen thought fit to encourage splendour and elaboration on the occasion of this annual pageant " [*i. e.*, the Lord Mayor's Show]. She did not confine this encouragement to the civic shows of London, as we shall see; how much direct influence she had on them, is doubtful — they had become pageantic before her reign.

[4] Holinshed, iv, p. 156; *Prog. Q. Eliz.*, i, p. 31. Wriothesley, ii, p. 142, says she entered London on 28 November; cf. Welch, i, pp. 204 f.

[5] *Prog. Q. Eliz.*, i, p. 34.

tells us that " in Christmas week scaffolds began to be made in divers places of the City for pageants against the day the queen was to pass through to her Coronation," which was to be January 15, " and the conduits to be newly painted and beautified." On Thursday, 12 January, 1558–59, the sovereign went from Westminster by water to the Tower; the Lord Mayor and aldermen in their barge, and the citizens with their barges, decked " with targets and banners of their mysteries," attended on her Grace.[1] " The Bachellers barge of the Lord Maiors companie, to wit the Mercers, had their barge, with a foist trimmed with three tops, and artillery aboord, gallantlie appointed to wait upon them, shooting of lustilie as they went, with great and pleasant melodie of instruments, which plaied in most sweet and heavenlie maner." [2]

ELIZABETH'S GREAT PROGRESS THROUGH LONDON BEFORE HER CORONATION

Accounts of the procession through London before the coronation of the queen, are numerous. The progress was made on Saturday, 14 January, 1558–59, and is especially interesting as it shows the affection of the queen for her people, and their love for her.[3] " . . . Entrying the Citie [she] was of the People received marueylous entierly as appeared by thassemblie, prayers, wishes, welcomminges, cryes, tender woordes, and all other signes. . . . And on thother syde, her grace, by holding up her handes, and merie countenaunce to such as stode farre of, and most tender & gentle lāguage to those that stode nigh to her grace, did declare

---

[1] *Prog. Q. Eliz.;* cf. Wriothesley, ii, p. 143; Holinshed, iv, p. 158.

[2] Holinshed and *Prog. Q. Eliz.*

[3] Contemporary descriptions are in the following pamphlets:

The Royall Passage of her Maiesty from the Tower of London, to her Palice of White-hall, with all the Speaches and Deuices, both of the Pageants and otherwise, together with her Maiesties Seueral Answers and most pleasing Speaches to them all. London, 1558 (B.M., C. 33. e. 7 (15)) — another edition, n.d. [1558–59] (B.M., C. 33. e. 7 (11)); a 1604 edition is in the Bodleian (Wood, 537).

The Passage of our most drad soueraigne lady Quene Elyzabeth through the citie of London to Westminster the daye before her coronacion. 4° B.L. London, 1558. (In the Guildhall Library.)

This pamphlet, published by Richard Tottill, is reprinted in *Prog. Q. Eliz.*, i, pp. 38 f., and in Arber, *Eng. Garner*, iv, pp. 217 f. My citations are made from the black-letter quarto in the Guildhall Library. (Cf. W. W. Greg, *A List of Masques, Pageants, etc.* (1902), p. ix.) Cf. also Sir John Hayward, *Annals of the first four years of the reign of Queen Elizabeth* (ed. from Harl. MS. 6021 (3) by John Bruce, for the Camden Society (London, 1840); here the entry is dated the 14th, and the coronation, Sunday the 15th).

For briefer accounts and references, see Holinshed, iv, pp. 159 f.; Wriothesley, ii, p. 143; J. G. Nichols, pp. 54 f.; Hone, *Anc. Mys.*, p. 241; Chambers, ii, p. 172; etc. Some expenses of the Carpenters on this occasion are recorded in Jupp, p. 51; and the Coopers' expenses are given in Firth, p. 99.

Neilson, *Court of Love*, p. 265, notes the appearance of personified abstractions in this spectacle, with the remark, " it is in pageants and the drama that the Court of Love left most traces in England." (He shows this influence on certain subsequent pageants and plays.)

her selfe no lesse thankefullye to receiue her peoples good wyll, than they louingly offred it vnto her . . . so that on eyther syde there was nothing but gladnes, nothing but prayer; nothing but comfort." [1]

Near Fenchurch was a rich scaffold whereon stood " a noyes of instrumentes "; and a child in costly apparell appointed to welcome Elizabeth on the whole city's behalf. When the queen came there, of her own will she commanded the chariot to be stayed, " and that the noyes might be appeased," until the child had spoken. As the last line of the poem [2] was ended, " the hole people gaue a great shout, wishing with one assent, as the chylde had said." The queen listened attentively, was touched and deeply grateful.

At the upper end of Gracechurch Street was a " gorgeous and sumptuous arke," containing historical figures: Henry VII and his wife Elizabeth, daughter of Edward IV, showed Lancaster and York united; Henry VIII with Anne Boleyn, the queen's mother; and — on the third and uppermost stage — Elizabeth Tudor herself.[3] " Out of the foreparte of this pageaunt was made a standyng for a chylde," who declared unto the queen the symbolism here shown: there was music, too; and all the " emptie places " of the pageant were covered with " sentences concerning unitie." This was called " The vniting of the two howses of Lancastre and Yorke," and it was covered with red and white roses. The characters were taken by children.

Because of the press of people, Elizabeth could hardly hear the child-interpreter, and as her chariot was stopped so that she could not well see the personages in the pageant, she had it moved back, and the whole matter explained to her; and she thanked the city, praising the fairness of the work, " and promised that she would doe her whole endeuour for the continuall preseruacion of concorde, as the pageant did emporte."

The next pageant showed " The Seat of Worthy Governance." It stood in the " nether end of Cornhill," and extended across the whole street. The queen, who was disposed to hear all that should be said to her, had the meaning expounded before she arrived — fearing that because of the people's noise she would hear nothing from the stage. Three gates there were, all open; [4] and above the middle one sat a child representing Elizabeth; she was supported by four Virtues — Pure Religion, Love of Subjects, Wisdom and Justice, each of whom trod its contrary vice under foot — Superstition and Ignorance; Rebellion and Insolence;

---

[1] Pamphlet, p. 1; cf. *Prog. Q. Eliz.*, i, p. 38; Arber, *Eng. Garner*, iv, p. 220.

[2] Which, written both in Latin and English, was fastened on a painted board to the scaffold. The child, however, spoke it only in English; the poem bade her welcome and wished her well.

[3] We have seen, before, a representation of the royal guests of the city in triumphs given for them; thus, both Henry VIII and Charles V appeared in 1522; Philip and Mary were both shown in 1554, etc.

[4] The " three-gated " arch seems to have been a common feature of Elizabethan pageantry. If it had been made with two doors, there would have been an obvious appropriateness in the style of architecture.

Folly and Vainglory; Adulation and Bribery, respectively. Each character was clearly labelled, besides being appropriately dressed; and sentences commending the virtues, and " defacing " the vices, " to the vtter extirpation of rebellion and to euerlasting continuaunce of quietnes and peace," covered the pageant.

After the child's speech, musicians played heavenly melody; again the queen thanked the city, and promised to maintain the virtues, and suppress the vices.

There is something pathetically tactful about the phrase " continuance of peace," considering that England, and Elizabeth herself, had suffered so much under " Bloody Mary." It is, however, good to know that this spontaneous expression of popular joy heralded a splendid age in British history. Perhaps the pageants — which must have made a deep impression on the young girl who found herself Queen of England — had a lasting influence on her. They were exhibited when her mind was keenly alive, even to slight impressions; we can see from her behavior, that she was much interested in the citizen's welcome, and we may conjecture the effect of this on her reign.

At Sopers-Lane end another pageant spanned the street, the three gates of which were also all open. Here sat eight children in three rows — one above, then three, then four — representing the Beatitudes. Another child expounded the meaning of this pageant to her majesty. What each child represented was written on a tablet over its head; and on the forepart of the pageant stood the name, as follows: " The Eight beatitudes expressed in the .v. chapter of the gospel of S. Mathew, applyed to our soueraigne Ladie Quene Elizabeth." At the Standard in Cheap were musicians, and near the Cross, on the porch of St. Peter's, stood the waits of the city. Ahead, at the Little Conduit, Elizabeth saw a paggeant, of which she immediately sought to know the meaning. " And it was tolde her grace, that there was placed Tyme. *Tyme?* quoth she, *and Tyme hath brought me hether.*"

The companies in their liveries had lined the road from Fenchurch Street to the Little Conduit; at the upper end of Cheap, the Recorder of the City gave her majesty a rich purse, with a thousand marks in gold. To his brief speech, asking her not to esteem the value of the gift but the mind of the givers, she replied " merueylous pithilie " in these words:

" I thanke my lord maior, his Brethren & you all. And whereas your request is that I should continue your good ladie & quene, be ye ensured, that I wil be as good vnto you, as euer quene was to her people. No wille in me can lacke, neither doe I trust shall ther lacke any power. And perswade your selues, that for the safetie and quietnes of you all, I will not spare, if nede be to spend my blood, God thanke you all."

This speech brought a " meruaylous showte and reioysing " from the crowd, as may well be imagined; one may suppose the people thought of Mary who had not hestitated to spend her subjects' blood to ensure her own " safety and quietness."

And so the queen moved on, to the two hills of the pageant at the Little Conduit: one represented " a decayed Commonweal," and the other, " a flourishing Commonweal ": and the causes of each state were written on tablets, affixed to the trees on the two hills. Time came out of a valley between them, leading his daughter, Truth; and, a child having explained the pageant, Truth gave the queen an English Bible, for which Elizabeth thanked the city, and said she would often read therein. In Paul's Churchyard, a child delivered a Latin oration and verses, to which the queen listened attentively; and the child gave the paper reverently to Elizabeth, who received it with thanks.

She then moved on to Ludgate, her approach announced by the playing of music; and so toward Fleet Bridge. " One aboute her grace noted the cities charge, that there was no coste spared: Her grace answered, that she did well consider the same, and that it should be remembred."

At the Conduit in Fleet Street was a stage, embattled with four towers, and in the same, a square plat, rising with degrees. And on the uppermost degree was a chair, and in it, " Deborah the judge and restorer of Israel," and on the other degrees stood two each of nobles, clergy, and commons. A child opened this pageant.

So the queen went on to Temple Bar; and at St. Dunstan's, she heard another Latin oration from a Blue-Coat Boy, and at Temple Bar she found the two giants, " Gotmagot " and " Corineus," who held Latin verses in their hands " evē aboue yᵉ gate ";[1] and on the south side were singing children, and one dressed as a poet, who bade her farewell.

The firing of guns accompanied her departure; and the shouting of the people, in whose ears her final promise echoed, — " Be ye well assured, I will stande your good quene." So " good Queen Bess " arrived at Westminster.

This triumph, in which most of the actors appear to have been children, is full of symbolism. The characters are historical, allegorical, and Biblical;[2] we find the giants of 1554 again at Temple Bar. The chief emphasis is on the allegory, which — as has been suggested — seems to have made more than a passing impression on Elizabeth, whose parting promise to her people was faithfully kept. The absence of classical characters in this show will be observed.

1559 — PAGEANTS AT CHENONCEAU AND MAY-GAMES AT GREENWICH

On Sunday, the last day of March, 1559, Francis II and Mary Stuart entered Chenonceau; the " triumphs " on this occasion included appropriately inscribed

---

[1] The reappearance of these giants probably indicates the fact that they were the same as those of 1554 (perhaps they had been borrowed by the Lord Mayor's Show — which, as we shall see in chapter vi, came into existence in the middle of this century). Former giants, prepared separately for each royal-entry, were apparently not kept — and so acquired no individuality.

[2] We may include Deborah and the Beatitudes under this head.

arches.[1] There were also fireworks; and the only speech was pronounced by a woman dressed as Pallas. In the same year we find forty-two men in armor, sent by the Ironmongers' Guild " to the May-game that went before the Queen's Majesty to Greenwich." [2] The next year, " a precept was received [by the Iron-mongers] from the Lord Mayor, requiring the Company to furnish ' xxiij hansom men, well and handsomely armed, and x whiffelers, to go with them to (feaching) ye Queenes Maigeste.' " [3]

1561 — Mary of Scotland Received at Edinburgh

On 2 September, 1561, Mary Queen of Scots was welcomed by the citizens of Edinburgh, and the crafts bore their share of the expenses.[4] Alexander Scott's *Ane new zeir gift*, which is printed, in part, in the Bannatyne Club volume, may not have been spoken at this entry; and although there was a " banquet and tryumphe " — to quote the *Records of the Burgh* — which cost the city a goodly sum, it is hard to say whether there was pageantry in the strict sense of the word; if there were, we do not know of what it consisted.

1563 — The Plague at London

In 1563 there was a great plague in London [5] which had not fully ceased in 1564. This year, the queen went to Cambridge; but although plays were given, orations and sermons delivered, and disputations carried on, no pageants were included in the entertainment.[6]

---

[1] See, for details, *Les Triomphes de Chenonceau*, reprinted from Le Plessis' contemporary pamphlet, by Prince Augustin Galitzin (Paris, 1857); this is in Fairholt's collection at the Society of Antiquaries.

[2] Nicholl, p. 75. Cf. above, p. 48, n. 2 (on p. 49).

[3] Nicholl, p. 77. It was in 1560, Chester being Mayor of London, that " musters of scholars " and other " open shows " were forbidden (see *Repertory* xiv, fol. 520 b); but the course of pageantry was only temporarily arrested, for soon it was ruled that the City Sta-tioners should follow the Poulterers in processions. (Fol. 552 b.)

[4] See, on this, *Documents relative to the Reception at Edinburgh of the Kings and Queens of Scotland A.D. MDLXI–A.D. MDCL* (pub. by the Bannatyne Club, 1822); also *Extracts from the Records of the Burgh of Edinburgh*, iii, pp. 119 f. Portions of Scott's poem are printed in the first work, pp. 9 f.; and the other records that the "banquet, triumphe, and propyne to the Quenys grace " cost the city 4000 marks (iii, p. 122). (*Propine* means " a present; a gift; drink money "; see Webster's *Glossary of Scottish Words and Phrases*.)

[5] Holinshed, iv, pp. 223 f., and *Prog. Q. Eliz.*, i, p. 147, going back to Stow's *Annals*. Holin-shed notes that no mayor's feast was held this year, for fear of spreading the disease through gathering a multitude together.

[6] Harl. MS. 7037, fols. 109 f., gives an account of "Queen Elizabeth's coming to Cambridge, 1564." Another account, collated with this, is printed in *Prog. Q. Eliz.*, i, pp. 151 f.; cf. also Holinshed, iv, pp. 225 f. The queen stayed from 5 to 10 August; she enjoyed her visit so much that she remained a day longer than she had intended. She delivered a Latin oration to the

1565 — The Queen at Coventry

On 17 August, 1565, Elizabeth visited Coventry, and was entertained with pageants. Sharp notes this as the last royal visit attended by their display. The queen was honorably received by the mayor and citizens " with many fair shows and pageants. The Tanners Pageant stood at St. John's Church; the Drapers at the Cross; the Smiths at Little Park-street; and the Weavers at Much Park-street." The Recorder presented Elizabeth with a purse worth about twenty marks, containing a hundred pounds in angels — and the hearts of all her loving subjects.[1]

1566 — Elizabeth at Oxford

In August, 1566, the queen visited Oxford University, but again there were no pageants. Among the plays presented was " Palæmon or Palamon Arcyte " by Mr. Richard Edwards. " This comedy was the last he made; for he died within a few months after." [2]

1571 — Charles IX Enters Paris

There was pageantry when, on 6 March, 1571, Charles IX entered Paris. " Et en toute diligence furent dressez des portiques, arcs triomphaux, figures, peinctures, & deuises en l'honneur de sa Majesté." [3] This passage, vague as it is, seems to show a tendency toward the *tableau* in France, which may be connected with the painting of the Worthies in 1554.[4] This kind of symbolical painting lies on the outskirts of our field.

University in St. Mary's Church; it surprised and delighted her hearers. This is printed by Holinshed, and by Nichols, *Prog. Q. Eliz.*, i, pp. 175, 176; the two versions differ somewhat from each other.

[1] Cf. *Prog. Q. Eliz.*, i, pp. 192 f., and Sharp, p. 158. "In August, 1566 [*sic*] Queen Elizabeth came to Coventry, on which occasion the Weavers' Pageant stood in Mint Park Street end. *MS. Annals.*"

Thus *The Presentation in the Temple* (a Pageant as originally represented by the Corporation of Weavers in Coventry . . . Edinburgh, printed for the Abbotsford Club, 1836), p. 27.

Chambers, ii, p. 175, suggests that the subjects represented on this occasion, as on that of Mary's visit in 1525, were those of the Corpus Christi plays of the crafts named. The subject of the Smiths' pageant was the *Trial, Condemnation and Crucifixion of Christ* (Sharp, pp. 13 f. — we must, however, note that they seem to have had a pageant (or prepared one) dealing with Samson, which they exhibited in 1461, to welcome Edward IV. See above, p. 151.) The Corpus Christi play of the Drapers was *Doomsday* (Sharp, pp. 66 f.); the Tanners' and Weavers' pageants, are mentioned by Sharp (p. 80) and the Abbotsford Club volume, referred to above, shows the subject of the Weavers' play. The Tanners' pageant, perhaps, stood at the Cross-cheaping when Arthur visited Coventry in 1498 (see above, p. 164).

[2] *Prog. Q. Eliz.*, i, p. 212. On this visit see Nichols's printing of a MS. account, i, pp. 206 f.; also Holinshed, iv, p. 230. This visit was the subject of an episode in the Oxford Pageant of 1907; see the *Book of Words*, pp. 89 f.

[3] Godefroy, pp. 483 f.   [4] Cf. above, p. 192.

1572 — A Triumphal Progress in the Provinces

In 1572, Elizabeth made a long royal progress, honoring many noble houses with her presence; but " few or no particulars are preserved of the various Masques and Pageants which were provided for her amusement," [1] save as connected with her majesty's visit to Warwick. Here she was welcomed by the chief city officials; the recorder made her an oration, after which the bailiff gave her £20, which she was loath to take, fearing to be a burden, but for which she gave gracious thanks. No pageants accompanied this entrance; [2] on her return to Warwick, however, after half a week's visit at Kenilworth, " a Dragon, flieng casting out huge flames & squibes," was intended to destroy a fort that had been built. By negligence, " or otherwise," a citizen's house was destroyed, instead of the fort.[3] Before the fireworks and the sham battle of the evening, the queen looked down from her window at the country people, who had come to see her; they danced in the castle courtyard, and both sovereign and subjects were delighted with each other.[4]

1573 — The Queen at Sandwich

In 1573, Elizabeth went to Sandwich,[5] where, " at Sandowne gate were a lyon and a dragon all gilt, set uppon ii posts at the bridge ende, and her armes was hanged up uppon the gate." The houses were decorated, and the streets strewn with rushes, herbs and flags; the town orator welcomed the queen, and gave her a " cup of gold of £100" and a Greek Testament. " And here it is to be noted, that upon every post and corner, from her first entrye to her lodginge wer fixed certen verses, and against the court gate all these verses put into a table

---

[1] *Prog. Q. Eliz.*, i, p. 309. Fleay, *Hist. Stage*, p. 19, notes the performance of a masque at Whitehall, 15–18 June, 1572, " in which Apollo, the Nine Muses (in a chariot), Lady Peace, Argus, and Discord were presented. . . . The castle for Lady Peace, or Lady Plenty, and the prison in which Discord is watched by Argus, are mentioned in the list of properties in 1572." Fleay thinks that this is a modified form of a 1562 masque; it is of interest to us only as it gives an example of the use of pageant-cars and castles in the masque.

[2] *Prog. Q. Eliz.*, i, pp. 309 f.; Nichols's account is taken from a MS., called *the Black Book*, belonging to the Corporation of Warwick. In 1898 this was edited by Thomas Kemp, deputy Mayor of Warwick; see this edition, pp. 86 f., for the account of the reception of the queen, 12 August, 1572. The Recorder's oration is printed in full, as is the sovereign's reply. Latin verses were handed (not spoken) to the queen by Mr. Griffin, preacher; these are printed by Kemp, pp. 92 f.

[3] Kemp, p. 96. Cf. the 1487 dragon on the Thames (above, p. 161). Episode X of the 1906 Warwick Pageant reproduces Elizabeth's entry (see *Book of Words*, pp. 50 f. History is invented or assumed (p. 52) when the boy, Will Shakspere, meets the queen.)

[4] Kemp. p. 95. On the " princely sports " made for Elizabeth at Kenilworth, see *Prog. Q. Eliz.*, i, p. 318.

[5] *Prog. Q. Eliz.*, i, p. 337.

and there hanged up." [1] The next day there was a mock battle, which the queen enjoyed.[2]

The day of her departure, " uppon a scaffold made uppon the wall of the Scolehowse yarde, were dyvers children, Englishe and Dutche, to the nombre of cth or vi score, all spynning of fine bay yarne; a thing well lyked both of her Majestie and of the Nobilitie and Ladies." [3]

1574 — The Queen at Bristol

At Bristol in 1574, the queen was received in pomp by the mayor, aldermen, and companies, formed under their proper ensigns.[4] At the High Cross " in a disguised manner " stood Fame, who addressed the queen in rimed heptameters. Three other boys, called Salutation, Gratulation, and Obedient Good Will, stood at the next gate, near the queen's lodging: all voiced the welcome of the inhabitants, and their joy at receiving the sovereign. After which speeches, Elizabeth was escorted to her host's dwelling by three hundred soldiers, and salutes were fired.

An elaborate sham-battle took place the next day. Dissention, "passyng between Wars and Peace " urged the capture of a little fort.[5] The speeches, which were intended to be spoken on this occasion, could not be heard by the " Prince," [6] and so were omitted. The triumph for that day, ending with the capture and destruction of the " little fort," lasted until nightfall, so that the queen was escorted back to her lodgings by torchlight; and there were fireworks.

The next day, the attack on the main fort began. Divers court gentlemen took part " for a better order of warre," assisting the fort, " which maed the shoe very gallant, and set out the matter mutch." A naval combat was combined with that on land, and when War waxed weary, Persuasion, setting forth the follies of civil broil, and the quietness which comes of mutual love, tried to bring about peace. The City replied, showing the blessings of peace and the value of the

---

[1] *Prog. Q. Eliz.*, i, p. 338.

[2] Apparently the citizens, or the soldiers of the " regular army," stormed the " fort " — which had been built " thother syde of the havon " — as an exercise or drill. In the fight at Warwick in 1572, nobles took part — the Earl of Oxford was governor of one fort, or castle.

[3] We shall have occasion to note many trade-pageants, even outside the Lord Mayor's Show. Cf. that at Norwich in 1578; that at Swansea in 1881, etc. In the *History of Preston* (1822) may be found a picture (pl. 6) of the Weavers' Company carrying a man working a loom.

[4] *Prog. Q. Eliz.*, i, pp. 392 f.; reprinted from *The Firste Parte of Churchyarde's Chippes* . . . (London, 1575), where Thomas Churchyard gives a full description of the queen's entertainment.

[5] This was either called Feeble Policy, or occupied by a character of that name; Churchyard's account is not clear. (Cf. *Prog. Q. Eliz.*, i, pp. 399 and 402.)

[6] *I. e.*, Elizabeth.

militia,[1] ending with a eulogy of Elizabeth. Amid cries of "God save the Queen," these triumphs and warlike pastimes ended. The sovereign liked them so well, that she sent the soldiers two hundred crowns for a "banket."

This kind of entertainment suggests a " pageantizing " of the muster, in much the same way that the tournament became pageantized. The participation of the courtiers was evidently as unexpected as it was welcome; and yet the affair was rather a citizens' muster than a tilt. The use of allegory in this " triumph " is noteworthy; and the storming of the forts may have some distant connection with the " Court of Love " elements.[2] The glorification of peace recalls the coronation pageant of Elizabeth.

" The Sunday next the Queen went to the Colledge to hear a Sarmon, whear thear was a speech to be sayd and an imme to be songe; the speech was left out by an occasion unlooked for, but the imme was songe by a very fien Boye." What the unlooked-for occasion was, we may guess from Churchyard's note:[3] " Some of these speeches could not be spoken, by means of a Scholemaister, who envied that any stranger should set forth these Shows."

" At her Highnes departuer, a Gentilman in the confiens of the Towns' Liberties spaek this speech that follows: The dolfull a Due."

1575 — THE GREAT SHOW AT KENILWORTH

When Elizabeth visited Kenilworth in 1575, a very elaborate entertainment was given for her; although this is not — strictly speaking — a pageant, it has pageantic features, and we may examine it here, where it belongs, chronologically.[4]

---

[1] Yet we have Soldyars, as you see, that stoers but when we pleas,
And sarvs our torns in howshold things, and sits in shop at eas.
And yet daer blaed hit with the best, when cawse of contrey coms,
And cals out courage to the fight by sound of warlike droms
We marchants keep a mean unmixt with any jarring part,
And bring boeth treble and the baess [*i. e.,* peace and war] in order still by art.

[2] That there is any close influence, I very much doubt; indeed, I think it unlikely that there is any; for forts were probably stormed in musters, long before they were given an allegorical name; and when the allegory appeared, it more likely came from the pageant than from literature directly. Here is political allegory.

[3] *Prog. Q. Eliz.*, i, p. 407.

[4] On this show see Laneham's letter to Humfrey Martin, reprinted in *Prog. Q. Eliz.*, i, pp. 426 f.; also by Furnivall, in *Captain Cox, his Ballads and Books, or Robert Laneham's Letter* . . . etc. (printed by the Ballad Society (vii), London, 1871). Cf. Nathan Drake, *Shakspere and his Times* (1817), ii, pp. 195 f.; Sir Walter Scott, *Kenilworth* (chs. xxx and xxxix); Strutt, *Sports* (1801), Introduction, § xxvii (p. xxxi); Kemp, pp. 203f.; Schelling, *Eliz. Drama*, ii, p. 97. Cf. also *The Princelye Pleasures at the Courte at Kenelwoorth*, by George Gascoigne (reprinted, *Prog. Q. Eliz.*, i, pp. 485 f.; cf. Greg, *A List, etc.*, p. 9) for the speeches on this occasion.

Reference has already been made to the giants of this show; cf. above, p. 51, n. 3.

Upon the queen's arrival, " one of the ten Sibills . . . cumly clad in pall of white sylk, pronounced a proper poezi in English rime and meeter; of effect, hoow great gladnesse her goodnesse prezenze brought into every stede whear it pleazed her too cum, and speciall now into that place that had so long longed after the same; ended with prophesie certain, of mooch and long prosperitee, health and felicitee." [1] After which the queen passed on to the tilt yard where a porter [2] pretended impatience that he might pay her a compliment; after which musicians played, and at the inner gate of the castle appeared the Lady of the Lake, with two attendant nymphs, floating to land from a movable island in the midst of " the pool." She welcomed the queen " with a well-penned meter," [3] telling the story of the castle and its owners; and she offered up her lake and her power therein, for which the queen thanked her with a gentle pleasantry. " This Pageaunt was cloz'd up with a delectable harmony of hautboiz, shalmz,[4] cornets and such oother looud muzik," and so the queen entered the castle over a bridge which bore gifts from Sylvanus, Pomona, Ceres, Bacchus, Neptune, Mars, and Phœbus. A Latin poem was written on a tablet over the castle gate, welcoming the royal visitor, and explaining the identity of those who gave her the fruits, fish, armor, and musical instruments which the queen had found on the bridge; for none of the gods appeared in person. As it was dark, and Elizabeth could not read the verses easily, a poet explained all orally.[5] A peal of " gunz," and fireworks, ended the reception.

A " one-man play " (Hombre Salvagio and Echo made up the cast), composed and acted by Gascoigne, ended the Monday's hunting:[6] on the following days the queen was entertained by dancing, bear-baiting, and elaborate fireworks at night; she also enjoyed seeing an Italian tumbler, a " Bride-ale," — including morris-dance and running at the quintain — and the Coventry Hox-Tuesday play.[7]

---

[1] *Prog. Q. Eliz.*, i, p. 430. Hunnes wrote these verses (p. 487).

[2] The verses were written and delivered by Master Badger, M.A., Oxon. (*Ibid.*, p. 491.)

[3] Nichols notes that these verses were written by M. Ferrers (*Prog. Q. Eliz.*, i, p. 492); they are in Gascoigne's *Princelye Pleasures*.

[4] *Shalm* or *shawm* is a psaltery or species of harp (Nichols).

[5] Muncaster (Mulcaster) wrote the actor's verses, and Paten, those over the gate. (*Prog. Q. Eliz.*, i, p. 493.)

[6] Nichols, i, p. 498.

[7] On this, see *Prog. Q. Eliz.*, i, pp. 446 f.; Furnivall, *Captain Cox*, pp. xii and 26; Scott's *Kenilworth*, ch. xxxix; Ward, *Hist. Eng. Dram. Lit.* (1875), i, p. 81; Sharp, pp. 125 f.; Strutt, *Sports*, Book iii, ch. 2 (p. 216) — [for the folk-customs of Hoke-day, or Hock-day, see Book iv, ch. 3 (p. 260). Cf. for detailed treatment of the subject, Denne's memoir on *Hokeday* in *Archæologia*, vii, pp. 244–268. Poole, *Coventry* (1870), pp. 50 f., remarks on the Hox-Tuesday play; he, too, goes back to Laneham. Drake, *Shakspere and his Times*, i, p. 149, notes that Hock-day " was usually observed on the Tuesday following the second Sunday after Easter-day," and cites Henry of Huntingdon's explanation of the term *hock*. (Cf. the explanation *hock-tide*, " expressive of the height of the festivity," i, p. 188, n. 2)]. Drake gives Laneham's account of the Hox-Tuesday play at Kenilworth in 1575, i, pp. 150 f.

MASQUE AT THE MARRIAGE OF SIR HENRY UNTON

On the second Monday of her stay, another entertainment followed the hunting; among the characters represented were Triton, Arion, the Lady of the Lake, and Proteus, who sat on a dolphin's back.[1] This was rather a danceless masque, or a plotless outdoor play with music, than a pageant in any sense of the word. But the dolphin suggests the pageantic animal.

Upon the queen's departure, the earl asked Gascoigne to devise some farewell entertainment worth the presenting; so Gascoigne himself, dressed like Sylvanus, met the sovereign as she went hunting, and delivered a long extempore speech, at times running beside her horse.[2] This was the prelude to a poetical address by Deepdesire, who spoke from a bush; then followed a concert.[3]

In all these shows provided for Elizabeth, there is nothing that can be called pageantry, although some have pageantic suggestions — such as the wild-man, the elaborate animals, and the " movable island," [4] from which the Lady of the Lake welcomed the queen. The popular background of pageantry is here lacking; [5] in the entertainment of a sovereign by one of her nobles, we could hardly expect to find what we could call, technically, a pageant, though we can expect — and often do find — a masque. The entertainments for Elizabeth at Kenilworth tend, on the whole, toward the outdoor masque.[6]

Laneham describes it in detail: Nichols, in a note, calls it " a tilting match, representing in dumb-shew the defeat of the Danes by the English." Strutt says it " was a kind of historical play, or *old storial show*, performed by certain persons who came for that purpose from Coventry. The subject of this show was the massacre of the Danes, a memorable event in the English history (on St. Brice's night, November 13, A.D. 1002) which was expressed ' in action and in rhimes.' " The spirit of it seems to have been that of the German *Erinnerungsspiele*, such as the *Meistertrunk* at Bavarian Rothenburg; it recalled events of interest in the local past.

[1] " And the dolphyn was conveyed upon a boate, so that the owers seemed to be his fynnes. Within the which dolphyn a consort of musicke was secretely placed, the which sounded; and Protheus, clearing his voyce, sang this song of congratulation . . ." *Prog. Q. Eliz.*, i, p. 500. The authors of this entertainment were Hunnes, Ferrers, and Goldingham (p. 502); for a full account, see the *Princelye Pleasures* (pp. 498 f.).

I omit mention of a " show " in two acts — really an operetta — written by Gascoigne to have been presented before her majesty in the forest; for some reason it was not given. Diana, nymphs, a wild man, etc., were in the cast (pp. 502 f.).

[2] *Prog. Q. Eliz.*, i, pp. 515 f.

[3] In connection with Sylvanus, I may refer to the woodmen at Worksop in 1603 (see below, p. 222).

[4] Which is called a " pageant " by Laneham (*Prog. Q. Eliz.*, i, p. 431).

[5] Save, possibly, in the Hox-Tuesday play.

[6] Compare Lord Knowles's reception of Anne, wife of James I, at Cawsome House near Reading, at the end of April, 1613. This is described by Thomas Campian, in *A Relation of the late Royal Entertainment given by . . . the Lord Knowles . . . to our most Gracious Queene, Queene Anne, in her Progresse toward the Bathe, vpon the seven and eight and twentie dayes of April, 1613* . . . (London, 1613.) Robin-Hood men took part in a dance (p. 5); and Sylvanus appeared in a masque performed in the evening before the queen.

1575 — Elizabeth at Worcester

In the same year, the queen visited Worcester; and the city records provide that the buildings be decorated, the streets cleaned, the four gates embellished with her majesty's arms, and " two Pageants, or Stages, to be set forward; *viz.*, the one at the Grass Crosse, and the other in St Alban's street end, at St. Helen's church." [1] Three boys spoke from each pageant, but their speeches are lost.[2]

1578 — The Royal Visit to Norwich

In August, 1578, the sovereign was received at Norwich by the mayor and three-score bachelors; in the procession was one representing King Gurgunt, the fabled king who built the Castle of Norwich and founded the city.[3] The city officers, the aldermen, the recorder, former sheriffs, etc., accompanied the mayor, while Gurgunt waited for Elizabeth near the city, in full view of the Castle. The others met her majesty about two miles out, where she was hailed by a joyful populace; after which, the mayor delivered an oration, and presented her with a cup, and £100 in gold.

So they all proceeded to the town: and at the Close were met by Gurgunt, whose speech was prevented by a shower of rain, whereat " hir Majestie hasted away."

The waits of the city were stationed at St. Stephen's gate, which had been " enriched and beautified"; and as the queen passed through, they "cheerfully and melodiously " welcomed her. Then she passed up St. Stephen's street, where the first pageant was placed.

This was the " artizan-strangers pageant," and was decorated with sentences explaining " the Causes of the Commonwealth " to be: God truly preached; Justice duly executed; Idleness expelled; the People obedient; Labor cherished;

---

[1] Cited in *Prog. Q. Eliz.*, i, pp. 533, 534.

[2] Pp. 537, 538. The queen received a purse with £20, on this visit.

[3] Cf. Ebrauc at York, and Bremmius at Bristol, in 1486.

On this Norwich visit, see *Prog. Q. Eliz.*, ii, pp. 136 f.; Francis Blomefield, *Hist. Norfolk* (1806), iii, pp. 319 f. ["A long contemporary account of this progress, by B. Goldingham and Thomas Churchyard, is printed by Blomefield, iii, 317, from Stow's Holinshed."—*Norf. Arch.*, vii, p. 295]; Stow's continuation of Holinshed, iv, p. 376; (cf., also, Greg, p. 8).

On p. 375, Stow mentions the queen's visit to Suffolk, which inspired Norfolk to ask her there. In Suffolk there were " feasting and bankets," and even " triumphs and devices." But of these no details are given; and as they took place at various private houses, we may presume they were rather masques than pageants — like the festivities at Kenilworth. On this Suffolk visit, see also Blomefield, iii, p. 318.

Verses addressed to Elizabeth were delivered to her " w't a payr of gold spurs " by William Downes, Lord of the Manor of Earlham, near Norwich, when the queen visited the latter city. They are to be found in Harl. MS. 890, fol. 282, from which manuscript they were printed in *Norf. Arch.*, vii, p. 214.

Universal Concord preserved. Various looms, with weavers, were painted on the pageant; girls spinning and knitting stood on the stage, with the men who made the "said several works." In the middle, a "pretie boy richly apparelled" represented the "Commonwelth of the Citie," and explained the pageant. It pleased the queen mightily, and she stopped to examine every detail; then, thanking the people, she went on to the second one.

This pageant "thwarted the streete" at the entrance of the market, and was divided into three gates. Musicians were stationed over the posterns; on the front, at one side of the main gate, were the arms of England; on the other side, the queen's badge — falcon with crown and sceptre. "The stage or Pageant was replenished with five personages apparelled like women. The first was the City of Norwich; the second Debora, the third Judeth, the fourth Esther, the fifth Martia, sometime Queene of England." Until Elizabeth arrived, the musicians played; upon her coming, Norwich welcomed her, and the other four spoke in turn. As the queen passed on her way, one of the musicians sang a song wishing "long raigne to Queene Elizabeth."[1]

The companies stood in their liveries on each side of the road, as the royal visitor crossed the market-place, and passed through the decorated streets to the Cathedral.

Churchyard had planned several devices for the queen's stay, some of which were prevented by the weather. It is Goldingham's masque, given on the Tuesday of her visit, which is referred to by Professor Neilson, in these words: " At Norwich . . . Venus and Cupid were represented as cast out of heaven and receiving ignominious treatment from a Philosopher, from Chastity, Modesty, Temperance and others. Elizabeth's *rôle* of the Virgin Queen naturally encouraged the irreverent treatment of the Love deities, and brought about an exalting of Diana at the expense of Venus."[2]

When the sovereign departed, the streets leading to St. Benet's Gates were decorated; and at the gates themselves a richly hung stage was erected, concealing a band of musicians. From this stage, " B. G." spoke a farewell poem, after

---

[1] The speeches and song were written by B. G. (*Prog. Q. Eliz.*, ii, pp. 145–150.) This is neither Bernard Goldingham nor Barnaby Googe, but Bernard Garter. (See *Prog. Q. Eliz.*, ii, p. 134 n. Goldingham's first name was Henry.) Greg, p. 8, says that part of the *Ioyfull Receyuing* was written by Henry Goldingham; Churchyard's part in the reception is shown by his pamphlet, reprinted in *Prog. Q. Eliz.*, ii, pp. 179 f. (Cf. Greg, p. 4.)

[2] *Court of Love*, p. 266. For details of this masque, see *Prog. Q. Eliz.*, ii, pp. 150 and 188 f.; Stow's Holinshed, iv, pp. 388 f. For other masques that took place during Elizabeth's stay at Norfolk, see *Prog. Q. Eliz.*, ii, pp. 136–214.

The gifts of the gods and goddesses, in Goldingham's " maske " for the Thursday night, remind us of the Kenilworth entertainment, where, however, the divinities did not appear.

Elizabeth's visit to Colchester in 1578 is the subject of Scene iv of Episode v in the Colchester Pageant of 1909 (see the *Book of Words*, pp. 47 f.). The queen also appears in the Bury St. Edmund's Pageant of 1907 (*Book*, p. 60).

which a " short dittie " was sung " in a very sweete voice." And so the queen
left Norwich with gratitude and regret, having sojourned there pleasantly.
" After so much mirthe succeeded as much sorrow. The traines of her majesty's
carriage being many of them infected, left the plague behind them," and it raged
in the city for a year and three quarters.[1]

1579 — James VI at Edinburgh

In 1579 James VI was welcomed to Edinburgh by his subjects. On 14 September of that year [2] it was ordered that " Robert Henrison, [3] chirugeon, and Robert
Kar, baillie, . . . speik the Frenche man, using William Stewart for his opinion in
devyse of the triumphe agane the kingis heir cuming." [4] On 7 October, " ordainis
Andrew Stevinson, thesaurer, to by sa mekill calk as will spargan all the tolbuythis [5] and the expensis thairof sal be allowit to him in his comptes." [6] On 14
October, " ordanis proclamatiounis to be maid be sound of tabourin throw this
burgh, commanding all the inhabitantis thereof[7] to hing their stairis with tapestrie
and ares warkis on Fryday nixt, and that nouther be nycht nor day ony fyre
ballis, fyre arowis, or uther ingynes of fyre be castyn [8] be ony maner of personis
heirefter, and for removing of red [9] tymmer, suyne and beggeris of the toune,
under the payne of puneshment of their [10] personis at the will and discretion of
the Jugis." [11]

On the day of the king's reception, " as he maid forder progres in the toun in
the streat that ascendis to the castell, thair is ane ancient port, at the whilk hang
a curious globe, that opnit artificiallie as the King came by, wharin was a young
boy that discendit craftelie, presenting the keyis of the toun to his Majestie, that
war all maid of fyne massie sylver, and thais war presentlie ressavit be ane of his
honourable counsall. During this space Dame Music and hir scollars exercesit hir
art with great melodie. Then, in his discense as he came fornent the hous of
Justice, thair shew thaymeselfis unto him, four gallant verteous ladeyis, to wit,
Peace, Justice, Plentie, and Policie, and aither of thayme had an oraison to his

---

[1] *Prog. Q. Eliz.*, ii, p. 214, n. 1 (quoting from Blomefield).

[2] My authorities are *Documents relative to the Reception at Edinburgh of the Kings and Queens of Scotland* [Bannatyne Club, Edinburgh, 1822], and *Extracts from the Records of the Burgh of Edinburgh*, iv.

[3] *Extracts*, iv, p. 117, reads *Heuisoun*, under date of 14 September, 1579; but cf. *Henrisoun*, *ibid.*, pp. 119 and 120.

[4] *Documents*, p. 16.

[5] " to by samekill calk as will spargten all the tolbuythis " — *Extracts*, iv, p. 122.

[6] *Documents*, p. 21.

[7] " thairof " — *Extracts*, iv, p. 124.

[8] " castin " — *Extracts*.

[9] *Extracts*, inserts a comma here.

[10] *Extracts*, has the following variations: *swyne, tovne, punesment, thair*.

[11] *Documents*, pp. 22 f.

Majestie. Tharefter, as he came towart the cheif collegiall kirk, thare Dame
Religion shew hirself desyring his presence, whilk he then obeyit be entring the
kirk. . . . Thareafter he came furth, and maid progres to the mercat croce,
whare he beheld Bacchus with his magnifik liberalitie and plentie, distributing of
his liquor to all passingers and behalders, in sic apperance as was plesant to see.
A littill beneth is a mercat place of salt, wharupon was erectit the genealogie of
the kings of Scotland, and a nomber of trumpets sounding melodiouslie, and
crying with loud voyce, Wealfayre to the King. At the East Port was erectit the
conjunction of the planets, as thay war in their degreis and places, the tyme of his
Majesties happie nativitie, and the same vivelie representit be assistance of King
Ptolomæ. And, withall, the haill streits war spred with flowres, and the forehowsis
of the streits be the whilks the King passit, war all hung with magnifik tapestrie,
with payntit historeis, and with the effegeis of noble men and wemen, and thus he
past out of the toun of Edinburgh to his palice of Halyruidhous." [1]

1581 — A Tilt at Whitehall with Pageantic Features

A tilt, which included disguising, and was not without pageantic features, took
place at Whitehall in 1581.[2] The Earl of Arundel, Lord Windsor, " Master "
Philip Sidney and " Master " Fulke Greville, calling themselves the Four Foster
Children of Desire, challenged the queen " that you will no longer exclude
virtuous Desire from perfect Beautie "; and they gave her warning that if she did
not yield, they would attack her fortress. On Whitmonday the attack took place;
a moving pageant, "which caried the name of a Rowling trench," on which
cannons of wood were mounted, and in which musicians were concealed, advanced
upon the Castle of Beauty.[3] With song, this was summoned to yield; with song
the alarm or refusal was given. The two cannon were then shot off, " the one with

---

[1] *Documents*, pp. 30 f. —from a MS. *Historie and Life of King James the Sext*. Maitland,
Hist. Edinb. (1753), p. 37, recounts this entry (from " Craw. Mem., pp. 356, 357 "): among
those who greeted the king were — according to this account — " Solomon, attended by a
numerous Train in *Jewish* Habits, with the Two Women striving for the Child "; and it was
Cupid, " who presented him [the king] with the Keys of the City-gates." Arrived at the
Tolbooth, he " was harangued by Persons representing Peace, Plenty, and Justice, in the
Greek, Latin, and *Scotish* Languages; and, at his entering *St. Giles's* Church, was addressed by
Religion in the *Hebrew* Tongue; and after Sermon, repaired to the Market-Cross, where
Bacchus, on a gilt Hogshead, was distributing Wine in Bumpers amongst the People . . .
At the *Netherbow* was erected the Nativity, and over it the Genealogies of the *Scotish* kings,
from Fergus I . . ."

[2] On this, see Stow's Holinshed, iv, pp. 435 f.; *Prog. Q. Eliz.*, ii, pp. 312 f.; Greg, p. 9;
Neilson, *Court of Love*, p. 266. There is a reference to this tilt in Drake, *Shaks. and his Times*,
ii, p. 189.

[3] " The Gallery, or place at the end of the Tilt-yard adjoining to her Majestie's house at
Whitehall, whereat her person should be placed, was called, and not without cause, ' The
Castle or Fortresse of Perfect Beautie ' . . ." *Prog. Q. Eliz.*, ii, p. 313.

sweet powder and the other with sweet water . . . and the noise of the shooting was verie excellent consent [1] of melodie within the mount." The castle was attacked with flowers, until the defenders arrived; and the tilting which followed was interrupted by appropriate speeches. The next day, the sport was resumed; and it ended by the submission of the four " foster-children of Desire " to the virtue of the queen.

This tilt is not a pageant: it is mentioned here to show how far the union of tournament and " disguising " — the origin of which we considered in an earlier chapter — had gone in Elizabethan times. This is really a " tournament-masque ": there is, however, an element of symbolism here; and it is of great interest to us because we see the moving pageant-car as well as the fixed castle.

When, in 1583, the Baron of Lasco visited Oxford, he was received with gifts; an oration was delivered; and musicians stationed in the Eastgate " made verie sweet harmonie " as he entered the town.[2] He heard disputations and saw plays; but no pageants were produced.

1588 — THE YEAR OF THE ARMADA

There is nothing to show whether or not pageants were included in " Certaine Devices and Shows " which were presented to her majesty by the gentlemen of Grays Inn, at Greenwich, 28 February, 1587–88.[3] In all probability this was a masque; and many masques had, by now, the pageant-car for a background.

When, on Sunday, 24 November, 1588, the queen entered London to return thanks at St. Paul's for the destruction of the Armada, the waits of the city were placed over Temple Bar; mayor, aldermen and the companies met her, and accompanied her to church, but there were no pageants.[4] A title was entered in

---

[1] Probably a misprint for either *consort* or *concert* — both of which mean the same thing.

[2] *Prog. Q. Eliz.*, ii, p. 405.

[3] *Prog. Q. Eliz.*, ii, p. 530. Says Nichols: " On the 28th of February, 1587–88, as appears by a publication entered in the Books of the Stationers' Company, ' Certaine Devices and Shows were presented to her Majesty . . .' " I can find no mention of this in Arber, *Stationers Register*, ii, *sub annis*, 1587, 1588; or in Greg.

[4] *Prog. Q. Eliz.*, ii, pp. 538 f.; cf. Segar, *Of Honor, Military and Ciuill* (1602) pp. 244 f. (Book iv, ch. xxv). W. M. Williams, *Annals Founders*, p. 218, citing from the London City Records, notes an order of 8 November, 1588, calling on the crafts to hold themselves in readiness to attend the queen on her visit to "Powles to heare a Sermon," on the 18th; further orders dated the 9th November referred to " your Standyng on Monday Morninge at Eight oClocke at the furthest " (*ibid.*, p. 219) may apply to this occasion; as the 24th was Sunday, the 18th would fall on a Monday.

The Carpenters " payed and layed oute " £3, 2s. on this occasion (see Jupp, p. 64); for the Coopers' expenses, see J. F. Firth, *Historical Memoranda . . . from the Records of the Corporation and the Books of the* [Coopers'] *Company, 1396–1848* (1848), p. 101. E. Conder, jr., *Records of the Hole Crafte and Fellowship of Masons* (1894), p. 121, refers to the procession of the 24th November — as well as to that of January, 1591, when Elizabeth again visited the

the stationer's books in 1588, called "An excellent Dyttie of the Queene's cominge to Paule's Crosse, the 24th daie of November, 1588." But this may not have been recited at the entry.[1]

1590 — ANNE OF DENMARK'S ENTRY INTO EDINBURGH

When Anne of Denmark, the bride of James VI, entered her husband's capital, there were hints of pageantry. "Upon the nyntein day of May, the Quenis Grace maid entrie in Edinburgh, at the West Poirt, and was ressavit, efter a certane speiche in Latine, and delyverie of the keyis, as use is, and wes convoyed throw the haill toun, under a paill, to Halyruidhous. Ther wes 42 young men, all cled in quhite taffetie, and vissours, of black cullour, on their faces, lyk Mores, all full of gold chenyies, that dancit befoir hir Grace all the way." [2]

1590 — A PAGEANTIC TILT

"On the 17 day of Nouember, *Anno* 1590, the honourable gentleman [Sir Henry Lea] together with the Earl of *Cumberland*, hauing first performed their seruice in Armes, presented themselves vnto her Highnesse, at the foot of the staires vnder her Gallery window in the Tilt yard at Westminster. . . . Her Maiesty . . . did suddenly heare a musicke so sweete and secret, as euery one thereat greatly marueiled. And hearkening to that excellent melodie, the earth as it were opening, there appeared a Pauilion, made of white Taffata, containing eight score elles, being in proportion like vnto the sacred Temple of the Virgins Vestall . . ." So writes Sir William Segar,[3] who describes the structure in detail, and reprints a prayer, *Elizæ*, which was fastened to it. Besides this " scripture," there was a song; gifts were then given to the queen, and the Earl of Cumberland besought her to accept him for her knight. After which, the " military exercises " began.[4]

---

city — under the head of " pageants." But he mentions none, using the word loosely in the sense of " spectacle."

[1] *Prog. Q. Eliz.*, ii, p. 544; cf. Arber, *Stationers' Register*, ii, p. 506, under 14 November. Arber notes: " Here is a book registered for publication before the event, which it described, happened." This was, it may be remarked, almost always the case with the descriptive pamphlets of the Lord Mayor's Shows, which may have served as programs.

Cf. also Arber, ii, p. 508, under dates of 25 and 26 November. Other songs and " sonnets " on this occasion were entered after the event had taken place.

[2] MS., cited in *Documents relating to Edinburgh*, p. 47, n.

[3] *Of Honor, Military and Ciuill*, Book, iii, ch. liv.

[4] The jousts before the queen in the Tiltyard in 1590 are described in detail in *Prog. Q. Eliz.*, iii, pp. 41 f.; they are called "triumphs" by Richard Brackenbury, in his letter to Lord Talbot (p. 70). Cf. Bullen's edition of Peele's *Works*, i, p. 282, where Peele's verses are printed; also Bullen's Peele, ii, p. 269, for an *Eclogue Gratulatory*, which seems to be another " interlude " rather than for a pageant.

The visit of Queen Elizabeth to Bath in 1590 is the subject of the fifth episode of the Bath Pageant of 1909. I can find no mention of this visit in *Prog. Q. Eliz.*, under 1590. It is unlikely

1591 — ELIZABETH AT COWDRAY AND ELVETHAM

In August, 1591, the queen was entertained by Lord Montecute at Cowdray, in Sussex;[1] the shows were much like those at Kenilworth in 1575. The details of her visit to Chichester, later in the same month, are, unfortunately, lost.[2]

Later in the same year, Elizabeth was entertained at Elvetham, in Hampshire, by the Earl of Hertford.[3] A poet delivered the welcoming oration, during which six virgins, representing the Graces and the Hours, removed blocks from her majesty's path, which Envy had placed there to impede Virtue's progress. After this, they strewed her way with flowers, singing the while. A discharge of firearms from the " Snail Mount " and the " Ship Isle " in the pond greeted her arrival at the castle.

After dinner the next day, the queen viewed some water-sports. From a bower, built at the further end of the pond, rose Nereus, Neptune, and Oceanus,[4] Phorcus and Glaucus with a pinnace, in which three virgins played Scottish jigs with their cornets. Neæra was in the pinnace with them; and lutes and voices in neighboring boats answered " by manner of echo " to the three singers and one lute who accompanied her. " The melody was sweet and the shew stately."

Nereus and Neæra presented jewels to the queen; the Snail Mount " nowe resembleth a monster, having hornes full of wildfire, continually burning "; and the fort in the pond was " round environed with armed men," while Sylvanus and his train lay in waiting in the woods nearby.

Nereus made an oration, in blank verse; he delivered his gift, after which a song was sung, " dialogue wise," with an echo's answer at the end of every fourth verse.[5] At the end of this, Sylvanus with his train appeared, saluted the queen, was enticed toward Neæra, and spilt into the lake by Nereus,[6] then ducked by the hooting sea-gods.[7] A fight began, in which the sea-gods squirted water, and the

---

that the researches of the Rev. C. W. Shickle, M.A., F.S.A. (which furnished much material to the author, the Rev. W. P. Hanks, M.A., F.R.S.L.) gave authority for the introduction in the episode, of Shakspere, Marlowe, and the band of players.

[1] *Prog. Q. Eliz.*, iii, pp. 90 f.

[2] *Ibid.*, p. 96.

[3] *Ibid.*, pp. 101 f., where a pamphlet, originally printed by John Wolfe in 1591, is reprinted. The " Engraving of the Great Pond," reproduced by Nichols, opposite p. 101, illustrates the pageants thereon. The visit is described in a pamphlet entitled: *The Honorable Entertainment gieven to the Quenes Maiestie in Progresse, at Eluetham in Hampshire by . . . the Earle of Hertford, 1591.* (London, 1591.) [B.M., press mark C. 33. e. 7 (9).] See *Prog. Q. Eliz.*, p. 76, for a reprint of John Davies' "Conference," or dialogue presented before the queen at Theobald's in 1591; cf. also J. P. Collier, *Hist. Eng. Dram. Poetry*, i, pp. 283–284.

[4] This may possibly show an influence from the water-processions of the Lord Mayor's Show, on the Thames.

[5] See *Prog. Q. Eliz.*, iii, p. 113.

[6] Whose interpolations in the oration of Sylvanus show incipient dialogue.

[7] Farce may evidently be included in an outdoor masque!

wood-spirits threw darts; Nereus at length "parted the fray with a line or two grounded on the excellence of her Majestyes presence, as being alwaies friend to Peace, and ennemy to Warre."

On the retreat of Sylvanus, (who frightened a number of the country people to the amusement of the courtiers,) Neæra presented her gift, and the gods departed with music.

This is clearly a masque, although fighting seems to have taken the place of dancing; despite the frightened country people, it has the exclusive character of the masque — as had the Kenilworth entertainment of 1575 — and was given on a " fixed stage." The presentation of gifts is common both to masque and pageant; the flattering address is an invariable companion of royalty on a visit. Yet the " Snail Mount " seems to show the development of pageantry in the hands of the masque; and the fort suggests the tournament and the " Court of Love." [1] There is probably some connection between the " wild-man " and Sylvanus; though this may be limited to cross-influences of one figure on the other, rather than the development of one from the other.

1592 — BISHAM AND SUDELEY

The " wild-man " who met Elizabeth " at the top of the hill going to Bissam " suggests Sylvanus, recalls the Hombre Salvagio of Kenilworth, and may show an influence of the " wodmen " of the Lord Mayor's Show.[2] He introduces Pan and two shepherdesses, whose dialogue — with the customary emphasis on the honorable state of virginity — turns into flattering references to the queen. Ceres, with her nymphs in a harvest cart, met Elizabeth at the foot of the hill;

---

[1] The next evening, there were fireworks from the three islands in the pond. " A castle of fireworks of all sorts, which played in the Fort "; a globe of all manner of fireworks " as big as a barrel " in the Snail Mount, etc.

A dance, with flattering songs sung by the Fairy Queen and her maidens, opened the next day's entertainment. The sovereign liked the masque so much that she commanded " to heare it sung and be danced three times over." When she departed, an hour later, Nereus and the sea-gods, Sylvanus and his company, the Graces and the Hours, appeared in the park " showing signe of sorrow," by wringing their hands; and the poet made a farewell speech. Nereus thanked the queen for her largess; and musicians hidden in a bower accompanied " two that were cunning " in their ditty called "Come again," which they sang "with excellent division."

[2] On this 1592 visit, see *Prog. Q. Eliz.*, iii, p. 131, from a contemporary publication by I. B., who apologizes to the reader for possible imperfections in the speeches, saying, " The matter of small moment, and therefore the offence of no great danger." Cf. also *A Handefvl of Gladsome Verses giuen to the Queenes Maiesty at Woodstocke this Prograce. 1592.* By Thomas Churchyarde. (Oxford, 1592. — [BM., C. 33. e. 7 (16)]) which tells of another visit paid this same year. The *Speeches Delivered to Her Maiestie this last Progresse at the Right Honorable the Lady Rvssels, at Bissam, the Right Honorable the Lorde Chandos at Sudley, at the Right Honorable the Lord Norris at Ricorte* (Oxford, 1592) may be found in the Brit. Mus. (C. 33. e. 7 (19)).

after a song, the goddess offered her a gift, with a speech of respectful homage and joyful welcome.

At Sudeley, also in September, 1592, an old Shepherd welcomed the queen.[1] During her stay, she saw a " sort of pastoral," [2] in which Apollo, Daphne, and shepherds took part. Daphne, chased by Apollo, flew to the Queen of Chastity for succor, and offered her, with wishes for her prosperity, adulatory verses. A woodland play, to be given by Melibœus, Nisa, and the Cutter of Cootsholde (which was full of flattery, and which ended with an appropriate address) was prevented by the weather.[3]

The same year, 1592, the queen visited Oxford again, and her entertainment did not vary much from the earlier visit.[4] She heard orations, attended disputations, and saw plays, but was not received with pageants. At Rycot [5] she was given gifts, which were accompanied by suitable addresses.

Sea-nymphs, Proteus, Thamesis, and Amphitrite, with other characters either already in the pageant or soon to be absorbed by it, appeared in a masque at Grays Inn in 1594.[6]

1594 — Pageants at the Christening Banquet of a Scottish Prince

In Edinburgh, symbolical devices were carried at the " mask," (which followed tilts between disguised knights) after the banquet on the occasion of the baptism of Prince Henry, son of James VI of Scotland, the same year.[7] A chariot with Ceres, Fecundity, Faith, Concord, Liberality, and Perseverance brought the dessert into the hall. It was followed by a ship, eighteen feet long, eight feet broad, and forty feet high, on board of which were Neptune, Thetis, and

---

[1] *Prog. Q. Eliz.*, iii, pp. 136 f. Episode V of the Gloucestershire Pageant of 1908 shows the visit of Elizabeth to Sherborne House in 1574 (see the *Book*, p. 51); among the characters shown are whifflers, a jester, dancers, and hobby horses. Tom the Shepherd, who welcomes the queen, is given a couple of speeches spoken by the Shepherd on the occasion of Elizabeth's visit to " Studeley " castle in 1592. Elizabeth's entertainment by Lord Howard of Effingham in 1592 is the subject of Episode VII of the Chelsea Pageant (1908).

[2] See Neilson, *Court of Love*, p. 266: " The love quibbling custom is exemplified in a sort of pastoral performed before the queen at Sudeley in 1592."

[3] *Prog. Q. Eliz.*, iii, pp. 140 f. This play was apparently named *The High Constable of Cotsholde*.

[4] *Prog. Q. Eliz.*, iii, pp. 144 f.

[5] *Ibid.*, pp. 168 f.

[6] *Ibid.*, pp. 309 f. Thomas Campion wrote some of the verses of this masque (p. 349). I may note here that Nichols (pp. 193 f.) reprints various masques performed before the queen, written by George Ferrers. (Cf. Neilson, p. 266.)

[7] *Prog. Q. Eliz.*, iii, pp. 353 f. Three Turks, three Christian Knights, three Amazons ("the Lord of Lendores, the Lord of Barclewch and the Abbot of Holy-roote-house," p. 356) and three Moors took part in the tilt, at which the Scottish queen was a spectator.

Triton, a taffeta-clad crew, and a pilot in cloth of gold. Fourteen musicians, and Arion with his harp, furnished music; and about the ship were sirens who kept time to the melody with their arms, singing the while. As the ship moved up to the table, ordnance was discharged from the stern: and this device " carried some morall meaning with it " — referring to the union of the king and queen by Neptune.

Such " enterludes " as this are really masques. Given in a hall, before courtly spectators, they have borrowed the car, and perhaps some of the characters, from the pageant; though, of course, the gods and goddesses of Greek mythology, and the allegorical figures, were borrowed by pageantry from literature, and are not necessarily the gift of pageant to masque, which probably borrowed them independently. It is possible that pageantry, by showing these figures personified, stimulated the masque, giving suggestions to those who planned the entertainments. The courtly nature of these festivities removes them from pageantry, even though they have taken the pageant-car and adapted it to their uses.

In 1595 Essex combined " devices " and " triumphs " with a tilt; and Francis Bacon, wrote the speeches, which were in prose.[1] The following year, the Seven Deadly Sins, the Sciences, the Nine Muses, and the Four Cardinal Virtues were combined with a tilt at the court of the Landgrave of Hessen;[2] Apollo, Normandy, an angel, Fame, and various mythological characters, who occupied an arbor resembling Apollo's temple, decorated with plaster figures and " scriptures," welcomed the King of France into Paris before his investiture with the Garter the same year.[3] It is interesting to see how the tournament has made even the morality-play contribute to its "cast of characters," and to note that in France such a heterogeneous collection of figures appeared upon the same stage.

On 14 November, 1597, Elizabeth was received in Westminster " by commandement of her Counsell " most royally by the Mayor of London, the Aldermen and Sheriffs in scarlet, and many wealthy citizens in velvet coats and chains of gold, " all on horsebacke, in the evening, by torchlight." She was again received by the mayor and his brethren, when she went to Whitehall in November, 1598, " a mile out of town "; but there does not seem to have been any pageantry, in the strict sense, on either occasion.[4] " On the 17 November [1599], the day whereon shee had been proclaimed Queene, and hadde now reigned 41 yeers, was great justings and other triumphs, which was not ended in divers dayes after." [5]

---

[1] *Prog. Q. Eliz.*, iii, pp. 371 f., Nichols prints the speeches from Bishop Gibson's papers in the MS. Library at Lambeth, v, no. 118, as published by Dr. Birch in *Letters, Speeches, &c., of Francis Bacon, Lord Viscount St. Albans, &c.* (1763). See *Prog. Q. Eliz.*, iii, p. 372, n. 2.

[2] *Prog. Q. Eliz.*, iii, p. 390.

[3] *Ibid.*, pp. 401 f.

[4] For the 1597 reference, see *Prog. Q. Eliz.*, iii, p. 423; for that of 1598, p. 431.

[5] *Ibid.*, p. 443.

1600 — Marie de Medicis at Avignon

That we may compare pageantry in France with that in England at the end of Elizabeth's reign, let us glance at the reception of Maria de Medici, wife of Henri IV, at Avignon, on 19 November, 1600.[1]

Stationary pageants, triumphal arches and a car (illustrated in the *Labyrinthe Royal*) were used in this entry; each arch of triumph was connected with a " theatre " on which the various characters spoke. Among the characters represented were Mars, Apollo, Jupiter, Minerva, Mercury, Diana, Venus, the Graces, and other classical figures; illustrious men of the Medici family, Charles Martel, and other famous ancestors of the king. The last-named hero, one of the " genies des hommes illustres deuanciers du Roy," was connected with the history of Avignon —

Jadis Charles Martel desbouta de ce lieu
De son bras foudroyant la race Sarazin . . .

Another ancestor was Charlemagne, who reëstablished the Cathedral Church at Avignon, profaned by the Saracens; in these characters the glorious past of the city was happily linked with its royal guest. Among those who addressed the queen were Louis VIII, Petrarch, Dante, and other "hommes doctes de Florence." A Temple of Janus was erected " au Change "; the fourteen principal cities and countries with which the house of Medici was allied, were personified at one of the arches; and each recited a Latin couplet from a gallery nearby. Seven angels represented the seven Medici cardinals, one of whom, Hippolyte, was Archbishop of Avignon in 1527. The car[2] was " vn char triomphal à l'Antique," and contained " les Genies du Roy & de la Royne," with a band of music at their feet, " sous la conduite de M. l' Æschirol organiste de l'Eglize Cathedrale." The car was drawn by elephants, guided by two Moors.

At the last arch, a tower replaced the " theatre," for the sake of variety; here there were three nymphs, Mariane, France, and Immortality, who led among them a little Henri V. The three nymphs sang an epithalamium to the king and his bride. The suggestion of the future, shown by the figure of Henri V, is not found in English pageants.

Conclusion

With the death of Elizabeth, the " Augustan age of pageantry " did not come to an end. As we shall see, the Lord Mayor's Show, which had been growing steadily in importance from the middle of the sixteenth century, reached the period of its greatest glory in these hundred years; the " royal-entry," it is true,

---

[1] A description of this welcome is preserved in a contemporary volume in the Fairholt collection in the Library of the Society of Antiquaries, entitled *Labyrinthe Royal de l'Hercule Gaulois triomphant*, etc., and published in 1601.

[2] Illustrated, in the pamphlet cited, opposite p. 16.

lost some of its importance, owing to the fact that royalty often honored the civic triumphs with its presence; and the festivities in which the citizens did not participate tended more and more to become masques, pure and simple. We have seen, in the chapter just ended, how the Elizabethan entertainments tended to draw from the pageant toward the masque — only, indeed, when the welcome to the queen was civic, could we expect to find real pageantry. As has been said, the " body " and the " soul " of pageant and masque have much in common; the differences lie in " spirit " and in " technique."

CHAPTER V

THE "ROYAL-ENTRY" IN THE SEVENTEENTH CENTURY — WITH NOTES ON A FEW SUBSEQUENT ONES

BEFORE turning to a consideration of the Lord Mayor's Show, which was at the height of its development in the seventeenth century, let us consider the "royal-entries" of the Stuart times, remembering always that, as the members of the Royal Family visited the Lord Mayor's Show very often, these entries declined in importance. We shall include in our survey some royal-entries of more recent years, without attempting to make the list exhaustive.

1604 — James I Enters his New Capital City

When, in March, 1603–04, King James I passed through the city of London to his coronation, Dekker, Jonson, and Stephen Harrison collaborated on the "show."[1] The entry was to have taken place on 25 July, 1603, but the plague

---

[1] A pamphlet, entitled "The True Narration of the Entertainment of his Royall Maiestie, from the time of his departure from Edenbrough; till his receuing at London: with all or the most speciall Occurrences. Together with the names of those Gentlemen whom his Maiestie honoured with Knighthood. At London, printed by Thomas Creede, for Thomas Millington. 1603," may be found in the Bodleian (Wood, 537). It is reprinted in Arber, viii, pp. 485 f., and in Nichols, *Prog. James*, i, p. 53.

This pamphlet gives an account of the king's progress from Edinburgh to London; there is no pageantry, in the technical sense, on this trip, though various orations were addressed to the new king, and gifts were presented to him. At York, "there was a conduit that all the day long ran white and claret wine, every man to drinke as much as he listed." (*The True Narration*, sig. D. 3; *Prog. James*, i, p. 78.) At Worksop, the Earl of Shrewsbury's house, the king was stopped in the park, "for there appeared a number of huntsmen all in greene, the chiefe of which, with a Woodman's Speech did welcome him, offering his Majestie to shew him some game, which he gladly condiscended to see; and, with a traine set, he hunted a good space, very much delighted." (*Prog. James*, i, p. 86.) Sir John Manners, the husband of Dorothy Vernon, was knighted by the king here. (*The True Narration*, sig. E b; Nichols, i, p. 88.)

Several minor textual differences between the pamphlet in the Bodleian and the version which Nichols prints, lead me to suppose that the latter used another edition of Millington's account.

On the king's passage through London see *The Magnificent Entertainment, given to King James, Queene Anne his wife, and Henry Frederick the Prince, vpon the day of his Maiesties Tryumphant Passage (from the Tower) through his Honourable Citie (and Chamber) of London, being the 15. of March, 1603. As well by the English as by the Strangers: With the speeches and Songs deliuered in the seuerall Pageants* . . . Tho. Dekker, London . . . 1604. This is in the Guildhall (A. 1. 5); Bodleian (Malone, 602); BM. (C. 34. c. 23). A second edition [entitled

prevented,[1] and the progress was postponed. Stephen Harrison was the artificer; the great poetic burden fell on Dekker's shoulders; but Jonson planned the Fenchurch Street pageant, and wrote the speeches of Genius Urbis and Tamesis; that at Temple Bar, with the speech of Genius; and that in the Strand, with Electra's speech. Middleton also contributed a speech.

Accompanied by his queen, the prince his son, and many nobles,[2] James crossed the city on the 15 March. Two armed knights, St. George and St. Andrew, opened the show, riding to meet the king. The passage of the procession was intèrrupted by the Genius of the City, who claimed he had the first right to welcome the king.[3] After this delay, the procession moved on to the gate erected at Fenchurch Street; on this were stationed twelve persons — Monarchia, Britannica, Divine Wisdom, Genius Urbis, and his daughters Veneration, Promptitude,

---

The Whole Magnifycent Entertainment, etc., " printed at London by E. Allde for Tho. Man the yonger. 1604 "] is in Bodl. (Gough. Lond. 122. 3; Douce D. 206); this is reprinted in Somers' *A Collection of Scarce and Valuable Tracts* (1751) third collection, i, p. 116; (1810), iii, p. 1; *Prog. James*, i, pp. 337 f. Another edition (" very rare ") printed at Edinburgh in 1604 is in Brit. Mus. (C. 33. d. 26.) Cf. also on this entry. *Prog. James*, i, pp. 325 f.; J. G. Nichols, pp. 59 f., Herbert, ii, p. 398; Drake, *Shakspere and his Times*, ii, p. 189; Howes, Stow's *Annals* (1615), pp. 836 f.; Harrison, *Illustrations of the Pageants in the 1604 coronation procession of James I. Together with two odes, by Thomas Dekker and John Webster, and the Speeches of Gratulation.* London, 1604. [The copy of this rare pamphlet in the Guildhall (A. 5. 2) lacks the title-page and one plate]; Jon[son], B[en], *His Part of King James his Royall and Magnificent Entertainement through his Honourable Cittie of London, Thurseday the 15. of March, 1603, so much as was presented in the first and last of their Triumphall Arch's. . . .* London, 1604. [Guildhall (A. 1. 5); Bodl. (Gough, Lond. 122.2.).] Cf. also Dugdale, *The Time Triumphant* (1604); his pamphlet is in Bodl. (Wood, 537), and is reprinted in Arber, *Eng. Garner*, v, pp. 648 f.; and in *Prog. James*, i, pp. 408 f. Nichols, p. 419, n., suggests that Dugdale was an eye witness of the progress he describes so enthusiastically.

Petowe's *England's Cæsar* (1603), the original of which is in the Brit. Mus., is reprinted in the *Harleian Miscellany*, x, pp. 342 f. This is a series of sonnets in honor of James—with some startling visions of Elizabeth in a Grecian heaven, presided over by Jove and Juno; they welcome her to her throne, " the chast *Dyana* bearing vp her traine." It gives no details of this 1604 ceremony; a reference in the next to last sonnet (or stanza) to the " famous Pageants (London's solemne pride) " is vague; and there is this prophecy —

" Where *Iames* shal ride, Conduits shal flow with wine
In honour of his state and happie time."

Dekker's volume, cited above, gives no credit to Jonson; but it notes that one speech was by Middleton — this, with a part of the prose description which precedes it, is reprinted in Dyce's Middleton (1840), v, pp. 207 f.; cf. Bullen's Middleton, i, p. xxvi; vii, pp. 219 f., 224.

The masques of James's reign are outside our province; the interested reader is referred to Brotanek, Evans, Reyher, and Nichols, *Prog. James*.

[1] Jupp. pp. 67 f. The expenses of the Carpenters on this occasion are given in Jupp, pp. 68 and 69; Welch, ii, p. 39, gives the Pewterers' expenses; Firth, p. 102, those of the Coopers.

[2] A list of these nobles is to be found in Addl. MS. 5758, fols. 115 f.

[3] In Dekker's 1604 pamphlet, the dialogue between the Genius and the Saints occupies a couple of pages.

Vigilance, Gladness, Loving Affection, and Unanimity; Thames, the Councell of the City, and the Warlike Force of the City were below.[1] Thames and the Genius spoke the gratulatory verses; the part of Thames was taken by one of the children of her Majesty's revels, and the Genius was done by "Mr. Allin (seruant to the young prince)." [2]

Then the king passed on to " the Italians' pageant " in Gracechurch Street.[3] Here he was addressed in Latin by an Italian. The procession then advanced to " the land of the seventeen provinces " where the Belgians were waiting to greet his Majesty.[4] This stood by the Royal Exchange. Seventeen young damsels, " sumptuously adorned after their countrey fashion " represented the seventeen "Provinces of Belgia." Other figures — men, women, and children — in Dutch habits, wove and spun; Time and Truth, Art, Sedulity, Labor and other like characters, occupied this arch. A boy, dressed in white silk, spoke the *sermo ad regem* — a Latin poem.

In honor of Queen Anne, who was a Dane, Danish music was played by nine trumpets and a kettledrum, stationed near St. Mildred's Church in the Poultry. At Soper-lane end stood another gate, called *Nova Felix Arabia* — England being figured " under the shape of Arabia." [5] Here the chief figures were Arabia-Britannica, Fame, the Five Senses; Detractio and Oblivion slept. The three Charities, or Graces, stood opposite the three " Hours " — Love, Justice, and Peace. Fame spoke as the king approached; the doleful music stopped, and the figures brightened as heavenly music began. Circumspection, " one of the choristers belonging to Paul's," welcomed James in heroic couplets.[6] After a song, the king passed through the gate, and received a gratulatory oration from the recorder of the city, in the presence of the city officials. Cups of gold were presented to all the royal family after the recorder's discourse; and Sylvanus, dressed in green ivy, with four other sylvans in attendance, welcomed James

---

[1] *The Deuice called Londinium* is described opposite the illustration of this " pegme " in Stephen Harrison's volume. The picture shows a model of the city on top of the arch. The speeches of Thamesis and the Genius are also printed here.

[2] Dekker's pamphlet; J. G. Nichols says, without giving his authority, that this was the celebrated Allen who founded Dulwich College. J. Nichols, *Prog. James*, i, pp. 320 and 344, is of the same opinion. Dekker says his speech " was deliuered with excellent Action, and a well tun'de audible voyce."

[3] " The Italians' Pegme stood in Gracious-streete," and we are told in Harrison's volume, where it is pictured, that the cost and invention of this were the Italians' own. The speech, both in Latin and English, is printed there. Cf., also, the frontispiece of J. G. Nichols, *Lond. Pag.*

[4] This is also called " the Pageant of the Dutch-men," by both Dekker and Harrison.

[5] This " device " is also described by Harrison, who gives the speeches of Fame, Euphrosyne, and Circumspection. He locates this " pegme " above the great Conduit in Chepe.

[6] Dekker's pamphlet records that Detraction and Oblivion were suddenly daunted at the approach of the king, and ceased their efforts to suck dry the Fount of Virtue, which then began to flow with " Milke, Wine, and Balme."

with music and a speech. " On his way neere to the Crosse " [in Cheap] nine boys of Paul's, as the Muses, sang to the accompaniment of viols, and other instruments; this was in the device called *Hortus Euporiæ*, or the garden of Plenty; which " pegme " was a " sommer Arbor," placed near the Little Conduit in Cheap.[1]

After the royal party had spent some time at the bower, delighted with the music and the workmanship of the place, they went on to St. Paul's where an anthem was sung by the choir, stationed on the battlements; then one of Master Mulcaster's scholars delivered a Latin oration at the door of the free school founded by the Mercers.

At the next arch of triumph above the Conduit in Fleet Street were Astræa (Justice) and Virtue. The four Cardinal Virtues were paired with the four kingdoms of Britain — England, Ireland, Scotland, and France. Envy made an unpleasant contrast to Virtue; Zeal, " whose personage was put on by W. Bourne, one of the seruants to the young prince," presented this device, with a speech written by Middleton.[2]

A song accompanied the procession to Temple Bar, where the king took leave of the mayor and the city. Here was the Temple of Janus,[3] on which were Peace, with Mars grovelling at her feet; Quiet, with Tumult at hers; Liberty treading on Servitude; Safety standing over Danger, and Felicity over Unhappiness. The Genius of the City — the same whom we found at Fenchurch Street — offered the heart of the city to the king,[4] and he departed.

In the Strand, the royal party found another pageant, which was provided by Westminster and the Duchy of Lancaster. This " pegme " was planned by Ben Jonson;[5] I quote a characteristic passage from his descriptive pamphlet:

---

[1] It is described, but not illustrated, in Harrison's volume, where the speech of Sylvanus is given. His followers played on cornets as the king approached; Peace, Plenty, Ceres, Pomona, the Nine Muses and the Seven Liberal Sciences occupied this pageant. Dekker's pamphlet records that here a " maister Gardner, and husband to Pomona," Vertumnus, was appointed to speak to the king.

[2] This arch is illustrated in Harrison's volume, where it is called " *Cozmoz Neoz — the New World*." The speech of Zeal is reprinted here, under the descriptive paragraphs.

[3] Dekker gives its dimensions; it was fifty-seven feet high, and eighteen broad.

[4] There is a suggestion of dialogue at the beginning of Genius's last speech, when he exchanges words with *Flamen*. Cf. *Prog. James*, i, p. 391. The Temple of Janus is illustrated and described in Harrison's volume where the dialogue between Genius and Flamen is reprinted. This soon beçomes a monologue, in which the latter is rebuked by the former, who compliments James in belitting Mars.

[5] Whose 1604 pamphlet describes it in detail. It is to be noted that Dekker's pamphlet does not credit Jonson with the pageants he planned; and that Jonson's pamphlet describes no others. Genius's first speech is paraphrased in Dekker's pamphlet, and that of Thames is not given at all. Dekker also prints paraphrases of the speeches of the Genius at Temple Bar, and of Electra in the Strand. It is perhaps worthy of remark that Jonson's pamphlet is full of notes and quotations from the classics.

" . . . The nature, and propertie of these Deuises being, to present alwaies some one entire body, or figure, consisting of distinct members and eache of those expressing it selfe, in the owne actiue spheare, yet all, with that generall harmony so connexed, and disposed, as no one little parte can be missing to the illustration of the whole: where also is to be noted, that the *Symboles* vsed, are not, neither ought to be simply *Hierogliphickes, Emblemes,* or *Imprese,* but a mixed Character, pertaking somwhat of all, and peculierly apted to these more magnificent Inuentions: wherein the Garments, and Ensignes deliuer the nature of the person, and the Word the present office. Neither was it becomming, or could it stand with the dignity of these shewes (after the most miserable & desperate shift of the Puppits) to require a Truch-man, or (with the ignorant Painter) one to write. *This is a Dog*; or, *This is a Hare*: but so to be presented, as vpon the view they might without cloude, or obscurity declare themselves to the sharpe and learned: And for the multitude, no doubt but their grounded iudgements gazed, said it was fine, and were satsfied."

Jonson's Strand pageant was " thought upon, begun and made perfect in twelve days ";[1] its invention was a rainbow, with the Moon, Sun and Seven Stars. Electra, in the guise of a Comet, gave the gratulatory speech.

1603–04 — HENRI IV RECEIVED AT METZ

In March, 1603, the citizens of Metz welcomed Henri IV to their city with pageantry.[2] There were triumphal arches, with inscriptions; two boys, representing victories, crowned the king, and recited verses. A pyramid or grotto[3] was unfinished; and there greeted the sovereign, " vne Compagnie de six vingts ieunes enfans ou enuiron, tous au dessous de dix ans, Nicolas Magvin fils du sieur Maistre Escheuin, en estoit Capitaine, lequel auoit pour Lieutenant François Praillon, & pour Enseigne Avgvste le Gavllon, qui portoit son Drapeau de Taffetas blanc parsemé de petits Dauphins en broderie d'or, pour tesmoigner que la Compagnie estoit de Monseigneur le Dauphin. . . . Tous les petits Soldats estoient . . . vestus de Soye, Satin, Taffetas, ou telle autre matiere . . . Ils auoient vn Fifre, & trois Tambours, dont les Caisses estoient argentées, & ces Fifres et Tambours vestus de mesme aux Soldats, & d'aage, & de taille semblable aux plus petits."[4] Their captain addressed the king, who replied kindly; they received the queen, and an illustration[5] shows them escorting her.

---

[1] *Prog. James,* i, p. 396.

[2] A contemporary account by Abr. Fabert (*Voyage du Roy à Metz, l'occasion d'iceluy* (illustrated) Metz, 1610 — in Fairholt's collection at the Society of Antiquaries) gives the details.

[3] Illustrated, opp. p. 36. It apparently would have been a *chef d'œuvre*, had it been completed.

[4] P. 41. [5] Opp. p. 56.

1606 — CHRISTIAN IV OF DENMARK VISITS LONDON

On 22 July, 1606, it was " ordered that Sir Stephen Soame and Sir John Garrard, knights, shall give their best advises, and join with the Committees lately appointed by act of common council for preparation of the pageants, shows and other services at the Royal passage of the King's most excellent majesty and King of Denmark through this city." [1]

On 31 July, King Christian was received by the City of London. He came from Greenwich with his royal host and Prince Henry; landing at the Tower Wharf, the royal party was met by Sir Leonard Holliday, the mayor, who delivered the sword unto his Highness; he graciously received it, and the party proceeded.[2]

As the kings, with their splendid train of followers, passed from Tower Hill, the companies of London in their livery, gowns, and hoods, lined the streets; the houses were decorated.

" In their passing at the great Conduit in Cheapside, was made with greene Boughes, a very artificiall Arboure, which was garnished with all sortes of delightfull Fruites.[3] In this Arbour was placed most sweete Musicke; which greatly delighted the hearers, and no doubt pleased his Maiestie.

" At the little Conduit as they proceeded, there was erected a most stately Pageant; such as for the rare deuice and beautie, was, and is to be admired, and hath seldome been seene: a matter of such state, and rare edifice, in so short time to be accomplished, the workmen and plotters thereof, hauing not past twelue dayes of respite, after their first warning.

"Heere these most famous Princes, and most admired Kinges stayed, beholding the deuises, and rarenesse of the same: vnto whom were deliuered (in the name of the Lord Mayre and his Brethren the Aldermen, which stood neere them in

---

[1] *Repertory* xxvii, fol. 247 b; W. M. Williams (in *Annals of the Founders*, p. 223) prints an entry from the City Records under date of 23 July, 1606 providing for the raising of £1000 from the companies. The expenses of the Carpenters on this entry seem to have been confined to a dinner before they " stood " in Fenchurch Street, and to £5 for the pageants. (Jupp, p. 73.)

[2] A pamphlet in the Brit. Mus., entitled: *The King of Denmarkes welcome: containing his arriual, abode, and entertainement, both in the Citie and other places.* London, 1606 (C. 33. e. 7 (5)) gives full details of this progress; it was " written in a discourse from a Gentleman to a friend of his in the northern parts." Another account, by Henry Robarts, is in the Guildhall Library; it is entitled: *The Most royall and Honourable entertainement, of the famous and renowmed* (sic) *King, Christiern the fourth, King of Denmarke, &c. . . . With the royall passage on Thursday the 31. of July, thorough the Citty of London, and honorable shewes there presented them, and maner of their passing.* By H. R. At London, printed for *H. R.* and are to be sold by *William Barley*, dwelling in Gracious streete, neere Leaden Hall gate. 1606. Cf. also Heath's *Account of the Grocers* (1854), pp. 86–89; [(1869), 87 f.]; Howes, Stow's *Annals* (1615), pp. 885 f.

[3] This was evidently symbolical of trade. Cf. the Grocers' " Paradise " of older shows.

their Scarlet Gownes, and all the Commons of the Citie,) a most pleasing speach: which ended, the Kinges gaue the Citie thankes, and proceeded, till they came to *Paules* Churchyard.[1]

" Where at the Schoole of the Worshipfull Companie of Mearcers, called *Paules* Schoole, there were other delightfull speaches deliuered: to which they graciously harkoned, and honorably accepted.

" Then rode they on without stay, to Fleet Conduit, which was garnished sweetely:[2] on the toppe was placed delightfull Musicke; and were presented with other speaches, which was graciously accepted.[3]

" When they came to *Saint Dunstans* Church, they were presented with a noyse of Cornets, which shewed their cunning to be excellent, and very pleasing to both their Maiesties.

" Heere-hence they proceeded to Temple-barre: where his Maiestie and his brother King, giuing many thankes to the Lord Mayre and Citizens, for their great charge and paines, deliuered the Sword to the Lord Mayre; and rode on their way to *Somerset* House: wherere (*sic*) they reposed themselues that night, and to their Gracious further pleasures (*sic*).

" The Lord Mayre returning, was mette by the Sheriffes and Aldermen of the Cittie, who accompanied him to his house." [4]

---

[1] It is to be regretted that Robarts gives no more details of this pageant, which is probably that described by the writer in the British Museum pamphlet, who records (p. 22) that from the corner of the Old Change " ouerthwart the whole breadth of Cheapside, was built and raised vp a most stately, and well conceyted Pegne or Pageant, into the depth and secrets whereof I do not intend to wade, because it is expected to bee published presently by the Authour that made it." It showed, the writer nevertheless goes on to tell us, the Isle of Britain in the sea, with nymphs, Neptune and " Mulciber, the god of mettals." Over the arches the rocks rose high, supported by two giants; and at the top were the arms of England and Denmark. Concord spoke as the kings approached; the " genious of the citie of London . . . deliuered to the kings a long speech in Latin, so did also Neptune; the Sea-Nymphs sang in Latin " (p. 23).

[2] *The King of Denmarkes welcome* records that this was a bower, occupied by a shepherd and a shepherdess, who sang a " moste excellent song sung dialogue wise " in English (p. 24). Instrumental and more vocal music followed; and then the kings took leave of the Mayor at Temple Bar, and departed (p. 25).

[3] Robarts does not seem to be a " finished writer."

[4] Robarts, pp. 24 f. The account in Howes's Stow's *Annals*, p. 886, adds little: at the " bower of the Muses " on the fountain in Cheap the Recorder made a Latin speech, and gave Christian a cup; " then the pageant after it had ceased her melodious harmonie, beganne to expresse the purpose thereof, *viz.* Divine concord as sent from Heaven, descended in a cloud from the toppe unto the middle stage, and with a lowd voyce, spake an excellent speech in Latine, purporting their hearty welcome . . . but through the distemperature of the unrulie Multitude, the kings could not well heare it, although they enclined their eares very seriously thereunto. At the faire Fountaine in Fleetstreete was a pleasant pastorall device, with songs, wherewith the kings were much delighted: this Fountaine and divers other ranne cleere wine. . . ."

PAGEANTIC FIREWORKS: THE DEADLY SINS BURNT

On 11 August, the English royal family visited King Christian's flagship, at anchor at Gravesend, where they were feasted. " About foure a clocke when the banquet was ended, and the said princes fully performed all kingly complements, K. James began to take his leave to depart, but his brother being loth to leave his royall presence so soone, having prepared against that time, for their entertainment, an ingenious device of his owne upon the water floting neere unto them, and would therefore have had the king, queene, and prince with the great assembly stayd untill the evening to have seene the rarenes of his invention but when he saw the king of great Brytane & his traine ready to depart, notwithstanding the brightnes of the sonne, hee caused fire to bee put unto it . . .

"The Device of wild fire was in pageant wise betweene foure round pillers uppon a lighter framed (*sic*) where the Seven deadly sinnes in their lively colours shape: and Caracters, sate chained fast, and for their wickednesse bound to endure eternall punishment, and over their heads in the midest of them, upon the top of a pinacle was a firece (*sic*) Lion cowchaunt, signifying sudden vengeance, holding in his teeth the loose ende of the chaine, which compassed them about, and from the Lyon's mouth the fire first did issue forth, and from thence without any confusion, or further ayde, by degrees and distinct proportion, descended into all parts, making sundry sorts of sounds, with loftie Rocketts, and fire flakes mounting in the ayre, and great number of thunder crackes like peales of ordinance (*sic*) and for the space of more than a quarter of an hower, the foresaid Images sate burning in Etnaes flame resembling hells endles torments prepared for such offendors, but in the end they were consumed and so were the foure great wooden pillers one after another being wel nigh three yeards in square distance from the rest, this nocturnall pastime of pleasant variable fireworkes lasted about halfe an hower, and only was disgraced by too much light wanting Egypts darknes to have made it bright." [1]

APRIL, 1610 — PRINCE HENRY AT CHESTER

On St. George's Day, 1610, Prince Henry witnessed the " famous show " given at Chester.[2] Two men " in green evies (*ivy*) " led the procession, scattering fireworks; [3] then followed —

---

[1] Howes, Stow's *Annals* (1615), p. 887. On this, cf. the Pope-burnings discussed below, chapter vii.

[2] Cf. on this Harl. MS. 2150, fols. 356 (this show is indexed (*ibid.*, fol. 3 b) as "Mr. Amory's new shew invented by him"). Cf. Richard Davies, *Chester's Triumph in honor of her Prince*, reprinted by the Chetham Society (Manchester, 1844); and *Prog. James*, ii, p. 291. (We may suppose that Davies was the poet on this occasion, and Amerie, or Amory, the planner — perhaps the engineer.) For mention of the show see Chambers, i, p. 224, n. 2; and for a description of it, see Ormerod (1882), i, p. 381, n. — his authority is Harl. MS. 2150, fols. 356 (pencilled numbering, fol. 186). This MS. is rather a " scenario " or plan of the show; the account in the pamphlet is fuller.

[3] I have already mentioned them — see above, p. 73, n. 1.

"It. one on horseback with the buckler and head-peece of St. George, and iij men to guide him, with a drum before him, for the honor of Englond.

"It. one on horseback called Fame, with a trumpet in his hand, and iij men to guide him, and he to make an oration with his habit, in pompe.

"It. one called Mercury, to descend from above in a cloude, his winges and all other matters in pompe, and heavenly musicke with him, and after his oration spoken, to ryde on horsebacke with the musicke before him.

"It. j called Chester, with an oration and drums before him, his habit in pompe.

"It. j on horsebacke, with the kynge's armes upon a shield in pompe."

Other figures on horseback, with orations " in pompe " followed. Then came St. George himself, " in complete armour with his flagg and buckler in pompe, and before him a noyse of drums." Peace, Plenty, Envy, and Love followed on horse-back.[1] A dialogue seems to have taken place between Envy and Love.[2]

A steeple climber cast fireworks " very delightfull," [3] and an artificial dragon, spouting fire, was later slain — to the great pleasure of the spectators.

MAY, 1610 — PRINCE HENRY AT LONDON

The next month Henry was created Prince of Wales and Earl of Chester. Hearing of the king's determination to do this, the mayor and aldermen decided " to meete him [the prince] in such good manner, as the breuitie of time would then permit them." [4]

In this water-show, " . . . out of his [Neptune's] spacious watrie wildernes, he then suddenly sent a huge Whale and a Dolphin, and by the power of his com-

---

[1] Ormerod. Harl. MS. 2150, fols. 356 b, ends the description with these verses (which are recorded in Ormerod, i, p. 382, note a):

"Amor is loue and Amory is his name
That did begin this pompe and princelye game
the Charge is great to him that all begun
let him be satisfyed now all is done."

The last line is crossed out, and beneath is written —

"Who now is sattisfied to here all so well done."

[2] Cf. *Prog. James*, i, p. 302; the Chetham Society's reprint has no numbered pages, but the passage is easily found therein.

[3] This seems to have been the Mercury already alluded to; for the accounts in *Prog. James* and the Chetham Society's pamphlet record that Mercury descended from heaven in a cloud, " artificially winged, a wheele of fire burning very cunningly, with other fire-workes, mounting to the height of the . . . steeple upon coardes; with the most pleasant and melodious harmonie at his approach " (*i. e.*, the Prince's).

[4] See Munday's *London Love, to the Royal Prince Henrie* (London, 1610) which is in both the British Museum and the Guildhall libraries. Dr. C. W. Wallace, writing in the London *Times* for 28 March, 1913 (p. 6, col. 1) records the fact that the latter text is imperfect, and says that he has heard there is another copy of the pamphlet at Exeter Cathedral, and that two more copies are in existence.

manding Trident, had seated two of his choycest Trytons on them, altring their de-formed Sea-shapes, bestowing on them the borrowed bodies of two absolute Actors, euen the verie best our instāt time can yeld;[1] & personating in them, the seuerall *Genii* of *Corinea*, the beautiful Queene of *Cornewall*,[2] and *Amphion* the Father of hermonie or musick.

" In these two well-seeming and richelye appointed persons, the Dukedome of *Cornewall*, and the Principalitie of Wales . . . caried some tipe or figure, and not improperly to them so applyed.

" For such representations and misticall vnderstandings, haue alwayes bin reputed lawfull, and are euermore allowed to holde and carrie correspondencie, with such solemne shewes and Triumphes; as before in Elder Antiquitie, so like-wise in Moderne and later vse.

"Let it suffice then, that thus was this goodly Fleete of Cittizens accompanied, and vshered the way so farre as *Chelseye*, where houering on the water vntill the Prince came: all pleasures that the times *interim* could afforde, were plētifully entercoursed, and no disorder or breache of arraye in the whole Nauie."

When the prince drew near, Corinea — " a very fayre and beautiful Nimphe, representing the Genius of olde Corineus Queene, and the Prouince of Cornewall " — mounted on her whale, greeted him in prose. Then, moving toward Whitehall, the prince being ready to land, Amphion, " a grave and iudicious Prophet-like personage . . . personating the Genius of Wales," appeared on his dolphin, and bade the prince farewell.

On 5 June of that year, " Itm. it is ordered that M[r]. Chamberlen shall pay vnto Mr. Burbage and John Rice the players that rode vpon the two fishes and made the speeches at the meeting of the high and mighty Prince the Prince of Wales vpon the River of Thames on Thursday last, seauenteen pounds tenn shillings six pence by them disbursed for robes and other furniture for adorning themselues at the same meeting, And that they shall receyue to their owne vses in lieu of their paynes therein taken all such Taffety, silke, and other necessaries as were provided for that purpose without any further allowance, And this shalbe M[r]. Chamberlen's warrant in that behalf.[3] On that day, also, it was "ordered that M[r]. Chamberlen shall pay vnto M[r]. Anthony Monday who was ymployed for the devising of two speeches to be deliuered to the prince and for divertions when my Lord Maior and Aldermen attended the prince the some of seauen and ffortie shillings by him disbursed for diuers necessaries concerning the same preparacoñ and ffowre pownds six shillings and ffowre pence for his paines and labour taken in the same amounting both to six pownds thirteene shillings and eight pence,

---

[1] These were Burbage and Rice; see below.   [2] Cf. Corineus, above, p. 58.

[3] *Repertory* xxix, fols. 232 b. This, as well as the following extract from the Records of the London Corporation, was cited by Dr. Wallace in his letter to the *Times* already referred to.

The order and solemnitie of the Creation of . . . Henrie . . . Prince of Wales, &c. (on 4 June, 1610), (London, 1610) may be found in the Brit. Mus. [C. 33. e. 7 (12)].

And this shalbe his warrant in that behalf." [1] Further expenses were — " vnto those persons that plaied one (*on*) cornetts within the devise made in the forme of a whale . . . for their paynes and Labor about the same the some of three pownds . . ." and to " such persons as plaied within the deuise made in the forme of a dolphin . . . the some of twentie two shillings for their paynes then taken." [2]

A Water-fight with Pageantic Features

On the Wednesday following the show, " after a most Royall and sumptuous Tilting, the water fight was worthilie perfourmed,[3] and by such reporte was as thereof made to me, thus it was ordered:

"A Turkishe Pirate prowling on the Seas, to maintaine a Turkishe Castle (for so their Armes and Streamers described them both to be) by his spoyle & rapine, of Merchants, and other Passengers; sculking abroad to finde a bootie: he descried to Merchants Shippes, the one whereof bearing to winde somewhat before her fellowe, made the pirate wafte her to strike sayle and come in, which the Merchant either not regarding, or no way fearing, rode still boldely on. The Pirate with drawen weapons and other menaces, wafts her againe to vayle her bonnet, but the Merchant still refusing: the Pirate sends a commanding shott, which the Merchant answered againe, encouraged thereto by her fellowe Merchant, who by this time was come neere her, and spake in like language with her to the Pirate. When he perceiued his hope defeated, and this bolde resistance returned; he sent shot vpon shot very fiercely, whereto they replyed as resoluedly: so that betweene them grewe a verie fierce & dangerous fight. Wherein the Merchāts wexing to be somewhat distressed (by reason that the Castle likewise often played vpon them) two men of warre happening then to be neere, made in to helpe and releeue their hard detriment.

" And now the fighte grewe on all sides to be fierce indeed, the Castle assisting the Pirate very hotly, and the other withstanding brauely and couragiously: diuers men appearing on either side to be slayne, and hurlled ouer into the Sea, as in such aduentures it often comes to passe, where such sharpe assaultes are vsed indeed.

"In conclusion, the Merchants and Men of warre, after a long and well fought skirmish, prooued too strong for the Pirate, they spoylde bothe him, and blewe vp the Castle, ending the whole batterie with verie rare and admirable Fire-works, as also a worthie peale of Chambers."

This is not a pageant; it savors of the courtly tilt, though it is fought on the water. If the arrangements were carried out on the Wednesday as they had been

---

[1] *Repertory* xxix, fol. 233.   [2] *Ibid.*, fol. 235.

[3] (It was postponed from the Monday, on account of the weather.) I am quoting from Munday's pamphlet, *London's Love*, before referred to. Perhaps Munday did not plan this part of the show; he seems to speak from " reporte."

planned for the Monday, Proteus, mounted on a sea-monster, delivered a pro-
logue to his Highness, explaining " the intent of the deuise." [1] That the city had
some connection with this is suggested by the entry, under date of 14 June, 1610,
in the Corporation records:

" Itm. whereas vpon the seuerall happy and blessed dayes appoynted for the
late triumphs of meeting the prince at Chelsey by my Lord Maior and the Companies in their Barges, As also for the creacoñ of the prince of Wales sondry kind
and gracefull offices were done by the clarkes of the counsell by Garter King at
Armes and by the ffowre principall gentlemen vshers to his ma[ty] wherein they all
shewed their foreward affections as occassions occurrently were offerred in their
severall places to grace and honor the citty in their speciall and respective services
by them don to the Lord Maior and Aldermen of this citty vpon both the said
dayes, it is therefore ordered that severall gratuities be sent them by M[r] Dyos, vizt.
to the clarke of the counsell ffowre pownds, ffive pownds to Garter King at Armes
who is to make a Recorde in his office of the whole buysines for the perpetuall
honor of this citty, and ffowre pownds to the ffowre gentlemen vshers w[ch] Mr.
Chamberlene is to pay." [2]

It is true that the city officials may merely have been present at this water-
fight; but the line between court and what we may call, for the moment, " folk,"
has been crossed. Proteus may be — as the sea-monster undoubtedly is — a
pageantic figure; and the merchantmen give a civic flavor to the contest.

1616 — CHARLES MADE PRINCE OF WALES

Prince Henry did not live to reign; four years after he was created Prince of
Wales, we find his brother Charles elevated to that position. On this occasion
Middleton wrote his *Civitatis Amor*, " an entertainment by Water at Chelsey and
Whitehall." [3] At Chelsea, London — sitting upon a sea-unicorn, with six Tritons
sounding before her, accompanied by Neptune, the Thames, and the Dee —
speaks as the prince appears. Neptune silences the Thames that London may be
heard; whereupon London wishes the prince a long and happy life, addressing the
future Charles I as the

> Treasure of hope and jewel of mankind,

and as the "glory of our days."

---

[1] *London's Love*, p. 23.

[2] *Repertory* xxix, fol. 238 b, *et seq.*

[3] *Civitatis Amor*. The Cities Loue. An entertainement by water, at Chelsey and Whitehall. At the ioyfull receiuing of that Illustrious Hope of Great Britaine, the High and Mighty
Charles To bee created Prince of Wales, Duke of Cornewall, Earle of Chester, &c. . . . London, 1616.

Copies of this pamphlet may be found in the Guildhall and British Museum. It is reprinted
in Bullen's Middleton, vii, pp. 269 f., Dyce's Middleton, v, p. 249, and in *Prog. James*, iii,
pp. 208 f. (Cf. Greg, p. 16.)

At Whitehall, London, the Tritons, Neptune and the two rivers are met by Hope and Peace, who await the prince's landing. Hope thanks London for awakening her " from the sad slumber of disconsolate fear "; and Peace sings a song of welcome as Charles lands. In the light of history, we find a certain pathos in these two characters who greet Charles a quarter of a century before the Civil War breaks out.[1]

When, in 1617, James visited York, the mayor and aldermen met him, and various speeches were addressed to the sovereign; he received gifts, but there were no pageants.[2] On 16 May of this year he was received at Edinburgh; here again there were no pageants.[3] This same year, however, at Stuttgart, there was a pageantic cavalcade to greet the Duke of Würtemberg on his entry into the city. Trumpeters; a two-faced Janus; children with wreaths on their heads; barefoot maidens with bows, arrows and lances; two figures suggesting Spring and Autumn; gryphons, with attendants wreathed in flames; children with hourglasses on their heads, and shields bearing Roman numerals up to xii represent the Hours; Indians with feathered headdresses; Moors, Centaurs and like figures took part in this procession.[4]   There were also cars: one elaborate one held Apollo and the Muses, and others suggested Biblical subjects.

1623 — CHARLES RETURNS FROM SPAIN

On 6 October, 1623, Prince Charles returned from Spain, and his welcome by the citizens of London, told by John Taylor, the Water-Poet, included bonfires, but apparently no pageants.[5] Two years later an elaborate welcome for Charles and his bride which had been planned, was stopped by the plague;[6] on 26 January, 1625–26, the Court of Aldermen ruled " vpon informacoñ given unto this Court by the maister and wardens of the company of Paynter-stayners London, and Mr

---

[1] On the next day but one — 6 November — there was a running at the ring.

[2] Francis Drake, *Eboracum*, pp. 121 f.

[3] The king received a gift of five hundred double angels, and heard a sermon preached by the Archbishop of St. Andrews; he also knighted the Provost. (See on this visit, *Documents relative to the Reception at Edinburgh of the Kings and Queens of Scotland* (publ. by the Bannatyne Club), 1822. Its account is taken " from a volume of the Records of the High Court of Justiciary).

In the introduction to the *Historical Account of his Majesty's Visit to Scotland* (Fourth edition, Edinburgh, 1822 — in the Fairholt Collection), this entry of James is dated 1618; it is recorded that Mr. John Hay, deputy town-clerk, addressed him " a learned oration," and that the king received 10,000 marks scots in double gold angels. (A mark is thirteen shillings, fourpence — see, p. 9, n.). [The above volume records the visit of George IV to Edinburgh in August, 1822].

[4] Which is illustrated in the second volume of Balthazar Küchler's engravings, in the Fairholt collection at the Society of Antiquaries.

[5] This account is reprinted in Somers, *Tracts* (second edition), ii, p. 550.

[6] Maitland, *History and Survey of London* (1760), p. 299.

Paule Isaacson and others of that company of abuses and badd workmanshipp in and about the contrivings and payntings of the Pagents, it is thought fitt and soe ordered by this courte, that Sr John Leman, Sr Edward Barkham, Sr Martin Lumley Knights, and Aldrēn Mr Aldrān Hackett, Mr Aldrān Johnson, Mr Aldrān Cambell, and Mr Aldrān Paynton or any foure or more of them shall togeather with the said M^r and Wardens and the said Mr Isaacson and such others as thye shall call vnto them veiwe the Pagents also the Crosse in Cheape, and the work done in the Exchange, and sufficientlie to informe themselves of the abuses any waie comitted in and aboute the workmanshipp thereof; and to certifie this court in writinge under their handes how theye fynde the same and theire opinions; and William Cunthrope to warne and attend them." [1]

On the 26 May, 1626, the Earl of Pembroke, Lord Chamberlain, wrote the Lord Mayor, saying that he and the Court of Aldermen " had been directed by letters from the Earl Marshal to prepare and erect in several places in the City sundry pageants for the fuller and more significant expression of their joy on the King and his Royal Consort's intended entrance through the City. His Majesty having altered his purpose, and directed him [the chamberlain] to signify so much to the Lord Mayor, he requested him to take notice thereof, and to remove such pageants which besides the charge they caused in the City, hindered the passage of coaches or carriages."[2] On the 8 June, the aldermen "takeing into consideracoñ the some of moneys alreadie disbursed and paid vnto Mr Christmas for the fynishing of the three pageants, and for the performance of the shewes that was intended att the solempniacoñ of his Ma^{ts} coronacoñ wch his Matie hath signified to bee forborne; It is thought fitt and soe ordered the said Mr Christmas and Mr Middleton referring themselues vnto this Court, that noe further moneys shalbe paid vnto either of them, but that Mr Christmas shall forthwith cause the said Pagents to bee taken downe, and to haue the same for his full satisfaccoñ."[3] On 22 June of the same year, " vpon further consideracoñ taken by this court [of aldermen] of the humble peticoñ of Gerrard Christmas who now wholly submitted himself unto this court is pleased to give him ye some of c li ouer and aboue what alreadie hee hath receiued out of the Chamber of London in full satisfaccoñ and demande for the settinge upp of three pageants. And Mr Chamberlen is hereby ordered to pay the same."[4]

It will be observed that only three pageants were provided for this progress which never took place; it may be that they were used in some Lord Mayor's Show so that Mr. Gerard Christmas did not make such a bad bargain, after all. But this is mere supposition.[5]

---

[1] *Repertory* xl, fol. 84, *et seq.*
[2] Overall, *Remembrancia* (1878), p. 417.
[3] *Repertory* xl, fol. 243.
[4] *Ibid.*, fol. 268.

[5] Pageant-cars and a triumphal arch which greeted Louis XIII at Paris in 1628 are illustrated in the first volume of Mr. Fairholt's scrapbook, now preserved in the library of the Society of Antiquaries. I mention this merely to show that French royal-entries are pageantic at a time when pageantry is dying out of those in England.

1629 — The Debt of the City for the 1626 Pageants Unpaid Four Years Later

The expenses which the city incurred on the occasion of Charles's coronation were not paid for several years afterwards. On 28 October, 1629, the Stationers "were called upon for £60, 4s., as their quota of £4300 expended by the City for pageants and other solemnities, and beautifying the City against the late entrance-time of his Majesty passing through the same for his Coronation, and for other necessary and public service of the City."[1] All the companies were called on for their share; on 26 August, 1630, the sum of £973, 10s., 4d., yet remained to be raised.[2] It was probably for this debt that the Carpenters contributed £21, 10s., on 2 April, 1630; not — as Jupp surmises — "on account of the peace with France and Spain, concluded about that time."[3]

1633 — Charles Crowned at Edinburgh

When Charles I entered Edinburgh for his coronation there, in 1633, pageants were exhibited, and there was considerable splendor.[4]

One account[5] describes a triumphal arch at the West Bow, on which "Caledonia appeared, in an ancient and rich attire, who in a copious speech[6] congratulated his Majesty on his safe arrival. At the west end of the Tolbooth, in the High Street, stood another triumphal arch, on which were painted the portraits of the Scottish kings: within the arch, Mercury appeared, conducting the first Fergus,[7] who bestowed much paternal and wholesome advice upon Charles. At the Cross appeared the rosy god, and issuing from the Cross streams of wine, which flowed copiously, "to the great solace of the commoners." At the Tron, a high mount was

---

[1] Nichols, *Literary Anecdotes of the Eighteenth Century* (London, 1812), iii, p. 575. W. M. Williams, *Annals of the Founders*, pp. 230, 231 (citing from the City Records) notes that on 11 October, 1629 it was determined that the sum of £4300, which the Chamber of London paid for the pageants and other solemnities at the coronation of Charles I, shall be raised among the different companies; the rates at which the companies are to be taxed follow.

[2] Williams.

[3] Jupp, p. 453. On 20 October, 1628, the Pewterers were taxed £12, 10s. for these pageants — see Welch, ii, p. 86.

[4] See the account, "from a MS., in the Advocates' Library, in the handwriting of Sir James Balfour," printed in *Documents* (ed. by the Bannatyne Club), pp. 115 f. This mentions no pageantry. In the "warrand to take the Heads aff the West Port — Mar. 14" (p. 109) — from Orders of the Privy Council of Scotland — the ceremonies were spoken of as "solemniteis and showes quhilks as to be made by the Magistrats of the burgh of Edinburgh . . . at his Majesties entrie."

[5] Which may be found in the introduction of the volume describing the visit of George IV to Edinburgh in 1822 (already cited).

[6] Printed in this pamphlet, appendix E, p. 335.

[7] *Quelle mélange!*

raised representing Parnassus, on the middle of which was a pyramid of great height, with a glass fountain, whence Hypocrene issued. In a cavern of the mountain sat two bands of vocal and instrumental music, with an organ to complete the concert, which performed a piece of music called Caledonia, composed for the occasion by the best masters. On the northern side sat Apollo and the Muses. When the divine harmony ceased, Apollo addressed himself in a panegyric to the king, and presented him with a volume of poetry composed by members of the University. As the procession advanced along the High-street, which was lined by the citizens, armed, and in their best apparel, his Majesty was saluted by peals of ordnance from the Castle, and by the joyous acclamations of his subjects." A banquet was given to the king, " the expense of which, and the other disbursements attending his entry, amounted to £41,489 Scots money." [1]

1637 — Two Splendid Spectacles at London

A pamphlet in the Guildhall Library, entitled, *The Arrivall and Intertainements of the Embassador, Alkaid Jaurar Ben Abdella, with his Associate, Mr. Robert Blake, &c.,*[2] tells of the ceremonies on the ambassador's arrival from Barbary on 19 October, 1637, and of those during his stay in England. The aldermen and sheriffs of London, in scarlet gowns, met the Barbary merchants; the torches and links made the streets " almost as light as day." On 5 November, the king received the ambassador; though both occasions were splendid spectacles, there seems to have been no pageantry on either.

1638 — An Example of the " Fighting Show "

While not a " royal-entry," the " Exercise performed the 18th of October, 1638, in Merchant-Taylors Hall, by certain Gentlemen of the Artillery Garden, London," may be considered here; it is interesting, because it shows the develop-

---

[1] Pp. 13 f. I can find no authority for some of this unknown author's statements — though for other details he uses the records reprinted in the Bannatyne Club publication already cited.

One further citation from this work may be made; the writer says (p. 13), that " the naturally fine genius of the poet of Hawthornden was, on this occasion, subjected to the severe drudgery of preparing speeches and poems to be recited to the king, stuffed with the most forced conceits, fulsome compliments, and extravagant imagery; though it must be confessed, that part of the poetry, if deficient in simplicity, possesses considerable vigour and even brilliancy."

The public entry of Ferdinand, Archduke of Austria, into Antwerp was accompanied by pageants, designed by Rubens.

Seven plates, " from the folio volume by Gervatius (published in 1642)," descriptive of the pageantry on this occasion may be found in the first volume of Fairholt's scrapbook, in the Society of Antiquaries' library. That Rubens's " sketches are preserved in the Antwerp Gallery " is noted by Fairholt; (they may have been moved, however, since the war began).

The date of this entry may be 1636, in which year " Ferdinand of Spain " was at Ghent.

[2] Published at London in 1637.

ment of the muster and like " fighting shows." [1] Eighty men took part in this
" exercise " — " *eighteen* with *Morions, Swords* and *Targets*; which encountred
nine against *nine*. Secondly 22 *Saracens*, that is to say, a *Captain, Lieutenant,
Ensign*, one *Serjeant, Pipe*, a *Turkey-Drum*, and 16 select *Saracens*. Thirdly 40
of the *Modern Arms; viz.* A *Captain, Lieutenant, Ensign*, 2 *Serjeants*, 1 *Phife*, and
2 *Drums*, 16 *Musquettiers* in Buffe-coats and Beaver Morions, and 16 *Pike-men*,
compleatly Armed in white Corselets, whole Pikes and Morions."

The banner of the Saracens bore the crescent, and " a motto in the Arabian
tongue and Characters." Both sides marched into the hall, and — after evolutions and countermarches before the " nobility, aldermen and gentry " who
were present, and a speech addressed to the spectators by a musketeer — various
manœuvres and " firings " took place; then followed a fight between the " Christians " and the " Saracens." It " contained (*sic*) a long time with great obstinacy
on either side, untill at length the advantage of the *Christians Arms* and number of
their *Souldiers* prevailing . . . the *Saracens* were forced to give ground." Re-
pulsed once, and forced from the hall, the Saracens returned; the fight was
renewed, and — after a valiant struggle — " they cryed for *quarter*; after the
Turkey manner, casting their *weapons* on the ground, and laying their *left hands*
on their *heads*, with a loud voice crying *Saybe-Sullam*." Taken captive, the Turks
were led about the hall triumphantly; and a soldier made a final speech, saluting
the nobility and citizens there assembled.[2]

This furnishes an interesting example of the step between the Elizabethan
" musters," and such fights as that the queen saw at Bristol in 1574,[3] and the
Royal Military Tournaments of our own day.[4] There is, probably, an influence
of the tournament in both — and both show the " soul " of pageantry.

1641 — THE RETURN OF THE KING TO LONDON

There was no sign of pageantry, save for the " armed-men " who rode at the
head of each company, when the city welcomed Charles on 25 November, 1641,
at his return from Scotland.[5] " Every Company had a horse-man which road

---

[1] My account is taken from William Barriffe's *Mars, his Triumph* (London, 1661 — in the
Guildhall Library [A. 1. 5]).

[2] Barriffe seems to have taken part in this " exercise " himself — as the lieutenant in the
" Christian " army (Cf. p. 5). From the Epistle Dedicatory, it appears that he published his
account only for the members of " our own company; as not being willing that so *rough* and
unpolisht a *draught* should be exposed to the *publick* view."

[3] See above, p. 206.

[4] See next volume.

[5] For accounts of this entry see *Ovatio Carolina*, London, 1641 (in the Guildhall library);
this pamphlet is reprinted in *Harl. Misc.*, v, pp. 86 f.; Maitland, pp. 341 f.; and John Taylor's
England's Comfort and London's Joy [of which pamphlet there are two copies in the Bodleian.
It is reprinted in the *Works of John Taylor, the Water Poet, Fourth collection*. (Spenser Society,
xxi (1877), no. 7)]. This last-named pamphlet contains three wood-cuts.

severally in front of each of them, which horse-man did likewise beare the Armes of such a one Company as hee attended, he being in all parts suited *Cap a pe* accordingly."[1] The king dined at Guildhall, after which he went to his palace through enthusiastic crowds — " there was no failing in expressions of love and loyalty by the people as appear'd by their shouts and acclimations (*sic*) as also by drinking of innumerable healths to his Majesty (which healths I hope will not prove sicknesse to any man)."[2] The fountains ran wine.

In 1642 the Civil War broke out, and in 1649 Charles was executed. We may well believe that the country was not, during these years, in the mood for pageantry; and the shadow of the king's death must have hung over Edinburgh when, in 1650, the city gave twenty thousand marks to Charles II on his entrance. Yet there seems to have been a dinner on this occasion, for we read that " the expensis of the desert bestowed upon his Majestie on Fryday last the second [of August] " amounted to £433, 16s., 8d.[3]

1653 — CROMWELL AT GUILDHALL

On Wednesday, 8 February, 1653, Cromwell was entertained in London. There were no pageants, but the companies turned out, and the recorder made the following speech:

" My Lord, there is one helpe more in Government, which God is pleased often to adde to the rest, which is the giving in of the affections of the People. The solemnity of this day, wherein the Citizens of this great City appeare in their severall Companies, as so many Cities within the City, speakes much to this; they leave it to other Nations to salute their Rulers and victorious Commanders with the names of *Cæsares* and *Imperatores*, and after triumphs to erect for them their *arcus Triumphales*; but if I mistake not, their end, this day, is not any such outward Pomp, or Glory, but that those who have beene delivered together, might rejoyce together, and to expresse their desires that the civill Sword might be as prosperous for publique ends, in the hand where it is placed, as the military Sword hath beene in the same hand. . . ."[4]

---

[1] Taylor, p. 3.

[2] Taylor, p. 5. The pamphlet includes " Verses Presented to his Majesty " which are both Biblical and loyal; a prose speech, spoken to the king (wishing him a long and happy reign — this on the eve of the Civil War!); and " Verses presented to the kings own Hand by John Taylor." (If this pamphlet be by Taylor, the author's name occurs in it nowhere else. The Spenser Society reprint refers to Hazlitt, *Bibliographical Hand Book*, no. 74.)

[3] From the records of the Town Council, in *Documents* (printed by the Bannatyne Club), p. 124.

[4] This speech was " printed by E. B. for Matthew Walbancke," in 1653 (5 pp). It is preserved in the Guildhall Library (A.1.5).

1660 — REJOICINGS AT LYONS, WITH REMARKS ON " FEUX D'ARTIFICE "

Before we notice the burst of pageantry that greeted Charles II, on his
return, let us refer to the celebrations at the return of peace in Lyons, 20 March,
1660. The elaborate *machines* on this occasion recalls the pageant, although the
latter was not usually made the basis of " feux d'artifice." Perhaps the construction which contained the Seven Deadly Sins, in 1606, was as much a pageant as
anything; and it obviously makes no difference — as far as our definition goes —
whether the pageant is burned, or simply torn to pieces after the show is over.[1]

The *machines* on this occasion were decorated with " scriptures," or inscriptions; and on them were placed allegorical, mythological, classical and symbolical figures — all more or less appropriate to the quarter of the town furnishing
the display, or to the occasion celebrated by the whole city.

Following the description of the show is printed *Advis Necessaires pour la
Conduite des Feux d'Artifice.*[2] From this, I quote. " Il y a trois choses à considerer
dans la conduite de ces Feux: le Sujet, l'Artifice, et les Ornemens. Le sujet peut
être Historique, fabuleux, emblematique, naturel, ou mêlé. . . . L'occasion est
ordinairement une Victoire, la Naissance d'un Prince, sa Majorité, son Mariage,
ses Alliances, sa Guerison, ou quelque auguste ceremonie. . . . Ces diverses
occasions demandent des sujets bien differens. On peut prendre pour une victoire
les Triomphes des Empereurs, les Nations subjuguées, & les Batailles gagnées.
C'est ainsi que les exploits de nos Monarques sont representés par le succés des
Armes glorieuses des Cesars & des Scipions. La naissance d'Hercule, & celle
d'Alexandre seroient des sujets propres de la naissance des Princes. Celle de cét
Empereur eût merveilleusement bien representé la naissance de sa Majesté,
pource que les Aigles, qui parurent sur le Palais où Olympias accoucha auroient
êté le Symbole des victoires de l'Allemagne, dont les Aigles vaincuës firent la
pompe du berceau de nôtre Monarque, & le Temple de Diane, qui brûla la nuit de
la naissance de cét Heros, tandis que la Deesse êtoit occupée à le receuoir, & à
seruir Olympias, seroit accomodé à la nature du Feu . . .

" Diuers Exemples des sujets Historiques.

" *Pour une Victoire*

" Achille & Vlysse mettans le feu à la Ville de Troye.

" Le jeune Annibal iurant la ruine de Rome sur les Autels.

" Carthage brûlée par Scipion . . ."

Various other suggestions are made, not only under this heading, but for the
birth of a prince, for his coming of age, for his coronation, etc., etc. The list

---

[1] This Lyonnais celebration is described in a pamphlet, preserved in the Fairholt collection
at the Society of Antiquaries, and entitled, *Les Rejouissances de la Paix faites dans la Ville de
Lyon, le 20. Mars 1660* (Lyons, 1660). It is illustrated with many plates, which show the
different " set-pieces "; and contains descriptions of each.

[2] Pp. 35 f.

includes such religious occasions as the canonization of a saint (where the suggestion is Elijah's journey to Heaven — " Ce transport est le vray symbole de l'Apotheose d'vne Ame sainte "), and " le sacré d'un Roy & d'un Prelat," for the first of which occasions " l'inauguration de Dauid & de Salomon " is suggested; " celle d'Aaron " for the prelate.

But " la Fable fournit des sujets plus agreables que l'Histoire, pource qu'elle reçoit plus de formes, & qu'elle fait des miracles qui passent les forces de la Nature. . . . Le Sujet Emblematique est le plus ingenieux, pource qu'il est de l'invention de l'Ouurier, qui est createur de sa matiere, à la façon des Poëtes; & qu'il n'est pas une simple application d'une chose faite, comme sont les sujets que l'on tire de l'Histoire & de la Fable . . . Le Sujet naturel est plus simple . . . Comme seroit un Phœnix sur son bucher, une Salemandre dans les flâmes, un Portique, vne Pyramide, vn Obelisque ou un Arc de Triomphe. . . . Le mêlé est composé de tous les autres."

That these *feux d'artifice* were fairly common, is shown by this *Advice*; my excuse for quoting as much of it as I do is to show how pageantic they have become. We shall, in a later chapter, return to pageantic effigy-burning, which — of course — has one root in folk-custom. It would not be surprising to find that it was stimulated by such celebrations as these — which are, after all, elaborate pageantic bonfires, and nothing else.

" L'une des principales obseruations qu'il faut faire en la conduite de ces Feux," says our Lyonnais author, " est de n'y mettre aucune figure, dont on puisse trouuer occasion de railler; & que comme on les fait ordinairement [1] brûler, on ne puisse faire la plainte que fait Monsieur Colletet en une de ses Epigrammes, à l'occasion d'un feu de Ioye fait en Gréve où l'on auoit brûlé les Muses l'an 1649.

> " Dedans un Siecle glorieux,
> On cherit les Filles des Dieux;
> Mais dans un lâche & ridicule
> On les mene en Gréve, on les brûle."

1660 — THE RESTORATION OF CHARLES II

At the end of May, 1660, Charles II was in Holland, but there was, apparently, no pageantry in connection with his visit.[2] Evelyn recounts, under the date of 29 May, 1660, the entry of the king into London.[3] There were no

---

[1] Not *toùjours*, notice.

[2] For details see *Relation, en Forme de Journal, du Voyage et Séjour que . . . Charles II . . . a fait en Hollande, depuis le 25 May, jusques au 2 Juin 1660* (the Hague, 1660). This illustrated pamphlet is in the Fairholt collection at the Soc. Antiq. library.

[3] *Diary* (ed. W. Bray, 1879), ii, p. 112.

An eight-page pamphlet in the Bodleian (Wood 398. 12), entitled *A True Relation of the Reception of his Majestie and Conducting him through the City of London . . . on Tuesday the*

pageants, but the fountains ran wine, and the mayor, aldermen and all the companies turned out to greet the monarch. On 5 July, Charles was entertained by the city; and there were pageants,[1] which are described in Tatham's *London's Glory*.[2] The city was decorated, and the companies, in gown and hood, lined the streets from " old Jury "[3] to Temple Bar. The city waits took part in the show. The mayor and aldermen, with their retinue, passed to Whitehall, whence the king " attended with the Lords of the Upper House, the Commons in Parliament, Lords of His Majesties most honourable Privy Councel," etc., " takes his way for *Guildhall*; and at *Fleetstreet* Conduit makes a stand, where He [4] is received by a person, representing *Time* in a very glorious Pageant, who Addresseth himself to His Majesty on his knee . . .

" And so His Majesty, the two Dukes, and the rest of the Noble Retinue and Gentlemen, pass on to *Pauls* Churchyard, where they are intertained (*sic*) by another Pageant, very much amplified and adorned, in which is seated *Truth* . . .

" Another Pageant presents its self at *Foster-lane*, being a large and goodly Fabrick, a Trumpetter placed on the Top, where it was intended *Fame* should speak; But at the great Conduit in *Cheapside*, *Fame* presents her speech.[5]

" At *Pauls Chain* is another Pageant in the Nature of a Droll; where is presented the Figure of Industry, and the Carders and Spinners, in relation to the Clothiers Company.

" At *Cheapside Crosse* another Droll, where *Pretty* and the Tumblers play their Tricks . . ."

---

29 of this instant May, being the Day of his Majesties Birth (London, 1660) gives full details of this show. The crafts and civic authorities took part in this welcome; there were bands stationed at Bridge Gate, the Exchange, St. Peter's in Cheap, Ludgate, and Temple Bar to play as the king passed; " and *Grace* church Conduit, Four spouts, *Cornhill* Conduit . . . Great and Little Conduits, and Standard in *Cheapside* and *Fleetstreet* Conduit, do all run with *Claret* Wine, as Tokens of Ioy." The expenses of the Pewterers on this occasion may be found in Welch, ii, p. 126.

[1] The MS. accounts of the Entertainment at Guildhall, 5 July, 1660, may be found in the Guildhall Library, MS. 289. The total cost was £7888, 2s., 6d.

[2] *London's Glory, Represented by Time, Truth and Fame: at the Magnificent Triumphs and Entertainment of His most Sacred Majesty Charles the II . . . at Guildhall on Thursday being the 5th day of July 1660, and in the 12th Year of His Majestie[s] most happy Reign. Together with the Order and Management of the Whole Days Business.* London, 1660. This pamphlet may be found in the Guildhall, Society of Antiquaries, Bodleian, and Cambridge University libraries; there are three copies of it in the British Museum. I make my outline from the pamphlet, which has been reprinted in Tatham's *Dramatic Works* (ed. J. Maidment and W. H. Logan, Edinburgh, 1879), p. 293.

[3] *I. e.*, Jewry.

[4] The capitalization is to be noted; it is a small, but none the less significant, sign of joy at the end of the Puritan *régime*.

[5] In Tatham's pamphlet, from which I have been quoting, may be found the three speeches of Time, Truth, and Fame.

After viewing these pageants, the king dined at the Guildhall; during dinner there was both instrumental and vocal music. When the banquet was over, the Lord Mayor and Aldermen attended the sovereign to Whitehall.

1661 — Charles's Progress across London on the Day before his Coronation

Charles II was crowned on 23 April, 1661; on the 22d he crossed the city and was greeted with pageants. John Ogilby was appointed " for the conduct of the Poetical part thereof, consisting in Speeches, Emblemes, Mottoes and Inscriptions." The architectural part was " by Mr. Peter Mills, surveyor of the city, and another person, who desires to have his name concealed." [1]

---

[1] *The Relation of His Majestie's Entertainment, Passing through the city of London to his Coronation: with a description of the Triumphal Arches, and Solemnity* (By John Ogilby. London, 1661.) is in both the Bodleian (Gough. Lond. 122.13, and Wood 398.18) and the Guildhall (A. 1. 3. no. 1). A 1662 edition, *The Entertainment of . . . Charles II* — with a greatly expanded text, giving the reasons and authorities for the symbolism — is illustrated; where it repeats the text of the 1661 edition it does so exactly, save that the present tense is usually (not always) changed to the past. This is in the Guildhall (Desk M). Another edition, *The King's Coronation* (London, 1685) is in the Guildhall (A. 1. 3. no. 5) and the Bodleian (Gough. Midd. 32, and Ashm. G. 10. vii. b); and a fourth (Edinburgh, 1685) is in the Guildhall (A. 1. 5). The quotations above, in the text, are from the 1661 edition — the page facing the title-page, and p. 32.

Cf. for other descriptions of this entry, Evelyn, *Diary*, ii, p. 126; J. G. Nichols, *Lond. Pag.*, pp. 74 f. (from three contemporary pamphlets).

In Ogilby's 1662 pamphlet, the procession is illustrated in a series of pictures; the four triumphal arches, and the coronation ceremony at Westminster Abbey, together with the procession thither from Westminister Hall, are also shown.

A five-page pamphlet in the Bodleian (Wood, 537.18) entitled *The Cities Loyalty Display'd: or the Four Famous and Renowned Fabricks in the City of London Exactly described in their several Representations, what they are, with their private meanings and perfect Actions at the day of publick View, which is not yet discovered. Together with a true Relation of that high and stately Cedar erected in the Strand bearing five Crowns, a Royal Streamer, three Lanthorns, and a rich Garland. Published for both Cities and Countreys Satisfaction* (London, 1661), gives a detailed description of the arches prepared for the coronation of Charles. The first — nearly eighty feet high — contained statues of James I, Charles I, and — above them — of Charles II himself, in robes of state. Behind him was drawn the Royal Oak.

The second was about the same height; its roof resembled " the leads of a Castle." On it four " kings " representing the four kingdoms; they bowed to his majesty as he passed. A turret above showed twelve angels at twelve casements; over it was placed the statue of Atlas. Under the gate were statues of Charles I, Charles II, the Dukes of York and Gloucester. The third represented the Temple of Diana; it contained goddesses and the Oracle of Apollo.

The Fleet Street pageant — the highest of all — was very elaborate. It was surmounted by a statue " like a blazing Comet glittering in the Air."

The Cedar in the Strand, commonly called the Maypole, was 134 feet high, and bore the king's arms. A morris dance " finely deckt, with purple Scarfs, in their half-shirts, with a Taber and Pipe the ancient Musick . . . Danced round about the Maypole, after that

On his way from the Tower to Whitehall, his Majesty was entertained by a band of eight waits, placed on a stage in Crouched Fryers; near Aldgate another band of six waits entertained him, in like manner, with music, from a balcony built for that purpose.

" In *Leaden-Hall*-Street, neer *Lime*-Street End, is erected the First Triumphal Arch, after the *Dorick* Order. On the North-side, on a Pedestal before the Arch, is a Woman personating *Rebellion*, mounted on a *Hydra*, in a Crimson Robe, torn, Snakes crawling on her Habit, and begirt with Serpents. . . . Her Attendant, *Confusion*, in a deformed Shape, a Garment of several ill-matched Colours, and put on the Wrong way. . . .

" On the South Pedestal is a Representation of *Brittain's Monarchy*, supported by *Loyalty*, both Women . . ." Their costumes are described; the paintings on the arch show Charles's landing, recall the ruined state of the kingdom under Cromwell, and show God's justice upon the rebels who murdered the king's sainted father. A picture of Usurpation, flying before Charles's calm advent, was placed over the arch; one of Usurpation's many faces was intended to represent the late Oliver Cromwell.

Rebellion made the first speech, rousing herself at Charles's approach; then Monarchy and Loyalty unveil themselves, and as the former consigns Rebellion to perdition, she sinks from sight.[1]

The East India Company's entertainment,[2] before the East India House in Leadenhall Street, showed a youth in the Indian habit, attended by two blackamoors; he addressed the king, while another youth, also in Indian costume, mounted on a camel led by blackamoors and other attendants, scattered jewels, spices and silks from his panniers among the spectators. He, in his turn, addressed the king.[3]

Danced the rounds of their Liberty " (p. 4). The Maypole also bore a royal purple streamer, and a garland with lanterns — one for James, Duke of York; one for the Admiral, and the third for the Vice-Admiral of England; they were to be lighted on dark nights, as long as the pole was to stand, to honor seamen.

For the expenses of the Pewterers on this occasion, see Welch, ii, p. 128.

What may be referred to as the " raw-material " of pageantry was seen at Bath when the citizens celebrated the coronation of Charles II. Four hundred virgins, who marched with the Lady Mayoress, " most in white Wastcoats and green Petticoats," bearing flowers, wreaths, and crowns; a conduit running wine; a parade of the civic authorities and militia, are all described in a pamphlet at the Bodleian (Wood, 537.17) entitled, *Of the Celebration of the King's Coronation-Day in the famous City of Bathe. A true Narrative in a Letter sent from thence to Dr. Charleton, Physician to his Majestie.* (London, Printed 29 April 1661.) This is signed " William Smith."

[1] The Edinburgh reprint, p. 3.

[2] " This Entertainment was designed, and the Speeches made by a Person of Quality." — Ogilby's note.

[3] " The two youths who speak to his Majesty as above, are John and Samuel Ford, sons of Sir Richard Ford, one of the Committees of the East India Company." Cf. J. G. Nichols, p. 74.

Near Leadenhall were more waits stationed; and on the top of the Cornhill conduit stood eight white-robed nymphs and a " noise of seven trumpets."

The second arch, " which is naval," stood near the Exchange in Cornhill. " On the *East* side are two Stages erected; on each side of the Street, one. In that on the *South* side is a person representing the River *Thames*; his Garment Loose and Flowing, Colour Blew and White, waved like Water, a Mantle over, like a Sayl; his Head crown'd with *London*-Bridg, Flags, and Ozier, like long Hair, falling o're his Shoulders; his Beard long, Sea-green, and White, curl'd; an Oar in his right Hand, the Model of a Ship in his left, an Urn beside him, out of which issues Water; four Attendants in White, representing the four fresh Streams which fall into the River *Thames*, viz. *Charwell, Lea, Colne,* and *Medway.*

" In the other *Stage* on the *North*-side, which is made like the upper Deck of a Ship, are three *Sea-men*, whereof one habited like a *Boat-swain.*" [1]

Neptune, Mars, Charles I, and Charles II are painted on the arch; but on pedestals are living figures of Europe, Asia, Africa, and America, " bearing the Arms of the Companies, Trading into those Parts." On the top of the arch is an Atlas, bearing on his back a terrestrial globe, on which is a ship under sail. " On the four *Niches* within the *Arch* are living Figures . . . representing *Arithmetick, Geometry, Astronomy,* and *Navigation.*" All are women.

The sailors entertain the passing nobility with a song; and six others, also habited like seamen, play wind-instruments. On the other side are more musicians, who " perform their Duty without Intermission, till such Time as His Majesty fronts the *Figure*, which represents *Thames*, and then cease "; Thames then speaks, after which the three sailors sing again.

At the Stocks there is a military band; the fountain there, " being after the *Thuscan* [*sic*] Order," vents wine and water; water and wine flow also from the great conduit in Cheap; on the towers of the Conduit are eight nymphs, and eight musicians: and at the Standard in Cheapside, six waits.

The third arch, near Wood Street end, " represents an Artificial Building of two Stories, one after the *Corinthian* way of Architecture, the other after the *Composite*, representing the *Temple of Concord.*" Two female figures, representing Peace and Truth, grace this building; there is also Concord with the four cardinal Virtues — each of whom has an attendant. In the Temple are the Goddess Concord [2] and eleven other " living figures "; behind the goddess stands a man in a purple gown " like a citizen of London," presenting " the *King* with an *Oaken* Garland, Over the *King's* Head, ' *Pater Patriæ*,' " and over the Citizen's, " *S.P.Q.L. ob cives servatos.*" [3]

---

[1] Ogilby (1661), p. 11.

[2] Called " the Goddess of the Temple " in the Edinburgh (1685) pamphlet (p. 6).

[3] It is not quite clear whether or not this be a " living picture." Perhaps Charles himself entered the temple, and stood beneath the inscription. There is, very likely, a connection between the " oaken garland " and the " Royal Oak " — cf. the Lord Mayor's Show for 1660 (below, chapter vi).

One of the figures which attends the goddess is named Truth;[1] another is Love, and there are nine " lesser Figures," with whom is mingled an orchestra of twenty-four violins. When the king comes, Concord, Love, and Truth sing a song (with chorus); then the former addresses the sovereign, and as he moves away, another song is rendered.

Nymphs occupied the Little Conduit; and in a balcony erected at the entrance of Paternoster Row were eight more musicians. Other musicians were distributed along the route; more nymphs in white graced the conduit in Fleet Street, on the " Lanthorn " of which was " the Figure of *Temperance*, mixing Water and Wine."

In Fleet Street, near Whitefriars, stood the fourth arch, representing the Garden of Plenty; it was of two stories — one Doric, and one Ionic. Bacchus, in appropriate dress, occupied the south side, in front of a painting which represented Silenus and dancing Satyrs; on the north side was Ceres, in front of a painting of Harvest, in a dragon-drawn chariot; Flora, in a various-colored habit, and Pomona, crowned with fruits, were on the west side, in front of paintings of garden and orchard; four figures representing the Seasons [probably artificial] stood above four living figures representing Eurus, Boreas, Auster, and Zephyrus. An artificial figure, on the top, represented Plenty; and there were many musicians. A woman, also named Plenty, attended by two virgins, addressed the king on his approach.[2]

At Temple Bar the king was " entertained with the view of a delightful Boscage full of several Beasts both Tame and Savage, as also several living Figures, and the Musick of eight Waits. . . ."[3]

This is one of the most elaborate entries of the century, and it is well to remark particularly the mixture of living figures with allegorical and historical paintings. The entertainment provided by the East India Company recalls the trade-symbolism so common in the Lord Mayor's Shows; the distribution of the jewels, spices, and silks among the spectators is an echo of the advertising common enough in the civic triumphs.

Evelyn [4] " spent the rest of ye evening in seeing the severall arch-triumphals built in ye streetes at severall eminent places thro' which his Majesty was next day to passe, some of which though temporary, and to stand but one yeare, were of good invention and architecture, with inscriptions." They were more elaborate than was usually the case with these pageants; and some of them — if not all —

---

[1] This suggests that the other Truth may be a statue; though the Edinburgh (1685) pamphlet calls her and Peace " two Figures in Female habits."

[2] It is hard to tell from Ogilby's description just which figures are alive, and which are effigies. Apparently there were two Concords on the third arch, as here there were two Plenties — one artificial, and one alive. From the illustration in Ogilby's 1662 volume (p. 139) I gather that Bacchus, Ceres, Flora and Pomona were either effigies or painted on the arch; Bacchus and Ceres look, in the drawing, as if they were painted.

[3] The Edinburgh (1685) pamphlet, p. 8.   [4] *Diary*, ii, p. 126.

stood for more than a year. On 27 May, 1662, the Court of Aldermen "thought fitt and ordered . . . that Sr Thomas Adams, Sr Thomas Aleyn, Sr John Robinson, Kts. & Baronetts & Sr Richard fford [1] Kt & Aldrañ do attend his Matie at Hampton Court to understand his pleasure touching the Pageants whether ye same shall bee continued for any further service or bee forthwith taken doune for prevencoñ of any further hindrance or annoyance to ye Inhabitants neare the same, And   to warne them." [2] On the 17 July, 1662, " it is ordered by this Court that the Citty workmen shall forthwith goe in hand to repaire the houses which have bene damaged and impaired by erecting and standing of ye Pageants before the same were taken downe." [3]

The author of *The Cities Loyalty Display'd* [4] makes this interesting comment: " And as for the glories of these renowned Fabricks, prepared against the blessed coronation, the fame thereof is sounded throughout all *Europe*; for I myself have seen a *French* Limner drawing the figures of them to send to *France*, so that I perceive we *English* have not altogether patterns from *France*, they take some from us, and they are even such, that I believe few in this age did ever see the like."

1662 — THE QUEEN'S PROGRESS ON THE RIVER THAMES

Both Evelyn and Pepys saw the queen's progress on the Thames 23 August, 1662. The latter restrains his enthusiasm — the former does not spare superlatives. " I was spectator," says Evelyn,[5] " of the most magnificent triumph that ever floated on the Thames, considering the innumerable boates and vessells dress'd and adorn'd with all imaginable pomp, but above all the thrones, arches, pageants, and other representations, stately barges of the Lord Maior and Companies with various inventions, musiq and peales of ordnance both from ye vessels and the shore, going to meete and conduct the new Queene from Hampton Court to White-hall, at the first time of her coming to towne. In my opinion it far exceeded all ye Venetian Bucentoras, &c., on the Ascension, when they go to espouse the Adriatic." [6] Pepys writes:[7] " All the show consisted chiefly in the number of boats and barges; and two pageants, one of a King and the other of a Queen with her Maydes of Honour sitting at her feet very prettily; and they tell me the Queen is Sir Richard Ford's daughter.[8] Anon come King and Queen in a barge under a canopy with 10,000 barges and boats, I think, for we could see no

---

[1] Whose sons took part in the entertainment of the East India Company.

[2] *Repertory* lxviii, fol. 120. The space is left in the MS.

[3] Fol. 155.

[4] The pamphlet mentioned above, p. 243, n. 1: the passage cited is on p. 3.

[5] *Diary*, ii, p. 150.

[6] In a note to this passage, Mr. Bray, the editor, refers to Tatham's *Aqua Triumphalis*, which we shall consider in a moment, and to the *Gentleman's Magazine*, xciv, ii, p. 516.

[7] Diary, ii, p. 316.

[8] Cf. above, p. 244, n. 3.

water for them, nor discern the King nor Queen. And so they landed at White Hall Bridge and the great guns on the other side went off." Tatham's description of his show goes into details.[1] The barges of the twelve companies were taken up early in the morning of the 23d to Chelsea: " Most of the Barges are attended with a Pageant, some more richly set out then [sic] the rest, but none remisse in shewing something of Affection and Loyalty.

" The Pageants are placed at the head of every Barge. That which attends the *Mercers* is thus set forth. Under a Canopy of State is seated a *Virgin*, on her head a silver Coronet. . . . Her attendants and three Maids of Honour and six Pages, . . . placed three of [sic] each side the Pageant.

" *The Drapers Pageant is thus set forth.* Under a Canopy of State is represented a Grave *Roman* Magistrate . . . His Attendants are four; *Loyalty, Truth, Fame,* and *Honour.* . . .

" *The Merchant Tailors Pageant is thus set forth.* The Stage (being 12. foot long, and 7. broad) is Arched with a wild Arbour, made in manner of a Wildernesse.

" The two Camels (supporters of the Companies Arms) are back'd with two *Indians.* . . . There are two Moores, that attend the camels as their guides.

" In the Wildernesse is seated an Aged Man, representing a Pilgrim, and habited accordingly. . . . This alludes to St. *John,* the Patron of their Company: for his Attendants he hath *Faith, Hope,* and *Charity,* who are placed before . . .

" *The Goldsmiths Pageant is thus set out.* Under a canopy of State sits *Justice,* her hair dishevell'd. She wears on her head a golden Crown, her Garment Gold-colour, girt with a girdle of Gold, in one hand she holds a Ballance, in the other a Touch-stone. At her feet is placed two Virgins [sic], their Hair dishevell'd, their Heads are encompassed with Wreaths of Flowers of severall Colours . . .

" It would be too tedious to insert here the bravery of the rest of the Pageants, and being streigthned in point of time, I shall omit it.

" The Barges are anchored some 40. or 50. yards distant in the middle of the River, behind them is left an open passage for Boats to passe, this side of the River is kept clear for their Majesties and their Trayn.

" Between 8. and 9. of the Clock, the Lord Mayor and Court of Aldermen, move towards *Chelsey,* where they attend their Majesties comming from *Putney,* and then the Lord Mayor leads the way down the River before their Majesties.

" The Grand Pageants appointed for the day are placed thus: The First at *Chelsey*; the second between *Fox hall* and *Lambeth*; the third at the private Staires at *Whitehall.*

---

[1] *Aqua Triumphalis; being a True Relation of the Honourable the City of London's Entertaining Their Sacred Majesties upon the River of Thames, and Wellcoming them from Hampton Court to White-hall. Expressed and set forth in several Shews and Pageants the 23. day of August, 1662,* written by John Tatham, Gent. (London, 1662.) Of this pamphlet the Guildhall and British Museum each possess one copy, and the Bodleian, three.

" Those three entertain their Majesties with Speeches, in their motion to *Whitehall*.

" There are two Drolls,[1] one of Watermen the other of Seamen, continually imployed in dancing and singing.

" The Droll of Watermen is placed between *Chelsey* and *Fox hall*.

" That of the Seamen between *Lambeth* and *White-hall*, cross the Thames, where there is several tricks of Activity performed, both on the Stage and the Rope.

" And the Seamen throw themselves into severall Antick postures and dances."

The first " entertainment " — presented at Chelsea, " in the head of the *Lord Mayors* and *Companies Barges* " — was a " Sea-Chariot, drawn with Sea-Horses. In the front whereof is seated *Isis*; . . . her head adorned with an *Anadem*, or Crown of all manner of Flowers. . . . In her left hand she holds a Watering pot, to denote her the Lady of the Western Meadowes, and Wife to *Tham*. At her feet are placed several infcriour Water Nymphs, belonging to small Rivolets, who are Contributaries to her . . ." When the royal barge approached, she hailed the royal pair; then they passed on to the " droll " of watermen, who sang a three-part song, after which one stepped forward and addressed their Majesties.

Then the king and queen moved on to the second entertainment, " which is a Pageant made in the manner of an *Island* floating, and presented between *Fox Hall* and Lambeth, with a *Lion* and a *Unicorn* standing in the Front, the Supporters of the *Armes* of *England*: upon whose backs are placed two bigg *Boyes*, the one a *Scotch*, the other an *English*, and habitted accordingly, with *Banners* in their hands, whereon is the *Armes* of either *Nation*.

" In the middle of this View is seated *Tham*, represented in an Old Man with long Hair and Beard, which may signifie the Weeds and Sedges of the River: On his head he wears a Crown of Flowers. . . . In his right hand he holds a *Trident*, as he is Viceroy to *Thetis* and King of Rivers. In his left hand he bears a Pitcher of Water, as he is Sonne to *Achelous* (the Father of Rivers) and Grandchild to *Oceanus*. . . . On his right hand is placed a Nymph of the Water on whose head is the Figure of *Greenwich Castle*. On his left hand another Nymph, on whose head is placed the Figure of *Windsor Castle* . . ."

Thames addressed the king on his approach; his speech is full of loyalty and flattery. His island, he says, shows Britain, which, with Portugal, is

> " . . . one in Fame,
> There is no difference 'twixt 'em but in Name,
> *Lisbon* is *London*, *Tagus Thames*, and then,
> The *Portugues* are become *Englishmen*,
> The *English*, *Portugues*, both meet in hearts,
> Thus *Providence* unites *remotest* parts."

---

[1] We shall find many of these in seventeenth century Lord Mayor's Shows.

With further compliments to both king and queen, Thames ended his speech; and
as the sovereigns moved on toward Whitehall, they were entertained by the
second " droll " of Indians and Seamen, who danced and sang.

The " third view " received the royal couple at the private stairs, when they
reached the palace. It consisted of " a *Sea Chariot* made in the manner of a
Scollop shell, drawn with two *Dolphins*, on whose backs are placed two *Tritons*.
In the front of the *Chariot* is seated *Thetis* . . . her Attendants are four Sea
Nymphs . . .

" *Thetis* addresseth her self to their Majesties . . . alluding to the *Storm*, and
Joy of the *Portugues*, which happened at one and the same time."

One of the explanations, which — like notes — follow the account of each
entertainment ("not," as Tatham says, " to inform the knowing person, but
to help such as are unacquainted with Poetical Authors and Historie"), is worth
recording. It shows the spirit of symbolism which permeates this show.

" Why *Thetis* drawn in a Sea Chariot, accompanied with *Tritons*, and *Sea
Nymphs*.

" By the Chariot, is meant the swift motion of the Sea, and by the diversity of
her Attendance, are (*sic*) understood the various sorts of Fishes, which are said to
wait upon the Sea Gods and Goddesses, because they have their being and habi-
tation in the Sea; But *Tritons* are commonly taken for *Neptunes* Trumpeters,
and sometimes for Sea Monsters. *Thetis* was also married to *Peleus* an excellent
Navigator, and therefore is presented with gray hairs, which is partly to intimate
the Antiquity of Navigation, and partly to shew the cares and fears of Seamen,
who are observed to become sooner Gray hair'd than others."

The songs of this triumph were " set by Mr. *John Gamble*, one of His *Majesties*
Servants, a Person well known in Musick.

" The Management and Ordering of this dayes Triumph was carried on by the
Judgement and Care of

" Mr. *Peter Mills*, Surveyor

" Mr. *Malin*, Water-Bayliff

" The two *City Painters*. Excellent in their quality

" Mr. *Thomas Whiting* Joyner ⎫
                                    ⎬ No lesse Excellent in their qualities."
" Mr. *Richard Cleere* Carver ⎭

This show has borrowed much from the Lord Mayor's Show of the times, as
might be expected; for Tatham had written many of the latter, and — it may be
presumed — was forced to use some of the properties already on hand. The
Island recalls the aquatic pageants of the Kenilworth entertainment almost a
century earlier; and the sea-chariots, with the dolphins and nymphs, show
nothing new in water shows. The adaptation of the pageantic animals to mercantile and national heraldry is to be noted; we shall see much of this kind of
thing in the civic triumphs which we shall examine in the next chapter. The
" drolls " seem to be a development of the tumblers whom we met in 1547

and 1553; in the Lord Mayor's Show they were often connected with the trade of the chief magistrate's guild — here, of course, they are fitted to the aquatic occasion.

It may be wondered how much of the poetry was heard, even by the sovereigns. That the noise of the crowds was greater on land than on this occasion may be doubted; it is likely, however, that the speakers were farther away from the king than was the case at a passage through the streets of the city. Perhaps it was owing to the difficulty in making king or mayor hear, that speech eventually faded both from the civic shows and the " royal-entry."

1665 — The Reception of the Duke of Ormond at Dublin

When the Duke of Ormond, Lord Lieutenant of Ireland, was received in Dublin on 17 October, 1665, there was " . . . a conduit in the Corn Market whence wine ran in abundance. At the New Hall was erected a scaffold, on which were placed half a dozen Anticks: by the Tollsell was erected another scaffold, whereupon was represented Ceres, under a canopy, attended by four virgins. At the end of the Castle street a third scaffold was erected, on which stood Vulcan by his anvil with four Cyclops asleep by it: and the last scaffold was raised at the entrance into the Castle Gate, whereupon stood Bacchus with four or five good fellows . . ."[1] Ordnance welcomed the governor, and there were fireworks in the evening. We cannot tell whether the characters mentioned above spoke to the duke — but there is nothing to let us assume they did. The mythological tendency here is noteworthy.

1672 — Triumphal Arch at Heidelberg

When Charles, Palatine of the Rhine, was married at Heidelberg in 1672, at least one triumphal arch was erected. An illustration of this may be found in the first volume of Fairholt's scrapbook, now preserved in the library of the Society of Antiquaries.

1679 — A Royal Passage through London

The precept of the mayor to the aldermen of the various London wards to prepare for the passage of the king through the city on his way from Flanders in November, 1679, is preserved in the Guildhall. No mention is made of pageants; but the houses are to be decorated, and the streets cleaned. A reference to the " late Precept for the prevention of Squibs and other Fireworks " may be noted.

---

[1] The Dublin correspondent's letter to *The Intelligencer* for 30 October, 1665 (no. 88; pp. 1062 f.).

1685 — Coronation of James and Mary

An account of the ceremonial at the coronation of their most excellent Majesties King James II and Queen Mary at Westminster the 23d of April, 1685,[1] makes no mention of pageantry.

William III at the Hague

There was pageantry when King William III made his first visit to Holland after the Revolution of 1688. It is described in a pamphlet [2] entitled " A Description of the Most Glorious and Most Magnificent Arches erected at the Hague, for the Reception of William the Third, King of Great Britain; with all the Mottoes and Latin Inscriptions that were written upon every one of the said Arches. Translated into English from the Dutch." Just what part speech played — if any — is hard to determine.

1692 — The Sovereigns Entertained at Guildhall

We shall have occasion to note, in the next chapter, the fairly frequent appearance of royalty at the seventeenth-century Lord Mayor's Shows. Here I may draw attention to " An acc[tt]: of Moneys Received towards the Entertainment of their maj[ties] King William and Queen Mary att Guildhall on the Lord Majors Day, 1692," [3] which shows receipts of £1114.

1697 — The King Received by the Citizens

A contemporary broadside describes a reception of the king by the citizens of London, 16 November, 1697.[4] It was very splendid, but there was no pageantry in the strict sense of the word. Besides the recorder's speech, there was a congratulatory oration addressed to the king by one of the Hospital boys; the houses were decorated, and in the evening there were illuminations and fireworks.

The next year Augustus II was crowned King of Poland; and triumphal arches were erected on this occasion.[5]

---

[1] A broadside in the Bodleian (Gough. Midd. 32), printed by Thomas Newcomb in the Savoy, 1685.

[2] Reprinted in the second edition of Lord Somers's *Collection of Scarce and Valuable Tracts* (ed. Sir Walter Scott), xi, pp. 595 f.

[3] Guildhall MS. 288. A painter's bill of £55, and a carpenter's of £80 suggest that some of this money went for the pageants. Edward Watts, Keeper of Blackwell Hall, received £2, 5s.

[4] *An Account of His Most Excellent Majesty's Splendid Reception into the Famous City of London, together with His Royal Entertainment in and through the said City on* Tuesday *the* 16th *of this Instant* November, 1697. (Guildhall, Broadsides, 7. 17) Cf. J. G. Nichols, p. 82.

[5] They are pictured in the Fairholt scrapbook before alluded to. An interesting plate illustrates a morris dance (" Der Mohren Tantz ") on this occasion.

By the end of the seventeenth century, the "royal-entry," which had been pretty elaborate until just after 1660, lost its pageantic features. This was probably chiefly due to the fact that the monarchs were not uncommonly visitors at the mayor's pageants; whatever the cause, the fact remains. The custom of riding through the city from the Tower to Westminister on the eve of their coronation fell into disuse at the end of this century; and the coronation ceremonies — which had never been, in themselves, pageantic — lost the prelude of pageantry which had marked the majority of coronations since that of Richard II in 1377. Instead arose the custom of a state visit to the Guildhall on the first Lord Mayor's Day in each reign. We shall see, in the next chapter, that Charles II witnessed several of these civic shows, and dined at the Guildhall after them, as did many of his successors; and it is, perhaps, due to this fact that the "royal-entry" was shorn of its pageantry, though not, of course, of its splendor.

Before we close this chapter, let us glance at some of the royal-entries of the later centuries, some of which will be found to have retained, for one reason or another, pageantic features. This survey obviously is not exhaustive.

1702 — Queen Anne at the Guildhall

On the first Lord Mayor's Day of her reign, Queen Anne visited the Guildhall; " An Account of moneys received towards the Entertainment of her Maj^tie Queen Anne att Guildhall on the Lord Mayor's day, 1702 "[1] shows expenses amounting to £1745, 1s., 6d.[2]

1714 — George Welcomed by the Citizens

In 1714, the Pewterers joined the other companies in welcoming George I on his passage through London; their expenses amounted to £48, 17s., 10d.,[3] but there seems to have been no pageantry on this occasion.

Aside from the participation of royalty in the welcome given to the Lord Mayor on his inauguration, I have found almost no instance, during the eighteenth century, of pageants used in connection with a welcome to a sovereign.

---

[1] Guildhall MS. 288. Mr. Watts, keeper of Blackwell Hall, received £2, 12s, and the " Queens Musick " received £20. The first item, undoubtedly, is connected with the Lord Mayor's Show.

[2] The same MS. accounts show that when the Duke of Marlborough was received at Goldsmiths Hall in 1704, Mr. Saunders [perhaps the creator of Gog and Magog—see above, p. 61, n. 4] was paid £3, and the " City Musick," £5; and one " Shipley for ye Musick w^thin, £56, 5s." The total cost of this entertainment was £868. In 1706, the Duke was entertained at Vintners Hall, on which occasion the city music received £8. In both cases this was probably for playing during dinner.

[3] Welch, ii, p. 180.

1803 — NAPOLEON AT ANTWERP; THE GIANT APPEARS

In 1803, Napoleon visited Antwerp, and was received with pageantry. Stationary structures, with inscriptions, welcomed him on his entrance; the city was illuminated every evening of his stay, and there were fireworks.[1]

On the first of Thermidor, in the afternoon, the *grooten Ommegang* was reviewed by the First Consul.[2] The giant appeared, "figure colossale de 26 à 28 pieds de haut, construite en 1534, par le peintre *Vanasselt*, sous la direction du grand *Rubbens*.[3] Il était traîné par six chevaux de brasseurs, les plus grands de la ville. . . . Il est vêtu à l'antique. . . . On lisait l'inscription suivante sur le piédestal où il est assis:

" *Mole meâ magnus sed tu, Bonaparte, triomphis.*" [4]

There was also, on this occasion, a car of triumph, on the highest part of which was a statue of Bonaparte; it carried appropriate mottoes. The " city music," habited as Mamelukes, played as they rode on this car.

A ship, named the *Deux Nêthes*, manned by cabin boys (*mousses*),[5] carried a motto, and was followed by " le char de Neptune. Le Dieu était représenté par un homme. A côté de lui était la Déesse Thétis sous l'apparence d'une jeune fille. Ils occupaient le fond du char attelé de chevaux marins conduits par deux Sirènes." Latin and French inscriptions were displayed.

Then came a whale, twenty-seven feet long and fifteen high; " portée sur un vaste flot qui renferme un réservoir d'eau et une pompe, ainsi que la mécanique qui la fait mouvoir, elle soufflait, par la bouche et les ouïes, une grande quantité d'eau sur les grouppes nombreux qu'elle rencontrait, ce qui était, pour le peuple, l'objet d'un divertissement très bruyant. Un joli enfant, vêtu en Triton, dirigeait malicieusement les jets des ouïes."

The car of Vulcan followed; a rock enclosing the forge of Vulcan, with figures representing " l'état militaire," religion and industry, it had also ten cyclops, who were forging " l'anneau d'une alliance étroite." Their hammers rang out an anvil chorus, while the smoke of an " encens exquis " issued from the forge. A

[1] See the *Relation de la Réception faite à Bonaparte . . . dans la Ville d'Anvers lors de son passage en l'an xi* (Antwerp, year 12—1804); this is in the Fairholt collection at the Soc. Antiq.

[2] The above-named account, pp. 34 f.

[3] MS. note, pencilled in the margin of Fairholt's copy: " !! Rubens was born 1577! "

[4] The pamphlet gives the supposed history of the figure, repeating the tradition of the giant named *petit Eckhof*, who " ranconnait les bateliers: mais le fameux Brabo, qui a donné son nom au Brabant, lui coupa la main (*hand*) et la jeta (*werpen*) dans le fleuve, d'où est venu *Handwerpen* ou, par corruption, *Antwerpen*, Anvers." This legend is repeated by Fairholt, in *L. M. Pag.* (pt. i, pp. xxxv f.)

[5] " Ces enfans qui appartenaient à d'honnêtes familles, qui les avaient habillés à leurs frais, étaient si bien instruits aux manœuvres, qu'ils satisfirent particulièrement le ministre de la marine, devant qui ils prirent à tâche de se distinguer." (p. 36.)

man in chains, behind the car, represented " l'envie cruellement tourmentée des succès du héros de la France."

Lastly came the car of Agriculture, or " l'enlèvement de l'Europe." This *char d'Europe* was built in 1767; it contained about forty young girls, in white, "placées en amphithéâtre." As on the other cars, there was here a suitable inscription.

" Il existe encore dans le magasin du *petit Eekhof* (*sic*) d'autres machines qui auraient fait partie de la fête, telles que la Géante, l'Elephant, les Dauphins etc. si leur grand état de dégradation eût permis de les réparer. La trinité, l'enfer, le jugement dernier, furent consumés par un incendie, il y a environ cinquante ans. Ces machines . . . ne sortaient jadis qu'aux deux kermesses ou fêtes patronales d'Anvers, jusques vers 1700 qu'on ne les vit plus qu'en 1728, 1744, 1767, lors de l'entrée des gouveneurs des Pays-Bas." [1]

Here we have a show which resembles closely the English royal-entries of the sixteenth century; although, of course, it was modernized with appropriate allusions to the city's guest of honor. Its giant, dating from the time of Henry VIII of England, was but one of the properties which was revived for the occasion; the *char de l'Europe* was only thirty-six years old, but perhaps replaced an earlier one. I have cited these details to show that in a city, which doubtless made many gifts to English pageantry, the love of this kind of thing was alive at a time when its parallel in England had lost much of its former glory.

1822 — GEORGE IV AT EDINBURGH

There were no pageants when Louis XVIII of France entered London on 20 April, 1814,[2] but in 1822, when George IV visited Edinburgh, there was a suggestion of pageantry.[3] Platforms and galleries were erected for the spectators, and triumphal arches were built. Two were put up at Leith, as soon as it was known that the king would land there; [4] another at the chief entrance of Dalkeith.[5]

The Lord Mayor of London in his State Barge, attended by the Goldsmiths' and Skinners' barges, bade George farewell on his departure from Greenwich.[6] After a sea-voyage, the king landed at Leith; much pomp there was in his entry

---

[1] P. 40.

[2] A MS. account of this entry, written on vellum, may be found in Addl. MS. 35,160.

[3] On this entry, see the *Historical Account of his Majesty's Visit to Scotland*. Fourth edition (Edinburgh, 1822). This is in the Faitholt collection at the Soc. Antiq.; it contans illustrations of the landing of George IV at Leith, 15 August, 1822; the royal procession passing by Picardy Place, on the same day; a view of the Grand Procession to the Castle, 22 August; the banquet given the king by the city, 24 August — and a plan of the same.

[4] They are described in the above-mentioned *Account*, p. 34.

[5] P. 37. Much poetry, including verses by Sir Walter Scott, John Mayne, and others — named and unnamed — was written for the occasion; it is reprinted, *ibid.*, pp. 49–67.

[6] P. 73. The State Barge was towed by " the Royal Sovereign Steam-boat."

into Edinburgh, but no pageantry; addresses were delivered, and fireworks displayed — the latter included "transparencies" and illuminations at Edinburgh, Dalkeith, and Leith. On the evening of the 16th, "inscriptions, ornaments, devices, and emblems were displayed in endless and dazzling variety" at Edinburgh.[1]

On the 22d, there was a splendid procession when the king went to the castle; but, though it is called a "pageant" more than once,[2] there were no pageantic features in the strict sense.

OTHER NINETEENTH CENTURY "ROYAL-ENTRIES"

Although arches were erected in the High Street, when Queen Adelaide visited Leicester 25 November, 1839, there was no other suggestion of pageantry, in its stricter sense, on that occasion. The city was decorated; the queen was greeted warmly by the citizens, and addressed by a school-boy — but there is nothing in this entry to detain us.[3]

When Queen Victoria and Prince Albert went to Scotland, in 1842, they were greeted everywhere with triumphal arches.[4] The next year the sovereigns visited Leicester; here again the pageantry was confined to triumphal arches.[5]

At the visit of the British Queen and Prince Consort to the King and Queen of Belgium, the same year, there were triumphal arches both at Brussels and at Antwerp. Ship and giants appeared in the cavalcade at the latter city; and there was also a "Whale Fountain."[6]

To celebrate the marriage of the Duke of Brabant with the Archduchess Marie of Austria, in 1853, there was held at Brussels an "historical procession." The "floats," or pageant-cars, seem to have carried not only historical *tableaux*, but also symbolical figures.[7] It is interesting to observe that the Lord Mayor's Show at London in November, 1853, showed a revival of pageantic features, which included the Car of Justice, and horsemen symbolizing various nations; a car representing Australia, and one of Peace and Prosperity.[8]

---

[1] P. 122.

[2] Pp. 191 f.

[3] See Kelly, *Royal Progresses and Visits to Leicester* (1884), pp. 512 f.; he cites the account of the Leicester *Journal* for 29 November, 1839, and appends various others, from local and metropolitan papers — some of them brief; others reflecting political prejudice.

[4] Cf. the *Lond. Illus. News* for 17 September, 1842, pp. 297 and 300; for 24 September, p. 312. These arches are pictured.

[5] They are illustrated in Kelly, *Royal Visits to Leicester*, pp. 557, 559, 561; his account is taken from the Leicester *Chronicle*.

[6] This visit is related in the London *Pictorial Times* for 30 September, 1843. The triumphal arches "Whale Fountain," ship and giants are illustrated in this periodical.

[7] For illustrations of this event, see the *Illus. Lond. News* for 27 August, 1853, p. 169.

[8] On this, see chapter vi, below.

It is not my purpose to record all the triumphal arches erected for royalty during the nineteenth century;[1] this was the common form of pageantry in the later " royal-entry." In 1881, however, when the Prince and Princess of Wales visited Swansea, there was a pageant which recalls the older castles; and several others recall the earlier trade-pageants. The Corporation address was delivered at a pavilion which had been erected on the boundary of the city. " The procession, joined by the Mayor and Corporation, then moved onwards through the streets of the town, which were crowded with delighted spectators. . . . The next halt was made near the Great Western Railway Station, where a Masonic Pavilion had been erected on one side of the road, whilst on the other was a grandstand, occupied by the Swansea Choral Society, 2000 strong, supplemented by some 200 youthful choristers in Welsh costume."[2] There were triumphal arches, parades, and illuminations at night, fireworks, bonfires, etc., and addresses and songs of welcome.

" The triumphal arch in Castle Bailey Street was a representation of the ancient Castle of Swansea, as shown on the borough arms, and was decorated with flags and spears." There was a " Tin Arch," and " the ' Wool Arch,' erected by Messrs. Parry and Rocke, woolstaplers, entirely at their own cost, was composed entirely of raw wool and yarn, weighing over six tons, the value being about £1000.[3] The sides consisted of bales of compressed wool, bound with gilded bars of iron; the other decorations were all of different various coloured yarns and raw wool, interspersed with a few evergreens, and upon the roof sat two women, in Welsh costume, busily engaged in knitting."[4]

A WORD ON RECENT CORONATIONS

Neither the visit of the Prince and Princess of Wales to the Guildhall on 5 December, 1901,[5] nor the " Royal Progress " of Edward VII through London on 25 October, 1902,[6] was pageantic. The latter event took place shortly after the coronation of the king[7] — the first coronation which England had seen in sixty-

---

[1] Cf. e. g., that erected on London Bridge in 1863 — pictured in the *Illus. Lond. News* for 21 March of that year.

[2] London *Graphic* for 29 October, 1881, pp. 435 f. This visit is also recorded and pictured in the *Illus. Lond. News* for 29 October, 1881, p. 416, etc.

[3] These arches are illustrated on p. 437 of the number of the *Graphic* referred to.

[4] We may compare these figures with the girls who spun and knitted at Norwich in 1578, and with the trade-pageant at Sandwich in 1573. We shall find the trade-pageant a common feature of the Lord Mayor's Show.

[5] A volume giving full details, with the speeches at the *déjeûner*, is preserved in the Guildhall library. A splendid spectacle the scene must have been — but it was not pageantry, in the technical sense.

[6] See Stone, *Festivals, Ceremonies and Customs* (1906), p. 42, for illustration and description of this event. Also see the contemporary press accounts.

[7] Which is described in detail in the London *Times* for 11 August, 1902.

four years. Within a decade Britain saw two king-emperors crowned, and the brilliancy of these spectacles has rarely been equalled in modern times. Both ceremonies may be considered symbolic of Britain's power; but even the symbolism of the Durbar, which followed the coronation of George V, will not bring the ceremony within the field of this discussion. Often what the press calls a " pageant " is merely a splendid show; this loose use of a word — which has too many legitimate meanings — adds to our difficulty.

In our consideration of the " royal-entry " — including those progresses of the sovereign across the city on the day before his coronation — it has been the passage, rather than the subsequent ceremony of crowning, which has interested us. When these processions were given up, toward the end of the seventeenth century, pageantry died out of the " royal-entry," save in the provinces. As recently as 1911, the Salisbury giant, St. Christopher, appeared in connection with the local fête celebrating the coronation of George V.

Until the time of Charles II, the Lord Mayor's Show — which had, about the middle of the sixteenth century, joined the folk-pageantry of the Midsummer festival to the trade-pageantry of the " royal-entry " — shared with the latter the floats and platforms with their symbolism, allegory, and history; since that time, pageantry in England has been, until the present century, chiefly confined to the London civic triumphs, which will be discussed in the next chapter.

END OF VOLUME I

Date Due

AG 1 '70				